Quiegolani Zapotec Syntax

A Principles and Parameters Account

SIL International and
The University of Texas at Arlington
Publications in Linguistics

Publication 136

Publications in Linguistics is a series published jointly by SIL International and the University of Texas at Arlington. The series is a venue for works covering a broad range of topics in linguistics, especially the analytical treatment of minority languages from all parts of the world. While most volumes are authored by members of SIL, suitable works by others will also form part of the series.

Series Editors

Donald A. Burquest
University of Texas at Arlington

Mary Ruth Wise
SIL International

Volume Editors

Mary Ruth Wise
Marilyn A. Mayers

Production Staff

Bonnie Brown, Managing Editor
Margaret González, Compositor
Hazel Shorey, Graphic Artist

Quiegolani Zapotec Syntax

A Principles and Parameters Account

Cheryl A. Black

A Publication of
SIL International
and
University of Texas at Arlington

©2000 by SIL International
Library of Congress Catalog No: 00-107439
ISBN: 1-55671-099-2
ISSN: 1040-0850

Printed in the United States of America

All Rights Reserved

09 08 07 06 05 04 03 02 01 00   10 9 8 7 6 5 4 3 2 1

No part of this publication may be reproduced, stored in a retrieval system, or transmitted in any form or by any means—electronic, mechanical, photocopy, recording, or otherwise—without the express permission of SIL International, with the exception of brief excerpts in journal articles or reviews.

Copies of this and other publications of SIL International may be obtained from

International Academic Bookstore
SIL International
7500 W. Camp Wisdom Road
Dallas, TX 75236-5699

Voice: 972-708-7404
Fax: 972-708-7363
Email: academic_books@sil.org
Internet: http://www.sil.org

Contents

Preface	xi
Abbreviations and Symbols	xiii
Map	xvi
1 Introduction	1
1.1 The data	3
1.2 Theoretical assumptions	5
1.2.1 The system of levels and rules	6
1.2.2 The system of constraints	7
1.2.2.1 The X-bar theory of phrase structure	7
1.2.2.2 Theta theory and Case theory	10
1.2.2.3 The theory of movement	13
1.2.2.4 Binding theory	15

Part I Grammatical Sketch

2 Morphology	21
2.1 Nominal morphology	21
2.2 Verbal morphology	24
2.2.1 Aspect marking and other prefixes	24
2.2.1.1 Stative aspect	25
2.2.1.2 Completive aspect	26
2.2.1.3 Habitual and Progressive aspects	26
2.2.1.4 Unreal mood	27
2.2.1.5 Potential mood	28
2.2.1.6 Future mood	29
2.2.1.7 Imperative constructions	31

2.2.1.8 Causative prefix	32
2.2.2 Verbal suffixes	32
2.3 Pronouns	33
2.3.1 The category of pronouns in QZ	36
2.3.2 Null pronominals	37
3 Syntax	45
3.1 Basic VSO word order	45
3.2 Sentences expressing states or existence	48
3.2.1 Existential sentences	48
3.2.2 Identificational sentences	49
3.2.3 Stative sentences	51
3.3 Constructions involving changes in argument structure	53
3.3.1 Passive constructions	53
3.3.2 Unaccusative constructions	57
3.3.3 Raising constructions	60
3.3.4 Causative constructions	61
3.4 Changes in word order due to movement	62
3.4.1 Focus and topic constructions	62
3.4.2 Question formation	64
3.4.3 Fronting of negative indefinite pronouns	66
4 Anaphoric or Binding Relations	69
4.1 Principles A and B: Distinguishing anaphors from pronouns	69
4.1.1 Isthmus Zapotec anaphora	69
4.1.2 Yatzachi Zapotec anaphora	71
4.1.3 Quiegolani Zapotec anaphora	73
4.2 Principle C: Binding restrictions on nominal phrases	75
4.2.1 Discourse considerations regarding the use of pronouns and nominal phrases	77
4.2.2 Bound nominal phrases and the null third-person pronoun	79

Part II Clause Structure and Ā-Dependencies

5 Theoretical Issues	89
5.1 How many functional projections are necessary?	89
5.2 How VSO word order is obtained	91
5.2.1 Verb Movement	92
5.2.2 Subject Adjunction	95
6 Focus and Topic Constructions	99
6.1 Focus versus topic syntactically and semantically	99
6.2 The focus marker	105
6.2.1 The category of the focus marker	105

Contents

6.2.2 The function of the focus marker	110
6.3 The phrase structure of focus constructions	112
7 Questions and Relative Clauses	**117**
7.1 Question formation and the *Wh*-Criterion	117
7.2 The structure of $CP_{[+wh]}$	121
7.2.1 QZ question formation	122
7.2.2 Inversion in pied-piping constructions	134
7.2.3 Featural distinction between clause types	138
7.3 Relative clauses	141
8 Constructions Involving Negation	**149**
8.1 The Zapotecan languages are Negative Concord languages	149
8.2 Analysis of the obligatory fronting	151
8.2.1 The limited negation system of QZ	151
8.2.1.1 Clause structure analysis: NegP and the Negative Criterion	153
8.2.1.2 Future mood as an Affirmative Polarity Item	158
8.2.2 The more complete negation system of Mitla Zapotec	159
8.2.1.1 Free negative words and the Negative Criterion	160
8.2.2.2 Negative quantifiers and the Negative Criterion	166
8.2.2.3 The interpretation of constituent negation as clausal negation	169
8.3 The negation constructions and Verb Movement versus Subject Adjunction	171
8.3.1 The Verb Movement account	172
8.3.2 The Subject Adjunction account	175
9 Interaction Between the Various Ā-Constructions	**181**
9.1 Questions and focus constructions may not co-occur in a clause	182
9.2 Relative positions of *wh*-phrases and negative phrases	186
9.3 Relative positions of focused phrases and negative phrases	191
9.4 Polarity phrase needed to account for clausal coordination	194
9.5 Proposed clause structure for QZ	200

Part III Phrase Structure and Constituent Constructions

10 Structure of Verb Phrases and Nonverbal Predicates 211
  10.1 The structure of VP. 212
    10.1.1 Auxiliary constructions with VP complements. . . 212
    10.1.2 Analysis of the apparent VP coordination
        constructions 217
        10.1.2.1 The Subject Adjunction account. 220
        10.1.2.2 The Verb Movement dilemma. 222
        10.1.2.3 Possible alternative analyses 227
  10.2 The structure of nonverbal predicates 234
11 Structure of Nominal Phrases. 241
  11.1 The DP structures parallel to the clause structure
     proposals 242
    11.1.1 The Verb Movement account 242
    11.1.2 The Subject Adjunction account 243
  11.2 Proposed DP structure for QZ 244
  11.3 Attested coordination within DP 250
12 Special Number-Marking Constructions 257
  12.1 Semantic interpretation 260
    12.1.1 The quantifier contribution 261
    12.1.2 Head type and inclusion 268
    12.1.3 The Person Hierarchy Effect and group
        reference 273
  12.2 Syntactic analysis of the contiguous structure. 275
    12.2.1 The clausal nature of the quantifier phrase 275
        12.2.1.1 The Subject = Possessor of Object
            Condition 276
        12.2.1.2 The Nonpronominal Head Condition . . 281
        12.2.1.3 Ordering restrictions between the DPs . . 285
    12.2.2 The constituency of the construction 289
    12.2.3 The internal structure of the mother DP and
        of the clausal adjunct 296
  12.3 Analysis of the separated construction 299
    12.3.1 Arguments for a base generation analysis
        in other languages 302
    12.3.2 Predictions made by a movement analysis 305
    12.3.3 The required coindexation and semantic
        construal 315
Appendix: A Parametric Account of Question Formation 319
  The *Wh*-Criterion alone is not sufficient. 319
  Parameterization of the *wh*-scope positions 325

Wh-chains account for partial *wh*-movement. 328
References. 333
Index 345

Preface

This study describes and analyzes many facets of the syntax of Quiegolani Zapotec (QZ), a member of the sparsely documented Otomanguean language family. It should be of interest to descriptive and comparative linguists, as well as to theorists. The analysis is presented within the Principles and Parameters framework, with some appeal to the more recent Minimalist Program. The theoretical issues addressed include the determination of how many functional projections are necessary and their relative nesting in the clause structure, the licensing requirements for Ā-dependencies, and QZ particular binding relations

Rather than concentrating exclusively on one small part of the syntax, this study seeks to cover a broad range of syntactic constructions in QZ. This wide scope investigation examines how effective a small number of principles or constraints can be in determining the full grammar of a language. At the same time, due to the number of constructions being considered, it is impossible to provide an exhaustive analysis of each one. It is my hope that this volume will provide the basis for future research into the areas which I am not able to fully account for here.

The description and analysis presented in this work are a revision of my Ph.D. dissertation, University of California at Santa Cruz, 1994. Working with my dissertation committee was a real joy, since I count each of them friends as well as mentors. I was especially pleased to have Sandy Chung as the chair of the committee. She encouraged me and challenged me to strive for excellence from the first class I took from her. Throughout the writing process, Sandy continued to cloak all her suggestions for changes with praise for the parts well done. This gave me encouragement to persevere. Jorge Hankamer is responsible for my undertaking graduate studies in Linguistics. The Syntax I class he taught completely captured my interest. Jorge has continued to be encouraging, as well as giving valuable help in clarifying my arguments. I am grateful to Bill Ladusaw for sharing his expertise and suggesting corrections where the analysis moves into the semantic realm.

Thanks are also due to the faculty of the Board of Studies in Linguistics at the University of California at Santa Cruz, all of whom had a significant impact in my linguistic training. Their ability to motivate students to excellence and their example of top-notch research were superb.

I am indebted to my colleagues in SIL International for their moral support and for giving me access to their data. Special gratitude is due to Randy and Sue Regnier and to Martín Hernández Antonio for sharing their knowledge of Quiegolani Zapotec. Special gratitude is due also to Mary Ruth Wise, Marilyn Mayers, Bonnie Brown, and Margaret González, the editors and compositor of this volume.

A graduate study program is difficult in itself, but for a wife and mother of four children it was especially challenging. My husband, Andy, and children, Kara, Lisa, Jeremy, and Matthew, deserve special recognition for their support and encouragement and for their help in keeping the house running. Andy's computer expertise was invaluable in the formatting of this study.

The study program would not have been possible without the financial support and prayers of our many friends, family, and supporters. I am especially thankful for my parents, Frank and Doris Ritchey, who always stood behind my endeavors. I am also grateful for support from UC Santa Cruz by means of grants and a teaching assistantship from the Humanities Division, a research assistantship under NSF Grant BNS-9021398, and logistic support provided by the Linguistic Research Center.

This work is dedicated to God, the creator of all things, including languages.

Abbreviations and Symbols

A	argument
Ā	nonargument
ASSOC	verbal suffix used to relate two events
C	completive
CAUS	causative marker
CL	class marker, in Jacaltec
Comp	complementizer
CP	complementizer phrase
def	definite determiner, in Tzotzil
DP	determiner phrase, used for nominal phrases
e_i	empty (null) category
ECP	Empty Category Principle
f	female
F	future
FocP	focus phrase
FM	focus marker
GB	Government and Binding Theory
H	habitual
IMP	imperative
INF	infinitive
INSTR	instrumental case
Infl	inflection

I⁰	head of inflection phrase
IP	inflection phrase, used for sentences
IZ	Isthmus Zapotec
JZ	Juarez Zapotec
LF	Logical Form
LM	loan marker
MORE	intensifying verbal suffix
MZ	Mitla Zapotec
NEG	negative marker
NegP	negation phrase
NOM	nominative case
NP	noun phrase
OPL	object plural marker
P	potential
PASS	passive
p.c.	personal communication
PF	Phonological Form
PL	plural
PolP	polarity phrase
POS	possessive prefix used with alienably possessed nouns
PP	prepositional phrase
PPC	Plural Pronoun Construction
PR	progressive
PRT	participle marker
Q	question marker
QP	quantifier phrase
QTZ	Quioquitani Zapotec
QZ	Quiegolani Zapotec
REP	repetitive, in YZ
S	stative
SC	small clause
SG	singular
Spec	specifier
SPL	subject plural marker
SS	S-structure
SZ	Santo Domingo Albarradas Zapotec
t_i	trace left after movement
U	unreal

VP	verb phrase
WH	demonstrative particle used in some *wh*-questions
XP, YP, ZP	phrases with unspecified or variable categories as their heads
YZ	Yatzachi Zapotec
1	first person
1EX	first person exclusive
1EXPL	first person exclusive plural
1I	first person inclusive
1IPL	first person inclusive plural
1SG	first person singular
2	second person
2DUAL	second person dual
2PL	second person plural
3	third person
3A	third person animate
3AO	third person animate object
3D	third person deity/baby
3I	third person inanimate
3IO	third person inanimate object
3M	third person masculine
3R	third person respectful
3RO	third person respectful object
3RS	third person respectful subject
*	ungrammatical example
??	questionable or disfavored readings
/	in gloss line indicates clear morpheme breaks cannot be made
!	exclamation

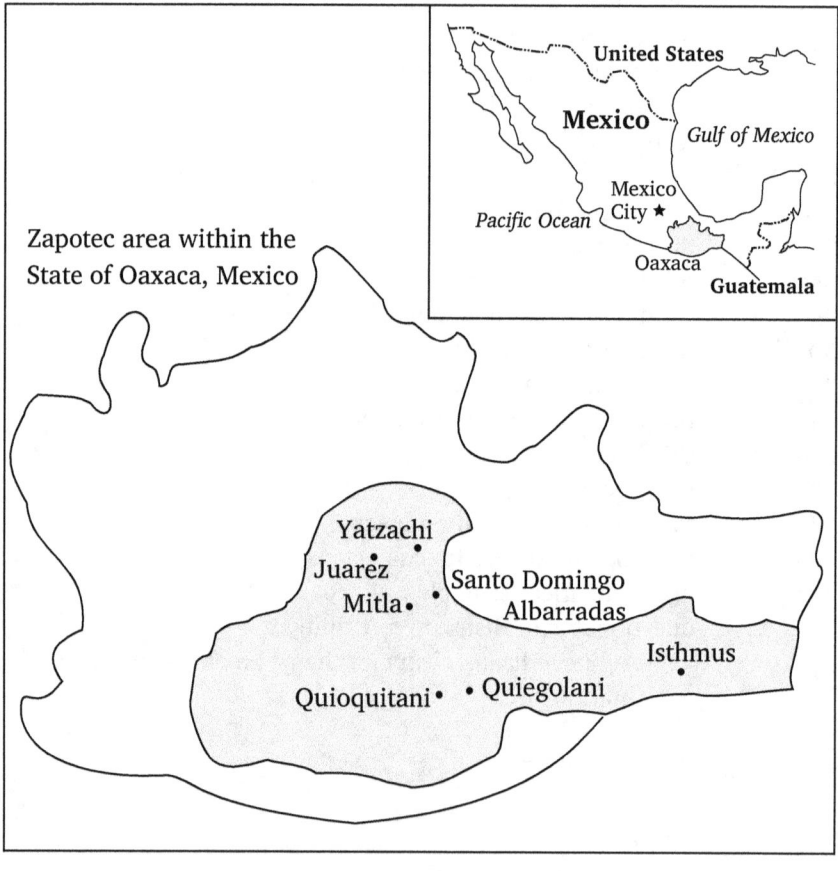

1
Introduction

The goal of this study is to describe and provide a coherent, explanatory analysis for many facets of the syntax of Quiegolani Zapotec (referred to throughout as QZ). Quiegolani Zapotec is one of over fifty distinct and mutually unintelligible dialects or related languages in the Zapotecan language family. Zapotec as a whole is part of the larger Otomanguean family. Zapotec speakers are found almost exclusively in the state of Oaxaca in Mexico. Total speakers of Zapotec number almost 500,000, though the number of speakers of any particular language varies from only about 1,000 to over 100,000. QZ is one of the smaller groups, with between two and three thousand speakers who live in south central Oaxaca. According to Grimes (1996), the official name of the language is Western Yautepec Zapoteco, though it is also known as Santa María Quiegolani Zapoteco and simply as Quiegolani Zapotec.

In some sections of this study, data are drawn from other Zapotecan languages, such as Isthmus Zapotec (IZ), Juarez Zapotec (JZ), Mitla Zapotec (MZ), Santo Domingo Albarradas Zapotec (SZ), Quioquitani Zapotec (QTZ), and Yatzachi Zapotec (YZ). All of these are also spoken in the state of Oaxaca in Mexico. In general, the Zapotecan family divides into five groups geographically and linguistically: northern, central, western, eastern, and southern. QZ is part of the southern group.

QZ, as well as the group of Zapotecan languages and the whole Otomanguean language family, has previously received little attention by syntacticians. There are some morphological sketches which describe word and phrase level phenomena, such as verb conjugations with the different aspect markers and the personal pronoun systems, including possessive and reflexive constructions (De Angulo 1926a, 1926b; Radin 1930; Pickett 1953a, 1953b, 1955, 1976; Leal and Leal 1954; Lyman 1964; Marks 1976; Speck and Pickett 1976; Butler 1976a, 1976b; Benton 1981; Marlett and Pickett 1985, 1987; López and Newberg 1990; Marlett 1993). In addition, a number of descriptive analyses of the phonology and of discourse elements are available, as well as texts and word lists in various Zapotecan languages. The literature dealing specifically with syntactic phenomena, especially at the clause level, is more limited. Juan de Cordova's 1578 grammar and an anonymous manuscript, dated 1823, are the earliest known studies of the grammar of a Zapotecan language. Since then, several studies have been done within the Tagmemic framework (Pickett 1959, 1960, 1967; Briggs 1961; Earl 1968) and descriptive grammars of several other Zapotecan languages have recently been completed (Nellis and Nellis 1983; Butler 1988; Stubblefield and Stubblefield 1991; Pickett, Black, and Marcial 1998). Many of these works were useful in my research. Rosenbaum (1974) is the only theoretical analysis done in the precursor to Government and Binding theory, transformational grammar. My three working papers, Black (1992, 1993, 1996) (parts of which are incorporated into the present study), a paper on the relevance of Binding theory by Piper (1993), and a paper on the clause structure of Amátlan Zapotec (Piper 1997) are the only other attempts that I am aware of to analyze Zapotecan syntax within the Principles and Parameters framework.

I am indebted to Randy and Susan Regnier for making available to me the language data they collected while studying Quiegolani Zapotec beginning in 1985. This data consists primarily of over forty glossed texts which have proved to be invaluable for this research. The majority of the examples used come from these texts, which were authored by at least three different QZ speakers. Some of the more unique aspects of QZ syntax, such as the special number-marking constructions, were discovered from the texts. The Regniers also made available their preliminary grammar analysis.

Since texts do not show the fringes of acceptability of a particular construction, or the full range of completely acceptable constructions, I worked personally on two separate occasions with QZ native speaker Martín Hernández Antonio to determine grammaticality judgments and to clarify the meaning of particular constructions. Spanish was used as the elicitation language (apart from QZ). Even during these elicitation sessions, whenever possible, the text examples and their slightly altered counterparts provided the basis for determining the range of acceptability of a particular

1.1 The data

construction. Translations from Spanish were only requested in a few cases where I needed to find out how something might be expressed in QZ and had found nothing like it in the texts.

The study is presented in three parts: a grammatical sketch in chapters 2–4; a discussion of clause structure and Ā-Dependencies in chapters 5–9; and a discussion of phrase structure and constituent constructions in chapters 10–12. While each part is distinct in nature, the latter parts crucially depend on the earlier ones. The major break comes between Parts I and II, where the shift is made from mostly description to theoretical analysis.

1.1 The data

All the examples of Zapotecan data are given in the form of glossed text, consisting of three lines each, as exemplified in (1).

(1)   *s-ya   men ru   x-yuu   men*   CWENT 14
      PR-go   3   mouth   POS-house   3
      He was going to his house.

The first line is the vernacular text in italics with morpheme breaks indicated by a hyphen (-). Each word in the first line is vertically aligned with its gloss on the second line. A gloss is given for each morpheme. All glosses consisting of numbers and/or abbreviations in small caps are explained in the list of abbreviations. Glosses in lower case letters are for roots. When a gloss requires more than one English word the two parts are separated by a period (.), as shown in (2) where *ex* is glossed as 'lying.down'. The third line gives a free translation of the text into English.

If the example is taken from the collection of glossed texts in Regnier (1989a), it is referenced with text name and line number at the far right on the first line.[1] If a letter follows the line number, it indicates that the data given is a slight modification of the text example obtained in consultation with a native speaker. Examples without text references are taken either from my own fieldwork or from Regnier (1989b).

There are a few cases where clear morpheme breaks cannot be made. In QZ this stems from one of two phonological processes. First is a process of antigemination, where like (or similar enough) consonants coming together results in the manifestation of only one. For example, the

---

[1] I have also used this field to indicate the reference number for a text taken from another author. In these instances, the author's name is given with the first letter in full caps, followed by the example number from their article.

Completive aspect marker *w-* added to the verb *wii* 'see' surfaces simply as *wii*. This will be glossed as shown in the first word in (2). The word *wii* on the first line is not split into morphemes, but the gloss shows that both the Completive aspect marker and the root are present in the word by separating the two morphemes with a slash (/).

(2) wii   mee laad men gol gin   n-ex   OLDMAN 26
    C/see boy FM   3   old this S-lying.down
    The boy saw that old man lying down.

The same slash notation is also used in the case of metathesis occurring between *w* and *b* when the Completive aspect marker is added to a verb root beginning with *b*. In this case /w+beree/ 'C-return' surfaces as *bweree*, as shown in (3).

(3) bweree   zhuzhey men   CWENT 3
    C/return uncle   3
    His uncle returned.

Ungrammatical examples are marked with an asterisk (*) before the first word and questionable or disfavored readings are noted with question marks (??). In each case, the free translation is given in parentheses.

The segmental inventory for the consonants of QZ is shown in (4).[2] The practical orthography, which is used in the examples throughout this volume, is cited according to place and type of articulation. The phonetic symbol (usually Americanist) is given in parenthesis when different from the orthographic symbol. In addition to the consonants listed in the chart, *f* and *j (h)* are used in Spanish loan words.

---

[2]The chart is based on Regnier (1993), which also includes information on the phonetic quality and distribution of each symbol and the contrasts and co-occurrence restrictions between symbols. See Black (1995) for a theoretical discussion of some aspects of QZ phonology.

1.2 The data

(4)

	Bilabial	Alveolar	Palato-Alveolar	Retro-flexed	Velar	Palatalized Velar	Labialized Velar
Stops	p	t			k	ky (k^y)	kw (k^w)
		d			g	gy (g^y)	gw (g^w)
Affricates		ts (c)	ch (č)	tx (c̣)			
			dx (ǰ)				
Fricatives		s		x (ṣ)			
		z		zh (ẓ)			
Nasals	m	n					
Laterals		l					
Approximants	b (β)		y	r			w

QZ has six vowels as shown in (5). Each vowel can also occur in a laryngealized (or glottalized) form, written as /VV/ in the orthography since QZ does not have any vowel clusters. QZ is a tonal language, but tone is not marked in the examples since it is not relevant to the discussion.

(5)

	Front	Back Unrounded	Back Rounded
High	i		u
Mid	e		o
Low	ë (æ)	a	

1.2 Theoretical assumptions

The theoretical analysis is presented in the Principles and Parameters framework, which was developed mainly by Chomsky (1981, 1982, 1986, 1991) beginning with Government and Binding theory (GB). A brief theoretical sketch is included here to introduce the key concepts and terminology and to clarify the starting points for the analysis. I emphasize only those parts of the theory which bear on the analysis of QZ syntax. This presentation gleans significant portions from the more thorough introductions to GB theory done by Sells (1985:19–76) and Baker (1988:24–75).

Chomsky assumes that a large portion of the grammar of any particular language is common to all languages, and is therefore part of Universal

Grammar. Cross-linguistic differences in a particular construction are accounted for via parametric variation, as in the account of question formation given in the appendix. Universal Grammar can be broken down into two main components: a system of levels of representation and rules, and a system of constraints.

1.2.1 The system of levels and rules

The framework uses a derivational model consisting of four levels of representation, as in (6). The lexicon lists the idiosyncratic properties of lexical items which constitute the atomic units of the syntax. These properties include what arguments the item subcategorizes for, etc. Lexical items are combined together at D-structure (underlying structure), which is the formal syntactic level of representation where thematic roles are mapped one-to-one onto syntactic arguments. D-structure generates S-structure, which is the syntactic representation that most closely reflects the surface order of the sentence. S-structure is not directly interpreted itself, but is factored into Phonological Form (PF) and Logical Form (LF). PF is the interface with the phonology where shapes, sounds, and groupings of items are directly represented. LF is the interface with the semantics. Predication relationships and the scope of quantifiers and operators of various kinds are explicitly represented in the phrase structure at LF.

(6)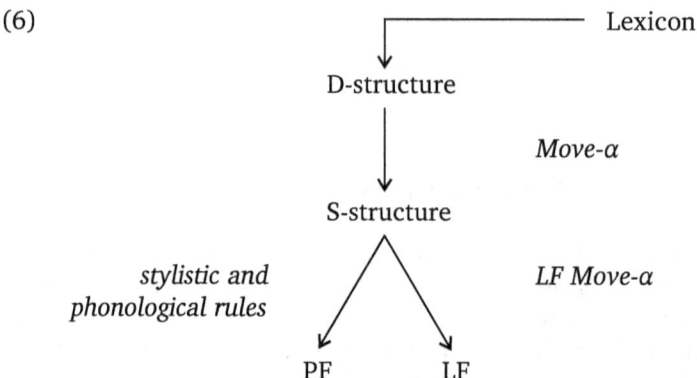

These levels are related to one another by rules—noted in italics in (6). A single movement rule, MOVE-α, maps between D-structure and S-structure and a similar rule maps S-structure into LF. Move-α is stated as a simple rule basically allowing anything to move anywhere, since the system of constraints is

1.2 Theoretical assumptions

responsible for correctly restricting this movement. Stylistic and other phonological rules are assumed to take place at PF.

The discussion and analyses in this study are concerned almost exclusively with the D-structure and S-structure levels of representation.

1.2.2 The system of constraints

The constraints are designed to restrict the system of levels and rules. These constraints or filters are divided into a number of subsystems that are developing theoretically in their own right, as shown in the subsections to follow. Like the rule of Move-α, the constraints are stated in the most general form possible. The interaction between the various constraints and the movement rule provides the restrictiveness needed in specific constructions.

1.2.2.1 The X-bar theory of phrase structure.
The X-bar theory constrains the type of representations allowed at each syntactic level. Instead of the numerous construction-specific phrase structure rules which were used in transformational grammar, X-bar theory allows only two phrase structure rules, given in (7), that show how lexical items project into phrases to generate the basic syntactic representations.[3] In (7), X, Y, and Z are variables ranging over category types, and asterisk (*) indicates that zero or more instances of that element may occur. XP is a maximal projection, X' is an intermediate projection, and X^0 is a head. The order of elements on the right side of each rule is subject to parametric variation.

(7) Basic rules of X-bar theory
 a. XP ⇒ YP* X'
 b. X' ⇒ X^0 ZP*

These rules produce the tree structure shown in (8). As illustrated, the maximal projection YP_1 which is the sister to X' is known as the SPECIFIER, X^0 is the HEAD, and the maximal projection ZP_1 which is the sister of the head is the COMPLEMENT. Both of these other maximal projections themselves have the same structure as in (8), so the tree expands recursively, as shown for Complement ZP_1.

---

[3] Rules allowing for adjunction and coordination are also necessary.

(8)   Basic X-bar structure

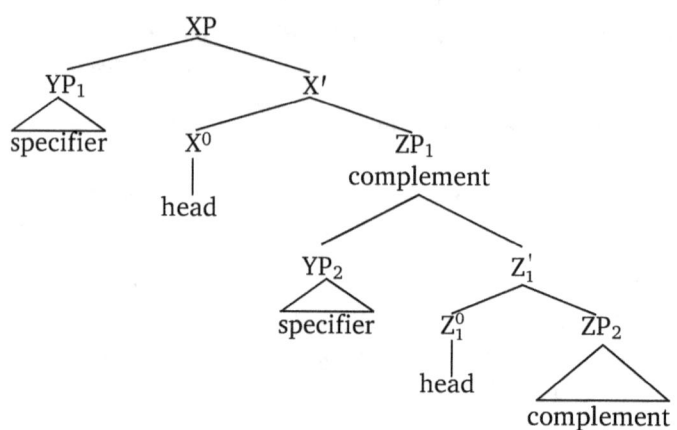

Several basic relationships crucial to other constraints are determined from the tree structure. The specifier and the head of a particular phrase normally share certain features. This specifier-head relationship is therefore important to both agreement and Case assignment. A second important relationship is that of C-COMMAND (Reinhart 1976), which formally expresses the notion of "higher in the tree than." A definition is given in (9), where α and β stand for particular categories. Applying this definition to (8), it is clear that the specifier YP_1 c-commands everything else in the tree except XP and the head X^0 c-commands its complement ZP_1 but not its specifier YP_1. The c-command relationship is especially important in Binding theory (§1.2.2.4).

(9)   α C-COMMANDS β iff

    a.   α does not dominate β, and
    b.   the first branching node that dominates α also dominates β

A related command relation[4] is M-COMMAND, as defined in (10). The only difference between m-command and c-command is that m-command allows a category α to command upward to the maximal projection as well as downward. Therefore, in (8) the head X^0 m-commands both its specifier YP_1 and its complement ZP_1, as well as everything within ZP_1. Note that crucially for both c-command and m-command, however, clause (a) prohibits a category α from commanding a category β which it

---

[4]See Barker and Pullum (1990) for theoretical discussion of the whole family of command relations.

1.2 Theoretical assumptions

dominates. Thus, ZP_1 does not c-command or m-command YP_2, Z'_{1}, Z^0_{1}, or ZP_2.

(10) α M-COMMANDS β iff

   a. α does not dominate β, and
   b. every maximal projection that dominates α also dominates β

The GOVERNMENT RELATION is a localized version of m-command. While m-command may hold between α and some β that is arbitrarily far down in a tree, government is much more local. As defined in (11), only heads may be governors and no maximal projection which is not subcategorized for by a lexical head ($=N^0$, V^0, A^0, or P^0) may intervene between the governor and its governee, since, in general, maximal projections are barriers to government.[5]

(11) α GOVERNS β iff

   a. α m-commands β, and
   b. α is a head ($=X^0$), and
   c. every maximal projection which is not a complement of a lexical head that dominates β also dominates α.

By this definition, the head X^0 in (8) governs both its specifier and its complement. If X^0 is a lexical head, it can also govern the specifier YP_2 of its complement, since the maximal projection ZP_1 would not be a barrier to government.

A similar type of government across a maximal projection is crucial for the analysis of *wh*-questions and focus constructions. This involves government by a FUNCTIONAL HEAD ($=$non-lexical, such as C^0, D^0, etc.) of a phrase which is adjoined to the maximal projection directly below it, as shown in (12), where the positions of α and β are being considered.

---

[5]A more technical definition of barriers, based on blocking categories, θ-government and L-marking is given in Chomsky (1986). A precise understanding of those details is not necessary for the analyses given here.

(12)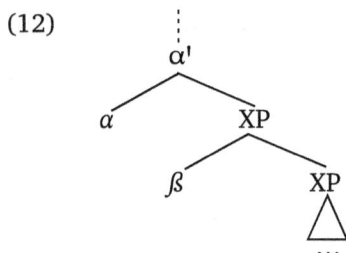

Since α is a functional head in this case, the maximal projection XP is not a complement of a lexical head, so direct application of the definition of government in (11) would rule out the possibility of α governing β in the configuration in (12). I appeal, therefore, to a general assumption about adjunction structures proposed by May (1985) and rephrased in (13), which claims that β is not really dominated by XP because the XP consists of two segments and β is not dominated by both of them. Therefore, the XP does not constitute a barrier for government and α governs β.

(13) β is DOMINATED by a maximal projection XP (or other category) iff it is contained in every segment of XP.

The application of the X-bar theory of phrase structure to every syntactic category of the grammar led to the assumption that sentences and clauses are projected from functional heads, I^0 and C^0, respectively. This approach was extended to nominal phrases under the DP Hypothesis (Abney 1987, Stowell 1989), which claims that nominals are projected from the functional head D^0 which takes NP as its complement. Pollock (1989) proposes further breakdown of the functional categories for inflection, and I argue that a projection for negation is needed in QZ. Once such a breakdown is undertaken, the question arises whether every morpheme should be a syntactic head. Baker (1989) explores such a proposal where the words are then put together via head movement. I also explore this possibility for the limited morphology of QZ. While such an account seems to provide an explanatory analysis for the aspect and the negation marking being realized on the verb, treating the adverbial suffixes as separate heads is problematic (see §9.5). Therefore, not all morphemes should be treated as syntactic heads.

1.2.2.2 Theta theory and Case theory. Theta theory determines the particular relationships between lexical items that allow them to be placed into the appropriate positions in the D-structure generated by the phrase structure rules under X-bar theory. Some of the principles within

1.2 Theoretical assumptions

this subarea also relate the levels of representation to one another. Case theory is responsible for much of the attested distribution of nominal phrases at S-structure.

A particular lexical item (head) is assumed to select not only the syntactic category of its arguments, but also their θ-roles, or thematic relations, such as Agent, Patient, etc. Each predicate may select θ-roles not only for its complements, known as "internal arguments," but also for its subject, the "external argument." The Theta-Criterion, stated in its simplest form in (14) (taken from Chomsky 1981) assures that there is a one-to-one mapping between the θ-roles selected by a head and the meaningful syntactic category to which they are linked.

(14) Theta-Criterion

Each argument bears one and only one θ-role, and each θ-role is assigned to one and only one argument.

A basic tenet of the framework is that the syntax is a "projection" of lexical properties. The Theta-Criterion and the Projection Principle, given in simplified form in (15) (Chomsky 1981), assure that the structure at each level of representation will reflect the subcategorization requirements of the heads, including both the relevant syntactic category and position in the tree and the proper thematic relationships.

(15) Projection Principle

Representations at each syntactic level are projected from the lexicon, in that they observe the subcategorization properties of the lexical items (both in the syntactic categories and the θ-roles assigned).

Taken together, these two principles constitute a strong restriction on the mapping between levels. A number of transformations posited under transformational grammar are ruled out. For example, movement to an object position is impossible, since that position would be subcategorized for and assigned a θ-role by the verb. At the same time, the Projection Principle forces the existence of empty categories, for otherwise any kind of movement of an argument would violate the principle.

In addition to the Theta-Criterion and the Projection Principle, I also assume the Uniformity of Theta Assignment Hypothesis, proposed by Baker (1988:46), which further restricts the assignment of θ-roles. Under this hypothesis, an argument which is assigned the Theme θ-role is always a

D-structure object in accord with its position in transitive clauses. Passive and unaccusative sentences must therefore be derived via movement.

(16)   Uniformity of Theta Assignment Hypothesis

Identical thematic relationships between items are represented by identical structural relationships between those items at the level of D-structure.

Burzio's Generalization (Burzio 1986:185) states that verbs which do not have external arguments cannot assign Case. This applies to passive and unaccusative verbs. The lack of Case assignment to the D-structure object position provides motivation for the movement of the object to the subject position, as made necessary by the Uniformity of Theta Assignment Hypothesis.

More generally, Case theory is responsible for determining much of the distribution of nominal phrases. The Case Filter, given in (17), rules out a particular structure if some nominal phrase fails to be in a position to which Case is assigned. The Case Filter is normally assumed to apply at S-structure, though more generally the filter must apply to chains,[6] where exactly one Case-marked position is included in the chain (usually the tail, as in normal *wh*-movement).

(17)   Case Filter

*NP (or DP under the DP hypothesis), if it has phonetic content and no Case.

Abstract Case is based on the traditional notion of morphological case, which is manifested in many languages. English is rather impoverished in this regard, since only the pronominal system distinguishes case, and QZ does not have any morphological marking for case at all. Technically though, based on assumptions about Universal Grammar, every nominal phrase must receive Case. It is assumed for English that verbs assign Case to their objects under the government relationship, while subjects receive Case via their specifier-head relationship with Infl ($=I^0$). Possessors are also assumed to receive Case from either the head noun or from D^0 (depending upon the position assumed for possessors) via the specifier-head

---

[6]In general, a chain consists of coindexed elements in a c-command relationship (Reinhart and Reuland 1993). As shown in the next section, a chain is formed between the moved element and the position it moved from. The topmost element is called the head of the chain and the lowest element is the tail.

1.2 Theoretical assumptions

relationship. Case assignment is thus accomplished under one of the two relationships which are local forms of m-command. It is important to note that in many languages, Case assignment requires the Case assigner to be adjacent to the element that receives Case (Stowell 1989), ruling out the intervention of adverbials, etc. This strict adjacency requirement has a part in several of the QZ constructions.

1.2.2.3 The theory of movement. Two basic types of movement of maximal projections are distinguished: A-movement and Ā-movement. A-movement, sometimes also called NP-movement, is movement to an (empty) argument position. Such A-movement is motivated by Case theory, normally involving either the object of a passive or unaccusative verb moving to subject position, or else the subject of a nonfinite embedded clause raising to the subject position in the matrix clause (since nonfinite Infl cannot assign Case to the embedded subject). Only very limited A-movement is attested in QZ, as shown in chapter 3.

Ā-movement is also referred to as *wh*-movement (this term arises from the movement to the front of the clause that takes place in question formation). Ā-movement comprises all movement to a non-argument position. It therefore includes movement to the specifier of a functional projection which is not normally filled by the subject (such as the specifier of CP) as well as movement to an adjoined position. Ā-movement is not motivated by Case theory, since the moved nominal phrase receives Case in its D-structure argument position (which is the tail of the chain created by the movement). Instead, Ā-movement takes place to assure the proper scope of semantic operators. The *Wh*-Criterion (May 1985, Rizzi 1991), given in (18), is one formalization of the motivation for Ā-movement. QZ exhibits extensive Ā-movement and chapters 6–9 and the appendix are concerned with its proper analysis.

(18) The *Wh*-Criterion

a. A *wh*-operator must be in a specifier-head configuration with an $X^0_{[+wh]}$ (i.e., a head bearing the feature [+wh]).
b. An $X^0_{[+wh]}$ must be in a specifier-head configuration with a *wh*-operator (i.e., a phrase bearing the feature [+wh]).

All movement is accomplished via the general rule of Move-α: "move anything anywhere." We have seen that the Theta-Criterion and the Projection Principle, coupled with X-bar theory, rule out many possible types of movement. Case theory can be seen as motivating A-movement, while at the same time ruling out other movement (unaccusative objects moving directly to the specifier of CP, for instance). Further constraints on the action of Move-α, restricting what can move, how far it can move, and where it can move, are presented here.

Given the Projection Principle, once some syntactic position exists, it must always have existed and must continue to exist, within the context of the derivation. This entails the existence of empty categories, or traces, which occupy the empty position vacated by Move-α. The trace is coindexed with the moved category, forming a chain. One of the major constraints on movement is a constraint on traces, called the Empty Category Principle (ECP), stated in (19).

(19) Empty Category Principle

A trace must be properly governed.

Within the Principles and Parameters framework, both conjunctive and disjunctive definitions of proper government have been argued for: traces must either be both lexically head governed and governed by an m-commanding antecedent, or only one of the two is sufficient (Lasnik and Saito 1984, Rizzi 1990, Cinque 1990, etc.). Further, there are differences across languages with respect to which categories are proper head governors. For the analysis presented here, I assume that government by a lexical head is required, but that P^0 and N^0 are not proper governors in QZ (to account for the lack of extractability of the possessor and the object of prepositions). Therefore, only the lexical [+V] heads are proper head governors in QZ.

It is also necessary to restrict long-distance movement. This is accounted for by SUBJACENCY, which is a locality constraint that restricts the application of Move-α. If more than one bounding node (or barrier) is crossed in a single movement, the result is marginal. The particular choice of bounding nodes varies with the language, but in general, movement is disallowed out of more than one nominal phrase or clause at a time. Long-distance movement in QZ is only touched on briefly, so subjacency will not be at issue.

The last set of restrictions in this subarea deal with the landing sites of movement. We have seen that the Theta-Criterion and the Projection Principle rule out movement to an argument position that is assigned a θ-role. A-movement is thus always to an empty specifier position that is reserved for arguments. Landing sites for Ā-movement include specifier positions not used as argument positions and adjoined positions.

1.2 Theoretical assumptions

General principles concerning adjunction restrict heads (X^0) to adjoin only to heads, while only maximal projections may adjoin to the higher-level projections, X', XP, and X^{max} (Rizzi and Roberts 1989). In addition, the Empty Category Principle (ECP) prohibits downward movement (if the conjunctive version requiring both head government and antecedent government is assumed), since the trace would not be m-commanded by its antecedent. A further stipulation, put forth by Chomsky (1986:6), prohibits adjunction to an argument. This prohibition will guide decisions about the clause structure and the structure of specific constituents in QZ.

Movement of intermediate projections is not allowed, but head movement deserves some consideration. Travis (1981:131) posited the Head Movement Constraint given in (20) which forces a moving head to observe a particularly strict version of locality. Baker (1985) argues that the Head Movement Constraint is not a separate principle, but instead falls out from the ECP requirement that a trace be governed by an m-commanding antecedent (if it does not meet the requirement of being governed by a head).[7]

(20) Head Movement Constraint

An X^0 may only move to the Y^0 which properly governs it.

Head movement of V^0 to I^0, and sometimes on to Neg^0 (or Pol^0) is crucial to the Verb Movement proposal for obtaining VSO word order adopted for QZ.

1.2.2.4 Binding theory. Binding theory characterizes the anaphoric relations between nominal phrases, covers the distribution of pronouns and reflexives, and is also used to determine the distribution of empty categories. BINDING is formally defined in (21).

(21) α BINDS β iff

   a. α c-commands β, and
   b. α and β are coindexed.

A-binding and Ā-binding can be further distinguished by requiring the binder α to be in an argument position for A-binding.

---

[7]A head cannot directly govern another head; instead the head governs the maximal projection containing the other head. This is why antecedent government is required for head movement.

Three principles which account for the distinct distributions of anaphors, pronouns, and other nominal phrases are given in (22), where the governing category is a local domain which, roughly speaking, denotes the minimal category which contains both a subject and an element that governs the element in question.[8]

(22) Principles of Binding Theory

    A. Anaphors (e.g., reflexives and reciprocals) must be A-bound in their governing category.
    B. Pronouns must not be A-bound in their governing category.
    C. Nominal phrases (or R(eferential)-expressions) must not be A-bound.

These principles thus recognize that the class of nominals is partitioned into three different types. These partitions are characterized by the two features [±anaphoric] and [±pronominal]. In this system, personal pronouns are labeled $[-a, +p]$, while reflexive and reciprocal pronouns are classified $[+a, -p]$, and full nominal phrases are assigned the features $[-a, -p]$.

It is an insight of the Principles and Parameters framework (dating back to Extended Standard Theory) that the chain coindexing established by Move-α is equivalent to the coindexing in binding relationships between overt nominals. Therefore, the Principles of Binding Theory are also applied to empty categories. Four types of empty categories are recognized, corresponding to the four possible feature specifications [±anaphoric] and [±pronominal]. The trace of $\bar{A}$-movement (also known as *wh*-trace) corresponds to the full nominal phrases, having the feature specification $[-a, -p]$ and being subject to Principle C.[9] The trace of A-movement (also known as NP-trace) corresponds to an anaphor in its need to be locally bound, therefore being classified as $[+a, -p]$ and being subject to Principle A. The empty counterpart of pronouns is filled by *pro*, which is the "missing" subject allowed in many languages where the verb shows person and number inflection. As such, *pro* is classified $[-a, +p]$ and falls under Principle B of Binding Theory. The final empty category does not have an overt counterpart, since it would have to be subject to both

---

[8]Again, more technical definitions have been proposed for the governing category, but these are not crucial to the analysis of QZ. We will see the need to parameterize some of the Principles of Binding theory, however, in chapter 4.

[9]Such traces are $\bar{A}$-bound but not A-bound.

1.2 Theoretical assumptions

Principles A and B simultaneously. The empty subject in control constructions, *PRO*, is assumed to be [+a, +p]. This feature specification and subsequent applicability of Principles A and B leads to the conclusion that *PRO* must be ungoverned and does not receive Case.

These binding relations are summarized and exemplified in the chart in (23) (a reordered and slightly modified version of Sells 1985:74). The examples for *pro* are given in Spanish, since English does not have an empty version of pronouns.

(23)

Nominal Type	Binding Features	Binding Principle	Examples
Overt			
anaphors	+a, −p	A	1. John$_i$ likes himself$_i$.
			2. *John$_i$ thinks that [I like himself$_i$].
			3. John$_i$ believes himself$_i$ to be sick.
			4. *John$_i$'s mother likes himself$_i$.
pronouns	−a, +p	B	1. *John$_i$ likes him$_i$.
			2. John$_i$ thinks that [I like him$_i$].
			3. *John$_i$ believes him$_i$ to be sick.
			4. John$_i$'s mother likes him$_i$.
			5. His$_i$ mother likes John$_i$.
nominal phrases	−a, −p	C	1. *He$_i$ likes John$_i$.
			2. *John$_i$ likes John$_i$.
			3. *He$_i$ thinks that [I like John$_i$].
Empty			
trace of A-movement	+a, −p	A	1. John$_i$ was seen e_i.
			2. *John$_i$ thinks that [I was seen e_i].
			3. John$_i$ seems [e_i to be here].
pro	−a, +p	B	1. *pro* habla inglés.
			2. *pro*$_i$ llegó Juan$_i$ ayer.
trace of Ā-movement	−a, −p	C	1. *Who$_i$ does he$_i$ like e_i
			2. *Who$_i$ does he$_i$ think that [I like e_i]?
PRO	+a, +p	A/B	1. John$_i$ tried *PRO*$_i$ to sleep.
			2. John thinks that it is inadvisable *PRO* to sleep.

Part I
Grammatical Sketch

2
Morphology

Nouns and verbs are the only word classes which exhibit affixes, with verbs being the most complex. Pronouns are also discussed, since they may appear attached to another word due to phonological dependence.

2.1 Nominal morphology

Nominal morphology in QZ is limited to the possessive prefix, *x-*, which occurs on alienably possessed nouns when they are possessed. Inalienably possessed nouns do not carry the prefix. Some examples are given in (24).[10] As the free translations indicate, number is not marked on the noun or the possessor, nor is there any morphological case marking.

(24) a. *x-yuu*   *men*
    POS-house 3
    his/her/their house(s)

   b. *x-pëëk*   *noo*
    POS-dog 1EX
    my/our dog(s)

---

[10]The addition of the possessive prefix to a root beginning with a voiced obstruent results in the devoicing of that consonant. This devoicing is reflected in the orthography.

c. *x-kayet   Biki*
   POS-cracker Virginia
   Virginia's cracker(s)

In each example in (24) the possessor follows the head noun. This is a fixed order. Other elements that may be present in a nominal phrase and the restrictions on their ordering are also presented here.

Nominal phrases do not carry any overt case marking, nor is there any way to indicate number except through the use of quantifiers. (Also, see chapter 12 for a description and analysis of the special construction used for marking number.) There are no clear definite nor indefinite articles in QZ, so many nominal phrases consist solely of a noun. In addition, a nominal phrase may contain a quantifier, one or more adjectives, a possessor, a demonstrative, and/or one or more relative clauses. Of these, the possessor and the relative clauses may themselves be embedded inside others of their same type. Normally, though, only one post-modifier is used. Only the quantifier (and any of its modifiers) precedes the noun.

Consider the following examples of nominal phrases. A quantifier can be modified by a following adverb, with both preceding the noun.

(25) *ndal yaa soldad*   SOLDADOS 2
     s/lots very soldier
     very many soldiers

The noun being quantified may also be modified by a demonstrative. In this case the quantifier is first, followed by the noun or pronoun, with the demonstrative last.

(26) *y-ra maa gin*   BENIT 19
     P-all 3A this
     all those animals

Possessors may be embedded, as shown by the bracketing in (27a). The possessor phrase follows the noun, though adjectives may intervene between the noun and the possessor, as shown in (27b).

(27) a. *x-yuu   [x-mig   [men]]*   MTLEMON 8
       POS-house POS-friend 3
       their friend's house

2.1 Nominal morphology

b. *x-pëëk   ngas   noo*
   POS-dog black 1EX
   my black dog

A quantifier may co-occur with a possessor. The quantifier occurs before the noun, while the possessor always follows the noun.

(28) *y-ra   x-kayet   Biki*   GRING 32
     P-all POS-cracker Virginia
     all Virginia's crackers

The possessor itself may include a demonstrative, which follows the noun expressing the possessor as expected.

(29) *xuz   [nzaap gin]*   CWENT 6
     papa   girl   this
     this girl's father

Finally, a nominal phrase may also be modified by a relative clause. (30a) gives an example where the relative clause modifies a quantified nominal phrase which includes an adjective, and (30b) shows a quantified possessive nominal phrase. Again we find the quantifier first, followed by the noun, then the optional adjective and optional possessor. The modifying relative clause, bracketed in each example, is last.

(30) a. *ndal   ngyed   gol   [w-u   mëëz]*   RANCHO 12
        lots   chicken old   C-eat   fox
        lots of old chickens that the fox ate

     b. *te   x-mig   noo [ne   r-laan   te   men*   HORTENS 4
        one POS-friend   1EX   that H-want   one   3

        [ne   r-nii   disa]]
        that H-speak   language
        a friend of mine that wants a person that speaks the language

Chapter 11 gives an analysis of the structure of QZ nominal phrases, where a version of the DP Hypothesis (Abney 1987 and Stowell 1989) is implemented in order to account for all the ordering restrictions and co-occurrence possibilities in QZ. Nominal phrases are therefore referred to as "DPs".

2.2 Verbal morphology

QZ verbal morphology consists of three prefixes and three suffixes. Of these, only the aspect marker is obligatory.[11] The next section describes the use of each aspect and mood marker, as well as the Imperative and Causative markers. Section 2.2.2 presents the three optional verbal suffixes and their usage.

2.2.1 Aspect marking and other prefixes

The three possible prefixes which may occur on a verb are an optional Imperative marker, an obligatory aspect marker, and an optional Causative marker. When present, they must occur in that order.

Except for the Causative, these prefixes are generally considered aspectual in nature throughout the Zapotec language family, but tense and mood also enter into the meaning at times.[12] The prefixes are traditionally divided between Realis and Irrealis moods, where the Stative, Completive, Habitual, and Progressive aspects are part of the Realis mood and the Unreal, Potential, Future, and the Imperative marker are under the Irrealis mood. It seems better, however, to make the distinction between aspect and mood instead, as shown in (31). Those prefixes normally considered part of the Realis mood are the true aspect markers which describe the internal structure of the action or event. In contrast, the mood markers, normally considered Irrealis, do not describe the internal structure of the action, but instead locate the event in some world that has a relation to the current real world (Chung and Timberlake 1985).

(31) **Aspect**   **Mood**

      Stative   Unreal
      Completive   Potential
      Habitual   Future
      Progressive   Imperative

All of the markers listed in (31) are informally referred to as aspect markers throughout this study and are assumed to be the head of IP (= I^0).

---

[11] In certain auxiliary or participial constructions the verb does not carry an aspect marker. Also, there are two existential and identificational verbs which do not take aspect, discussed in §3.2.

[12] Most of the information in this section is taken from Regnier (1989b), including all examples without text references.

2.2 Verbal morphology

2.2.1.1 Stative aspect. The Stative aspect marker *n-* is used most frequently on the two copular verbs, *uu* 'be' and *ak* 'become', and on most adjectives and some quantifiers when they function as predicates. Examples of each usage are given in (32).

(32) a. *n-uu gyët*   GRANDMA3 24
     S-be tortilla
     There were tortillas.

   b. *n-uu naal yaa nis*   MTLEMON 44
     S-be much very water
     There was a lot of water.

   c. *n-dal play n-ak ru nis*   BENIT 41
     lots beach S-become mouth water
     There are many beaches at the shore of the water.

   d. *n-gaal-o*   MEXICO 20
     S-fresh-3I
     It's fresh.

   e. *n-dux xnaa noo lo noo*   SNAKHAIR 4
     S-angry mother 1EX face 1EX
     My mother was angry with me.

   f. *ndal yaa soldad*   SOLDADOS 2
     S/lots very soldier
     There are lots of soldiers. *or* The soldiers are many.

In addition, the Stative aspect is frequently used with the verb *an* 'know', as shown in (33).

(33) a. *n-an-t noo-w*   GRING 37
     S-know-NEG 1EX-3I
     I don't know.

   b. *n-an-t men dex-til*   GRANDMA2 8
     S-know-NEG 3 word-Spanish
     They didn't speak any Spanish.

c. dxe   n-an   de chene y-zhiin   be ru   MARTRIST 26
   already s-know 2 when P-arrive 1I mouth

   x-yuu   x-mig   noo y-xob noo te disk
   POS-house POS-friend 1EX P-put 1EX one record
   You already know that when we arrive at my friend's house,
   I'm going to play a record.

Due to semantic incongruity, the Stative marker may not occur on all verbs. However, it may occur on some active verbs, where it forms a depictive adjunct, as shown in (34).

(34) z-ëëd   men n-bib   men gway
     PR-come   3   s-mount   3   horse
     He comes riding on a horse.

2.2.1.2 Completive aspect. *W-* is the QZ prefix for the Completive aspect. When this aspect marker is used, the action in question was completed prior to utterance time, or prior to some other point of time mentioned in the utterance. Example (35) shows two uses of the Completive aspect. The first usage indicates that the speaker finished returning prior to utterance time, while the second usage sets the completion of the hair changing to snakes as prior to the speaker's return.

(35) chene w-a noo s-te   w-ak-o   mëël   SNAKHAIR 9
     when C-go 1EX F-one C-become-3I   snake
     When I went again, it (the hair) had become snakes.

2.2.1.3 Habitual and Progressive aspects. Use of the Habitual aspect prefix *r-* expresses that the action is not closed with respect to some point in time. The Habitual aspect is thus the opposite of the Completive aspect. For most QZ verbs, the prefix *r-* is ambiguous between habitual action and present progressive action.

(36) a. r-a   noo skwel
        H -go 1EX school
        I go to school (every day). *or* I am going to school.

     b. r-oo   noo nis
        H-drink 1EX water
        I drink water (regularly) *or* I am drinking water.

2.2 Verbal morphology

When the Completive and the Habitual aspects are used in combination in a sentence, the Completive aspect marks an event that takes place completely within the span of time of the event or action marked by the Habitual aspect. An example is given in (37), where John finished arriving during the time Mary was reading the book.

(37) or   ne   w-lenza Zwa r-ool   Mblid liber
     hour that C-arrive John H-read Mary book
     When John arrived, Mary was reading a book.

A restricted set of QZ verbs, consisting solely of five verbs of motion, has two separate prefixes to distinguish between habitual and progressive action. For these verbs, the meaning of the prefix *r-* is narrowed to cover only habitual action. A different prefix, *z-*, is used to express progressive action. (38) gives examples of the two separate forms used with the verb *zob* 'sit'.

(38) a. r-zob men lgyeey yzhe   yzhe
        H-sit 3   market tomorrow tomorrow
        He sits in the market every day.

    b. zob   noo
       PR/sit 1EX
       I am sitting.

2.2.1.4 Unreal mood. There are two phonologically conditioned allomorphs for the Unreal mood: *n-* occurs on consonant-initial verbs, and *ny-* occurs on vowel-initial verbs. The Unreal mood marker is used in two major contexts in QZ. First, it is used in contrafactual conditions, as shown in example (39).

(39) a. che-bel   ny-oon-t   Min   ny-oon-t   Lawer
        when-if U-cry-NEG Yazmin U-cry-NEG Laura
        If Yazmin would not have cried, Laura would not have cried.

    b. che-bel   ny-oon-t   Min   ny-u   Lawer
       when-if U-cry-NEG Yazmin U-eat Laura
       If Yazmin would not have cried, Laura would have eaten.

The Unreal marker is also used on complements of the verb *laan* 'want' in two situations. The first case is where the wanted action never occurred, as indicated by the Habitual aspect marking on *laan* 'want' and by the negative marker on the verb in the second conjunct in (40a). The complement of *laan* 'want' may also carry the Unreal marker when the thing wanted did happen, as in (40b), though it is also grammatical with the Potential mood.

(40) a. *r-laan   noo   ny-u   noo-w   per   w-u-t   noo-w*
       H-want 1EX U-eat 1EX-3I but C-eat-NEG 1EX-3I
       I wanted to eat it, but I did not eat it.

   b. *w-laan   noo   ny-a   noo   no   w-a   noo*
      C-want 1EX U-go 1EX and C-go 1EX
      I wanted to go, and I went.

2.2.1.5 Potential mood. The Potential prefix is used as a miscellaneous marker in any situation that is not covered by one of the other mood prefixes, but it never refers to the past.

The Potential prefix has three allomorphs: *y-* used with regular consonant-initial verbs, *g-* used with regular vowel-initial verbs, and *ts-* which is used for some irregular vowel-initial and *z-*initial verbs.

The Potential marker is used in habitual future events, as shown in (41a), and in one-time future events, as in (41b).

(41) a. *s-te   iz   ne   z-ëët   ts-a   men   skwel*
       F-one year that PR-come P-go   3   school
       Next year, which is coming, he will go to school.

   b. *yzhe   g-ool   noo   liber*
      tomorrow P-read   1EX   book
      Tomorrow I will read a book.

The Potential marker is also used to express purpose, as in (42).

(42) *r-a   me r-ka   me gyus na   g-eey   x-nisyaa   me*   SANJOSE 2
     H-go 3R H-buy 3R pot   which P-cook POS-food 3R
     She went to buy a pot to cook her food in.

In addition, the Potential prefix is used in various subordinate clauses. (43a) gives an example of its use in a time clause and (43b) shows the Potential prefix in a conditional clause.

2.2 Verbal morphology

(43) a. *chene y-dxiin may y-beree noo*
 when P-arrive May P-return 1EX
 When May comes, I will return.

 b. *che-bel y-beree de ts-a-b Laa*
 when-if P-return 2 P-go-1I Oaxaca
 If you return, we will go to Oaxaca.

QZ also uses the Potential marker for polite commands and for negative commands. These uses are discussed in §2.2.1.7. The next section gives additional information about the Potential marker as it relates to the Future prefix.

2.2.1.6 Future mood. The Future prefix is *s-*. There does not seem to be any clear distinction in meaning between the Potential and Future moods. Sometimes the meaning seems exactly the same, as in the first occurrence of the word meaning "eat" (in bold type) in the examples in (44), which are taken from the same text.

(44) a. *laa de y-na bel ne **g-u** noo men* MANSNAKE 34
 FM 2 P-say if that P-eat 1EX 3

 o g-u-t noo men
 or P-eat-NEG 1EX 3
 You say whether I should eat him or I should not eat him.

 b. *porke w-dxiid loo men noo* MANSNAKE 51
 because C-come extract 3 1EX

 *laa de y-na bel ne **s-u** noo men o g-u-t noo men*
 FM 2 P-say if that F-eat 1EX 3 or P-eat-NEG 1EX 3
 Because the man came to get me, you say whether I should eat him or I should not eat him.

There are, however, several clear distributional differences between the two mood markers. For example, the Future marker is used in Yes/No questions, while the Potential prefix never is.

(45) a. *pe s-oo de nis*
 Q F-drink 2 water
 Will you drink water?

b. *pe g-oo   de nis
   Q P-drink 2   water
   (Will you drink water?)

A positive response to a Yes/No question is also always in the Future mood, as shown in (46).[13]

(46) a. s-oo   noo nis
        F-drink 1EX water
        I will drink water.

   b. *g-oo   noo nis
       P-drink 1EX water
       (I will drink water.)

A negative answer to a Yes/No question, however, will always be in the Potential mood. The Future prefix is never used in negative contexts.

(47) a. g-oo-t   noo nis
        P-drink-NEG 1EX water
        I will not drink water.

   b. *s-oo-t   noo nis
       F-drink-NEG 1EX water
       (I will not drink water.)

This positive/negative distributional scheme is followed in other situations as well. One example is given in (48) and additional examples will be seen in the Imperative constructions.

(48) a. zim   s-yab gyo
        perhaps F-fall rain
        Perhaps rain will fall.

   b. zim   g-yab-t   gyo
      perhaps P-fall-NEG   rain
      Perhaps rain will not fall.

---

[13]The marking of (46b) as ungrammatical is intended to relate to the context of a response to a Yes/No question only. In isolation or in other contexts (46b) is grammatical.

2.2 Verbal morphology

2.2.1.7 Imperative constructions. QZ has two kinds of commands: negative and positive. The positive commands are further classified into strong and mild types, where the mild command is more polite than the strong command.

Negative commands are formed by prefixing the Potential marker and suffixing the negative marker to the verb. The subject is always overt in negative commands.

(49) y-laa-t   de ze-gwa
P-do-NEG 2 how-that
Don't do that!

Mild positive commands also use the Potential marker. The subject is optional in this case, as shown in (50). In (50a) the second person subject is overt, but in (50b) it is not expressed.

(50) a. g-e de men naap wzëë y-beree noo
P-tell 2 3 soon afternoon P-return 1EX
You tell him I will return soon this afternoon.

b. ts-uu zëd-o
P-be salt-3I
Add salt to it.

For strong commands, the Imperative marker *gu-* is used. Vowel-initial verbs and irregular consonant-initial verbs prefix both the Imperative marker and the Potential marker, as shown in (51). For regular consonant-initial verbs, the Imperative marker is used in place of an aspect marker, as shown in (52). As verified by (52b), strong commands never have overt subjects.

(51) r-e ngyed gu-g-u men
H-say chicken IMP-P-eat 3
The chicken said, 'Eat him!'

(52) a. gu-nii disa
IMP-speak language
Speak Zapotec!

b. *gu-nii de disa
IMP-speak 2 language
(You speak Zapotec!)

2.2.1.8 Causative prefix.

The one remaining prefix is the Causative marker *gu-* (*gw-* before a vowel-initial root). This prefix must follow the aspect marker. In QZ the Causative morpheme is almost exclusively used with an unaccusative verb to add an Agent θ-role. Some examples are given in (53).

(53) a. *w-gw-et   men mëël*   AGOSTO 56
C-CAUS-die 3 snake
They killed the snake.

b. *per w-gw-et-et   men maa*   MENMAAC 12
but C-CAUS-die-NEG 3 3A
But he didn't kill the dog.

c. *r-gw-eey   men kafe*   DEATH 10
H-CAUS-cook 3 coffee
They make coffee.

Chapter 3 gives more details about the distribution of the Causative morpheme and shows that the QZ causative constructions are formed lexically rather than syntactically.

2.2.2 Verbal suffixes

There are only three morphemes which can be attached following the verb root. These consist of the negative marker *-t*, already used in several examples,[14] and two adverbials. The verb in example (54) contains all three morphemes. The suffix glossed 'MORE' intensifies the action of the verb. The suffix glossed 'ASSOC' has the meaning of associating the event being expressed by this clause with the action of someone else, i.e., if someone is (or is not) going to do something, *-ke* 'ASSOC' is used if someone else is (or is not) going to do the same thing. All three suffixes are optional and are independent of one another.

---

[14]See chapter 8 for a more complete description and analysis of the constructions involving negation.

(54) g-oo-t-re-ke   noo nis
     P-drink-NEG-MORE-ASSOC 1EX water
     I will not drink more water either.

2.3 Pronouns

In §2.2 all the possible verbal affixes in QZ were presented. None of them cross-reference or indicate agreement with either the subject or the object.[15] Though a few of the pronouns occur attached to the verb, these arguably are not affixes, but rather phonological clitics which simply attach to whatever precedes them in the sentence. These pronouns are not agreement markers (QZ completely lacks marking for agreement and does not license *pro*-drop); they remain separate syntactic entities filling an argument position and receiving a semantic role. It is ungrammatical to have both an attached pronoun and an additional nominal filling the same grammatical function in the sentence.

The chart in (55) shows the distribution and features of the pronouns in QZ.

---

[15]There is a third person plural subject agreement marker that is prefixed to the verb in some of the Zapotecan languages. For example, YZ (Butler 1976a, 1988) has the subject plural marker, *asaʔa*, which is used to pluralize a third person subject. (Only first and second person pronouns distinguish number in YZ.) This is the only type of agreement marker used in Zapotec, other than the resumptive pronouns which follow the verb when the subject is focused in some languages. QZ does not make use of either of these mechanisms.

(55) QZ Pronouns

Person	Features	Form	Phonological status
First	exclusive	*noo*	free
	inclusive	*be*	attaches / V__
Second		*de*	free
Third	general	*men*	free
	masculine	*zaa*	free
	respectful	*me*	attaches / V__
	animate	*maa*	free
	inanimate	*w(e) / o*	attaches -w / V__
			-o / C __
	deity/baby	*ne*	attaches / V__

The pronouns consisting of only a consonant and a regular vowel may attach to the preceding word (usually a verb) if it ends in a vowel. If they do attach, the final *e* is dropped, presumably indicating the QZ preference for closed syllables.[16] The third inanimate pronoun is the only one which has an alternate form so that it may also attach to words ending in a consonant. The second person pronoun *de* is an exception; even though it has the same phonological shape as the others that attach, *de* '2' is always a free standing word. The form of the other free pronouns is either a closed syllable or a syllable ending in a laryngealized vowel. These are syllables that normally bear stress, which explains why these pronouns do not cliticize.

Some examples of verbs with pronouns attached are given in (56).[17]

(56) a. *r-na-w*
    H-say-3I
    it says

b. *ts-a-b*
    P-go-1I
    let's go

---

[16] An alternative analysis involving an epenthetic *e* is also possible.
[17] The third person respectful pronoun, *me* '3R', is also used in cases where the indefinite pronoun *one* is used in English as shown in (56e).

2.3 Pronouns

   c. *g-u-b*
      P-chat-1I
      let's chat

   d. *gu-zëët-o*
      IMP-relate-3I
      tell it!

   e. *g-e-m-o*
      P-say-3R-3I
      one says it

Note that in (56a–c) the subject pronoun has attached to the verb root. In (56d) it is the object pronoun that has attached, but the subject cannot be overtly expressed since the use of the Imperative indicates it is a strong command. In (56e) both the subject and object pronouns have attached, but the VSO order must be maintained.

Across the Zapotecan language family, there are variations as to which pronouns may attach to the verb, but two things are constant: (1) each language has some forms which are always free and some forms which must attach, and (2) those forms that do attach to the verb must attach in the order V-S-O. This means that if a free form or a full nominal phrase is used for the subject, the object may not attach to the verb. In order to observe these constraints, most Zapotecan languages have a base root that can be inserted to "carry" a dependent object pronoun, since there is not a complete duplication between free and dependent forms in any of the languages. QZ does not have a base root; instead the dependent pronouns may attach to any immediately preceding word. Thus, the dependent pronouns may attach not only to a verb, but also to a pronoun or a noun, as exemplified in (57), or to any other word which is allowed to precede it syntactically. This behavior verifies the status of the dependent pronouns as phonological clitics.[18]

(57) a. *n-an-t   noo-w*   GRING 37
        S-know-NEG 1EX-3I
        I don't know.

---

[18]See Marlett (1993) for a description of the pronoun systems in seven other Zapotecan languages. Of those languages, the QZ system is most like that of Santa Catarina Xanaguía Zapotec, which is also from the southern group.

b. *ts-uu zëd-o*
P-be salt-3I
Add salt to it.

In addition to this distinction between free and dependent pronouns, QZ pronouns differ in crucial ways from pronouns in English. As indicated in the chart in (55), QZ pronouns lack any marking for morphological case.[19] Further, they are not marked for number either, though they can be quantified, as the next section demonstrates.

2.3.1 The category of pronouns in QZ. Pronouns in QZ have no overt case marking, nor is there a reflexive distinction or any number marking on the pronoun itself. All the QZ pronouns can be quantified without having a partitive meaning, as in (58). The reading is one of cardinal description of a group, rather than expressing that this is one part of a larger group.

(58) a. *z-a gaay mil men*
PR-go five thousand 3
Five thousand people are going. (lit.: Five thousand they(s) are going.)

b. *z-a gaay mil zaa*
PR-go five thousand 3M
Five thousand males are going. (lit.: Five thousand he(s) are going.)

The third person pronouns often seem to have a generic noun interpretation rather than a definite article interpretation.[20] In contrast to first and second person pronouns, third person pronouns can be modified by a demonstrative as well as a quantifier, as seen in (59a). First and second person pronouns can only be quantified. Third person pronouns can also be modified by an adjective (59b) or a possessor (59c).

(59) a. *y-ra maa gin* BENIT 19
P-all 3A this
all these animals

---

[19]Some of the other Zapotecan languages have limited case marking on their pronouns. For example, JZ distinguishes between genitive and nominative case in some forms and YZ distinguishes between nominative and accusative case in third person pronouns.

[20]Postal (1966) argues that pronouns in English are a form of definite article, and therefore, should be determiners or the head of DP, but pronouns in QZ do not function in this way.

b. *n-ak   noo men win*   GRANDMA1 6
   S-become 1EX 3   small
   I was a child.

c. *men La Merse*   GRANDMA1 12
   3   La Merced
   men/people of La Merced

There is evidence that at least some of the third person pronouns are shortened forms of the nouns they are related to, similar to the formation of pronouns from the noun classifiers in Jacaltec and Kanjobalan discussed by Craig (1991).

An alternative to analyzing QZ pronouns as definite articles is to posit that they function as group referents, where the person feature of the pronoun determines who may be included in the group. The additional characteristics of the third person pronouns, such as animal, human, familiar, male, baby, deity, and inanimate, serve to further define the group. I assume, then, that third person QZ pronouns are basically generic nouns with the category N, while first and second person pronouns have the category NP.

2.3.2 Null pronominals. QZ syntax is somewhat restricted with respect to empty categories. As far as traces go, syntactic A-movement is limited to unaccusative constructions and a single case of a passive verb (see §3.3.1); there is no evidence for raising. Ā-movement is quite productive in questions, focusing, and negation constructions, however, so *wh*-traces are clearly operative (see §3.4 and chapters 6–8). The availability of null pronominals is very limited, as detailed below.

I claim that QZ is not a *pro*-drop language, since there is no agreement marking on the verb to license *pro*-drop (see Jaeggli and Safir 1989) and in the vast majority of cases all arguments are required to be overt. This is definitely the unmarked situation. Therefore, referential *pro* is not normally licensed in QZ. The only places where *pro* (or its anaphoric counterpart) may be licensed are in some special anaphoric constructions (see §§4.1 and 12.2.1.1).

The situation is unclear with respect to nonfinite PRO. All Zapotecan languages have only minimally attested nonfinite verb forms. In Yatzachi, Choapan, and Atepec Zapotec a special verb form that has been called the infinitive occurs in purpose clauses after a motion verb. An example from YZ, taken from (Butler 1988:112), is given in (60) with the infinitive form in bold type. In these constructions, the infinitive may not have an expressed subject.

(60) gw-yej̈-e? **gü-ib** lachə-?
C-go-3R INF-wash clothes
S/he went to wash the clothes.

The other Zapotecan languages, including QZ, use the Potential marker on the embedded verb in that situation. Thus, only verbs with the Potential marker can possibly be analyzed as nonfinite.[21] But the use of the Potential does not necessarily mean that the clause is nonfinite, since there are many examples where the Potential mood is used in the main clause, as in example (61).

(61) a. *g-aa noo gyaan* LIFEINQ 12
P-wash 1EX plate
I'll wash the plates.

b. *ts-a-no noo de gyoow Santyoo* TRIPTOQ 58
P-go-take 1EX 2 river Santiago
I'll take you to the Santiago River.

Further, many embedded clauses in which the verb is inflected for the Potential mood and the English translation is a nonfinite construction still have overt subjects in QZ (see the examples in 62). Only clauses with a missing subject which are inflected for the Potential mood are therefore analyzed as possibly nonfinite here. Even in these cases, there may be an alternative analysis, as discussed below.

Some possible candidates for nonfinite clauses are given in (62), with bracketing and coindexing added to aid the reader. (62a–b) illustrate the very common usage of *g-an* 'P-know' in an embedded question. This form of the verb 'know' never has an expressed subject; it basically means '*PRO* find out', where *PRO* is coreferent with the subject of the immediately higher clause. This verb form is also sometimes used in the main clause where the null subject has an arbitrary reference (either PRO_{arb} or pro_{arb}), giving a reading of 'it will be found out' or 'we'll see', as in (62c).

---

[21]Embedded verbs carrying the Unreal mood marker would normally be considered nonfinite also. In QZ these verbs always have an expressed subject, so PRO is not involved.

2.3 Pronouns

(62) a. [n-a men$_i$ [g-an PRO$_i$ [pe [r-laan-t   noo [ts-a noo   HORTENS 3
      S-say 3   P-know   Q   H-want-NEG 1EX P-go 1EX

    [y-laa noo dxiin Estados Unidos]]]]]
    P-do 1EX work States United
    She asked if I wouldn't want to go and work in the United States.

b. [r-laan noo [ts-a noo$_i$ [g-an   PRO$_i$ LIFEINUS 3
   H-want 1EX P-go 1EX P-know

   [pe-zee n-ak-o]]]]
   Q-how S-become-3I
   I want to go to find out how it is.

c. [g-an   PRO/pro$_{arb}$ [pe [s-na   de   TRIPTOQ 8
   P-know   Q   F-want 2

   [g-aa   de lyu o g-aa   de lo daa]]]
   P-lie.down 2 land or P-lie.down 2 face petate
   We'll see if you will want to lie down on the ground or on a petate.

In (62) it is the verb *g-an* 'P-know' itself that requires the null subject; it is not selected by the higher verb. Thus, whether these clauses count as nonfinite or not, it is clear that their form is not due to control by a higher predicate.

Saxon (1989) makes a distinction between two distinct phenomena that have been been labeled 'control'. One phenomenon is the presence of obligatory control predicates, like *try* in English, which entail the presence of an obligatorily controlled DP. QZ does not appear to have such predicates. For example, there is no word meaning 'try' in QZ. The closest one can come in expressing a sentence such as "I am trying to learn Zapotec" is given in (63), where the verb *laan* 'want' is used. The subject of the embedded verb is overtly expressed. Further, its reference is not obligatorily controlled, as shown in (64).

(63) *r-laan noo y-seed noo disa*
      H-want 1EX P-learn 1EX language
      I want to learn the language.

(64) r-laan   noo   y-seed   Jose   disa
     H-want 1EX   P-learn   José language
     I want José to learn the language.

See (67)–(68), though, for discussion of the verb *xaal* 'send' as an obligatory object control predicate.

A separate source of "control effects", Saxon says, is the existence of empty subject DPs which always receive interpretations of coreference with a higher DP. *G-an* 'P-know' selects an external argument which must be null and must find its reference from a higher DP, if available. Further evidence of the unique character of *g-an* 'P-know' is that it cannot be inflected for negation or for any of the adverbial suffixes. The Stative form of the verb is inserted to carry these markers, as shown in (65). Also, *an* is the only verb that can select an embedded question. (See §7.2.1.)

(65) n-an-t-er   noo$_i$ g-an   PRO$_i$ pa   go   sar   BRU 83
     S-know-NEG-MORE 1EX   P-know   what   thing follow
     I don't know anything more about what happened.

The example in (66) also shows a "control effect" where there is an empty subject embedded under the verb meaning 'want'. Examples such as (66) are rare since almost every sentence containing the verb *laan* 'want' has the subject of the embedded verb expressed overtly. Further, there is no coreference requirement between the subject of *laan* 'want' and the subject of the selected verb. (66) could read 'One time an American woman wanted her brother (i.e., someone else) to take a Mexican woman to the United States'. Therefore, there is again no evidence of an obligatory control predicate.

(66) teb   tir   [[te   wnaa   gring]$_i$ r-laan   GRING 1
     one   time   one   woman   gringa   H-want

     [ts-a-no   PRO$_i$ te   wnaa   mejikan   Estados Unidos]
     P-go-take   one   woman   Mexican   States United
     One time a gringa (American woman) wanted to take a Mexican woman to the United States.

The best example of what might truly be an obligatory control predicate is shown in (67) which involves "object control". This example contains some of the more complex constructions allowed in QZ. The phrase in the lowest clause of this example *y-rup de men* 'P-two 2 3' is an example

2.3 Pronouns   41

of the special number-marking construction. (See chapter 12 for its analysis.) The clause *y-xaal x-pee noo* 'I'll send my boy' is an example of a construction in which the subject of any transitive clause may be covert if it is coreferent with the possessor of the object of the clause (see §§4.1 and 12.2.1.1). Thus, the subject is the first person exclusive pronoun *noo* because it is coindexed with the possessor of the object. Note that the subject of *y-xaal* 'P-send' is not coreferent with the subject of the clause above it. The clause which is selected by *xaal* 'send' contains *karëz* 'call' which is a transitive verb and is followed only by its object, the second person pronoun. The Potential marker is used, so this can be analyzed as a nonfinite clause. The understood subject is *x-pee noo* 'my boy', so the PRO subject of *y-karëz de* 'to call you' is controlled by the object of the clause above it.

(67) *per   yzhe   dxe   n-an   de*
     but   tomorrow   already   S-know   2

    *[y-xaal **pro**$_i$ [x-pee   [noo]$_i$]$_j$ [y-karëz **PRO**$_j$ de*
    P-send   POS-boy   1EX   P-call   2

    [chiid   de [g-u   de diiz   y-rup   de men$_k$]]]]
    P-come   2   P-chat   2   word   P-two   2   3
But tomorrow you already know that I'll send my boy to call you to come and chat with him.

In constructions like these where *xaal* 'send' takes a human object and a clausal complement, the subject of the embedded predicate must be coreferent with the object of 'send'. Normally, though, the coreferent subject is overtly expressed, as shown in the rewording of (67) in (68).

(68) *per   yzhe   dxe   n-an   de*
     but   tomorrow   already   S-know   2

    [y-xaal noo   Jose$_i$ [y-karëz Jose$_i$ de
    P-send   1EX   José   P-call   José   2

    [chiid   de [g-u   de diiz   y-rup   de Dolf]]]]
    P-come   2   P-chat   2   word   P-two   2   Rodolfo
But tomorrow you already know that I'll send José to call you to come and chat with Rodolfo.

This usage of *xaal* 'send' may be seen as an obligatory object control predicate, due to the required coreference between the direct object of *xaal* 'send' and the subject of its clausal complement. However, the controlled DP need not be (and in QZ usually is not) empty. Thus (as Saxon 1989 proposed), some predicates may select a clause containing a [+anaphor, +pronominal] subject, even though the clause is finite. Therefore, PRO could be active in QZ in the very limited sense seen (though using *pro*$_{[+anaphor]}$ would probably be more accurate).

The question still arises as to why the null subject occurs in examples like (66) and (67), when the normal situation is for all DPs to be overt. I conjecture that the distinction is dependent upon the antecedent. QZ seems to have a hierarchy of nominal phrases which distinguishes between pronouns on the one hand and full nominal phrases on the other. Proper names and nominal phrases consisting solely of a bare noun fit in the middle. In every case where there is a null subject (other than as subject of *g-an* 'P-know'), the antecedent is a full nominal phrase. For example, in (66) the antecedent is *te wnaa gring* 'one gringa (American woman)' and in (67) it is *x-pee noo* 'my boy'. This type of antecedent is able to license a null pronominal. In fact, repeating the full nominal phrase is highly disfavored, especially when the full nominal phrase contains a quantifier; either an overt or null third person pronominal is acceptable. Just the opposite is true when the antecedent is a pronoun. In that case, repetition must occur. If the antecedent is a proper name or a bare noun, all three options are available: the proper name or bare noun may be repeated, or it may be replaced by either an overt or a null third person pronoun. This phenomenon will be analyzed further in chapter 4.

QZ also seems to have an expletive *pro* which is very similar to the expletive *it* in English, though the QZ version is not overt.[22] The examples in (69) show the types of constructions that allow the expletive *pro*, with bracketing added for clarification. Again, the use of this null pro-form is quite rare.

(69) a. *[s-ak*   **pro-exp** *[[ts-a de lo lbanyil]*   BENIT 57
     F-become   P-go 2 face builder

     o *[ts-a de [y-chux de mëlbyuu]]]]*
     or P-go 2 P-peel 2 fish
     It could be that you can go to the builders or go to peel shrimp.

---

[22]Jaeggli and Safir (1989) report that this same distribution of allowing PRO and the expletive *pro* but not licensing referential *pro* via agreement features is also found in German, Icelandic, and Faroese.

2.3 Pronouns

    b. *[w-yen   **pro-exp** diiz*   AGOSTO 71
       c-look.for   word

       [laa Dolf   n-uu Pwert   y-rup x-unaa   Dolf]
        FM Rodolfo s-be Salina.Cruz P-two POS-woman Rodolfo
       It was heard (or somebody heard) that Rodolfo and his wife were in Salina Cruz.

Meteorological constructions in English also use the word *it* in a non-referential way. Note that in QZ the constructions used to describe the weather are regular unaccusative constructions, as shown in (70), and thus do not involve an expletive element.

(70) a. *r-yab gyeey noze ngich   x-too   gyeey*   LIFEINUS 63
      H-fall ice   only s/white POS-head mountain
      It snows such that it's all white on the mountain.

    b. *per r-yab gyo*   OLDMAN 11
      but H-fall rain
      But it rained.

    c. *xiid   zeeb   noo axta-ge   gyët   gin nga*   MTLEMON2 38
      PR/come lower 1EX until-that down this there

       dxe   w-yeep gyo
       already c-raise rain
      We arrived below when it quit raining.

    d. *bwëz   noo axta w-yeep gyo*   MTLEMON2 42
      c/wait 1EX until c-raise rain
      I waited until the rain quit.

3
Syntax

This chapter begins by establishing the strict VSO word order of QZ and discussing the positions in which adverbial elements may be found.

Section 3.2 describes existential, identificational, and stative sentences. Section 3.3 then moves to passive, unaccusative, raising, and causative constructions.

Finally, §3.4 covers the clear cases involving overt movement. These are focus constructions, questions, and negative constructions. (See also chapters 6–9.)

3.1 Basic VSO word order

The basic clausal word order is VSO, as seen in the transitive clauses in (71). The verb is first, followed immediately by the subject, which is followed by the direct object.

(71) a. *w-eey Benit mël*   BENIT 4
C-take Benito fish
Benito took a fish.

b. *r-laa noo dxiin yzhe yzhe*   BENIT 11
H-do 1EX work tomorrow tomorrow
I do work every day.

    c. *r-u   mëëz ngyed*   AGOSTO 18
       H-eat fox   chicken
       The fox is eating the chicken.

This VSO order is quite strict and is used to determine the grammatical functions of the nominal phrases, since there is no morphological case marking. None of the sentences in (71) above can be interpreted with VOS order.

In intransitive sentences (both unergative and unaccusative), the verb is initial and is followed immediately by the subject, as shown in (72). The examples in (72)–(74) also illustrate the form of QZ prepositional phrases, which have the same type of head-initial structure seen with verbs. These prepositions are usually body part terms, e.g., *ru* 'mouth' in (72b), *chu* 'belly' in (72c), and *lo* 'face' in (73a–b) and (74).

(72) a. *s-ya   men*   SAMUEL 13
       PR-go 3
       He is going.

    b. *s-ya   men ru   x-yuu   men*   CWENT 14
       PR-go 3   mouth POS-house 3
       He is going to his house.

    c. *chu   tank zob   giblew ne   r-len   nis   za*   BATHROOM 5
       belly tub   PR.sit faucet that H-bear water warm
       In the middle of the tub sits a faucet that bears warm water.

The examples in (73) show that the indirect object follows the direct object in ditransitive clauses, thus normally appearing at the end of the clause. The preposition *lo* 'face' is required with indirect objects.

(73) a. *w-dee men bal   lo   ngol*   CWENT 45
       C-give 3   bullet face vulture
       He shot a vulture (lit.: He gave a bullet to the vulture).

    b. *w-nii   men disa   lo   noo*   HORTENS 38
       C-speak 3   language face 1EX
       She spoke Zapotec to me.

In normal ditransitives, the order of V-S-O-IO is fixed. The indirect object directly follows the subject, however, when the object has the form of a

3.1 Basic VSO word order   47

direct quotation, as shown in (74). Presumably, this shift in order is due to Extraposition of the direct quote object. Direct quotations may also be fronted.

(74) r-e   Samwel lo   Javyer ay   SAMUEL 19
      H-say Samuel face Javier   ah
      Samuel said to Javier, 'Ah!'

The only morphemes that can occur between the verb and the subject, or between the subject and the object or other complements of the verb are the three verbal suffixes discussed in §2.3. Free adverbials occur either sentence-initially or clause-finally only, as shown in (75a–d). The locative can also be fronted as (75e), but it cannot occur between the verb and the subject (75f).

(75) a. *yzhe   ts-a   noo Mejiko*
        tomorrow P-go 1EX Mexico
        Tomorrow I will go to Mexico City.

   b. **ts-a yzhe   noo Mejiko*
        P-go tomorrow 1EX Mexico
        (I will go tomorrow to Mexico City.)

   c. **ts-a noo   yzhe   Mejiko*
        P-go 1EX   tomorrow Mexico
        (I will go tomorrow to Mexico City.)

   d. *ts-a   noo Mejiko yzhe*
        P-go 1EX Mexico tomorrow
        I will go to Mexico City tomorrow.

   e. *Mejiko ts-a   noo yzhe*
        Mexico P-go 1EX tomorrow
        To Mexico City I will go tomorrow.

   f. **ts-a Mejiko noo yzhe*
        P-go Mexico 1EX tomorrow
        (I will go to Mexico City tomorrow.)

There is thus a strict adjacency requirement between the verb and its arguments, including the subject as well as the complements of the verb.

3.2 Sentences expressing states or existence

QZ allows various constructions for expressing existence, identification, and states of being. These constructions are discussed in turn in the following sections.

3.2.1 Existential sentences

Existential sentences usually contain the copular verb *uu* inflected with Stative aspect, *n-uu* 'S-be', but sometimes the other copular verb, *ak* 'become', is used as in (76d). These sentences can have the normal verb-initial order, as shown in (76a–c), or the subject may be fronted, as in (76d–f).

(76) a. *n-uu gyët*   GRANDMA3 24
       S-be tortilla
       There were tortillas.

     b. *n-uu naal yaa nis*   MTLEMON 44
         S-be much very water
         There was a lot of water.

     c. *n-uu ndal yag bduu ru lgyëëz Santyoo*   TRIPTOQ 63
         S-be lots tree banana mouth town Santiago
         There are lots of banana trees in the town of Santiago.

     d. *ndal play n-ak ru nis*   BENIT 41
         lots beach S-become mouth water
         There are many beaches at the shore of the water.

     e. *ndal yaa yag gyer n-uu*   MTLEMON2 18
         lots very tree pine S-be
         There were lots of pine trees.

     f. *le mdxin n-uu len yuu*   YENEGU 31
         FM deer S-be inside house
         The deer is in the house.

In addition, existentials may be expressed without a verb being present at all. For example, in (77) the quantifier *ndal* 'lots' acts as the predicate.

3.2 Sentences expressing states or existence

(77) ndal   yaa   soldad   SOLDADOS 2
     s/lots very   soldiers
     There are lots of soldiers. *or* The soldiers are many.

QZ also has a negative existential verb, *yët*. This verb is one of two that does not take any aspect marking. Examples of its use are given in (78) (see §8.2.1 for more examples and possible analyses of the negative existential verb).

(78) a. *per   yët   dxiin*   GRANDMA3 7
       but   not.be work
       But there wasn't any work.

     b. *per   yët   loon*   TRIPTOQ 7
       but   not.be bed
       But there aren't any beds.

3.2.2 Identificational sentences

The other verb which does not take aspect marking is *la* 'call' used in identificational sentences, as in (79). This verb is used to specify the name of a particular individual or to give a definition of a term. It is not fully identificational in the sense that *la* would not be used to say "That man is a doctor." The copular verbs or a construction with a nominal phrase acting as the predicate, as in (83), would be used in that case.

(79) *n-a   men noo   la   Susan*   HORTENS 39
     S-say 3   1EX   call Susan
     She said, "My name is Susan."

These identificational sentences can have the expected order with the verb first, followed by the two arguments being equated (80a). In the majority of the text examples, though, the surface word order is nominal phrase-*la*-proper name, as shown in (79) and (80b–e), where I assume that the nominal phrase has fronted via Ā-movement. (80f) verifies that the proper name may be fronted instead.

(80) a. *la   men   Lawer*   AGOSTO 3
       call 3   Laura
       She was called Laura.

b. *mëëd la Karmita* GRING 5
   baby call Carmita
   The baby's name was Carmita.

c. *te men la Samwel* SAMUEL 11
   one 3 call Samuel
   One man was called Samuel.

d. *x-mig men la Danyel* MTLEMON 12
   POS-friend 3 call Daniel
   His friend's name is Daniel.

e. *le wnaa ne mejikan la Gecha* GRING 3
   FM woman that Mexican call Lucrecia
   The Mexican woman was called Lucrecia.

f. *Tomas la te mgyeey* AGOSTO 11
   Thomas call one man

   ne w-tsa-nya xsaap Manwel
   that C-give-hand daughter Manuel
   Thomas is the name of the man who married Manuel's daughter.

The verb *la* 'call' is also used in giving definitions. Such definitions can follow an existential statement, as shown in (81)–(82), where the (a) example in each case is an existential and the (b) example gives the definition.[23]

(81) a. *n-uu refineri* BENIT 35
       S-be refinery
       There is a refinery.

   b. *refineri la led-ne r-boo men petrolye* BENIT 36
      refinery call body-that H-extract 3 kerosene
      A refinery is where they extract kerosene.

(82) a. *n-uu ndik* BENIT 38
       S-be dry.dock
       There is a dry dock.

---

[23]This text is a conversation between two friends. One of the men has returned from working in the city and he is describing it to his friend, who has never been there.

3.2 Sentences expressing states or existence

    b. *ndik   la   led-ne   r-la-wen   men bark*   BENIT 39
       dry.dock call body-that H-do-good 3   ship
       A dry dock is where they fix ships.

Identificational sentences not involving a name can be expressed without a verb, as shown in (83). In this case the nominal phrase *x-bur noo* 'my burro' acts as the predicate and the pronoun used to refer to animals, *maa*, is the subject.

(83) *per x-bur   noo   maa*   BRU 27
       but POS-burro 1EX   3A
       But it's my burro.

3.2.3 Stative sentences

Several of the preceding examples used the copular verbs and Stative aspect. In addition to giving an existential reading, a state of being may be expressed using the copular verbs *n-uu* 'S-be' or *n-ak* 'S-become'. Text examples of this type all have the adjective first, followed by the Stative verb and then the item being described, as shown in (84).[24]

(84) a. *barat   n-uu   zhob*   GRANDMA3 25
          cheap   S-be   elote
          Elote (corn) was cheap.

      b. *kontent   n-uu lextoo mër   gol*   MARTRIST 40
          contented S-be liver   pigeon male
          The male pigeon was content.

      c. *zhaandxe n-ak   Estados Unidos*   LIFEINUS 4
          pretty   S-become States   United
          The United States is pretty.

      d. *zhaandxe n-ak   x-too   gyeey   gin*   LIFEINUS 61
          pretty   S-become POS-head mountain this
          It's pretty at the top of this mountain.

The difference in usage between the two copular verbs is not completely clear, though in general *uu* only appears with the Stative aspect and is used to express existence or a (fairly) permanent state. In contrast,

---

[24]The sentence in (84b) literally means that his liver was content. For most Zapotecs, the liver is recognized as the center of emotions.

ak usually occurs with adjectives which are more temporary, such as 'pretty' in (84c–d) above.[25] Also, *ak* may carry other aspect markings besides the Stative aspect, as shown in (85), where its gloss of 'become' is clearer.

(85) a. *g-ak   men x-unaa   de*   MARTRIST 29
P-become 3   POS-woman 2
She will become your wife.

  b. *noze byu   w-ak   gyus*   SANJOSE 9
only piece C-become pot
The pot was only pieces.

  c. *pur mëël w-ak   gits x-too   noo* SNAKHAIR 10
pure snake C-become hair POS-head 1EX
My hair had become pure snakes.

The adjective itself can also serve as the predicate in a stative sentence. Neither copular verb is present in the examples in (86). The Stative aspect marker is usually found on the adjective in these constructions, though a subset of the adjectives do not carry it.

(86) a. *n-gaal-o*   MEXICO 20
S-fresh-3I
It's fresh.

  b. *n-gaa den*   MEXICO 21
S-green ranch
The ranch is green.

  c. *n-dux xnaa   noo lo noo*   SNAKHAIR 4
S-angry mother 1EX face 1EX
My mother was angry with me.

  d. *kesentyent n-yag x-too   gyeey   gin* LIFEINUS 68
much   S-cold POS-head mountain this
It was very cold on the mountain top.

---

[25]The distinction between the two copular verbs thus corresponds somewhat to the stage-level versus individual-level distinction (Kratzer 1989). There is no discernible difference in the position of the subject, however.

3.3 Constructions involving changes in argument structure

These next two sections deal with the constructions which are analyzed to involve movement. The possibilities for movement to an argument position (A-movement), including passive, unaccusative, raising, and causative constructions, are considered in this section.

3.3.1 Passive constructions

Passive constructions are only minimally attested throughout the Zapotecan language family. Marlett and Pickett (1987:413–414) claim that Isthmus Zapotec does not have any passives. In contrast, Yatzachi, Texmelucan, and Choapan Zapotec have a passive morpheme that attaches to a normally transitive verb. In this case the underlying direct object bearing the Theme θ-role surfaces in the subject position and no Agent θ-role is expressed. An example from YZ (Butler 1988:120) is given in (87), where the transitive verb is shown in (87a) and its passive counterpart is given in (87b).

(87) a. *ch-aʔo-boʔ-on*
   H-buy-3F-3I
   He buys it.

   b. *ch-d-aʔo-n*
   H-PASS-buy-3I
   It is bought.

QZ does not have such an affix to indicate that a normally transitive verb has become passive. In certain situations where it is clear from the semantics which role the participants are playing, focusing the object gives it more prominence, which is similar to the effect in a passive construction. The subject argument is still present and has not changed form so that this is simply an object focus construction and not a true passive construction.

There is one QZ verb which is underlyingly passive, however. This is the verb *zël* 'be.found'. *Zël* only takes one argument and that argument may not be the Agent. Some examples are given in (88).

(88) a. dxe   w-ak   xe   r-ye   noo men   MARTRIST 5
       already C-become   F.day   H-search 1EX 3

   per r-zël-t   men
   but H-be.found-NEG   3
   Already another day has passed that I've been looking for her
   (a wife) but she hasn't been found.

b. dxe   w-zël   x-nobye   mër   gol   MARTRIST 41
   already C-be.found   POS-fiancee pigeon   male
   Already the male pigeon's fiancee was found!

c. r-zël-t   led-ne   g-u-gwe   noo   MTLEMON2 36
   H-be.found-NEG   body-that   P-eat-lunch   1EX
   A place we could eat lunch was not found.

d. dxe   w-zaa zek chup tson gbiz w-zël   Mblid AGOSTO 64
   already C-walk as   two three day C-be.found Mary
   After two or three days Mary was found.

When the finder or the Agent is expressed, the preposition *lo* 'face' must be used, as shown in (89a). This is equivalent to adding the *by*-phrase in English to express the Agent. (89b–c) verify that the Agent may not be added as a second DP following the verb, either before or after the Theme, *Karmita*. These sentences are simply nonsense.

(89) a. r-zël-t   Karmita lo   men   GRING 40
       H-be.found-NEG   Carmita face 3
       They didn't find Carmita. (lit.: Carmita was not found by them.)
       *(Carmita didn't find them.)

   b. *r-zël-t   Karmita men
       H-be.found-NEG   Carmita 3
       (They didn't find Carmita)
       (Carmita didn't find them.)

   c. *r-zël-t   men Karmita
       H-be.found-NEG   3   Carmita
       (They didn't find Carmita)
       (Carmita didn't find them.)

3.3 Constructions involving changes in argument structure 55

Additional examples of this passive verb where the Agent is expressed via the prepositional phrase are given in (90).

(90) a. *chene w-zël   Karmita lo Biki*   GRING 41
    when C-be.found Carmita face Virginia

    la Karmita n-uu axta-ge   leen ofisin
    FM Carmita S-be until-that inside office
    When Virginia found Carmita, Carmita was inside the office.
    (lit.: When Carmita was found by Virginia...)

b. *w-zël-t   x-mgyeey men lo men*   RANCHO 46
   C-be.found-NEG POS-man 3   face 3
   She didn't find her husband. (lit.: Her husband wasn't found by her.)

I assume that since this verb *zël* is always passive, its lexical entry specifies that it subcategorizes for a complement bearing the Theme θ-role and for an optional Oblique Agent, but that it does not assign an external argument.

There is another verb in QZ which has a similar meaning to *zël* 'be.found'. This verb *tsalo* which is glossed 'find' is a normal transitive verb taking two arguments which correspond to the Agent and Theme θ-roles. Some examples are given in (91).

(91) a. *w-tsalo mëëk te   mëël*   MENMAAC 37
    C-find dog one snake
    The dog found a snake.

b. *chu den Gyak w-tsalo men te mëël*   RANCHO 23
    belly ranch Gyak C-find 3   one snake
    In the middle of the Gyak ranch they found a snake.

c. *w-tsalo maa te   meedx axta-ge x-too   gyeey*   RYENEGU 4
    C-find 3A one lion   until-that POS-head mountain
    He (a deer) found a lion on the mountain top.

d. *per nëz w-tsalo men tson mgyeey*   CWENT 34
   but road C-find 3 three man

   ne n-ak ngbaan
   that S-become thief
   But on the way he encountered three men that were thieves.

e. *w-tsalo men te ngyed*   MANSNAKE 29
   C-find 3 one chicken
   They met a chicken.

From these examples it is clear that the meaning of *tsalo* is more that of 'encounter by chance' or 'meet', whereas *zël* was the result of being searched for purposely. The verb *tsalo*, though a fixed form now, most likely derived from the verb *ts-a* 'P-go' and the preposition *lo* 'face'. The addition of the preposition (with its argument) to the intransitive verb produces a transitive verb taking the normal two arguments.

Another case where this type of lexical preposition incorporation has occurred, with a concomitant change in argument structure, is the verb *a-nal* 'go-with', as shown in (92).

(92) a. *gu-ts-a-nal men*   HORTENS 23
      IMP-P-go-with 3
      Go with him!

   b. *w-a-nal noo men*   MTLEMON 3
      C-go-with 1EX 3
      I went with them.

   c. *y-ra zhiin men w-a no noo w-a-nal men*   TEXAS 17–18
      P-all child 3 C-go and 1EX C-go-with 3
      All their children went and I went with them.

I assume that this incorporation is lexical rather than syntactic, since *nal* 'with' is never used as a separate preposition and since these verb-preposition compounds have a very limited distribution. The preferred way of expressing the comitative relationship in QZ is via the special number-marking constructions (analyzed in chapter 12) like those shown in (93).

(93) a. ts-a   de y-rup de Susan   TRIPTOQ 80
       P-go 2   P-two 2   Susan
       You can go with Susan.

   b. le koyot s-ya y-rup men   MANSNAKE 64
      FM coyote PR-go P-two 3
      The coyote went with the man.

It is practically impossible to tell whether there has been actual movement of the Theme argument to the subject position, or whether the Theme simply remains in place in QZ. To remain in place would contradict Case theory, which is assumed to be universal. Likewise, base generating the single argument of passives or unaccusatives in subject position would violate the Uniformity of Theta Assignment Hypothesis. The natural assumption, then, is that QZ behaves like other languages studied and movement to subject position does occur. There is, however, some empirical evidence that the Theme argument does occupy the surface subject position in other Zapotecan languages with more overt marking of morphological case and plural agreement. This evidence will be presented after the discussion of the unaccusative constructions.

3.3.2 Unaccusative constructions

There are a number of verbs in QZ which are unaccusatives in the sense that they are intransitives which select only a Theme argument. No Agent is present. Some examples are given in (94).

(94) a. w-yëkwen gyëël men   OLDMAN 32
       C-heal   well   3
       He healed nicely.

   b. lex   w-yab gits x-too   noo leen gyoow   SNAKHAIR 3
      later C-fall hair POS-head 1EX inside river
      Later, my hair fell into the river.

   c. w-ats   te   bla   tabel lo   pwent   OLDMAN 15
      C-break one piece plank face bridge
      A piece of the planking on the bridge broke.

d. *dxe w-eey bëël wen wen ndxee nagon*   MOLE 2
already C-cook meat good good very however

chene g-yu ngob
when P-mix dough
After the meat is cooked very well, you mix the dough.

e. *w-et mëël*   SAMUEL 27
C-die snake
The snake died.

These unaccusative verbs are almost exclusively the verbs which are used in the QZ causative constructions, discussed in §3.3.4.

There is no evidence which indicates that the argument bearing the Theme θ-role in the unaccusative and passive constructions occupies the subject position, rather than remaining in the object position, at S-structure. Neither is there counter-evidence to the normally assumed A-movement for these cases. Other Zapotecan languages provide some evidence. In YZ the third person subject pronouns must be used in unaccusative constructions, as shown in (95),[26] which is consistent with Burzio's Generalization that verbs which do not assign external arguments cannot assign Case to their complements. (96a) then shows the two forms of pronouns in a ditransitive construction, and (96b–c) verify that the object form of the pronoun can be used without a preceding subject pronoun in an imperative or infinitive construction. This difference in morphological case marking indicates that movement to the subject position from the D-structure position which is assigned the Theme θ-role must occur in unaccusative constructions.

(95) a. *bg^{w}ix:-e?*
C/fall-3RS
He fell.

b. **bg^{w}ix:-ne?*
C/fall-3RO
(He fell.)

(96) a. *b-nežR^w-e?-(e)ne?-(e)b*
C-give-3RS-3RO-3AO
He gave it to him.

---

[26]The YZ examples are taken from Butler (1976a, 1988) or obtained from her personally.

3.3 Constructions involving changes in argument structure

b. *gʷ-dao-n*
C-eat-3IO
Eat it!

c. *š-aʔa   go-ye-b*
F-go/1S INF-care-3AO
I am going to care for it (an animal).

Also, there is a verbal prefix indicating plural agreement, *əsəʔə*,[27] which is used with third person plural subjects only. (97) illustrates the use of this subject plural marker for transitive subjects and for intransitive subjects which bear the Agent role. This marker is used with the Theme argument of unaccusative verbs as well, as shown in (98), indicating that A-movement has taken place.

(97) a. *b-osoʔo-nežRʷ-eʔ-(e)neʔ-(e)b*
C-SPL-give-3RS-3RO-3AO
They gave it to him.

b. *b-esəʔə-sed-eʔ*
C-SPL-study-3RS
They studied.

(98) a. *g-osəʔə-bix:-eʔ*
C-SPL-fall-3RS
They fell.

b. *g-osəʔə-tas-eʔ*
C-SPL-sleep-3RS
They slept.

I therefore claim that the QZ passive and unaccusative constructions are best analyzed as involving A-movement of the underlying direct object bearing the Theme θ-role to the S-structure subject position, in accord with the normal assumptions of the Principles and Parameters framework.

---

[27]There is variation in the realization of the vowels in this morpheme when the root begins with a consonant, ranging from the given form through *esəʔə, osəʔə,* and *osoʔo*. Further variations occur with vowel-initial roots.

3.3.3 Raising constructions

Constructions containing "raising" verbs are not frequently used in QZ. Since the complement of the verb *zem* 'seem' is not necessarily nonfinite in QZ, the subject of the embedded verb can receive Case in its original position, and raising is not needed. The sentences given in (99a), and (100a) were solicited from my language consultant and are interpreted as given in the free translation. As is evident from the (b) and (c) examples in each case, the lower subject may not be raised up to follow the verb *zem* 'seem'.

(99) a. *kesentyent   zem   n-gan   disa*
   much   seem s-difficult language
   Zapotec seems very difficult. *or* It seems that Zapotec is very difficult.

   b. **kesentyent   zem   disa   n-gan*
   much   seem language s-difficult
   (Zapotec seems very difficult.)

   c. **kesentyent   zem   disa   gan   disa*
   much   seem language difficult language
   (Zapotec seems very difficult.)

(100) a. *zem   r-laan   Jose   ts-a   men   Laa*
   seem H-want José P-go   3   Oaxaca
   José seems to want to go to Oaxaca. *or* It seems that José wants to go to Oaxaca.

   b. **zem   Jose   r-laan   ts-a   men   Laa*
   seem José H-want P-go   3   Oaxaca
   (José seems to want to go to Oaxaca.)

   c. **zem   Jose   r-laan   men   ts-a   men   Laa*
   seem José H-want 3   P-go   3   Oaxaca
   (José seems to want to go to Oaxaca.)

Apparently, *zem* 'seem' subcategorizes for a clausal complement and does not assign an external argument. Its subject position may not be filled by raising, but only by the expletive *pro*, similar to the example in (101).

3.3 Constructions involving changes in argument structure   61

(101) s-ak   ***pro-exp*** ts-a de lo   lbanyil   BENIT 57
      F-become   P-go 2   face builder

      o   ts-a de y-chux de mëlbyuu
      or P-go 2   P-peel 2   fish
      It could be that you can go to the builders or go to peel shrimp.

As long as we assume that embedded clauses with Potential marking may be (and usually are) finite, the subject of the embedded clause can receive Case in its D-structure position, making raising unnecessary.

3.3.4 Causative constructions

The addition of the Causative prefix *gu-* (*gw-* before a vowel) to an unaccusative verb adds an external argument with the Agent θ-role.[28] Examples of this type of causative construction are given in (102).

(102) a. w-gw-et   men mëël   AGOSTO 56
         C-CAUS-die 3   snake
         They killed the snake.

      b. per w-gw-et-et   men maa   MENMAAC 12
         but C-CAUS-die-NEG 3   3A
         But he didn't kill the dog.

      c. swer   r-gw-eey   me   QUESO 20
         suero H-CAUS-cook   3R
         She cooks the suero.

      d. chene r-beree   noo   lët me dxe   w-gw-eey   kafe   LIFEINQ 4
         when   H-return 1EX FM 3R already C-CAUS-cook coffee
         When I returned, my mother had made the coffee.

The only other type of example in the QZ texts where the Causative prefix is used is given in (103), with the crucial parts in bold type.

---

[28]The Causative prefix cannot be added to the underlyingly passive verb *zël* 'be.found' since the Agent θ-role is already present in the optional oblique argument.

(103) laz   noo chene r-et te   men$_i$ r-kaa   men$_j$ kwib DEATH 1
      homeland 1EX when H-die one 3   H-touch 3   bell

   chin   ga-gu-nan   yra   men$_k$ ne   w-et   men$_i$
   so.that P-CAUS-know P-all 3   that C-die 3
   In my homeland, when someone dies, they ring the bell, so that everyone will know that the person died.

As we saw in §2.3.2, when the Potential marker is used with the verb meaning 'know', *g-an*, no overt subject is expressed. The addition of the Causative prefix in this example causes the "knowers" to be expressed overtly and to be different from the reference they would have in a control situation. As in the case of adding the Causative prefix to unaccusative verbs, the Causative is added here to a verb which does not assign an Agent θ-role itself, allowing the Agent to be expressed.

No other types of causative constructions are attested in the QZ texts. Specifically, there are no examples where the Causative prefix is used with an underlyingly transitive verb nor any examples where it is used with an underlyingly intransitive verb which assigns an Agent θ-role. This distribution argues for a lexical account of the causative construction, rather than a syntactic account, since one would expect syntactically to simply be able to add an additional argument to any type of verb. Comrie (1985) would classify the causative constructions in QZ as morphological causatives.

3.4 Changes in word order due to movement

A number of QZ clauses do not surface with VSO word order. This is due to movement to a non-argument position, called Ā-movement. These constructions, involving focus and topic constructions, question formation, and the fronting of negative indefinite pronouns, are described briefly here. Chapters 6–9 give the analyses of these constructions.

3.4.1 Focus and topic constructions

Example (104) shows that SVO order is an alternative to the usual VSO order. I analyze this as the result of focusing the subject. A focus marker

3.4 Changes in word order due to movement

optionally occurs directly before the focused constituent, as in (104b),[29] and has the effect of highlighting a single participant out of several in a text. The underscore (_) in the examples indicates the normal position of the phrase.

(104) a. **y-ra maa gin** r-dil _ noo   BENIT 19
     P-all 3A this H-fight 1EX
     All those animals are bothering me.

   b. **le Manwel** w-ruu _ dxe ne w-et x-maa men   AGOSTO 68
      FM Manuel C-leave day that C-die POS-3A 3
      Manuel left the day that his animal died.

Alternatively, the object may be focused, yielding OVS order. This is less common and may only be done when it is clear either from the context or from the argument structure which nominal phrase is the subject, as in example (105).

(105) *noze* **laa-w** r-ap-kwent men _   SEMBRAR 7
    only FM-3I H-have-watch 3
    Only it they watch.

The examples in (106) verify that long-distance focusing is possible. In (106a) the indirect object has been focused out of an embedded clause, and in (106b–c) either the subject or the direct object of an embedded clause has been focused.

(106) a. **lo Jose** r-e Mblid y-dee men/Mblid liber _
     face José H-say Mary P-give 3/Mary   book
     To José, Mary said she will give the book.

   b. **Susan** r-e Mblid y-xaal _ Jose ts-a-ye bzaan men
     Susan H-say Mary P-send José P-go-search brother 3
     Susan, Mary said, sent José to look for her brother.

   c. **Susan** r-e Mblid y-xaal Jose _ ts-a-ye bzaan men
     Susan H-say Mary P-send José   P-go-search brother 3
     Susan, Mary said, José sent to look for her brother.

---

[29]The focus marker usually has the form *laa*, as in (105). Though quite a bit of phonetic variation is possible, including the forms *laad*, *lat*, *lët*, *le*, and *la*, there is no meaning difference associated with this variation. Instead, the difference is apparently phonologically based.

In contrast to the focus constructions in (104)–(106) in which a constituent has moved to the front from a position after the verb, there is no gap in the clause in example (107).

(107) *per laa Gecha   w-on-t   Gecha*   GRING 25
　　　but FM Lucrecia C-hear-NEG Lucrecia

　　　porke   ndal   yaa   men n-dxin
　　　because   s/lots very 3   s-there
　　　But as for Lucrecia, Lucrecia didn't hear because there were lots of people.

In this case the first constituent *per laa Gecha* 'but as for Lucrecia' is marking a change in topic to Lucrecia (the Mexican woman), since up to this point the text had been explaining what Virginia (the American woman) was doing. No movement is needed here; we may simply assume that topics are base generated adjoined to a regular clause, similar to the proposal in Aissen (1992a) for Tzotzil and Jacaltec.

3.4.2 Question formation

To form Yes/No questions in QZ a question marker *pe* is inserted at the beginning of the question, as shown in (108).

(108) *r-e   Javyer pe w-u   maa nii   de*   SAMUEL 28
　　　H-say Javier Q   C-eat 3A   foot 2
　　　Javier asked, "Did the snake eat your foot?"

Content questions in QZ are formed by moving a *wh*-phrase to the beginning of the clause. (109) gives examples of interrogative constructions in both main and embedded clauses, showing that the *wh*-words always move to the beginning of their clause. In these examples, *pa* seems to be a *wh*-determiner, meaning 'what'.

(109) a. *pa   go   r-laa de*   GRING 34
　　　　 what thing H-do   2
　　　　 What are you doing?

　　　b. *n-an-t   men pa   nëz   z-a   Biki*   AGOSTO 59
　　　　 s-know-NEG   3   what road PR-go Virginia
　　　　 They don't know which way Virginia is going.

3.4 Changes in word order due to movement

Additional examples are given in (110), using the QZ words meaning 'how' (110a), 'why' (110b), 'where' (110c–d), and 'who' and 'how much' (110e), where in each case the *wh*-phrase is fronted to the beginning of its clause.[30]

(110) a. **pe-zee** n-ak   no   BENIT 32
      Q-how s-become there
      How is it there?

    b. **pe n-ak**   g-u   de   noo   MANSNAKE 20
        Q s-become P-eat 2   1EX
        Why are you going to eat me?

    c. **pa**   g-u-gwe   noo   MTLEMON2 33
        where P-eat-lunch 1EX
        Where were we to eat lunch?

    d. **go**   Karmita   GRING 35
        where Carmita
        Where is Carmita?

    e. **txu** n-an   **palal**   zek n-on   yag   GRANDMA3 21
        who s-know how.much   as   s-cost tree
        Who knows how much the tree is worth?

The examples in (111) show that long distance *wh*-movement is possible.

(111) a. **txu** n-a   Jose   wii   noo __
      who s-say José c/see 1EX
      Who does José say that I saw?

    b. **txu** n-a   Jose   wii   __   noo
        who s-say José c/see   1EX
        Who does José say saw me?

---

[30]Questions asking 'when' are formed by using *pa or* 'what hour', *pa gbiz* 'what day', etc. *Chene* 'when' is normally only used in adverbial phrases in QZ.

    c. **pa nëz zhe** n-a xe-mgyeey noo
       what road WH S-say POS-man 1EX

       y-nëëz noo _ ne ts-a noo den
       P-take 1EX   that P-go 1EX ranch
       What road did my husband say I should take to go to the ranch?

3.4.3 Fronting of negative indefinite pronouns

In addition to focus constructions and *wh*-questions, a third type of construction also involves fronting in QZ. This construction is a negative clause which contains a negative indefinite pronoun. The negative indefinite pronoun must be fronted, as shown in (112)–(113), and it must co-occur with the negative suffix on the verb.

(112) a. *pa   go   r-laa   de*   GRING 34
       what thing H-do 2
       What thing are you doing?

    b. **bet** *r-laa-t noo*
       nothing H-do-NEG 1EX
       I am not doing anything.

    c. ***bet** *r-laa noo*
       nothing H-do 1EX
       (I am doing nothing.)

    d. *r-laa-t noo **bet**
       H-do-NEG 1EX nothing
       (I am not doing anything.)

(113) a. *pa ts-a de*
       where P-go 2
       Where are you going?

    b. **bat** *ts-a-t noo*
       nowhere P-go-NEG 1EX
       I am not going anywhere.

3.4 Changes in word order due to movement

c. *****bat**   ts-a   noo*
   nowhere P-go 1EX
   (I am going nowhere.)

d. **ts-a-t*   *noo* ***bat***
   P-go-NEG 1EX nowhere
   (I am not going anywhere.)

4
Anaphoric or Binding Relations

The anaphora facts in QZ and two other Zapotecan languages, IZ and YZ, are described in this chapter to show the variation in these constructions throughout the language family. While IZ distinguishes reflexive and nonreflexive pronouns and uses each in accordance with Binding theory, YZ expresses reflexive, reciprocal, and reflexive of possession constructions only by means of a special syntactic configuration in which the subject is unexpressed if it is coreferent with the possessor of the object. QZ makes even fewer morphological or syntactic distinctions than either of the others, with pronouns being used both reflexively and nonreflexively, resulting in ambiguity. This chapter also investigates the question of which elements can have a nonpronominal antecedent.

4.1 Principles A and B: Distinguishing anaphors from pronouns

Cross-linguistically, the "normal" situation is for anaphors to be used to signal coindexation and for pronouns to signal disjoint indexing, within a local domain.

4.1.1 Isthmus Zapotec anaphora

IZ is a member of the eastern group of Zapotecan languages. In IZ and most of the central, eastern, and western languages, as well as the

Mixtepec dialect in the southern group, the reflexive construction is formed by a base word, *laka* (which may mean 'same' but is glossed here simply as REFL for reflexive), followed by a pronoun which is coindexed with the antecedent. This pronoun acts as the possessor of *laka*. The antecedent is always overtly expressed. Examples (114a–b) show the reflexive construction in IZ, while (114c) demonstrates that a disjoint reference reading is obtained when the simple third person pronoun is used.[31]

(114) a. *gu-diñe-e laka na*
C-hit-1SG REFL 1SG
I hit myself.

    b. *gu-diñe bašdu laka laa*
C-hit child REFL PN-3
The child hit himself/herself.

    c. *gu-diñe bašdu laa*
C-hit child PN-3
The child$_i$ hit him/her$_j$.

The reflexive marker *laka* is also used in emphatic expressions, as shown in (115).

(115) *laka la-be b-išni-be ni*
REFL PN-3H C-do-3H 3I
He himself did it.

In contrast to the reflexive, the reciprocal is expressed by verbal morphology.[32] When the suffix *sa* is added to a transitive verb, it changes the verb's valence to allow only one argument. The subject is required to be plural, as exemplified in (116).

(116) *ka-giñe-sa ka-be*
PR-hit-RECIP PL-3H
They are hitting each other.

---

[31] Note that *laa* is really the pronoun base, which carries dependent pronouns, followed by a null third person pronoun. Compare (114b–c) with (115). *Laa* is shortened to *la* in (115) since laryngealized (or glottalized) vowels are only realized in stressed syllables (the foot is iambic).

[32] Only Texmelucan Zapotec, part of the western group, uses a reciprocal pronoun similar to the reflexive construction rather than using verbal morphology for the reciprocal.

4.1 Principles A and B: Distinguishing anaphors from pronouns

This use of a derivational suffix to express reciprocity forces the anaphora relationship to be subject oriented and local, though this relationship is only expressed via a verbal affix rather than being realized by structural coindexing.

4.1.2 Yatzachi Zapotec anaphora

YZ is a member of the northern group of Zapotecan languages. All the data presented in this section are taken from Butler (1976a). There are three anaphoric constructions in YZ, each having the same structural shape: the true reflexive, the reciprocal, and the reflexive of possession.

The true reflexive construction is based on an intrinsically possessed noun k^wiN 'self of'.[33] This construction involves a portmanteau realization of the subject and the possessor of k^wiN, where the subject position is empty. The possessor of the noun k^wiN may be a clitic pronoun, as in (117a–c), or a full noun phrase following the noun, as in (117d).

(117) a. *b-čog k^wiN-aʔ*
   C-cut self.of-1SG
   I cut myself.

   b. *b-čeč k^wiN-boʔ*
   C-hit self.of-3F
   He hit himself.

   c. *j-leʔi k^wiN-toʔ*
   H-see self.of-1EXPL
   We see ourselves.

   d. *b-e-xot   k^wiN   beʔe-naʔ*
   C-REP-kill self.of person-that
   That person reportedly killed himself (suicide).

The reciprocal construction in YZ also contains a portmanteau realization of the subject and the possessor of an item, in this case the possessed noun $lR^wežR$ 'fellow of'.[34] (118) gives examples of this reciprocal construction.

(118) a. *j-e-xalə? g-akəlen   lr^wežR-jo*
   H-REP-owe P-help   fellow.of-1IPL
   We must help one another.

---
[33]This form is also used in six other northern group languages.
[34]The symbols R^w and R indicate uvular fricatives. N is an unspecified nasal.

b. *ǰ-ge?i-ne? nada? na? bito ǰ-ne lRʷežR-to?*
H-hate-3RS 1SG and not H-speak fellow.of-1EXPL
She hates me and we do not speak to one another.

c. *bižčen? ǰ-bažə? lRʷežR-le*
why H-hit fellow.of-2PL
Why do you hit one another?

d. *ba-ǰ-əsə?ə-le?i lRʷežR bžin? ka?*
already-H-SPL-see fellow.of mule those
Those mules have already seen one another.

The third anaphoric construction is the reflexive of possession. Here any possessed noun may occur with the portmanteau realization of the subject and the possessor. The examples in (119) show the normal construction, where the subject and possessor of the object are expressed separately.[35] This contrasts with the examples in (120) (compare especially (119a) with (120a) and (119b) with (120b)) showing this reflexive of possession construction.[36]

(119) a. *čin-a? xičR-bo?*
P/comb-1SG head-3F
I will comb his hair.

b. *ǰ-labo? libř če-bo?*
H-read/3F book of-3F
He$_i$ is reading his$_j$ book.

(120) a. *čin xičR-a?*
P/comb head-1SG
I will comb my hair.

b. *ǰ-lab libř če-bo?*
H-read book of-3F
He$_i$ is reading his$_i$ book.

---

[35] (119b) could be used in a case where the subject and the possessor of the object are coindexed, since the null subject is not absolutely required for coindexation. When there is a null subject, there is forced coreference between the subject and the possessor of the object. Therefore, to avoid ambiguity and in conformity with Gricean principles, (119b) would normally be used only for cases of disjoint reference, since (120b) clearly expresses forced coreference.

[36] Nouns which are not of the class that is normally possessed in YZ require *če* or *či* 'of' before the possessor.

4.1 Principles A and B: Distinguishing anaphors from pronouns 73

c. ba-ĵ-gʷia   liš   Bed-ən?
   already-H-look.at paper Peter-the
   Peter$_i$ is already looking at his$_i$ paper.

d. ž-rə-nab   kařt   či-a?   kořeo-n?
   P-go-ask letter of-1SG post.office-the
   I will go ask for my letters at the post office.

e. bito   b-nežR^w bgʷex   če no?ol-ən?
   not   C-give   broom   of woman-the
   The woman$_i$ did not lend her$_i$ broom.

These anaphoric constructions fit the usual characteristics of anaphors in that the portmanteau realization of the subject and the possessor structurally enforces subject-orientation. The locality constraint on antecedents of anaphors is also enforced, if it is assumed that the null subject is the antecedent and the possessor or possessed object is the anaphor. The subject and the possessor of the direct object or of an oblique object are always within the same IP. No other possibilities for antecedent-anaphor relations are available in YZ. No morphological marking is used to distinguish pronouns from anaphors; this special syntactic configuration is employed instead. The major concern with these syntactic anaphoric constructions is how the null subject is licensed. The construction seems backwards, since it is normally the antecedent that carries the identifying information. Section 12.2.1.1 details the theoretical problems posed by this construction and points in the direction of a possible analysis.

4.1.3 Quiegolani Zapotec anaphora

In contrast to both IZ and YZ, which differentiate between anaphors and pronominals via either morphological or syntactic structure, QZ and at least four other southern group languages do not make such a distinction (Piper 1993). The regular pronouns are used in both subject and object position. In the case of first or second person pronouns, the coindexing is clear and an anaphoric reading is given (121a) (though singular versus plural is still a problem in QZ). In (121b), however, there is no way to distinguish coreference from noncoreference with third person pronouns.[37]

(121) a. *r-wii noo noo*
    H-see 1EX 1EX
    I see myself. *or* We see ourselves.

  b. *r-wii men men*
    H-see 3 3
    She/he/they see(s) herself/himself/themselves/her/him/them.

Because of the ambiguity caused by this lack of distinction between anaphors and pronominals, speakers of these languages prefer to use proper names or common nouns rather than third person pronouns. This practice will be discussed in §4.2.

QZ also allows a construction just like the reflexive of possession construction in YZ, where the subject may be null if it is coindexed with the possessor of the object. Some examples are given in (122), where an underscore indicates the position of the missing subject. (122d) verifies that the possessor may be a full nominal phrase, not just a pronoun, and that the possessor of the object of a preposition counts as well for this construction. (See also §12.2.1.1).

---

[37] According to Regnier (1989b), QZ speakers have developed some idiomatic expressions to indicate an anaphoric usage. "He sees himself" can be idiomatically expressed as in (i). Another idiomatic expression that can be used in a reflexive situation is shown in (ii). This expression can also be used in a nonreflexive situation, as shown in the text examples in (iii)–(iv).

  (i) *r-wii men lo   gyewan*
       H-see 3   face mirror
       He/she sees himself/herself. (lit.: He/she looks in the mirror.)
  (ii) *w-niiz men x-kwent   men*
       C-give 3   POS-account 3
       He/she hit himself/herself. (lit.: He/she gave his/her own account.)
  (iii) *r-niiz men x-kwent   noo*   ESCUELA 29
        H-give 3   POS-account 1EX
        He (the teacher) beats me. (lit.: He gives my account.)
  (iv) *w-niiz xnaa   noo x-kwent   noo*   SANJOSE 10
        C-give mother 1EX POS-account 1EX
        My mother hit me. (lit.: My mother gave my account.)

Another strategy for a clear reflexive interpretation is to use the morpheme *-ke* (usually a verbal suffix), meaning 'association' or 'also', attached to the focus marker with the subject focused, as in (v).

  (v) *laa-ke   noo r-wii*
       FM-ASSOC 1EX H-see
       I see myself.

This construction apparently alters the argument structure of the verb to take only one argument, as in 'I self-see'.

4.1 Principles A and B: Distinguishing anaphors from pronouns

(122) a. *r-dxiin-t* _ *x-ten men*   RANCHO 9A
H-arrive-NEG   POS-ranch 3
They$_i$ didn't arrive at their$_i$ ranch.

b. *r-e noo r-laan noo ts-a noo per che-bel*   HORTENS 17
H-say 1EX H-want 1EX P-go 1EX but when-if

y-na de g-weey _ x-pëëd noo
P-say 2 P-take POS-child 1EX
I said, "I want to go, but only if you say that I can take my daughter."

c. *dxe w-dxiin _ x-ten men*   MENMAAC 3
already C-arrive POS-ranch 3

w-kaa _ x-kix men chu yag
C-put POS-bag 3 belly tree
When he$_i$ arrived at his$_i$ ranch, he$_i$ put his$_i$ bag on a tree.

d. *s-ya _ ru x-yuu mër gol*   MARTRIST 42
PR-go mouth POS-house pigeon male
The male pigeon$_i$ went to his$_i$ house.

The fact that both IZ and YZ have ways to express reflexive and reciprocal constructions which obey locality constraints and are distinct from regular pronominal constructions is consistent with at least the spirit of Principles A and B. For QZ and other southern Zapotecan languages, however, there is no overt distinction between anaphors and pronominals morphologically, and QZ only makes a structural distinction in the reflexive of possession construction. I leave the question of whether Principles A and B apply for further research. (See Piper 1993 for a proposal on how the Binding theory could be reformulated to account for these southern group languages.)

4.2 Principle C: Binding restrictions on nominal phrases

Perhaps a more striking departure from the Principles of Binding theory is that bound proper names and common nouns occur in a sentence as common practice. The QZ texts are full of examples like those in (123).

(123) a. w-eey **Benit** mëlbyuu ne y-ged **Benit**   BENIT 5
C-take Benito fish that P-give Benito

    lo x-mig **Benit** Jasint
    face POS-friend Benito Jacinto
    Benito took a fish, which he gave to his friend, Jacinto.

  b. r-e **Mblid** lo xsaap **Mblid**   BRU 14
    H-say Mary face daughter Mary
    Mary said to her daughter:

  c. per n-an-t **Merse** pa go r-zak **Merse**   BRU 34
    but S-know-NEG Mercedes what thing H-have Mercedes
    But Mercedes didn't know what she had.

  d. per chene w-dee **Biki** r-e **Biki**   GRING 33
    but when C-pass Virginia H-say Virginia
    But when Virginia entered, she said...

  e. w-chug **mëëk** duu porke w-laan **mëëk** nis   MENMAAC 35
    C-cut dog rope because C-want dog water
    The dog cut the rope, because he was thirsty.

  f. z-a ye **mëëk** nis g-oo **mëëk**   MENMAAC 36
    PR-go search dog water P-drink dog
    The dog went to look for water to drink.

These examples are very similar to those given for Vietnamese and Thai in Lasnik (1986). Lasnik argues for parameterization of Principle C, stating that while a proper name or nominal phrase must always be free in English, in Vietnamese it must be free in its governing category, and in Thai there is no restriction. QZ is like Thai, since (123b) verifies that a proper name may be bound even within the same minimal IP.

Lasnik further notes that neither Thai nor Vietnamese can allow a nominal phrase to be bound by a pronoun, since the same sentences which are grammatical with repeated proper names or nominal phrases are very ungrammatical when the antecedent is replaced by a pronoun. This is also true in QZ, as shown in (124).

4.2 Principle C: Binding restrictions on nominal phrases

(124) a. *r-e   **men** lo   xsaap   **Mblid**
      H-say 3   face daughter Mary
      (She$_i$ said to Mary$_i$'s daughter...)

  b. *per n-an-t   **men** pa   go   r-zak   **Merse**
     but s-know-NEG 3   what thing H-have Mercedes
     (But she$_i$ didn't know what Mercedes$_i$ had.)

  c. *z-a   ye   **maa** nis   g-oo   **mëëk**
     PR-go search 3A   water P-drink dog
     (It$_i$ went to look for water for the dog$_i$ to drink.)

QZ, therefore, confirms Lasnik's proposal that Principle C is really two conditions, one which needs to be parameterized across languages and one which appears to be universal. The correct condition for QZ seems to be only the universal condition given in (125) (reworded from Lasnik 1986).[38]

(125)   A nominal phrase may not be A-bound by a pronoun.

4.2.1 Discourse considerations regarding the use of pronouns and nominal phrases

As mentioned earlier, QZ speakers prefer repeating proper names or nominal phrases over switching to pronouns due to the ambiguity caused by the lack of morphological distinction between anaphors and pronominals. This is especially true in isolated situations. In a discourse, pronouns may be used to refer back to a previously introduced individual as long as there are not two individuals being referred to by the same pronoun at the same time. Consider the opening sentences of two texts for examples of this. Excerpts from the first text are given in (126).

(126) a. te   mgyeey ne   la   Benit   n-uu   Pwert   BENIT 1
     one man   that call Benito s-be Salina.Cruz
     One man whose name is Benito lived in Salina Cruz.

---

[38]Though see §4.2.2 for an additional condition on quantified nominal phrases.

b. *z-a   men g-un men inbitar x-mig   men*   BENIT 2
   PR-go 3   P-LM 3   invite   POS-friend 3

   ne   la   Jasint   n-uu San Jose
   that call Jacinto S-be San Jose
   He$_i$ went to invite his$_i$ friend whose name is Jacinto and who lived in San Jose.

c. *chene w-dxiin Benit   ru   x-yuu   Jasint*   BENIT 6
   when C-arrive Benito mouth POS-house Jacinto

   r-e   Benit payus Jasint
   H-say Benito hi   Jacinto
   When Benito arrived at Jacinto's house, Benito said, "Hi, Jacinto."

In sentence (126a) Benito is introduced. The general third person pronoun *men* is then used three times in (126b) to refer to Benito, and Jacinto is introduced as distinct from the pronoun referent. In sentence (126c), since there are two distinct referents which could be coindexed with the pronoun, the names are repeated instead.

Excerpts from the beginning of the second text are given in (127).

(127) a. *teb tir   te   men ts-a   men g-oob   giix*   MANSNAKE 1
         one time one 3   P-go   3   P-clean weed.patch
         One time a man went to clean the weeds.

   b. *r-loob men lyu let-ne   g-uu men bni*   MANSNAKE 2
      H-clean 3   land side-that P-sow 3   seed

      chene w-on   men w-zob-tsaa   te   maa
      when C-hear 3   C-sit-shout   one   3A
      He was cleaning the land where he plants seed, when he heard an animal sitting shouting.

   c. *te   mëël   n-uu te   leen yag*   MANSNAKE 6
      one snake S-be one in   tree
      A snake was in a tree.

4.2 Principle C: Binding restrictions on nominal phrases

  d. r-ob-tsaa   mëël   MANSNAKE 7
     H-sit-shout snake
     The snake was sitting shouting.

In this text, a folktale, no names are given. Instead, the human character is introduced by referring to him specifically with a pronoun in (127a) and assigning him that reference for the remainder of the story. In (127b) the pronominal phrase *te maa* 'one animal (3A)' is introduced. This animal is shown to be a snake in (127c–d). In this case, three other animals will be a part of the story, so for clarity *mëël* 'snake' is now used in each reference to the snake, and the other animals are also referred to by common nouns, as shown in (128).

(128) r-e   mëël   lo   ngyed   MANSNAKE 30
      H-say   snake face chicken

      men-ree   z-ëd-no   noo   men
      3-this   PR-come-take   1EX   3
      The snake said to the chicken, "This man came to take me with him."

On a discourse level, then, the basic consideration seems to be a desire for clarity of reference. Pronouns will normally be used for only one referent in the sentence, unless confusion is avoided by person or animacy distinctions.

4.2.2 Bound nominal phrases and the null third-person pronoun

In the discussion regarding control constructions in chapter 2, it was pointed out that QZ seems to have a hierarchy of types of nominal phrases.[39] In this hierarchy full quantified, possessed, or modified nominal phrases are at the top, with pronouns at the bottom. Proper names and unmodified common nouns fit in between.

We have seen that the same forms are used for both pronouns and anaphors. Nominal phrases consisting of proper names or common nouns may be freely repeated in QZ, as seen in (123); subsequent instances may also be changed to pronouns, subject to the discourse considerations just discussed. These types of nominal phrases make up the middle tier of the hierarchy. When considering whether quantified, possessed, or modified nominal phrases may be bound, the results are much different. Quantified

---

[39]See Stenning (1987:167–168) for a related hierarchy of class inclusion. Stenning shows that antecedents must be subordinate to or coextensional with their anaphors. Superordinate antecedents, such as *the creature* or *it*, are not allowed to antecede a subordinate anaphor like *the cat* or *Patrick's pet*.

phrases, which fill the top level of the hierarchy, may not be bound without yielding highly unnatural readings, as shown in (129). In the text example (129a), the second clause has a null subject which is coindexed with the subject of the main clause. My language consultant prefers the reading in (129b), where an overt pronoun fills the subject position in the embedded clause. (129c), with the bound quantified nominal phrase, however, is highly unnatural.[40] Further variation on the same text is shown in (130) to demonstrate that strong DPs behave the same as weak DPs in this regard. Therefore, the restriction against bound quantified nominal phrases is not simply due to the novelty requirement for weak DPs.

(129) a. *teb   tir   te   wnaa   gring   r-laan*   GRING 1
       one time one woman gringa H-want

   ts-a-no   _   te   wnaa   mejikan   Estados Unidos
   P-go-take   one   woman   Mexican   States United
   One time a gringa (American woman) wanted to take a Mexican woman to the United States.

b. *teb   tir   te   wnaa   gring   r-laan*
   one time one woman gringa H-want

   ts-a-no   men   te   wnaa   mejikan   Estados Unidos
   P-go-take   3   one   woman   Mexican   States United
   One time a gringa (American woman) wanted to take a Mexican woman to the United States.

c. ?? *teb   tir   te   wnaa   gring   r-laan   ts-a-no*
      one time one woman gringa H-want   P-go-take

   te   wnaa   gring   te   wnaa   mejikan   Estados Unidos
   one   woman   gringa   one   woman   Mexican   States   United
   (One time a gringa (American woman) wanted to take a Mexican woman to the United States.)

---

[40](130c) is improved somewhat if the quantifier is omitted in the consequent to read simply *wnaa gring* 'American woman'.

4.2 Principle C: Binding restrictions on nominal phrases

(130) a. *teb   tir   **y-ra wnaa   mejikan** r-laan*
      one time P-all woman Mexican H-want

   ts-a-no   __   Biki   San Jose
   P-go-take   Virginia San Jose
   One time all the Mexican women wanted to take Virginia to San Jose.

b. *teb   tir   **y-ra wnaa   mejikan** r-laan*
   one time P-all woman Mexican H-want

   *ts-a-no   **men** Biki   San Jose*
   P-go-take   3   Virginia San Jose
   One time all the Mexican women wanted to take Virginia to San Jose.

c. *??teb   tir   **y-ra wnaa   mejikan** r-laan*
   one time P-all woman Mexican H-want

   *ts-a-no   **y-ra wnaa   mejikan** Biki   San Jose*
   P-go-take P-all woman Mexican Virginia San Jose
   (One time all the Mexican women wanted to take Virginia to San Jose.)

Example (131) shows a similar distribution and verifies that the options for the subject position in an embedded clause are not dependent upon the aspect marker in the clause; Habitual aspect is definitely not nonfinite. Again, the reading in (131b) with an overt pronoun is preferred over the use of the null pronoun (131a) and both of the former are much better than allowing the bound quantified phrase (131c). (132) is included to underscore the lack of distinction between strong and weak DPs in their ability to be bound.

(131) a. *r-a   **txup tson   wnaa**   r-ka   __   gyus*   SANJOSE 2A
      H-go   two three woman H-buy   pot

   ne   y-gw-eey   x-nisyaa men
   that P-CAUS-cook POS-food 3
   A few women went to buy a pot that they can cook their food in.

b. r-a **txup tson wnaa** r-ka **men** gyus
H-go two three woman H-buy 3 pot
A few women went to buy a pot...

c. *??* r-a **txup tson wnaa** r-ka **txup tson wnaa** gyus
H-go two three woman H-buy two three woman pot
(A few women went to buy a pot...)

(132) a. r-a **y-ra wnaa** *San Jose* r-ka __ gyus
H-go P-all woman San Jose H-buy pot
All the women of San Jose went to buy a pot...

b. r-a **y-ra wnaa** *San Jose* r-ka **men** gyus
H-go P-all woman San Jose H-buy 3 pot
All the women of San Jose went to buy a pot...

c. *??* r-a **y-ra wnaa** *San Jose* r-ka **y-ra wnaa San**
H-go P-all woman San Jose H-buy P-all woman San

Jose gyus
Jose pot
(All the women of San Jose went to buy a pot...)

The hierarchy may need to be further divided to place possessed phrases lower than quantified nominal phrases, since there are text examples which contain repeated instances of possessed nominals, as in (133). The second instance of *xnaa noo* 'my mother' could also be replaced by an overt pronoun, as in (134), or possibly by a null third person pronoun, as in (135).

(133) *chene* w-uu **noo** *lgyëz* y-ra **xnaa noo** r-a **xnaa**   SANJOSE 1
when C-be 1EX town P-all mother 1EX H-go mother

noo *San Jose*
1EX San Jose
When I lived in town with my mother, my mother went to San Jose.

(134) *chene* w-uu **noo** *lgyëz* y-ra **xnaa noo** r-a **men** *San Jose*
when C-be 1EX town P-all mother 1EX H-go 3 San Jose
When I lived in town with my mother, she went to San Jose.

4.2 Principle C: Binding restrictions on nominal phrases 83

(135) *chene w-uu noo lgyëz y-ra xnaa noo r-a _ San Jose*
when C-be 1EX town P-all mother 1EX H-go San Jose
When I lived in town with my mother$_j$, she$_j$ went to San Jose.

Example (134) could also be understood to mean that someone else went to San Jose, which may be why the possessed phrase was repeated in the text.

Two proposals are needed to account for this behavior. First, an account is needed for the fact that bound quantified nominal phrases (and other modified nominals to some extent) yield unnatural readings which are similar to Principle C violations in English. This can be achieved by limiting the type of nominal phrases that must be free. The Principle C restriction relevant in QZ, in addition to the prohibition against binding by a pronoun in (125), is given in (136).

(136) A quantified nominal phrase must not be bound.

Secondly, an account is needed for when an argument can be null. Leaving aside the QZ version of the YZ reflexive of possession construction (which is further discussed in chapter 12), whenever the antecedent is a pronoun, all coindexed nominals must also be overtly realized as a pronoun. The prohibition in (125) rules out the possibility of a nominal phrase having a pronominal antecedent (at least one that is also a binder). Further, the data show that the coindexed consequent of a pronoun may not be null. Since a nominal which has a pronominal antecedent must be overtly realized, and first and second person are always expressed by pronouns, the only arguments which can possibly be null are third person. I believe that QZ has a null third person pronominal which must have a nominal phrase as its antecedent. If this view is correct, it accounts for the fact that null subjects may be found outside of control constructions and local anaphoric constructions, as well as for the fact that the null arguments are always third person.

Cases where a null object appears confirm that the antecedent of the null pronoun need not be local. In examples (137)–(140) the antecedent is in bold type in each case, with the null pronoun indicated by an underscore.

(137) a. *g-ix de **tapet** lyu* BATHROOM 20
P-put 2 rug land
Put the rug on the floor.

b. *g-ix-nii   de _*   BATHROOM 21
   P-put-foot 2
   Put your foot [on the rug].

(138) a. *s-ya   **Benit***   BENIT 75
         PR-go Benito
         Benito went.

   b. *la Jasint   z-a-nal   _*   BENIT 76
      FM Jacinto   PR-go-with
      Jacinto went with [him].

(139) a. *bwoo   men **teb gix gee   zaa***   SAMUEL 5
         C/extract 3   one bag each elote
         They each harvested a bag of elote (corn).

   b. *w-eey   men y-rup   men _*   SAMUEL 6
      C-take 3   P-two   3
      They each carried [one].

(140) a. *w-nëëz   men **txup mëëk***   MANSNAKE 82
         C-catch 3   two   dog

         ne   maz-re   n-dux-re   ne   r-ap   men
         that more-this S-angry-MORE that H-have 3
         The man caught two dogs that were the wildest that he had.

   b. *w-see   men _ te   leen   **kotens***   MANSNAKE 83
      C-throw 3   one   inside sack
      He threw [them] into a sack.

   c. *w-dxiin   n-eey   men _   lo   koyot*   MANSNAKE 84
      C-arrive S-take   3   face   coyote
      The man brought [the sack] to the coyote.

In these examples, the null object pronoun has a nominal phrase as its antecedent, but not as a binder. C-command cannot hold across sentence boundaries in the discourse.

4.2 Principle C: Binding restrictions on nominal phrases

We need to ask, then, whether QZ distinguishes between null subjects and null objects, or whether they have the same distribution.[41] This involves two questions: (a) Can a null object have a nominal phrase as its binder as well as its antecedent? and (b) Can a null subject occur outside of the c-command domain of the nominal phrase antecedent? The examples in (141)–(142) verify that the answer to both questions is "Yes." (141) shows that a null object pronoun may be bound by the subject of the higher clause.[42]

(141) *per n-an   y-rup mgyeey gin*   BRU 50A
      but s-know p-two man   this

    y-guu xdiiz   _   chigiib te   xman o   chii gbiz
    p-sow official   jail   one week or ten   day
    But those two men knew the officials would throw them in jail for a week or ten days.

(142) gives a text example where two null subjects find their antecedent across sentence boundaries.[43]

(142) a. *per la **Biki**   n-eey   ne   g-u   Karmita*   GRING 19
      but FM Virginia s-take that p-eat Carmita
      But Virginia had brought Carmita's food.

   b. *n-eey   _   gayet*   GRING 20
      s-take   cracker
      She had crackers.

   c. *n-eey   _   **nex***   GRING 21
      s-take   fruit
      She had fruit.

---

[41]Both Chamorro and Japanese allow null subjects to be routinely bound by a c-commanding antecedent, whereas null objects are licensed by antecedents that are not binders (Chung, p.c.). QZ does not appear to follow this pattern.

[42]As in several earlier examples, though (141) is acceptable, my language consultant prefers to have the overt third person pronoun *men* in place of the null pronoun. The word for 'official', *xdiiz*, may etymologically consist of the possessive marker *x-* and the root *diiz* 'word', indicating that the town officials are the possessors of words.

[43](142) provides an example of the antecedent being found across sentence boundaries, similarly to the examples of null objects, since it is not easily reanalyzed as sentence-level coordination. A null subject in a coordination construction also provides evidence that the null subject pronoun need not be bound by its antecedent, since c-command cannot hold from within one conjunct into another conjunct either. See §10.1.2 for this type of example.

I therefore conclude that there is only one null third person pronoun in QZ (which can act either as a subject or an object) and that it must have a nominal phrase as its antecedent, but not necessarily as its binder.

Part II
Clause Structure and Ā-Dependencies

5
Theoretical Issues

Given the basic understanding of QZ provided by the grammatical sketch, this part undertakes the task of deciding on the overall clause structure of QZ and providing analyses for the various Ā-dependencies attested. The overarching theoretical issue addressed is the question of how many functional projections are needed in the overall clause structure and how these projections are ordered with respect to one another (§5.1). Included also is a discussion of how the specifier position in each projection is utilized, and how its use is correctly restricted. Section 5.2 moves to the independent question of how VSO word order is generated within X-bar theory.

5.1 How many functional projections are necessary?

Pollock (1989) first advocated splitting IP into the separate projections of TenseP, AgrP, and NegP. Others have since proposed additional projections, such as a distinction between subject agreement and object agreement for languages that manifest both types. Similarly, Hendrick (1991) argues that aspect heads its own AspP projection.

The inflectional (Infl) elements in Zapotec are quite restricted; only aspect is marked, so TenseP and AgrP are not needed. I present evidence that there is, however, a NegP projection above IP (= AspP) in Zapotec in chapter 8. In addition, the data for focus constructions (chapter 6) and question formation (chapter 7) indicate that another Ā landing site is needed. The interaction of these various constructions with one another and with clausal coordination clarifies the picture, as shown in chapter 9. I claim that Zapotec clause structure has only two functional projections above IP, as well as allowing an adjoined position. These consist of a polarity phrase (PolP), which is the ± counterpart of NegP,[44] and the usual complementizer phrase (CP). PolP is immediately above IP and below CP. An additional position for Ā-movement is left-adjoined to PolP, directly below CP, as shown in (143)

(143)
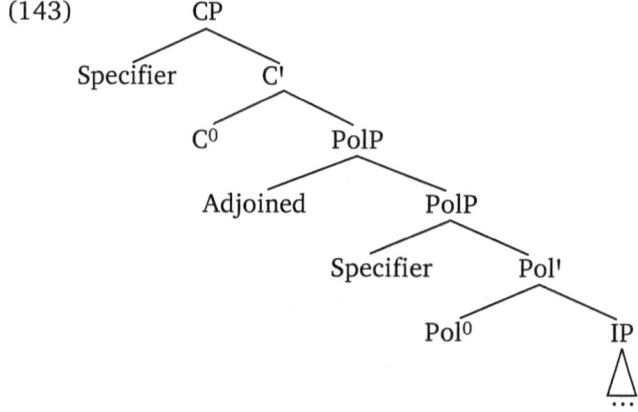

Looking at (143), one might wonder what the three specifier or adjoined positions are used for.[45] This issue has largely been left unanswered in the proposals which advocate additional functional projections. Two options are normally seen: either the specifier positions and single bar projections are omitted from the tree structure so that only the heads and maximal projections are visible, or, in SVO languages, the specifier positions are shown and the subject is assumed to raise successively through each specifier position to the highest one (Koopman and Sportiche 1991). NegP is an exception to this, since the French *pas* is assumed to occupy the specifier of NegP, and this is probably true of English *not* as well (Pollock 1989 and Zanuttini 1991, among others).

This is not the scenario in Zapotec. One of the main reasons for positing the projection in each case is to make use of its specifier position. Each specifier or adjoined position, with the possible exception of the specifier

---

[44]PolP seems similar to the proposal of ΣP in Laka (1990), but the two proposals are distinct. See §9.4.

[45]In addition to the specifiers of CP and PolP and the adjoined position, the specifier of IP under the Verb Movement proposal must also be considered.

5.1 How many functional projections are necessary?

of CP, has a unique use as a landing site for movement. Further, there need to be restrictions on exactly what can or must fill each specifier position. The requirement that the *Wh*-Criterion and the Negative Criterion hold at S-structure, discussed in chapters 7 and 8, respectively, accounts for two crucial facts. First, only a phrase which carries the relevant feature may occupy the specifier or adjoined position. Second, these phrases are required to front. While the normal specifier-head relationship holds for a Neg^0 and its specifier, a $C^0_{[+wh]}$ requires that the fronted *wh*-phrase follow it in a minimal government relationship. Focused phrases occupy the same adjoined position as *wh*-phrases do.

5.2 How VSO word order is obtained

Greenberg (1963) documented three basic word orders for natural language: SVO, SOV, and VSO (with VOS and OVS also occurring rarely). In 1978 Derbyshire and Pullum documented OSV order also although, again, it is rare. All of these word orders, except VSO and OSV, can be accounted for by positing that the verb and its object form a verb phrase (VP) and the subject occurs on one side of the VP. This means that the clause structure for all except VSO and OSV languages would be as shown in (144) (except for possible linear reordering of the verb and its object within VP and/or reordering of the subject with respect to VP).[46] The C^0 position is for complementizers and the I^0 position is filled by one or more inflectional elements, such as tense, aspect, and/or agreement.[47]

---

[46]Likewise, OSV order can be obtained by using a mirror image of the proposals discussed for VSO order.

[47]Under the theory of Chomsky (1981, 1982, 1986), the subject would begin in the specifier of I^0 position, as (148) shows. An alternative to this is to place the subject in the specifier of V^0 position, following the Internal Subject Hypothesis argued for by Kitagawa (1986), Kuroda (1986), Diesing (1990), Koopman and Sportiche (1991), McNally (1992), Burton and Grimshaw (1992), and others.

(144)

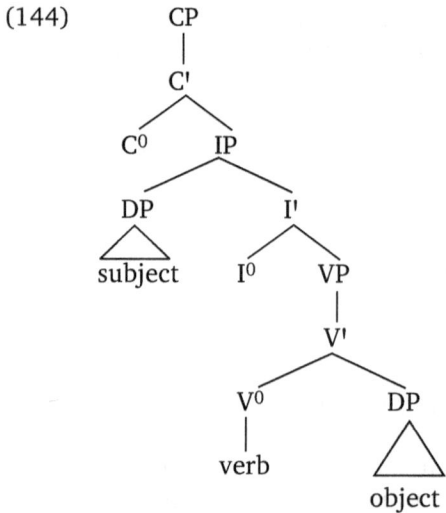

Beginning with this basic clause structure, two major proposals have been made within the Principles and Parameters framework to account for VSO word order.[48] The two proposals differ in the position assumed for subjects and in whether it is the subject or the verb that moves. The Verb Movement proposal involves movement of the verb upward over the subject, while the Subject Adjunction proposal assumes that the subject lowers to adjoin to the verb. These proposals are presented and evaluated in turn.

5.2.1 Verb Movement

The Verb Movement proposal incorporates a version of the Internal Subject Hypothesis, as presented by McCloskey (1991), Koopman and Sportiche (1991), and many others. Under this approach, the subject begins in the

---

[48]There are two additional proposals that I do not consider here. The first of these is akin to Germanic-type Verb-Second movement, where the subject occupies the specifier of I^0, then the verb undergoes obligatory V^0-to-I^0-to-C^0 movement (Emonds 1979, Sproat 1985, Haider and Prinzhorn 1986). One reason for eliminating this proposal from consideration is that V^0-to-I^0-to-C^0 movement is posited in the Germanic languages only when there is no overt complementizer, whereas VSO order occurs in Zapotec regardless of the presence of an overt complementizer. Further, McCloskey (1992b) argues on the basis of the position of the verb with respect to IP-adjoined adverbials that the verbal complex in I^0 does not move on to C^0 in VSO languages.

The second proposal, by Woolford (1991), is that VSO order is base generated within V', where the verb, subject, and object are sisters, and both the specifier of V^0 and the specifier of I^0 are empty (though Woolford argues that A-movement can move the subject to the specifier of I^0 position in the clauses that have SVO order). This proposal seems to offer no clear benefits for Zapotec and goes against the X-bar theory of clause structure, so I do not consider it further.

5.2 How VSO word order is obtained

specifier of V^0 and still occupies this position at S-structure. V^0-to-I^0 movement produces the standard VSO surface order. The D- and S-structures are shown in (145), where the specifier of I^0 position is assumed to be empty and possibly available as a landing site for movement. Following McCloskey (1991), I use the V^{max} over V^n notation in (145) to remain neutral, at least for now, on the question of whether the predicate phrase which is the sister to the subject is nonmaximal i.e., V' as Kuroda (1986), Huang (1990), and Speas (1991:179–183) have argued, or maximal (i.e., VP) as argued for by Koopman and Sportiche (1991).

(145)   D-structure   S-structure

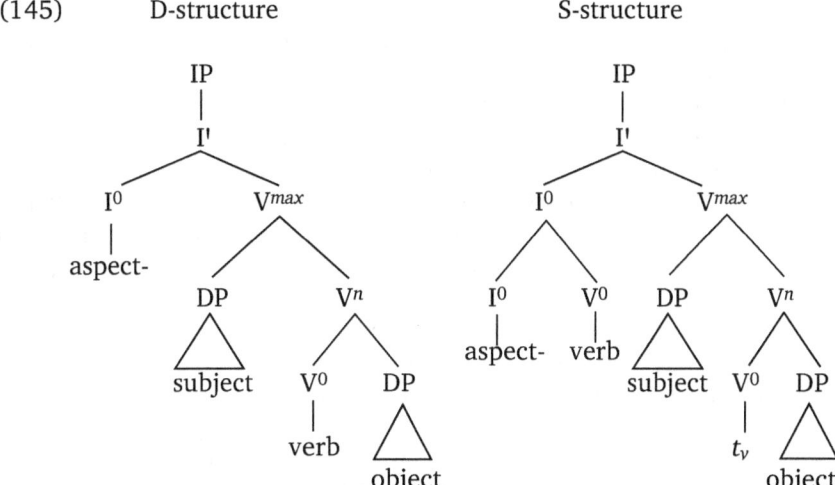

Evaluating how the Verb Movement proposal fares with respect to the theory of phrase structure depends partially on whether the subject is actually in the specifier within the minimal VP projection (as sister to V'), or whether it must be adjoined to the VP (i.e., within V^{max} as noted above). As Emonds (1985) and Kuroda (1986) argue, if the subject is the specifier of the minimal XP predicate, this is a plus for the theory of phrase structure, since the fact that there is otherwise no specifier for VP is an embarrassment within the X-bar theory of phrase structure. Positing either an additional bar-level, as in X^{max} over XP, or that the subject adjoins to the XP predicate, however, complicates (rather than enhances) the theory of phrase structure. Such a move is argued to be necessary by Koopman and Sportiche (1991:239–244) since some languages require the object to be in the specifier of VP position. Further, McCloskey (1991:286) notes that possible movement of the predicate phrase without the subject in clefting constructions in Irish indicates that the predicate phrase is maximal.

Similar evidence that the predicate phrase must be maximal in Zapotec nonverbal predicates is shown in some examples of negative fronting in chapter 8.[49]

Regardless of the bar-level status of the predicate phrase containing the subject, the Verb Movement proposal faces another drawback with respect to the theory of phrase structure. This is the fact that the specifier of IP position is empty. If, however, it can be shown to be the landing site for either A-movement or Ā-movement, this drawback will be eliminated.

The Verb Movement proposal shines with respect to the theory of movement. Movement of V^0 to I^0 is an instance of head-to-head movement allowed as substitution in Chomsky (1986:4 and 73) and extended to "incorporation" or adjunction in Baker (1988:309–310). Furthermore, the proposed movement is leftward and upward, so it meets the normal restrictions imposed upon its trace by the Empty Category Principle (ECP).

As for the question of what motivates the movement of V^0 to I^0, three possible explanations have been put forth. One rationale for why French verbs and English auxiliaries raise to Infl, yet full verbs in English do not raise, is that French has a strong agreement (AGR), whereas English AGR is weak (see Emonds 1979, Pollock 1989 and Chomsky 1989).[50] Strong AGR is assumed to be able to "attract" all verbs, causing V^0-to-I^0 movement, whereas weak AGR can only "attract" auxiliary elements. If English AGR is weak, however, then Zapotec AGR is even weaker because it is completely nonexistent. This cannot be the motivation for V^0-to-I^0 movement in Zapotec.[51]

A second possible explanation for why the verb must move to Infl involves Case theory. Koopman and Sportiche (1991:227–232) claim that there are two distinct mechanisms available for Case assignment that may be chosen by a particular category within a particular language. Case may either be assigned by a head to its complement or the specifier of its

---

[49]This complication of X-bar theory might be minimized by adopting an amendment along the lines of the proposal by Fukui and Speas (1986) where functional categories have a single specifier and a single complement but lexical categories may have multiple specifiers and complements, limited only by the projection Principle and the subcategorization requirements of the head.

Another alternative is the proposal by Bowers (1993) that there is an additional predicate phrase (PrP) in every clause. Under this view, the subject is the specifier of PrP and VP is usually its complement. Verb Movement would be V^0-to-Pr^0-to-I^0, yielding VSO order without violating strict X-bar theory.

[50]Pollock (1989) uses the terms "transparent" and "opaque" instead of "strong" and "weak".

[51]Vikner (1991:137) cites Platzack and Holmberg (1989:73–74) as noting the idea that Infl must include a substantial number of distinctive features to trigger V^0-to-I^0 movement must be an implicature, or one-way correlation, not an equivalence. Therefore, a strong AGR may imply V^0-to-I^0 movement but the presence of V^0-to-I^0 movement does not imply the presence of a strong AGR.

5.2 How VSO word order is obtained

complement under government, or it may be assigned to its own specifier under agreement via the specifier-head agreement relationship. In English and French finite clauses, Infl is specified as assigning Case only under the agreement relation, not by government. Koopman and Sportiche (1991) maintain that this requires the subject to move up to the specifier of IP position in English and French, since it cannot receive Case in the specifier of VP (which is the D-structure position of the subject in all languages under the Internal Subject Hypothesis they are arguing in favor of). In contrast, in finite clauses in VSO languages such as Irish and Welsh, Infl may only assign Case under government, not by specifier-head agreement. Therefore, the subject can receive Case in its D-structure position and no A-movement of the subject is called for. Note, however, that this difference in Case assignment mechanisms, in itself, accounts only for the different S-structure positions of the subject, not for the S-structure position of the verb. In order to use Case theory to explain why the verb must move to Infl in VSO languages and in French, we must also assume that in these languages Infl alone is not sufficient to assign Case to the subject; Infl must be supported by the verb as well. Once V^0-to-I^0 movement has taken place, the subject can receive Case by the mechanism prescribed.

Additionally, it is an overriding assumption of this study that (at least a portion of) the morphology is reflected in the syntax. Therefore, the fact that Infl (which is simply the aspect marking in Zapotec) is morphologically marked on the verb can be seen as consistent with incorporation of the verb into Infl via head movement of V^0-to-I^0. This idea of a direct relationship between the morphology and the syntax is a basic tenet of Baker (1988), as well as being maintained in Chomsky (1986, 1991) for inflectional morphology. Rizzi and Roberts (1989:18–19) specifically claim that all head movement is substitution, where the incorporation host morphologically subcategorizes for the incorporee. Specifically for V^0-to-I^0 movement, Infl has the subcategorization frame [__ + V^0], so a slot for V^0 is base-generated within I^0, which triggers the substitution of V^0 during the derivation. The complex head created by this incorporation remains I^0, so no problems are created for the Projection Principle.

Overall, the Verb Movement proposal seems to be on basically solid ground theoretically. It has some weak points in the area of phrase structure, but is very strong in complying with the theory of movement.

5.2.2 Subject Adjunction

The Subject Adjunction proposal was developed for Chamorro in Chung (1990) and was originally proposed by Choe (1986) for Berber. In this case, the subject begins in the specifier of I^0 and then right-adjoins to the verb, leaving behind a coindexed expletive *pro*. The D- and S-structures under this proposal are shown in (146).

(146)

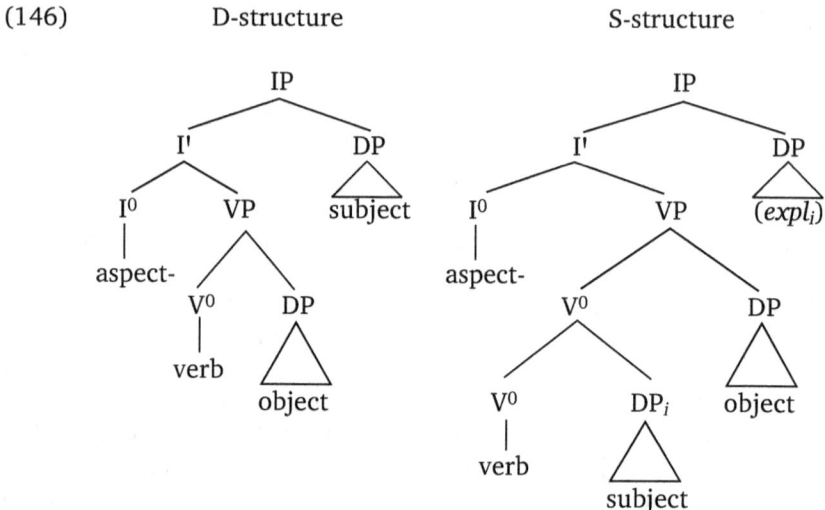

The Subject Adjunction proposal clearly fares best in terms of the theory of phrase structure. The proposed D-structure in (146) complies perfectly with X-bar theory in that each projection has both a specifier and a complement.[52] Further, the notion that the clause is projected from Infl, in which the subject serves as its specifier and the predicate XP is its complement, is maintained under this proposal.

In contrast, the proposed adjunction of the subject to the verb at S-structure is clearly problematic for the theory of movement. First, the adjunction of a maximal projection to a head is disallowed by the constraints on movement in Chomsky (1986:4). Second, the movement is downward (though it is leftward), which means that the trace could not be governed by its antecedent, in violation of the ECP. This necessitates the claim that a coindexed expletive *pro* is left behind in the specifier of IP position, rather than a trace.[53] The use of a coindexed expletive *pro* seems to be a powerful mechanism which is invoked chiefly to legitimize what would otherwise be an ECP violation.

Exactly what might motivate Subject Adjunction, other than the need to account for surface word order, is unclear. Case theory is not involved

---

[52]With the otherwise known exception that there is not a clear specifier for VP.

[53]Also proposed by Rizzi (1982) and Burzio (1986) to deal with free inversion of subjects in Italian.

5.2 How VSO word order is obtained

here, since the subject would have to receive Case in its D-structure position from Infl. Likewise, we cannot assume that the syntactic movement is "caused" by morphological requirements, since the verb and subject do not form a single word. Instead, Chung (1990:615–616) speculates that the motivation might be due to the need to resolve a conflict between the underlying head-initial (VOS) structure of the clause and the near universal preference (noted in Greenberg 1963) for subjects to precede objects. Subject Adjunction might be a way of resolving this dilemma.

Overall, the Subject Adjunction proposal faces serious problems under the theory of movement, while maintaining the theory of phrase structure. Strictly from a theoretical point of view, the Verb Movement proposal seems more attractive. This means that, if the empirical coverage is equivalent between the two, the Verb Movement hypothesis would be chosen.[54]

A basic task of this part of the study is to determine which of these proposals for obtaining VSO order, or combination thereof, fully accounts for the clause structure of QZ. In chapter 8 we will see that the negation constructions prompt the decision to adopt the Verb Movement proposal, since these constructions show evidence for head movement of the verb. Chapter 10 presents additional evidence in support of this choice.

---

[54]Chung (1990) shows quite conclusively that the empirical coverage is not always equivalent, which merits the choice of Subject Adjunction for Chamorro.

6
Focus and Topic Constructions

This chapter begins the look at Ā-dependencies by presenting and contrasting focus and topic constructions. Section 6.1 shows how the two types of constructions can be distinguished syntactically and discusses the semantics of each construction. Section 6.2 looks at the focus marker itself. Section 6.3 gives two possible phrase structure analyses for focus constructions. The decision between these analyses is made in chapter 9.

6.1 Focus versus topic syntactically and semantically

The most common alternative to standard VSO order is SVO order, which I analyze as the result of focusing the subject. Some examples with SVO order are given in (147). A focus marker may occur directly before the focused subject.

(147) a. ***y-ra maa gin*** *r-dil*   *noo*   BENIT 19
P-all 3A   this H-fight 1EX
All those animals are bothering me.

   b. ***le Manwel*** *w-ruu   dxe ne   w-et   x-maa men*   AGOSTO 68
FM Manuel C-leave day that C-die POS-3A 3
Manuel left the day that his animal died.

c. **laad men La Merse** w-dee lgyëz   GRANDMA1 8
FM 3 La Merced C-give town
The people of La Merced burned the village.

d. *per* **la Biki** n-eey ne g-u Karmita   GRING 19
but FM Virginia S-take that P-eat Carmita
But Virginia had brought Carmita's food.

e. **laad x-unaa Dolf** dxe z-u nga   HORTENS 37
FM POS-woman Rodolfo already PR-stand there
Rodolfo's wife was already standing there.

f. **lët me** r-diix-o   LIFEINQ 7
FM 3R H-turn.over-3I
She turned them over.

The object may be optionally focused instead, yielding OVS order. This is less common and may only be done when it is clear either from the context or from the argument structure which nominal phrase is the subject, as is the case in each of the examples in (148).

(148) a. **noze laa-w** r-ap-kwent men   SEMBRAR 7
only FM-3I H-have-watch 3
Only it they watch.

b. **pur le yuu** r-kaa zhich men   GRANDMA2 26
pure FM bundles H-put back 3
Just the bundles they carried on their backs.

c. **teb gix mank** w-eey men   OLDMAN 10
one bag mango C-take 3
He took a bag of mangos.

d. **y-ra ngyed win** w-u msii   RANCHO 13
P-all chicken small C-eat eagle
An eagle had eaten all the young chickens.

In QZ, there is no resumptive pronoun following the verb in a focus construction regardless of whether the fronted phrase is a subject or an object. Other Zapotecan languages vary greatly in this regard; some require a resumptive pronoun only for fronted subjects, some for both subjects and objects, and others allow it optionally. Resumptive pronouns most commonly appear when the fronted nominal is a first or second person pronominal subject. QZ focus constructions involve Ā-movement of the fronted nominal with only a trace left in its D-structure position.

In contrast, in QZ topic constructions there is a constituent corresponding to the initial constituent in its normal position following the verb. The examples in (149) show that this repeated constituent in the standard position is not simply a resumptive pronoun. (149a) shows that the repeated constituent may be a name, and (149b–c) demonstrate that it may be a common noun phrase. The subject in normal position is a pronoun in (149d) only because the topic is also a pronoun. This repetition of the nominal phrase rather than changing the subsequent entry to a pronoun relates to the overall distribution of pronouns and nonpronominals in QZ (discussed in chapter 4). Proper names and common nouns may be freely repeated, even in bound positions, rather than undergoing pronominalization. (149b) shows the effect of the hierarchy of nominal phrases, however, in that the possessed nominal phrase in the topic position is not repeated in the argument position: only the common noun is used.[55]

(149) a. *per* **laa** *Gecha* *w-on-t* *Gecha*   GRING 25
    but FM Lucretia C-hear-NEG Lucretia

    porke   *ndal*   *yaa*   *men*   *ndxin*
    because s/lots very 3 there
    But as for Lucretia, Lucretia didn't hear because there were lots of people there.

b. *no* *x-pëëd* *le* *de* *g-an*   *pe-zee* *n-eey* *de* **mëëd** TRIPTOQ 10
   and POS-baby FM 2 P-know Q-how S-take 2 baby
   And your baby, we'll see how you take the baby.

---

[55]I have no data involving a topic phrase which is a quantified nominal phrase, but I assume that the full quantified nominal phrase would not be repeated, similarly to (149b). Instead it would be replaced by the common noun or a pronoun. The presence of the null third person pronoun (discussed in §4.2.2) brings up a problem in that nonpronominal topic phrases could antecede this null pronoun. In that situation, topic constructions and focus constructions would be indistinguishable since both would have an empty category in argument position. Such structural ambiguity could apply in (148d), for example. Topic constructions with overt DPs in argument position are clearly distinct from focus constructions, however.

c. *per* **laa mdxin** *nagon*   *dxe*   *n-an*   **mdxin**   RYENEGU 33
   but FM deer   however already s-know deer

   no   *ne*   *y-gw-et*   *meedx*   *mdxin*
   there that P-CAUS-die lion   deer
   But as for the deer, however, the deer already knew that the lion was going to kill him.

d. *re*   *Jasint*   **laa** *de* **naa**   BENIT 23
   H-say Jacinto   FM   2   DEM

   pe r-laan   *de*   *y-laa*   *de*   *dxiin*   *nee*
   Q H-want   2   P-do   2   work   here
   Jacinto said, "And you, do you want to work here?"

Syntactically, then, while the QZ focus constructions involve movement of a constituent from its unmarked position following the verb, the topic constructions do not involve any movement; the topicalized constituent is still in its normal position in the clause as well as being appended to the front of the sentence. I assume that the syntax of topic phrases is simply that they are adjoined to a matrix clause, following Aissen (1992a).

An adjunction analysis predicts the possibility of multiple topics, however, which (150) verifies is not allowed.

(150) a. **per [laa Gecha]*   *[x-pëëd   Gecha]*   GRING 27A
       but   FM Lucretia   POS-baby Lucretia

   w-ni-t-leech   *Gecha*   *x-pëëd*   *Gecha*
   C-lose-NEG-liver Lucretia   pos-baby Lucretia
   (But as for Lucretia, her baby, Lucretia had forgotten about her baby.)

b. **per [laa mdxin]* *[meedx]* *nagon*   RYENEGU 33A
   but FM deer   lion   however

   dxe   *n-an*   *mdxin*   *no*   *ne*   *y-gw-et*   *meedx*   *mdxin*
   already s-know   deer   there that P-CAUS-die lion   deer
   (But as for the deer, the lion, however, the deer already knew that the lion was going to kill him.)

6.1 Focus versus topic syntactically and semantically

The limitation of only one topic per sentence may be accounted for by the semantics. Since the semantics of topic constructions is that of designating a particular referent to be the topic of conversation (i.e., who or what is being talked about) in the following discourse, it seems intuitive that there could be at most one topic per matrix clause. This semantic or discourse constraint allows the syntactic adjunction analysis to remain valid, even though the syntax alone would predict the possibility of multiple topics.

The semantics of the focus constructions is less clear, as it moves further into the realm of discourse. The construction definitely highlights the referent of the fronted nominal, but there seems to be no clear distinction as to whether the focused phrase is presupposed or whether it introduces a new referent. Discourse analyses done on other Zapotecan languages show that the fronted nominal may be either old or new information. In his paragraph analysis in Amatlán Zapotec, Riggs (1987) found that fronting was used more than it usually is in the peak paragraph to drive home the point. In nonpeak paragraphs, fronting signals a new participant or focuses on some known participant. Newberg (1987) found that in Yalálag Zapotec, fronting in narrative discourse serves to highlight the referent of the fronted nominal in relation to the other participants or in relation to the development of the plot. He gives the examples in (151), translated from texts, where all the clauses have the unmarked VSO order except where noted.

(151) a. The lion wanted to kill the mouse but the MOUSE (fronted) begged for mercy.
  b. They took the coffee pot, poured water in it, prepared it, set it on the ground and thought it would boil; but in fact it was the kind that needs fire. PETER (fronted) had tricked them.

Focus constructions are also limited to a single phrase being focused. Though some of the other Zapotecan languages allow both the subject and the object to be fronted in a focus construction, this is not allowed in either order in QZ, as shown in (152).

(152) a. *[pur le yuu]   [zhich men] r-kaa _ _   GRANDMA2 26A
       pure FM bundles   back   3   H-put
       (Only the bundles on their backs they carried.)

b. *[zhich men] [pur le yuu]   r-kaa _ _   GRANDMA2 26B
   back 3   pure FM bundles H-put
   (On their backs only the bundles they carried.)

c. *[laad men La Merse] [lgyëz] w-dee _ _   GRANDMA1 8B
   FM   3   La Merced town   C-give
   (The people of La Merced the village burned.)

d. *[lgyëz] [laad men La Merse] w-dee _ _   GRANDMA1 8C
   town   FM   3   La Merced C-give
   (Their village the people of La Merced burned.)

Although neither multiple topics nor multiple focused phrases are allowed in QZ, it is possible under very limited circumstances to have both a topic phrase and a focus phrase in the same clause, with the topic phrase (the one which has an overt coindexed argument in its normal position) obligatorily occurring first. In general, although these constructions are seldom used, a topic phrase and a focused phrase may occur in the same clause when both refer to humans, as shown in (153a). (153b–c) verifies that the topic phrase and the focused phrase must have distinct referents and (153d–e) shows that ungrammaticality results when one of the phrases is nonhuman. This demonstrates that topic phrases and focused phrases must have syntactically distinct positions, though the limitations on their interaction will again have to relegated to the semantics.

(153) a. *per [Karmita] [laa Biki]   n-eey _ ne g-u   GRING 19A
        but Carmita   FM Virginia S-take that P-eat

        Karmita
        Carmita
   But as for Carmita, Virginia had brought Carmita's food.

b. *per [Biki]   [le Biki]   w-yan _ fwer   GRING 18A
   but Virginia FM Virginia C-stay outside
   (But as for Virginia, Virginia had stayed outside.)

6.1 Focus versus topic syntactically and semantically

c. *per [laa mdxin] nagon   dxe   [mdxin]   RYENEGU 33B
   but FM deer however already deer

   n-an _ no   ne   y-gw-et   meedx mdxin
   s-know   there that P-CAUS-die   lion   deer
   (But as for the deer, however, the deer already knew that the lion was going to kill him.)

d. *[laad men La Merse] [lgyëz] w-dee men _   GRANDMA1 8A
   FM   3   La Merced   town   C-give 3
   (As for the people of La Merced, the village they burned.)

e. *per [msii] [y-ra ngyed win] w-u   msii   _   RANCHO 13A
   but eagle P-all chicken small C-eat eagle
   (But as for the eagle, all the young chickens it had eaten.)

6.2 The focus marker

The analysis of the focus marker is broken down into two parts: its syntactic category, and why it is used in some constructions and not in others.

6.2.1 The category of the focus marker

As discussed above, the focus marker not only marks focus phrases, but also appears in topic phrases. This argues against the assumption that the focus marker is a complementizer, and that the focus position is immediately after the complementizer. More evidence against the complementizer analysis is provided in (154). (154a) shows the focus marker following *pur* 'only', which is itself a semantic type of focus marker. In (154b) the focus marker follows *chene* 'when', which makes it unlikely that the focus marker is a complementizer if *chene* is analyzed as a complementizer itself.[56] Note that there is a focus marker on the fronted constituent in each clause in (154b). (154c) gives a clear example where a focused phrase, marked with the focus marker, follows the overt complementizer *ne* 'that' in an embedded clause. Thus, the focus marker cannot be a complementizer.

---

[56]Alternatively, *chene* 'when' could be analyzed as a preposition which takes a sentential complement.

(154) a. *pur* **le** **yuu**   *r-kaa zhich men*   GRANDMA2 26
       pure FM bundles H-put back 3
       Only the bundles they carried on their backs.

   b. *chene* **le** **gyo** **bni** *g-yab nagon*   **le** **men**   GRANDMA4 20
      when FM grain seed P-fall however FM 3

      g-uu bni
      P-sow seed
      When it rained seed, however, they planted the seed.

   c. *bweree x-yag   men w-nii   lo   xuz   nzaap gin*   CWENT 6A
      C/return nephew 3 C-speak face father girl this

      ne **la** **xsaap**   *men y-ka men*
      that FM daughter 3 P-buy 3
      His nephew$_i$ returned and said to this girl's father$_k$ that his$_k$ daughter he$_i$ would marry.

Further, the focus marker can occur in positions other than the front of the clause. (155a) shows that it can occur with the object of a preposition, while in (155b) it occurs with the possessor in a topic, and in (155c) it is part of the possessor in a conjoined DP subject which has not been fronted.

(155) a. *r-e   Benit nee n-eey noo te   bëd mël por* **laa** **de**   BENIT 12
       H-say Benito here S-take 1EX one little fish for FM 2
       Benito said, "Here, I have a little fish for you."

   b. *no x-pëëd* **le** **de** *g-an   pe-zee n-eey de mëëd* TRIPTOQ 10
      and POS-baby FM 2 P-know Q-how S-take 2 baby
      And your baby, we'll see how you take the baby.

   c. *w-u tson bech   Dolf   s-te   bzaan Dolf*   TEXAS 13
      C-eat three brother Rodolfo F-one sister Rodolfo

      xuz **le** **Dolf**   *xnaa* **le** **Dolf**
      father FM Rodolfo mother FM Rodolfo
      Rodolfo's three brothers, another sister his father and his mother ate.

6.2 The focus marker

The lack of fronting of the focus-marked phrases in these cases is illustrative of the general lack of extractability of possessors and objects of prepositions, indicating that these positions are not properly governed. We will see in chapters 7 and 8 that pied-piping of the whole prepositional phrase or possessed nominal is required in *wh*-movement and negative fronting. Examples (156a and c) demonstrate that pied-piping is possible, while extraction of the focus-marked prepositional object or possessor alone is highly questionable (156b and d).

(156) a. r-e   Benit **por laa de** n-eey noo te bëd mël   BENIT 12A
     H-say Benito for FM 2 S-take 1EX one little fish
     Benito said, "For you I have a little fish."

    b. ??r-e Benit **laa de** n-eey noo te bëd mël por   BENIT 12B
     H-say Benito FM 2 S-take 1EX one little fish for
     (Benito said, "You I have a little fish for.")

    c. **tson bech le Dolf**   w-u   TEXAS 13A
     three brother FM Rodolfo C-eat
     Rodolfo's three brothers ate.

    d. ??**le Dolf**   w-u tson bech   TEXAS 13B
     FM Rodolfo C-eat three brother
     (Rodolfo's ate three brothers.)

Further, (157) verifies that fronting of focus-marked phrases is required for subjects and direct objects. It must, therefore, be the lack of direct extractability which accounts for the acceptance of the in situ focus-marked phrases in (155).

(157) a. *w-yan **le Biki**   fwer   GRING 18B
     C-stay FM Virginia outside
     (Virginia had stayed outside.)

    b. *per n-eey **la Biki**   ne   g-u Karmita   GRING 19B
     but S-take FM Virginia that P-eat Carmita
     (But Virginia had brought Carmita's food.)

    c. *r-ap-kwent   men **noze laa-w**   SEMBRAR 7A
     H-have-watch 3   only FM-3I
     (They watch only it.)

The distribution of the focus marker is much more that of a determiner than a complementizer. Analyzing the focus marker as a type of determiner would account for the fact that only DPs can be marked with the focus marker in QZ.[57] The determiner analysis would also allow for the occurrence of the focus marker on DPs that have not been fronted, or which occupy the topic position above CP, as seen in (155).

Examples like (158a) show that the focus marker is not simply a determiner, however, since it may co-occur with a quantifier which otherwise seems to be the head of DP. (158b) verifies that the focus marker must occur outside of the quantifier.

(158) a. **laa y-rup meedx** z-umbës-te-ke — RYENEGU 37
FM P-two lion   PR-stay-MORE-ASSOC

y-ruu   mdxin
P-leave deer
The two lions were just waiting for the deer to leave.

b. ***y-rup laa meedx** z-umbës-te-ke _ y-ruu mdxin
P-two FM lion   PR-stay-MORE-ASSOC   P-leave deer
(The two lions were just waiting for the deer to leave.)

I assume, therefore, that the focus marker can adjoin to (or within) a DP, similarly to the usual analysis for term negation, as in *not one man*.

There are also ordering restrictions between the focus marker and the words meaning 'pure' or 'only'. There seem to be three QZ words translated as 'only': *pur*, *nonchee*, and *noze*. Of these, *pur* is limited to modifying nominal phrases. It can be used on a fronted phrase, as in (159a), or on a phrase left in place (159b–c).

(159) a. *per* **pur** *men* Santyoo n-uu nga   TRIPTOQ 62
but pure 3   Santiago s-be there
But only people from Santiago are there.

---

[57]Which types of phrases can be focus-marked varies somewhat throughout the Zapotecan language family. For example, in SZ both DPs and VPs can be preceded by the focus marker. In the case where it is preposed to a verb, the effect is one of emphasizing the action (Kreikebaum 1987). The distribution of the focus marker in SZ is similar to the distribution of *only* in English. It is also similar to the distribution of two words meaning 'only' in QZ, *nonchee* and *noze*, to be shown further below. MZ exemplifies the other end of the distribution in not having a focus marker at all (Stubblefield, p.c.).

b. nga   lo   play   zob   restawran   BENIT 45
   there face beach PR/sit restaurant

   ne   r-too men **pur** **mël**
   that H-sell 3   pure   fish
   There at the beach is a restaurant in which they only sell fish.

c. teb-o   w-uu   **pur** **mgyeey**   MTLEMON 32
   one-3I   C-be   pure   man
   One was only men.

In contrast, *nonchee* and *noze* can also be used to directly modify (or focus on) the predicate, as shown in (160).

(160) a. r-e   Javyer gu-kwëw   **nonchee** g-u-b   SAMUEL 39
        H-say Javier IMP-wait only   P-eat-1I
        Javier said, "Wait until after we eat."

     b. **noze** r-on   noo   diiz   n-ak   noo men win   GRANDMA1 6
        only   H-hear   1EX   word   S-become   1EX   3   small
        I only heard it, when I was a child.

     c. r-yab   gyeey   **noze**   n-gich   x-too   gyeey   LIFEINUS 63
        H-fall ice   only   S-white   POS-head   mountain
        It snows such that it's all white on the mountain.

However, when these words meaning 'only' are used with a DP which is marked with the focus marker, the focus marker must occur closest to the DP, as shown in (161) and (162).

(161) a. **pur** **le** **yuu**   r-kaa   zhich   men   GRANDMA2 26
        pure   FM   bundles H-put   back   3
        Only the bundles they carried on their backs.

     b. *****le** **pur** **yuu**   r-kaa   zhich   men
        FM   pure   bundles H-put   back   3
        (Only the bundles they carried on their backs.)

(162) a. *per chene wii mdxin r-u-t meedx* RYENEGU 22
but when c/see deer H-eat-NEG lion

    noze laa mdxin r-u
    only FM deer H-eat
But when the deer saw that the lion wasn't eating, only the deer was eating...

b. **per chene wii mdxin r-u-t meedx*
but when c/see deer H-eat-NEG lion

    laa noze mdxin r-u
    FM only deer H-eat
(But when the deer saw that the lion wasn't eating only the deer was eating...)

If both the focus marker and the words meaning 'only' are analyzed as adjoining to a DP, what accounts for the ordering restrictions between them? The best account seems to be that the focus marker is most like a determiner and can therefore fill the D^0 position itself or adjoin to an already filled D^0 position. In contrast, the words meaning 'only' could be a type of phrasal projection which adjoins to a DP[58] (or to IP in the case of *noze* and *nonchee*).

6.2.2 The function of the focus marker

It appears that the focus marker in QZ has the discourse function of picking one referent out of a group to highlight. There needs to be more than one discourse familiar referent present or the focus marker would not be used, though fronting of the constituent is still possible. For example, (163)–(164) show that focus constructions with and without the focus marker are both syntactically grammatical although they would be used in different contexts. The (a) examples would only be used when other possible referents were already mentioned in the discourse. The focus marker serves to highlight the marked referent out of this group. In contrast, the (b) examples make no claim about there being more referents in the discourse.

---

[58]This is probably adjunction to D' to avoid the problem of adjunction to an argument (Chomsky 1986:6).

6.2 The focus marker

(163) a. **le Manwel** w-ruu dxe ne w-et x-maa men AGOSTO 68
FM Manuel C-leave day that C-die POS-3A 3
Manuel left the day that his animal died.

b. **Manwel** w-ruu dxe ne w-et x-maa men
Manuel C-leave day that C-die POS-3A 3
Manuel left the day that his animal died.

(164) a. **laad x-unaa Dolf** dxe z-u nga HORTENS 37
FM POS-woman Rodolfo already PR-stand there
Rodolfo's wife was already standing there.

b. **x-unaa Dolf** dxe z-u nga
POS-woman Rodolfo already PR-stand there
Rodolfo's wife was already standing there.

The focus marker is not normally used when a referent is first introduced into a discourse, which further restricts the marked referent to one which has been previously identified. (165) shows that adding the focus marker to the introductory statement in a text is highly questionable.

(165) a. teb tir **te mër** zob lo yag MARTRIST 1
one time one pigeon PR/sit face tree

r-oolbaan maa te-tee maa
H-sing 3A one-one 3A
One time a male pigeon sat in a tree singing all by himself.

b. ??teb tir **laa te mër** zob lo yag
one time FM one pigeon PR/sit face tree

r-oolbaan maa te-tee maa
H-sing 3A one-one 3A
(One time a male pigeon sat in a tree singing all by himself.)

The focus marker may occur on a topic phrase where it has exactly the same function: that of picking out one specific referent from a group of discourse familiar referents. All of the topic constructions in (149) are also syntactically grammatical without the focus marker. The use of the focus marker in a given example indicates that there are other discourse familiar referents present.

6.3 The phrase structure of focus constructions

Even though we have shown that the focus marker itself is a type of determiner, it is still necessary to account for the position of the fronted focused phrase and for the fact that phrases marked with the focus marker normally must front. Example (154c) illustrates that when the focus marker co-occurs with an overt complementizer, the complementizer is first. Thus, a position below that complementizer is needed for focused phrases. This can be accomplished by positing either an adjoined position or a two-level projection, as shown in (166). In (166a) the focused phrase occupies the specifier of FocP directly below C⁰, and the head of FocP is always null. We could assume that the focused phrase in the specifier position licenses the null head. The focused phrase would then be in a specifier-head relationship within FocP. In contrast, (166b) has the focused phrase simply adjoined to the phrase below C⁰. The only relationship between the focused phrase and a head here would be government by C⁰. Both of these structures are plausible and the determination of which one is best is postponed until chapter 9, where the interaction between the various constructions involving Ā-movement is studied.

(166)   a. CP over FocP   b. IP adjoined

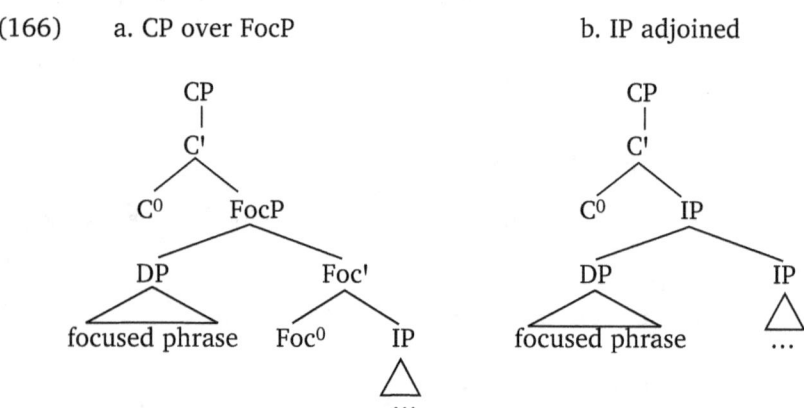

The issues of what motivates the fronting of a focused phrase, and what limits the fronting to a single phrase remain to be dealt with. If we adopt the CP over FocP configuration in (166a), we could assume that the focus marker carries a [+*foc*] feature that must be in a specifier-head relationship with a Foc⁰ at S-structure to be licensed. This is parallel to the *Wh*-Criterion that has been proposed for questions (May 1985, Rizzi 1991). The limitation of FocP to a single specifier would correctly limit the number of phrases that could be fronted.

6.3 The phrase structure of focus constructions

The same basic assumptions could be applied to the adjoined configuration in (166b), except that the required licensing relationship would be a minimal government relationship,[59] where the C^0 must be the closest governor for the focused phrase and no other phrase(s) may intervene. This is similar in spirit to Relativized Minimality (Rizzi 1990:7), though this relationship involves government by a functional head rather than a lexical head and the barred intervention is by a closer potential governee rather than a closer potential governor. The minimal government relationship defined here also encompasses the strict adjacency requirement noted in McCloskey (1991:291–292).

The configuration in (167) illustrates how this minimal government relationship disallows adjunction of another phrase from meeting the requirement. Crucially assuming that ZP is not a barrier for government since all segments of ZP do not dominate XP (May 1985), the head C^0 governs XP in a minimal government relationship, as indicated by the coindexing in (167). C^0 cannot also minimally govern YP, however, since another potential governee (XP) intervenes between C^0 and YP.

(167) *Multiple Adjunction to ZP

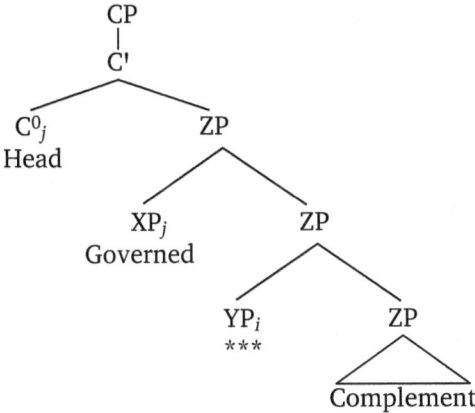

This licensing requirement would thus both motivate the fronting of a focus-marked phrase and limit the fronting to a single phrase.

---

[59]See Rudin (1993) for discussion of a similar licensing requirement by the focus marker in Bulgarian which must also be discharged by S-structure. In Bulgarian, the canonical focus position is adjoined to IP and the topic position is adjoined to CP, just as in the analysis presented here. The focus marker *li*, used in questions, is analyzed as a complementizer, however, with subsequent movement of the focused phrase to the specifier of CP.

Dealing with the case of focused phrases not marked by the focus marker is more complex, and I do not have a fully satisfactory account to propose. We can assume syntactically that Move-α allows the phrase to move. The problem is how to limit such movement to a single phrase and how to assure that it ends up in the proper position only.[60] The CP over FocP proposal (166a) can assume that there is a single specifier position present, so only one phrase can move there. However, without feature marking on the moved DP, we cannot be assured that the moved phrase lands in the specifier of FocP position instead of somewhere else. The account involving an adjoined position for focus phrases (166b) faces similar problems. It seems necessary to posit that a DP that is not already a semantic operator (i.e., is [-wh, -neg]) becomes [+foc] when it moves. This $DP_{[+foc]}$ would then be required to adjoin below C^0 to be licensed. Further, a second phrase could not front since it could not meet the minimal government relationship.

Apparently, QZ has a strong desire to have scope relations readable at S-structure, which motivates the fronting of focused phrases as well as other semantic operatore. This means that LF movement in QZ is very limited. As far as focus constructions go, a focus-marked phrase is only allowed to remain in situ if its movement would violate the ECP. We will see in the next chapter that wh-movement absolutely must take place at S-structure and chapter 9 will show that the negtive indefinite pronouns are also required to front at S-structure. At least one of the quantifiers, zhi (or sometimes zhindxe) 'few', must be fronted at S-structure as well, as shown in (168)–(169). (169c) shows that a similar statement could be expressed using txup-tson 'two-three' instead of zhi 'few' with the quantified argument remaining in situ.

(168) a. zhi   maa   gin   r-dil   _   noo
few   3A   this   H-fight   1EX
Those few animals are bothering me.

    b. *r-dil   zhi   maa   gin   noo
H-fight   few   3A   this   1EX
(Those few animals are bothering me.)

(169) a. zhi   ngyed   win   w-u   msii   _
few   chicken   small   C-eat   eagle
An eagle had eaten a few small chickens.

---

[60]The same questions that I raise here for QZ apply to English and other languages as well.

6.3 The phrase structure of focus constructions

b. *w-u   msii   zhi   ngyed   win
   C-eat eagle few chicken small
   (An eagle had eaten a few small chickens.)

c. w-u   msii   txup-tson   ngyed   win
   C-eat eagle two-three chicken small
   An eagle had eaten two or three small chickens.

We can analyze this required fronting by saying that the quantifier *zhi* must assume its scope position at S-structure also. Analyzing the fronted position of this quantified phrase as the same as the focus position accounts for the fact that nothing else may be fronted along with the quantified phrase, as shown in (170). The required fronting can then be subsumed under the licensing requirement for focus phrases by assuming that *zhi* is [+*foc*].[61]

(170) *zhi   ngyed   win   msii   w-u
      few chicken small eagle C-eat
      (An eagle had eaten a few young chickens)

---

[61] The focus marker may not occur either before or after *zhi* though it can occur before a numeral quantifier. The difference seems to be that the phrases with numeral quantifiers may be referential.

7
Questions and Relative Clauses

This chapter focuses on the formation of questions and relative clauses in QZ. As expected from the typology in Greenberg (1963) content questions are formed in QZ by fronting a *wh*-phrase (§3.4.2). Only one *wh*-phrase may be present per clause. In §7.1 this restriction is shown to follow from the requirement that both clauses of the *Wh*-Criterion hold at S-Structure. Section 7.2 then shows that QZ does not follow the widely attested pattern of having the fronted *wh*-phrase in the specifier of CP position, above the $C^0_{[+wh]}$. Instead, the complementizer is first, with the *wh*-phrase following it (similar to the position of focused phrases). In the appendix I readdress the issue of the motivation for and restrictions on *wh*-movement. The investigation reveals that the QZ facts are part of a much larger picture. I propose there a replacement for the *Wh*-Criterion which should account for the full range of cross-linguistic variation.

Section 7.3 presents the data for relative clauses. The possibility of separation of a relative clause from its head foreshadows the analysis in chapter 12 of similar facts in the special number-marking constructions.

7.1 Question formation and the *Wh*-Criterion

QZ is a tonal language and does not have a distinct intonation for questions. Therefore, syntactic marking is needed. To signal a Yes/No question, *pe* is added to the front of a sentence which is otherwise in the normal VSO order. To signal that an information question is being asked, a *wh*-phrase must be fronted (171a). A *wh*-phrase may never remain in situ (171b), even if the question marker *pe,* used in Yes/No questions, is added (171c). Further, no multiple *wh*-questions may be formed. (171d) shows that multiple *wh*-questions are impossible when one phrase is fronted and one remains in situ, and (171e) shows that fronting more than one *wh*-phrase is equally unattested. Finally, (171f) shows that QZ does not allow multiple *wh*-phrases to remain in situ.

(171) a. **pa**   **go**   *r-laa   de*   GRING 34
what thing H-do   2
What are you doing?

   b. **r-laa   de*   **pa**   **go**
H-do   2   what   thing
(You are doing what?)

   c. **pe   r-laa   de*   **pa**   **go**
Q   H-do   2   what   thing
(You are doing what?)

   d. ***pa**   **go**   *r-laa   de*   *lo*   **txu**
what   thing   H-do   2   face   who
(What are you doing to whom?)

   e. ***pa**   **go**   **txu**   *lo*   *r-laa   de*
what   thing   who   face   H-do   2
(What are you doing to whom?)

   f. **r-laa   de*   **pa**   **go**   *lo*   **txu**
H-do   2   what   thing   face   who
(What are you doing to whom?)

The pattern shown in (171) can be accounted for by two basic assumptions: First, the obligatory fronting means that QZ only allows *wh*-movement in the syntax; no further movement can take place at LF. This can be seen to follow from the requirement that both parts of the *Wh*-Criterion hold at S-structure. Second, the fact that only a single *wh*-phrase may be fronted can be accounted for by assuming that only a single position is available which fulfills the required licensing configuration.

7.1 Question formation and the *Wh*-Criterion

The *Wh*-Criterion was originally proposed by May (1985); Rizzi (1991) made it compatible with the theory of COMP in Chomsky (1986). I cite Rizzi's version in (172).[62]

(172) The *Wh*-Criterion
 A. *wh*-operator must be in a Spec-head configuration with an $X^0_{[+wh]}$.
 B. An $X^0_{[+wh]}$ must be in a Spec-head configuration with a *wh*-operator.

Rizzi (1991:23) describes the *Wh*-Criterion as "a general well-formedness condition on *wh*-structures, which is also ultimately responsible for the SS distribution and LF interpretation of *wh*-operators." It expresses the fact that, at the designated level of representation, interrogative operators must be in the specifier of a $CP_{[+wh]}$, and a $C^0_{[+wh]}$ must have an interrogative operator as its specifier, in the familiar configuration shown in (173).

(173)
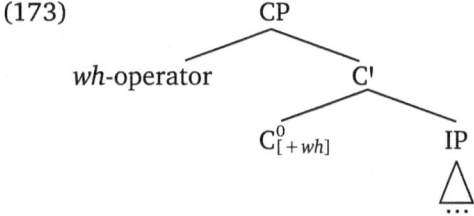

Clause B of the *Wh*-Criterion has the effect of requiring a single *wh*-phrase to front to the specifier of a $C^0_{[+wh]}$. May (1985) assumed for English that Clause B must be fulfilled at S-structure, whereas Clause A, which requires all *wh*-phrases to front, only holds at LF. This asymmetric application allows a second *wh*-operator to remain in situ in a multiple *wh*-question as long as one interrogative operator has fronted to the specifier of $C^0_{[+wh]}$. May (1985) thus assumes the definition of operator given in Cinque (1990:73) following Chomsky (1981:102), whereby all *wh*-phrases are *wh*-operators:

(174) Operator = $_{def}$ bare quantifiers, *wh*-phrases, and null NPs in Spec CP.

Rizzi (1991:29–32) takes a different view and claims that both clauses of the *Wh*-Criterion apply at S-structure in English. In order to account for

---

[62]The version appropriate to QZ will require some slight modifications (see §7.2).

the possibility of *wh*-phrases remaining in situ in multiple *wh*-questions, he redefines the notion of *wh*-operator, as shown in (175).

(175) *Wh*-operator $=_{def}$ a *wh*-phrase in a scope position, where scope position $=_{def}$ a left-peripheral Ā-position.

Rizzi shows that the requirement that both clauses of the *Wh*-Criterion apply at S-structure, coupled with the definition of *wh*-operator in (175), explains why the second *wh*-phrase in a multiple *wh*-question cannot move to an intermediate Ā-position in the syntax.[63] Instead, it must remain in situ until LF, as shown in (176)–(177) (taken from Rizzi 1991:31).

(176) a. Who thinks [C [Mary saw whom]]?
    b. *Who thinks [whom C [Mary saw *t*]]?

(177) a. Who believes that John, Mary likes *t*?
    b. *Who believes that whom, Mary likes *t*?

While these moves provide a nice account of the facts in (176)–(177),[64] the effectiveness of the *Wh*-Criterion in forcing movement at LF of *wh*-phrases remaining in situ is lost. Rizzi notes that the stronger definition of operator (174)[65] will have to be used and the *Wh*-Criterion would have to reapply at LF to cause the raising of *wh*-phrases remaining in situ at S-structure.

Further, Rizzi's account provides no explanation for the difference in distribution of *wh*-phrases between English and QZ. I assume instead that all *wh*-phrases are *wh*-operators, as in (174). This definition of operator, coupled with the requirement that both clauses of the *Wh*-Criterion hold at S-structure, entails that no *wh*-phrase may remain in situ, correctly predicting the obligatory fronting.

It is still necessary to insure that multiple fronting is not allowed. If movement is to a specifier position, it could be specified that CP only has a single specifier. Then only one *wh*-phrase could qualify as meeting the special relationship required by the *Wh*-Criterion. If movement is instead to an adjoined position, as was posited as a possibility for focus

---

[63]Rizzi credits the observation of this generalization, exemplified in (176), to Aoun, Hornstein and Sportiche (1981). Lasnik and Saito (1984, 1992) pointed out the similar facts in (177).

[64]The full analysis proposed in the appendix accounts for the facts in (176)–(177) by positing a universal filter constraining the presence of *wh*-elements in intermediate Ā-positions.

[65]Perhaps limited to non-discourse-linked phrases, following Pesetsky (1987).

constructions, the minimal government relationship required for licensing only allows a single fronted phrase.

As already hinted at, the QZ data seemingly allow the overt presence of both a *wh*-phrase and a *wh*-complementizer in some cases, which adds complications to the overall clause structure. Exactly where this "specifier position" for *wh*-phrases is located relative to the *wh*-complementizer is discussed in the next section.

7.2 The structure of $CP_{[+wh]}$

In Chomsky (1986), the theory of COMP underwent significant restructuring, as illustrated in (178). Instead of the S' category previously used, a Complementizer Phrase (CP) projected from COMP = C^0 and following X-bar theory was proposed.

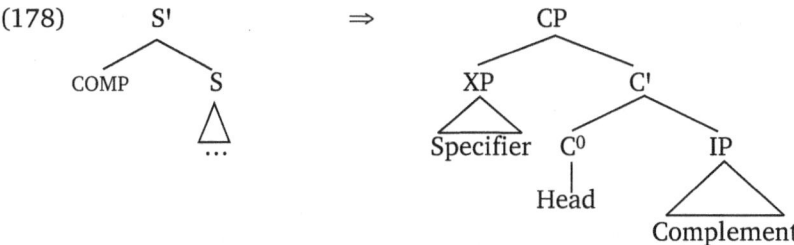

The new structure for CP revolutionized the analysis of second position clitics and also that of Verb Second languages, since these clitics or verbal elements can now be seen as occupying C^0 at S-structure, with the phrase they attach to residing in the specifier position: see Emonds (1979), Sproat (1985), and Haider and Prinzhorn (1986) on V-2; Klavans (1982, 1985), Marantz (1989), and Anderson (1992) on 2P clitics; and H. A. Black (1992) on both topics.

Further, most of the familiar languages have a requirement that disallows the presence of both an overt C^0 and a fronted *wh*-phrase in a $CP_{[+wh]}$, thus trivially conforming to the new configuration in (178). Some languages, such as Chamorro and Irish, allow both the specifier and head positions to be overtly-filled under some conditions, and these cases provide evidence for the structure in (178). As documented in Pullum (1979) and Pullum and Postal (1979), however, there are also a number of languages which allow both the specifier and the head position to be overtly-filled, but for which (178) does not seem to be correct. QZ and Samoan are two of these languages.

7.2.1 QZ question formation

Yes/No questions are formed in QZ by inserting a question marker *pe* at the beginning of a regular declarative sentence, as shown in the independent clause questions in (179).

(179) a. *r-e   Javyer pe w-u   maa nii   de*   SAMUEL 28
       H-say Javier Q   C-eat 3A   foot 2
       Javier asked, "Did the snake eat your foot?"

   b. *pe r-laan   de s-aa   de ts-a-b   Estados Unidos*   HORTENS 16
      Q H-want 2   F-walk 2   P-go-1I States United
      Do you want to go together to the United States?

The question marker *pe* also occurs in embedded questions in the position of a complementizer. Further, it never co-occurs with the other known complementizer *ne* 'that'. This lends credence to the claim that *pe* is itself a complementizer.

(180) a. *n-a   men g-an   pe r-laan-t   noo*   HORTENS 3
       S-say man P-know Q   H-want-NEG 1EX

   ts-a noo y-laa noo dxiin Estados Unidos
   P-go 1EX P-do 1EX work States United
   She asked if I didn't want to go and work in the United States.

   b. *g-an   pe s-na   de g-aa   de lyu*   TRIPTOQ 8
      P-know Q   F-want 2   P-lie.down 2 land

   o   g-aa   de lo   daa
   or   P-lie.down 2   face petate
   We'll see if you want to lie down on the ground or lie down on a petate.

Content questions in QZ are formed by moving a *wh*-phrase to the beginning of the clause. Some of the *wh*-phrases may not co-occur with the question marker, *pe*, making them unproblematic for the normal CP structure (178). These *wh*-phrases use the *wh*-words *pa* 'what', *txu* 'who', *palal* 'how much', and *pa* or *go* 'where'. *Pe* may not occur either before or after these *wh*-phrases.

7.2 The structure of CP$_{[+wh]}$

(181) a. **pa** **go** r-laa de   GRING 34
       what thing H-do 2
       What are you doing?

   b. n-an-t   men **pa** **nëz** z-a Biki   AGOSTO 59
      S-know-NEG 3   what road PR-go Virginia
      They don't know which way Virginia is going.

   c. **txu** n-an **palal** zek n-on yag   GRANDMA3 21
      who S-know how.much as S-cost tree
      Who knows how much the tree is worth?

   d. **pa** g-u-gwe noo   MTLEMON2 33
      where P-eat-lunch 1EX
      Where were we to eat lunch?

   e. **go** Karmita   GRING 35
      where Carmita
      Where is Carmita?

There is another set of *wh*-words in QZ, however, which must co-occur with the question marker *pe* used in Yes/No questions. *Zee* means 'how', but it always occurs with the question marker *pe* whenever it is expressing a question. Note especially that the *wh*-word comes after the complementizer, and not the other way around.

(182) a. **pe-zee** n-ak no   BENIT 32
       Q-how S-become there
       How is it there?

   b. *****zee** n-ak no
      how S-become there
      (How is it there?)

   c. *****zee pe** n-ak no
      how Q S-become there
      (How is it there?)

'Why' is expressed by using the question marker *pe* followed by the stative verb *n-ak* 'S-become'.

(183) *pe n-ak*   *g-u de noo*   MANSNAKE 20
      Q S-become P-eat 2   1EX
      Why are you going to eat me?

In addition, *zh* seems to be a *wh*-demonstrative which can occur in combination with some of the other *wh*-words. In (184a), the *wh*-phrase *dxiin zhe*[66] has fronted to the position after the question marker *pe*. (184b–c) show *zh* used with *txu* 'who' or its complement, and (184d) shows it used with *go* 'where'. The use of *zh* adds a discourse-linked reading to the *wh*-phrase it attaches to (Pesetsky 1987) since something about the questioned item must have been previously identified in order for *zh* to be used. Note, however, that its position is always after the normal *wh*-word, rather than before it, where *pe* is found.

(184) a. *r-e   Benit **pe dxiin zhe** r-laa de na-ree*   Jasint   BENIT 15
        H-say Benito Q work WH H-do 2 which-this Jacinto
        Benito said, "What work are you doing with this, Jacinto?"

     b. *w-a-ke   mee wii g-an   **txu-zh** ne*   OLDMAN 25
        C-go-ASSOC boy see P-know who-WH 3D
        The boy went to see who he was.

     c. *lex   n-uu lexto men   **txu maa-zh** maa*   MANSNAKE 3
        later S-be liver 3   who 3A-WH   3A
        Then he wondered, "What animal is it?"

     d. *r-e   doktor **go-zh**   men naa*   SAMUEL 43
        H-say doctor where-WH 3   DEM
        The doctor said, "Where is the man?"

There are various possible analyses to consider for this data. The most straightforward alternative is to assume that the complexity lies in the morphology, rather than in the syntax. This would mean that *pe* is a complementizer for Yes/No questions, but that it may also be a *wh*-determiner in examples like (184a). Further, *pe-zee* would not be analyzed as a combination of the question complementizer *pe* and the

---

[66] I assume that the morpheme is simply *zh*, since it occurs in this form whenever it can be syllabified as the coda of the final syllable of the preceding word. In (184a) this is not possible, so an epenthetic vowel *e* is added to allow syllabification. Alternatively, it could be *zhe* underlyingly but be a phonological clitic which can only attach following a vowel, like the first person inclusive pronoun *be*. Truncation of the final vowel occurs when the clitic is able to attach to the preceding word, since it is incorporated into the final syllable of that word.

7.2 The structure of CP$_{[+wh]}$

adverb *zee* 'how', but instead simply as a *wh*-adverb meaning 'how' consisting of a single morpheme. Likewise, 'why' would be simply *penak*, rather than a combination of morphemes. The *wh*-marker *zh* would either simply be a *wh*-demonstrative that must only occur in a discourse-linked *wh*-phrase, or it could possibly be a *wh*-complementizer that can be used in discourse-linked content questions (whereas *pe* would be restricted to Yes/No questions).[67] This analysis would allow QZ to form questions using the normal CP configuration in (178), and would therefore be the most likely analysis if all other languages followed that pattern.

A second possibility is that *pe* is not a complementizer at all, but is simply adjoined to a regular clause to signal a question. Some of the other Zapotecan languages have both an initial and a final question marker, which seem to function like the syntactic analogue of intonation. For example, in IZ (Pickett 1979:143–144), *ñee* is used optionally at the beginning of a Yes/No question and *la* is required at the end (185a). Further, *la* is also used in the middle of a sentence to mark a pause between two units (185b). A different marker, *ya'*, is used at the end of content questions (185c). Similarly, *xa* appears sentence finally to indicate strong emphasis or exclamation (185d). Since there is no audible intonational difference in Zapotec between a question and a declaration or an exclamation, these markers signal to the hearer what type of phrase is being uttered.

(185) a. *(ñee) n-uu dxita* **la**
      Q   s-be egg   Q
      Are there any eggs?

   b. *después de ngue* **la** *u-yaa México*
      after   of this Q   C-go Mexico
      After this, I went to Mexico.

   c. **paraa** *cheu'* **ya'**
      where   PR-go   WH
      Where are you going?

   d. *zeeda be* **xa**
      F-sell 3   !
      He will sell it!

---

[67]Pickett (1979) reports that IZ has different markers for Yes/No questions and for content questions.

The final position of these markers seems unusual for a complementizer, since the complementizer is a head, and all other heads in Zapotec are initial. At the same time, the fact that these markers occur in embedded questions is problematic for the hypothesis that they are simply adjoined to the clause. This is because at least some embedded CPs$_{[+wh]}$ that are introduced by *pe* are selected as an argument of the higher predicate. Adjunction of *pe* to such CPs would be disallowed by the principle prohibiting adjunction to arguments, taken from Chomsky (1986:6).

(186) Adjunction is possible only to a maximal projection that is a nonargument.

Instead, we can take the view that at least the markers in final position actually are morphemes that signal intonation, and as such they need not have any syntactic representation at all. Thus, the IZ morphemes *la*, *ya'*, and *xa* would be analyzed as attaching to the right edge of an intonational phrase of the appropriate type.

There is now quite a body of literature on the relationship between prosodic structure and syntactic structure: for examples, see Selkirk (1978, 1984, 1986,) Nespor and Vogel (1986), Hayes (1989), and the articles in Inkelas and Zec (1990). Selkirk (1986) proposes an edge-based theory for mapping S-structure into prosodic structure which allows reference to an edge of an X'-constituent. This is extended by Hale and Selkirk (1987) for Papago to include reference to the government relation, and by Aissen (1992a), following their lead, for the Mayan languages. Aissen (1992a:57) claims that the algorithm for determining intonational phrase boundaries in Tzotzil maps the right edge of an ungoverned X^{max} to the right edge of an intonational phrase. This algorithm correctly predicts the distribution of the Tzotzil clitics *un* and *e*.

A similar algorithm for determining intonational phrase boundaries may be correct for Zapotec. However, the IZ intonational morphemes differ from the Tzotzil clitics in not simply attaching (optionally) to the end of any intonational phrase, but only to certain types of phrases. For example, although the use of *la* in (185b) is to simply indicate a pause (which coincides with an intonational phrase boundary), *la* in (185a) indicates a Yes/No question; it would not be used in final position of a declarative sentence, even though the end of a sentence is clearly the edge of an intonational phrase. Further, *ya'* is only used with content questions, and *xa* is used with exclamations.

These morphemes make it clear that it is crucial to know what type of phrase an intonational phrase is. However, neither the edge-based theory

7.2 The structure of $CP_{[+wh]}$

(Selkirk 1986) nor the relation-based theory for mapping syntactic structure to prosodic structure (developed by Selkirk 1984, Nespor and Vogel 1986, and Hayes 1989) has any mechanism for obtaining this necessary information. Hyman (1990) suggests that features such as [+wh] and [+imp] must be marked on the intonational phrases if the syntactic phrases they contain are so marked. This seems workable, though the details remain to be specified. Of further interest here is that the IZ morphemes point out the need to posit distinct features for content questions and Yes/No questions, as well as distinguishing each type of question from exclamations. We will see in §7.2.3 that these same distinctions are also necessary to correctly limit the application of the Wh-Criterion.

In QZ, the question marker *pe* is initial in the normal position of a head and it is syntactically required as a complementizer in embedded clauses. This fact rules out an adjunction analysis, either at the intonational phrase level or syntactically. Several other possible syntactic configurations need to be considered.

One possibility is that the normal CP structure (178) is the D-structure,[68] but that after *wh*-movement QZ allows the specifier to right-adjoin to the head. Such movement would be string vacuous if there is no overt complementizer, but it would be visible (and required) when the complementizer is overt. This analysis, diagrammed in (187), is equivalent to assuming that Subject Adjunction-type movement also applies within CP.

(187)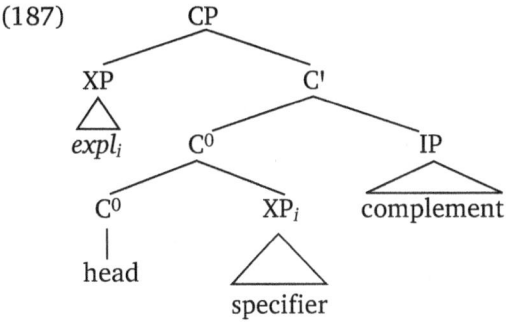

The appeal of such an analysis would be greater if the Subject Adjunction proposal was shown to be best for QZ clause structure on independent grounds.

Within the Verb Movement hypothesis, the head-specifier-complement order exhibited by these questions would seem to call for a double CP structure or another additional projection. The double CP structure, also known as

---

[68]Or a version of (178) with the specifier on the right.

CP-recursion, has been proposed for embedded CPs that have the characteristics of matrix clauses. Specifically, it has been proposed to account for embedded V2 phenomenon in Germanic (Haider and Prinzhorn 1986), embedded *qué*+Question constructions in Spanish (Suñer 1993 and Fontana 1993), and the embedded I^0-to-C^0 movement (i.e., Subject-Aux inversion) allowed in negative contexts in standard English (Rizzi and Roberts 1989) and more freely in Hiberno-English (McCloskey 1992a). (196) diagrams how this double CP account could be applied to QZ. The *Wh*-Criterion could be met in the lower CP ($=CP_2$) via the normal specifier-head relationship, and then head movement of the $C^0_{[+wh]}$ to the head of the higher CP_1 projection would produce the surface order.

(188)
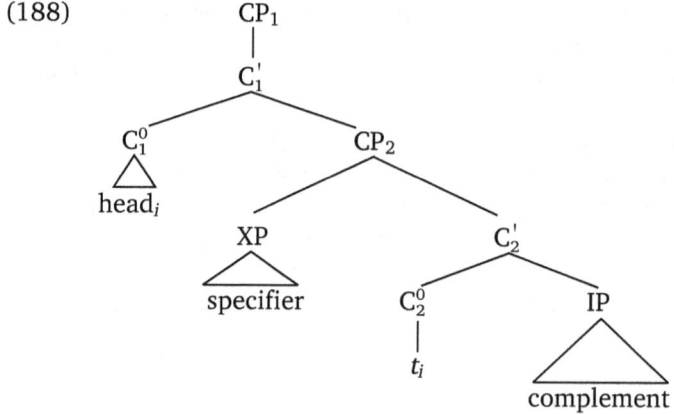

It is unclear why such head movement is needed, however, since the higher CP_1 would be selected as $[+q]$ in an embedded structure, and thus *pe* would already be expected to lexically fill that head position. Alternatively, we could assume that the *wh*-morpheme *zh* fills the C^0_2 position (when present), while *pe* occupies the C^0_1 position in (188). Then no head movement would occur, eliminating the problem of lack of motivation noted above (but also eliminating the parallel with the Verb Movement proposal). In this alternative as well, the *Wh*-Criterion would be met within CP_2.

Use of such an account would require a double CP structure to be available in both matrix and embedded question contexts. The extension of the double-CP structure to matrix questions does not appear to be theoretically problematic. More crucial is the restriction on embedded questions noted in the above references, which calls for the double-CP structure to be limited to embedded interrogative contexts in which a true question is expressed. McCloskey (1992a) (see also Berman 1989, discussed below) summarizes this distinction by saying that verbs like *wonder* and *ask* always select a true

7.2 The structure of CP$_{[+wh]}$

question of the same semantic type as a matrix question, while verbs such as *know, discover,* and *find out* select a semi-question. Complements of this second type of predicate can have the true question interpretation if the matrix clause is an interrogative, and possibly also when the matrix clause is negated.[69]

The question then, is whether this type of selectional distinction is also seen in QZ. The basic generalization is that only the verb *an* 'know' selects a *wh*-question complement.[70] (189) gives examples of *an* 'know' with interrogative CP complements: in (189a–d) the complement is a *wh*-interrogative, and in (189e) it is an indirect Yes/No question. (190) shows that *an* can also take a declarative CP complement.

(189) a. **n-an-t**   men pa   go   r-zak   men   AGOSTO 2
       s-know-NEG 3   what thing H-have 3
       Nobody knew what she had.

b. *r-laan   noo   t-sa   noo   **g-an**   pe-zee   n-ak-o*   LIFEINUS 3
   H-want 1EX P-go 1EX P-know Q-how S-become-3I
   I want to go find out what it's like.

c. *mejor   s-aa   noo   ts-a-b*   MARTRIST 11
   better F-walk 1EX P-go-1I

   g-an   pa   ts-a de
   P-know where P-go 2
   It's better that I go, we should go together, to find out where you are going.

d. *por negin* **n-an-t**   *noo* **g-an**   *pa   or   chiid   de* CARTA 6
   for this   s-know-NEG 1EX P-know what hour P/come 2
   Because of this, I don't know when you will come.

---

[69]Though there is both language variation and individual variation in the acceptability of these complements. For instance, Spanish does not allow the interpretation as a true question for complements of *know*, etc., even if the matrix clause is interrogative, but Spanish does allow it with manner-of-speaking verbs such as *whisper* and *shout* (Suñer 1991, 1993).

[70]*An* 'know' with the Stative aspect marking is a regular transitive verb with an expressed subject and either a DP or CP complement. When it has the Potential marking and takes a CP complement, however, *g-an* 'P-know' acts as a nonfinite verb and takes either a controlled *PRO* or a *PRO$_{arb}$* subject (even in the matrix clause). Its meaning is more like '*PRO* find out'. In (190b) there is an overt subject with the verb marked with the Potential because of the causative construction. This distinction was noted earlier in §§2.3.2 and 3.3.4.

e. *che-bel chiid de **g-an** pe s-u de gyët*   TRIPTOQ 11
   when-if P/come 2 P-know Q F-eat 2 tortilla

   porke no r-u men gyët
   because there H-eat 3 tortilla
   If you come, we'll see if you eat tortillas, because there they eat tortillas.

(190) a. *per laa mdxin nagon dxe **n-an** mdxin no*   RYENEGU 33
   but FM deer however already S-know deer there

   ne y-gw-et meedx mdxin
   that P-CAUS-die lion deer
   But the deer, however, already knew that the lion was going to kill him.

   b. *laz noo chene r-et te men r-kaa men kwib*   DEATH 1
   homeland 1EX when H-die one 3 H-touch 3 bell

   *chin **ga-gu-nan** y-ra men ne w-et men*
   so.that P-CAUS-know P-all 3 that C-die 3
   In my land, when someone dies, they ring the bell, so that everyone will know that the person died.

Verbs of speaking can take complements that are direct quotations, including questions. They can also take complements that are Yes/No indirect questions, as shown in (191a). My language consultant prefers the reading given in (191b), however, where the indirect question complement is further embedded under *g-an* 'P-know'. The text example in (191c) gives a further example where the indirect question complement is embedded under *g-an*.

(191) a. *laa de y-na pe s-u noo men o g-u-t noo men*   MANSNAKE 43
   FM 2 P-say Q F-eat 1EX 3 or P-eat-NEG 1EX 3
   You say whether I should eat him or not.

   b. *laa de y-na **g-an** pe s-u noo men o g-u-t noo men*
   FM 2 P-say P-know Q F-eat 1EX 3 or P-eat-NEG 1EX 3
   You say whether I should eat him or not.

7.2 The structure of CP[+wh]

    c. n-a   men **g-an**   pe r-laan-t   noo   HORTENS 3
       S-say 3   P-know Q H-want-NEG 1EX

       ts-a   noo y-laa noo dxiin Estados Unidos
       P-go 1EX P-do 1EX work States United
       She asked if I wouldn't want to go and work in the United States.

This embedding strategy is required for indirect *wh*-questions under a verb of speaking.

(192) a. w-zëët de **g-an**   pe-zee n-ak   nëz ro   BENIT 60
       C-say 2 P-know Q-how S-become road this
       You said how it is there.

    b. *w-zëët de pe-zee n-ak   nëz   ro
       C-say 2 Q-how S-become road this
       (You said how it is there.)

    Embedding of *g-an* 'P-know' is also used to express an embedded *wh*-interrogative when the main verb is *wii* 'see'.

(193) a. w-a-ke   mee wii **g-an**   txu-zh   ne   OLDMAN 25
       C-go-ASSOC boy see P-know who-WH 3D
       The boy also went to see who he was.

    b. *w-a-ke   mee wii txu-zh   ne
       C-go-ASSOC boy see who-WH 3D
       (The boy also went to see who he was.)

(194) a. r-e   mdxin ts-a   noo wii **g-an**   RYENEGU 6
       H-say deer   P-go 1EX see P-know

       pe-zee r-naa   gyeey   ne r-yab gyo
       Q-how H-appear mountain that H-fall rain
       The deer said, "I'm going to see how the mountain appears where the rain is."

b. *r-e   mdxin   ts-a   noo   wii
   H-say   deer   P-go   1EX   see

   pe-zee r-naa   gyeey   ne   r-yab gyo
   Q-how   H-appear   mountain that H-fall rain
   (The deer said, "I'm going to see how the mountain appears where the rain is.")

QZ uses an idiomatic expression, *n-uu lextoo* 'S-be liver' to express the same basic meaning as *think* or *wonder*, as shown in (195).[71] This predicate can take a direct quotation interrogative complement (195b) but not an indirect question complement without embedding *g-an*. (195c) gives a similar example using the expression *z-a lextoo* 'PR-go liver' to mean 'remember' with the embedded *g-an* before the indirect *wh*-interrogative complement.

(195) a. *noo n-uu lextoo noo wen-dee   Pwert*   BENIT 28
         1EX S-be liver 1EX good-more Salina.Cruz
         As for me, I think it's better in Salina Cruz.

      b. *lex   n-uu lextoo men txu   maa-zh maa*   MANSNAKE 3
         later S-be liver   3   who   3A-WH   3A
         Later he wondered, "What animal was it?"

      c. *z-a   lextoo Susan **g-an**   pa   gos   w-dee men lo   Susan*
         PR-go liver Susan P-know   what thing C-give 3   face Susan

         chene w-zaa   Susan iz
         when   C-complete   Susan year
         Susan remembers what things she received when she had her birthday.

Therefore, the distribution of embedded *wh*-interrogative complements is clearly limited by lexical selection in QZ, since such complements are only allowed embedded directly under the verb *an* 'know'. This verb is not the same type as the normally cited *ask* and *wonder*, however. Berman (1989) notes

---

[71]The liver is the center of the emotions for the Zapotec. In addition to the expression shown in (195), there is also a word *pazer* glossed 'I think' which is used as a parenthetical or qualifying expression, as shown in (i).

(i) *zhaache n-ak-o   pazer*   TRIPTOQ 77
     pretty   S-become-3I I.think
     It's pretty, I think.

Pazer does not select any type of complement.

7.2 The structure of CP[+wh]

that the specific difference between verbs like *wonder* and verbs like *know* is that only the latter group may have clear variable readings, due to their factivity. The factive verbs presuppose their complements, making a distinction in the readings available for (196a) versus (196b) (examples from Berman 1989:33, 37).

(196) a. Sue mostly remembers what she got for her birthday.

b. Sue mostly wonders what she got for her birthday.

In (196a) the quantificational force of the embedded interrogative is that of a variable under the scope of the adverb, giving a reading of 'Sue remembers most of the presents...'. Also available is the universal reading that 'Most of the time, Sue remembers all of the presents...'. In contrast, (196b) with the nonfactive verb only allows the universal reading with the adverb being equivalent to 'most of the time'. QZ does not have adverbs equivalent to 'mostly' or 'occasionally' to test for the readings obtained. Adverbs expressing similar meanings are either tied directly to time, as in *n-uu or* 'S-be hour' meaning 'there are times', or else tied directly to a thing, as in *ndal* 'lots' (used with count nouns) or *naal* 'much' (used with mass nouns). The factivity of *g-an* seems to disallow an analysis of the QZ embedded interrogative clauses as matrix questions, though, thus eliminating a CP-recursion structure for embedded questions.

The QZ matrix question data seems compatible with either a double CP structure (197a) where the top CP might bear the feature [+q] while the embedded CP would be [+wh],[72] a CP over another projection, such as a focus phrase (FocP) (197b), or simply a CP with an adjoined position immediately below it for the *wh*-phrase to occupy, as shown in (197c).

---

[72] I assume that [+q] indicates a question, which may be either a Yes/No question or a content question. In contrast, [+wh] indicates a construction involving *wh*-movement.

(197) a. Double CP   b. CP over FocP   c. IP adjoined

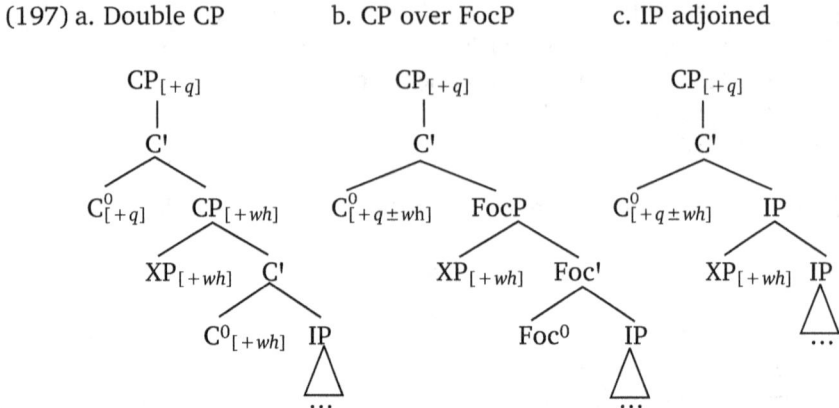

Since we have determined that the embedded questions cannot involve the CP-recursion structure because the embedding verb *an* 'know' is not of the right semantic type, I prefer not to pursue the double CP structure (197a) for matrix questions either. The choice between the other two configurations is dependent on the interaction between question formation and focus constructions and negative constructions which will be dealt with in chapter 9, so a definite decision cannot be made as yet. Certain facts are clear, however. In both (197b and c) the specifier of the top CP projection is empty—with the possible exception of the pied-piping constructions shown below in (198)—and the moved *wh*-phrase occupies the position immediately below the $C^0_{[+q]}$, rather than the normal specifier position. I claim that QZ utilizes a minimal government relationship (as defined in §6.3 to include the strict adjacency requirement noted in McCloskey 1991:291–292) to license its *wh*-phrases, instead of the usually assumed specifier-head relationship.

The only case where the specifier-head relationship might possibly be at work in QZ questions is in a construction involving pied-piping. This special case is considered in the following subsection.

7.2.2 Inversion in pied-piping constructions

There is a phenomenon called "Pied-Piping with Inversion", shown by Smith Stark (1988) to be prevalent throughout Mesoamerica, in which both the [+wh] object of a prepositional phrase and the [+wh] possessor in a possessed nominal move out of their normal position in a pied-piped phrase. This is shown in (198a–c) for prepositional phrases, where (198a) gives the normal order in a declarative sentence and (198b–c) show that the *wh*-word must be first when the phrase is pied-piped, reversing the

7.2 The structure of CP$_{[+wh]}$

normal order. The similar facts for questioning the possessor are given in (198d–e). The examples in (199) verify that this inversion does not occur with focused prepositional phrases, while (200) shows that inversion must occur in negation constructions, just as in questions.

(198) a. n-dux   xnaa   noo lo   noo   SNAKHAIR 4
       s-angry mother 1EX face 1EX
       My mother was angry with me.

     b. *lo   **txu** n-dux   xnaa   noo __
        face who s-angry mother 1EX
        (With whom was my mother angry?)

     c. **txu** lo   n-dux   xnaa   noo __
        who face s-angry mother 1EX
        With whom was my mother angry?

     d. *xnaa **txu** n-dux __ lo   de
        mother who s-angry   face 2
        (Whose mother was angry with you?)

     e. **txu** xnaa   n-dux __ lo   de
        who mother s-angry   face 2
        Whose mother was angry with you?

(199) a. lo   Jose n-dux   xnaa   noo __
       face José s-angry mother 1EX
       With José, my mother was angry.

     b. *Jose lo   n-dux   xnaa   noo __
        José face s-angry mother 1ex
        (With José, my mother was angry.)

(200) a. *lo   rut   w-gwed-et Susan kart __
       face nobody C-give-NEG Susan letter
       (Susan didn't give the letter to anybody.)

     b. rut   lo   w-gwed-et Susan kart __
        nobody face C-give-NEG Susan letter
        Susan didn't give the letter to anybody.

The analysis of this inversion in pied-piped phrases is not at all clear, but a possible analysis is sketched here. We can assume that when the pied-piped phrase has fronted to the position immediately below the $C^0_{[+wh]}$, the *wh*-phrase is too deeply embedded to meet the strict adjacency requirement. This prompts further fronting of the *wh*-phrase, either to fill the specifier of CP position as diagrammed in (201a) (then meeting a specifier-head relationship with the $C^0_{[+wh]}$), or possibly left-adjoining to the pied-piped phrase and thus being immediately below the $C^0_{[+wh]}$ as shown in (201b) (in which case the government relationship would still hold).

(201) a. In Specifier of CP   or   b. Adjoined below C^0

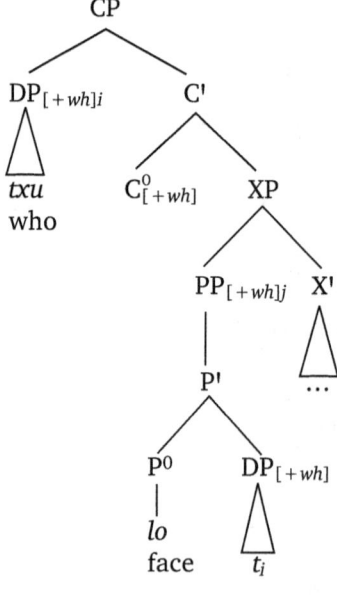
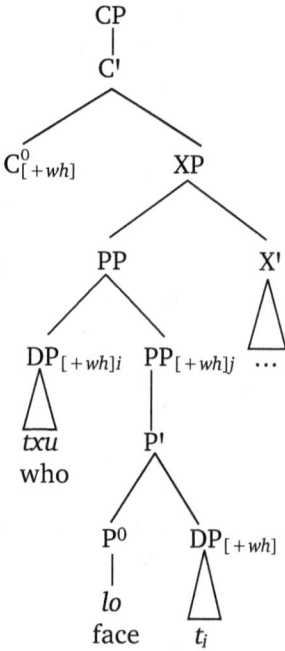

If we restrict our attention only to *wh*-questions, the account in (201a) where the inverted *wh*-phrase is in the specifier of CP seems preferable; it allows the pied-piped phrase to meet the adjacency requirement of the government relationship and it provides a use for the specifier of CP position (though it is perhaps odd to have the position utilized only in this special case). The fact that inversion also occurs in cases of negative fronting makes the adjunction account in (201b) more probable, however,

7.2 The structure of $CP_{[+wh]}$

since the fronted negative phrase already occupies the specifier position within the negative projection (see chapter 8).

Problematic for this analysis is the fact that pied-piping is required in QZ; extraction of a possessor or the object of a preposition yields highly unnatural to ungrammatical results. I assume this is due to P^0, N^0, and D^0 not being proper governors. Why, then, can the *wh*-phrase be extracted out of a pied-piped phrase? Rizzi (1992:appendix 2) suggests that movement to the specifier position[73] triggers abstract agreement with the head, which then turns the head into an appropriate head governor for the trace. For QZ, however, the possessor already occupies the specifier of NP position, and there is agreement between the possessor and the head overtly marked for alienably possessed nouns, yet the possessor cannot normally be extracted. Thus, Rizzi's suggestion does not explain the difference in extraction possibilities between the normal possessors and prepositional objects and pied-piped ones. I can only suggest that perhaps this is a case of the need for ranking of constraints (see also §12.2.1.1), where the requirements of the *Wh*-Criterion (and the Negative Criterion) outrank the ECP requirement that traces be properly governed. Such a ranking would need to be formulated so that the ECP is strong enough to block direct extraction of the possessors and prepositional objects, but the licensing criteria force pied-piping to occur. Within the pied-piped phrases, the ranking would then force further fronting, in violation of the ECP.[74] In the case of the fronting involved in focused phrases seen in the last chapter, however, the ECP is stronger than the licensing requirement on focused phrases. This ranking allows focus-marked phrases to remain in situ only in these two positions; pied-piping is not required. Further, when pied-piping does occur, no further fronting out of the pied-piped phrase is required or allowed.

---

[73]One might wonder whether the inversion might instead be due to movement of the *wh*-phrase to the specifier of P^0 within the pied-piped prepositional phrase, as has been suggested to account for inversion in Sluicing constructions such as (i) (Chung, Ladusaw, and McCloskey 1994:footnote 1).

(i)   He left but I don't know [who with].

Aissen (1996) combines movement to the specifier of P^0 with abstract agreement for similar constructions in Tzotzil.

Such an analysis is not plausible for QZ, since the specifiers of all [–V] projections, PP, NP and DP, are on the right (see chapters 10 and 11). Thus, neither movement of the object of a preposition to the specifier of PP nor movement of the possessor to the specifier of DP would result in the desired change in word order.

[74]This idea of ranked and violable constraints is developed under Optimality Theory (Prince and Smolensky 1991,1992, and 1993, and McCarthy and Prince 1992, 1993; see also H. A. Black 1993 for an implementation within a derivational framework). A recent Optimality Theory account of this phenomenon in San Dionicio Ocotopec Zapotec is presented in Broadwell (1999).

Thus, two changes need to be made in order to account for QZ questions. First, the required specifier-head relation must be changed to a minimal government relationship for the normal case. This can be seen as simply a parameter: some languages require a specifier-head relation, some require instead a government relationship, and some allow both types for licensing *wh*-phrases in scope position. Koopman and Sportiche (1991) claim that nominative case assignment exemplifies a parallel type of variation in that SVO languages assign nominative case via the specifier-head relationship while VSO languages assign nominative case under a government relationship. The same strict adjacency requirement for Case assignment under government is also noted.

The second change needed in the *Wh*-Criterion is that the required relation must only hold for *wh*-questions, not for Yes/No questions as well. The next section explores how this distinction can be made, and a proposal for the QZ version of the *Wh*-Criterion is given.

7.2.3 Featural distinction between clause types

Yes/No questions do not require a *wh*-phrase to be fronted; a *wh*-phrase may not even be present in the clause. This is illustrated in the familiar English examples of embedded Yes/No questions in (202). The grammatical example (202a) has a complementizer *whether*, indicating that a question is being asked, but there is no corresponding *wh*-phrase in the specifier of CP, as is required if the *Wh*-Criterion is applicable. (202b) verifies that the presence of a *wh*-phrase in the specifier position is ungrammatical, and (202c) demonstrates that it is equally bad to have a *wh*-phrase remain in situ.

(202) a. I wonder whether you saw it.

b. *I wonder what whether you saw___.

c. *I wonder whether you saw what.

Under the S' over S system, where there was only a single position in COMP, examples such as (202b) were ruled out since COMP was already filled by *whether*. In the CP system proposed in Chomsky (1986), examples like (202b) have been accounted for either by saying that *whether* begins in C^0 and then moves to the specifier position[75] (due to its *wh* morphology), as illustrated in the S-structure tree in (203a), or that *whether* licenses an empty

---

[75]This proposed movement of a head to a specifier position is clearly suspect given the constraints on movement given in Chomsky (1986:4).

7.2 The structure of CP$_{[+wh]}$

operator in its specifier position (203b). Either of these options provides a filled specifier of CP position, which accounts for the weak island effects seen when extraction out of the embedded clause is attempted.

(203) a. Movement of *whether*   or   b. Licensed empty Operator

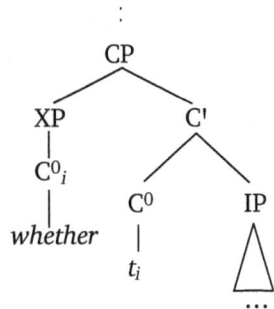 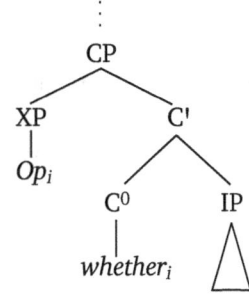

But this filled specifier analysis, by itself, would not account for the ungrammaticality of (202b–c), as the schematic forms for (202), shown in (204), illustrate. All three cases have a filled specifier, yet two are ungrammatical.

(204) a. I wonder   *Op*   whether   [you saw it]

     b. *I wonder   what$_i$ whether   [you saw t$_i$]

     c. *I wonder   *Op*   whether   [you saw what]

If *whether* were simply a C$^0_{[+wh]}$, the moved *wh*-phrase in (204b) should be allowed, assuming that the empty operator is only used if an overt operator is not available. Even if we assume instead that either movement of *whether* or the presence of the empty operator precludes movement of the *wh*-phrase (in the syntax), there would still be nothing to disallow (204c), where the *wh*-phrase remains in situ at S-structure and presumably moves to adjoin to CP or to the specifier of CP at LF. This is the analysis for the grammatical examples in (205).

(205) a. I wonder   what$_i$ Ø   [you saw t$_i$ where]

     b. I wonder   who$_i$ Ø   [t$_i$ saw what]

Therefore, we must be able to distinguish between Yes/No questions and *wh*-questions. Also, questions must be distinguished from relative clauses and exclamations, which also involve *wh*-movement but are subject to different constraints (Grimshaw 1979). All of the above must be kept distinct from regular declaratives. Rizzi (1990:67–68) suggests a two-feature system (±*wh* and ±pred) which allows *wh*-questions to be featurally distinct from *wh*-relatives, 'that'-relatives, and declaratives. This system is a move in the right direction, but it does not draw enough distinctions. Specifically, Yes/No questions are not distinguished from content questions as crucially needed here, and exclamations are not distinguished from the other types. I suggest here a three-feature system which makes all six distinctions needed, as shown in (206).[76]

(206)
+q	−wh	−rel	Yes/No questions
+q	+wh	−rel	content questions
−q	+wh	−rel	exclamations
−q	−wh	−rel	declaratives
−q	−wh	+rel	'that'-relatives
−q	+wh	+rel	*wh*-relatives

Besides making the six individual distinctions noted, the feature specifications shown in (206) divide the constructions into natural classes: questions are separated from nonquestions by the [±q] feature, relative clauses are separated from nonrelatives by the [±rel] feature, and constructions with *wh*-phrases are distinguished from those without by the [±wh] feature.

Given this feature system, we can assume that matrix verbs subcategorize for a $CP_{[+q]}$ rather than for a $CP_{[+wh]}$, explicitly recognizing that +q (=question) is distinct from +wh (=must acquire a moved *wh*-phrase). We can then account for the distribution of Yes/No questions in (202). Since *whether* is used only with Yes/No questions, it would be specified [+q, −wh]. As an $X^0_{[-wh]}$, Clause B of the *Wh*-Criterion does not apply, so no *wh*-phrase is required in its specifier position and (202a) is correctly predicted to be grammatical. Further, a *wh*-phrase may not occupy the specifier position above *whether* (202b), since there would be a clash of *wh*-features, in violation of Clause A of the *Wh*-Criterion. Clause A

---

[76]There are two possible feature specifications missing in (217): [+q, −wh, +rel] and [+q, +wh, +rel]. These are not possible specifications given the restriction +q ⇒ −rel, which expresses the intuition that a construction cannot be both a question and a relative clause simultaneously.

7.2 The structure of $CP_{[+wh]}$

also rules out the *wh*-phrase remaining in situ (202c). If Clause A is assumed to hold at S-structure for English, then the *wh*-phrase is only grammatical if it is in a specifier-head relationship with a $C^0_{[+wh]}$. Even if Clause A is not required to apply until LF, the *wh*-phrase cannot be licensed by *whether*, since it is [−*wh*]. The presence of *wh*-phrases in a Yes/No question is thus correctly prohibited.

Returning to QZ, recall that *pe* is used in Yes/No questions and it also co-occurs with some of the *wh*-phrases. I propose that *pe* be specified [+*q*, α*wh*] to allow it to be in the proper licensing relationship with a *wh*-phrase when appropriate, but not require the presence of a fronted *wh*-phrase itself. This featural specification eliminates the need to posit an empty operator and reduces the statement of the *Wh*-Criterion for QZ to a single clause, as given in (207).

(207) Revised *Wh*-Criterion for QZ

A *wh*-operator (=*wh*-phrase) must be in a minimal government relationship with a $C^0_{[+wh]}$ at S-structure.

As noted earlier, this minimal government relationship includes a strict adjacency requirement, McCloskey (1991:291–292)[77] which limits the fronting to a single *wh*-phrase. The fact that the *Wh*-Criterion holds at S-structure prohibits any *wh*-phrases from remaining in situ. The attested distribution of questions in QZ is thus accounted for.

The differences seen between QZ and English as to what licensing relationship is required between the head and the *wh*-phrase, how many positions are available, and at what level the licensing restrictions apply are part of a much larger cross-linguistic picture. The appendix contains a proposal for a more general, parameterized treatment of *wh*-movement.

7.3 Relative clauses

The normal *wh*-words used in questions are not used in QZ relative clauses. Many QZ relative clauses use the finite complementizer *ne*, as in

---

[77]A more formal version of the definition of the minimal government relationship is given in (i) than that given at the end of chapter 6.
  (i) X^0 MINIMALLY GOVERNS YP iff
     a. X^0 governs YP, and
     b. X^0 is the closest potential governor for YP, and
     c. no closer potential governee ZP intervenes between X^0 and YP.

(209), which also introduces 'that'-clauses, as (208) demonstrates. In (208a) the embedded CP introduced by *ne* is an adjunct, while in (208b) it is an argument.

(208) a. r-e   men lo   x-mgyeey men   RANCHO 52
H-say 3   face POS-man 3

    pa   nëz w-a de **ne** w-zëlt   de
    what road C-go 2 that C-be.found-NEG 2
She said to her husband "Which way did you go that I didn't find you?"

b. per laa mdxin nagon   dxe   n-an   mdxin no   RYENEGU 33
but FM deer however already s-know deer   there

    ne y-gw-et   meedx mdxin
    that P-CAUS-die lion   deer
But as for the deer, however, the deer already knew that the lion was going to kill him.

(209) a. chu tank zob   giblew **ne** r-len   nis   za   BATHROOM 5
belly tub PR/sit faucet that H-bear water warm
In the middle of the tub sits a faucet that bears warm water.

b. r-ap   noo te x-mig   noo **ne** r-laan te   men   HORTENS 4
H-have 1EX one POS-friend 1EX that H-want one person

    ne r-nii   disa
    that H-speak language
I have a friend who wants a person who speaks the language.

c. yët   yag **ne** n-gaa   per n-uu pur yag   LIFEINUS 93
not.be tree that S-green but s-be pure tree

    byaa   chi
    cactus prickly.pear
There aren't any trees that are green, but purely (lots of) prickly pear tree cactus.

This type of relative clause can be analyzed as a normal 'that'-relative in which the gap in the relative clause is coindexed with a null operator in

7.3 Relative clauses

the specifier of CP and the operator is also coindexed with, and identified by, the head NP. I assume the normal analysis that the specifier of CP is filled in relative clauses to account for the inability to extract from a relative clause.

Na 'which' may be used in relative clauses instead of *ne* 'that'. *Na* is restricted to occurring with heads which are inanimate[78] and is not otherwise used as a complementizer. Examples of this type of relative clause are given in (210). I assume that *na* originates in the position of the gap and moves to the specifier of CP position, as is normally assumed for *wh*-relative clauses.

(210) a. *r-a   me r-ka   me gyus na   g-eey x-nisyaa me*   SANJOSE 2
H-go 3R H-buy 3R pot which P-cook POS-food 3R
She went to buy a pot which her food would cook in.

   b. *n-guxkwaa tank na   r-az   men*   LIFEINUS 17
S-make   tub which H-bathe 3
A tub in which they bathe is made.

   c. *n-uu pur byaa na   win   ger*   LIFEINUS 94
S-be pure cactus which small very
There is a lot of cactus which is very small.

   d. *w-tsoow x-unaa   men gyët-guu   na*   RANCHO 29
C-make POS-woman 3   tortilla-tamale which

      g-u   men
      P-eat 3
His wife made tamales which he would eat (on his trip).

Examples of what appear to be null-headed relative clauses are given in (211).

(211) a. *la men ne la Danyel w-eey ne g-u noo y-ra noo* MTLEMON 21
FM 3   that call Daniel C-take that P-eat 1EX P-all 1EX
The man called Daniel took that which we all ate.

   b. *w-ka men ne g-u-gwe   noo*   MTLEMON2 6
C-buy 3   that P-eat-lunch 1EX
They bought that which we would eat for lunch.

---
[78]Thus, the only way to form a relative clause modifying an animate or human head is by using *ne* as in (209b).

An explanation for these examples comes from Regnier (1989b). He notes that while all of the other pronouns may be modified by a relative clause, the third person inanimate pronoun cannot be. He cites the following example, where in (212a) the inanimate pronoun -w may occur without a modifying relative clause, or the same idea may be expressed using a null-headed relative clause, as in (212b). But (212c) shows that the presence of both the inanimate pronoun and the relative clause is ungrammatical.

(212) a. *w-az y-ra-w leen yuu*
 c-wet P-all-3I inside house
 Everything in the house was wet.

 b. *w-az y-ra ne n-uu leen yuu*
 C-wet P-all that S-be inside house
 Everything that was in the house was wet.

 c. **w-az y-ra-w ne n-uu leen yuu*
 C-wet P-all-3I that S-be inside house
 (Everything which was in the house was wet.)

This restriction makes it seem probable that all examples of null-headed relatives, as in (211), can be analyzed as headed relatives with the third person inanimate pronoun (which is null only in this case) as the head.

This relative clause data should not be problematic for either of the theories of clause structure considered here. Of interest to the theory of Ā-movement in QZ, however, is the fact that the head of a relative clause may be fronted or focused (see chapter 6), leaving behind the CP. Text examples of this separation are given in (213). Just as in English, either the 'that' complementizer *ne* or the relative pronoun *na* must be present for this separation to be allowed.

(213) a. *s-te giblew zob gya ne regader*   BATHROOM 7
 F-one faucet PR/sit high that showerhead
 Another faucet that is the showerhead sits higher.

 b. *txup maa n-ak ne r-e g-u maa noo*   MANSNAKE 74
 two 3A S-become that H-say P-eat 3A 1EX
 There were two animals that said the snake should eat me.

7.3 Relative clauses

    c. ***s-te maa*** *nagon n-ak*   MANSNAKE 75
       F-one 3A however S-become

       na r-e g-u-t maa noo
       which H-say P-eat-NEG 3A 1EX
       There was another animal, however, which said the snake should
       not eat me.

    d. ***koyot*** *n-ak* ***ne*** *w-sa-laa* ***x-bit noo***   MANSNAKE 77
       coyote S-become that C-fall-escape POS-life 1EX
       The coyote was the one that saved my life.

    e. ***ndal edifisyo*** *n-uu* ***ne*** *ndal yaa pis*   MEXICO 23
       lots building S-be that lots very floor
       There are lots of buildings that have lots of floors.

All of the separated examples in (213) contain either stative or existential verbs. Separation of the head from the relative clause is not possible when the main verb is active, as shown in (214).

(214) a. *r-a me r-ka me* ***gyus*** *na g-eey x-nisyaa me*   SANJOSE 2
       H-go 3R H-buy 3R pot which P-cook POS-food 3R
       She went to buy a pot which her food would cook in.

    b. **r-a me* ***gyus*** *r-ka me* ***na*** *g-eey x-nisyaa me*
       H-go 3R pot H-buy 3R which P-cook POS-food 3R
       (She went to buy a pot which her food would cook in.)

    c. *w-tsoow x-unaa men* ***gyët-guu***   *na*   RANCHO 29
       C-make POS-woman 3 tortilla-tamale which

       g-u men
       P-eat 3
       His wife made tamales which he would eat (on his trip).

    d. *****gyët-guu*** *w-tsoow x-unaa men* ***na*** *g-u men*
       tortilla-tamale C-make POS-woman 3 which P-eat 3
       (His wife made tamales which he would eat (on his trip).)

In the DP structure I propose, the CP part of the relative clause is adjoined to either NP or to D' (see chapter 12). We cannot assume that the

CP is adjoined to the entire DP, since this would violate the prohibition against adjunction to arguments (Chomsky 1986:6) given earlier in (186). For example, the structure of the full relative clause in (213b) would be one of the options shown in (215), depending on the choice of adjunction site.

(215)

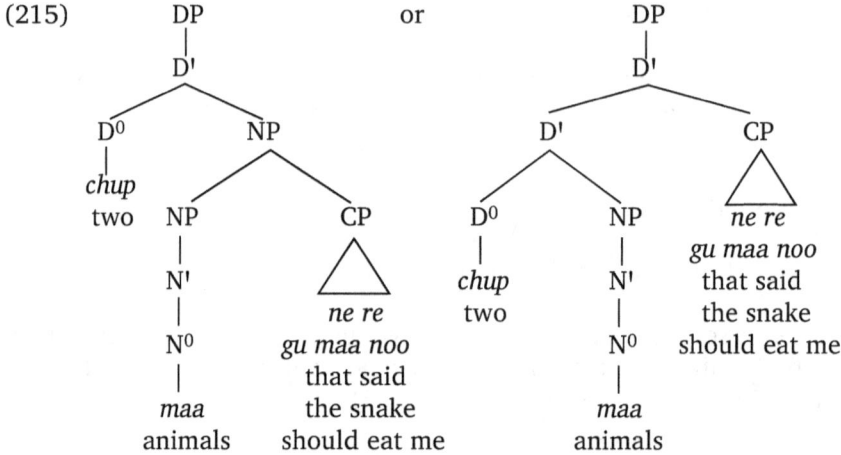

It is clear from these structures that the quantifier and noun which have been fronted in (213b) either do not form a constituent at D-structure or are only a single-bar constituent, so direct movement of these elements is not allowed. Under a movement analysis, we must assume instead that the CP is allowed to extrapose, thus leaving the remaining DP free to be fronted. This is the same type of Extraposition from DP movement allowed in English for comparatives and for some relative clauses,[79] as shown in example (216).

(216) a. **More angels** were in the sky over Bethlehem that night **than anyone could count.**

b. **Two men** approached the sheriff **who were wearing gunbelts.**

c. **Two men** approached the sheriff **that were wearing gunbelts.**

---

[79]There are also restrictions on this Extraposition from relative clauses in English. One of these is that the separated constructions are more acceptable when the head NP is indefinite.

7.3 Relative clauses

Similar types of separated structures involving fronting of the head and extraposition of the clausal adjunct are very common in the quantifier structures analyzed in chapter 12. See §12.3 for discussion regarding whether the separation arises via movement or whether it is base generated.

8
Constructions Involving Negation

Negative constructions in most of the Zapotecan languages have the same two crucial characteristics as seen for *wh*-questions: (a) a negative phrase must be fronted and (b) only one negative phrase per clause is allowed.[80] The analysis proposed will therefore be very similar as well (see §8.2). There are also two major differences between negative constructions and questions. First, the fronted phrase is always found **before** the negative head, allowing the normal specifier-head relationship to hold within a single projection in this case. Second, since the negative head is realized on the verb in most cases, these constructions provide important data for the decision regarding the best proposal for obtaining VSO order (see §8.3).

We first need to provide a backdrop for the Zapotec negation constructions by placing them within the larger context of Negative Concord languages.[81]

8.1 The Zapotecan languages are Negative Concord languages

All languages have the ability to express negation, though there is great variation in how it is done. A major division exists between Multi-Negation languages, like standard English, where the effect of each negation is cumulative, and Negative Concord languages, in which a single negation reading results from multiple markings of negation. For example, in standard English

---

[80] QZ actually allows a second negative phrase in limited circumstances. See §8.2.1.
[81] Much of the content of this chapter appeared in Black (1993), though it has been updated by further fieldwork.

the sentence *I didn't see nothing* really means 'I did see something'. In contrast, in a Negative Concord language like some varieties of nonstandard English, *I didn't see nothing* means the same as 'I didn't see anything' in standard English. The Zapotecan languages are Negative Concord languages.

Zanuttini (1991) and Ladusaw (1992, 1993), have noted that it is a deep property of Negative Concord languages that negation must be expressed on or above the head of the clause. This means that a negative pronoun in a complement position alone is not grammatical; a higher negation which either m-commands or is part of Infl is also required, as shown in (217a–b) for Italian. In contrast, if the negative pronoun is in subject position, as shown in (217c), it can express negation by itself, without the separate negative word.[82]

(217) a. *Mario **non** ha visto **nessuno***
Mario NEG has seen nobody
Mario has seen no one.

b. **Mario ha visto **nessuno***
Mario has seen nobody
(Mario has seen no one.)

c. ***nessuno** ha visto Mario*
nobody has seen Mario
Nobody has seen Mario.

Most of the Zapotecan languages follow not only this general restriction that negation must be expressed above the head of the clause, but also require fronting of all negative words. Thus, in a sentence meaning roughly the same as (217a), QZ requires the order shown in (218a), where the negative pronominal object has fronted before the verb which carries the negative marker, and the subject follows the verb in its usual position. The order given in (218b), which has a parallel structure to (218a) with the negative object pronoun in situ, is not allowed. Further, even when it is the subject, the negative pronoun must be fronted with negation still marked on the verb, yielding exactly the same surface form in (218c) as in (218a). The ambiguity arises from the obligatory fronting coupled with the normal VSO order and the lack of morphological case marking in the

---

[82]The separate negative word, *non* is not allowed to be present in this case in Italian. As noted by Ladusaw (1993), Negative Concord languages vary in whether the "Infl"-negation can be overt if there is a negative word higher in the clause: Italian does not allow it, Catalan allows it optionally, and Rumanian requires it to always be overt. This fact is thus simply a parameterization of an independent constraint.

language. The meaning of a particular utterance would need to be sorted out from the context.

(218) a. **rut**   wii-t   Maryo _
        nobody c/see-NEG Mario
        Mario saw nobody.

   b. *wii-t   Maryo **rut**
      c/see-NEG Mario nobody
      (Mario saw nobody.)

   c. **rut**   wii-t   _ Maryo
      nobody c/see-NEG   Mario
      Nobody saw Mario.

8.2 Analysis of the obligatory fronting

The analysis is presented in two parts. First, the basic clause structure including a NegP projection and the obligatory fronting of negative pronouns, resulting in compliance with the Negative Criterion at S-structure, is developed for the limited system of marking negation available in QZ. Then in §8.2.2 the more complex negation system available in MZ, which is part of the central group of Zapotecan languages, is examined, and the basic analysis given for QZ is shown to extend to MZ.

8.2.1 The limited negation system of QZ

Most Zapotecan languages have at least one free negative word as well as having a negative marker which cliticizes to the verb, negative indefinite pronouns, and negative quantifiers. QZ is more limited in its negative markers.[83] The normal way to express negation in QZ is via the verbal clitic -*t*, as shown in (219).

(219) r-ool-t   noo liber
      H-read-NEG 1EX book
      I am not reading a book.

---

[83]In §2.2.2 the negative marker -*t* is described as a verbal suffix. Here it is treated as an enclitic to facilitate discussion of negation in other Zapotecan languages. See §9.5 for further discussion of negation in QZ.

In addition to this negative clitic, QZ can express negation in three other ways:

    a. Through use of the negative indefinite pronouns, *bet* 'nothing', *rut* 'nobody', *bat* 'nowhere', and *nunk* 'never', in combination with either a verb followed by the negative clitic or the negative existential verb *yët*,

    b. By using the negative existential verb alone, or

    c. By using the negative adverbial *gart* 'still no', which can be combined with the negative indefinite pronouns but not with the negative verbal clitic nor with the negative existential verb.

Each of these uses is exemplified below.

The negative indefinite pronouns are always fronted, just as *wh*-words are.[84] These negative indefinite pronouns are frequently used in responses to questions, as shown in (220)–(221).[85]

(220) a. pa   go   r-laa de
       what thing H-do 2
       What thing are you doing?

    b. **bet**   r-laa-t   noo
       nothing H-do-NEG 1EX
       I am not doing anything.

(221) a. pa   ts-a   de
       where P-go 2
       Where are you going?

    b. **bat**   ts-a-t   noo
       nowhere P-go-NEG 1EX
       I am not going anywhere.

---

[84]This is similar to the use of *wh*-words as indefinite pronouns in Tzotzil. Aissen (1992b) reports that they must be fronted in either usage. In QZ, however, the negative indefinite pronouns do not double as *wh*-phrases.

[85]Note also that the negative pronoun by itself cannot be used to answer a question; the full sentence is required.

8.2 Analysis of the obligatory fronting   153

Example (222a) shows the negative indefinite pronoun *rut* 'nobody' with the negative existential *yët* and (222b) shows the negative existential verb used alone.

(222) a. **rut**   **yët**   ts-a-ron   gyët   g-u   men
   nobody not.be P-go-leave tortilla P-eat 3
   There isn't anybody to take the food for them to eat.

   b. *per* **yët**   *dxiin*   GRANDMA3 7
   but not.be work
   But there wasn't any work.

Exmaple (223a) shows the usage of the adverb *gart* 'still no' by itself and (223b) demonstrates that it can be combined with the negative indefinite pronoun *nunk* 'never', which was borrowed from Spanish but is used according to the syntactic rules of QZ.

(223) a. *por fabor gu-cheree x-kwiich   noo g-an*   CARTA 7
   for favor IMP-return POS-paper 1EX P-know

   pa   gos   r-zak   de ne   **gart**   chiid   de
   what thing H-happen 2 that still.no P/come 2
   Please answer my letter so I can know what happened to you that you still haven't come.

   b. *Jasint* **nunk** **gart**   *ts-a Jasint   Pwert*   BENIT 29
   Jacinto never still.no P-go Jacinto Salina.Cruz
   As for Jacinto, he had never gone to Salina Cruz.

8.2.1.1 Clause structure analysis: NegP and the Negative Criterion.
Both the required word order and the single reading of negation can be accounted for via specifier-head agreement, if the negative indefinite pronouns are seen as occupying the specifier of NegP at S-structure. The verbal clitic -*t*, the negative existential verb *yët*, and the negative adverb *gart* are mutually exclusive heads which must occupy Neg⁰ at S-structure.

Under the Verb Movement hypothesis, the basic clause structure for a QZ negative clause would be as shown in (224), where the verb moves to I⁰ and then to Neg⁰ to carry both the aspect marking and negation, and a negative indefinite pronoun moves to the specifier of NegP.

(224)   S-structure

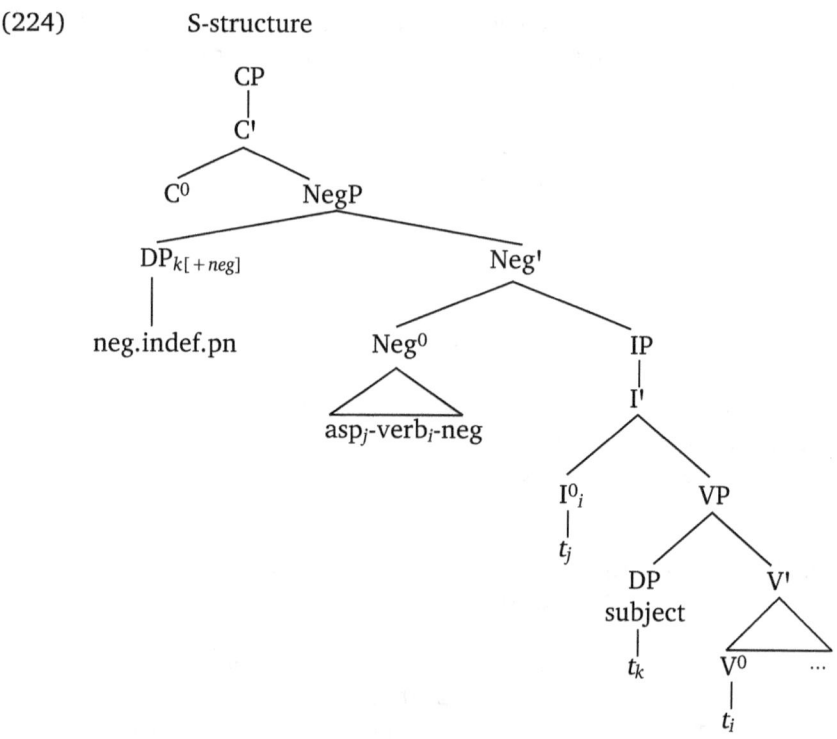

The movements posited in (224) will clearly obtain the surface word order of a sentence like (218c) and can be straightforwardly extended to also obtain (218a), where the object has fronted. An account of why (218b), where the negative indefinite pronoun has remained in situ, is ungrammatical is still needed. Rizzi (1991:33) claims that this can be explained by the same basic mechanism which assures that *wh*-phrases must move to the front. He expresses this extension of the *Wh*-Criterion informally as, "Affective operators must be in a spec-head configuration with a head marked with the relevant affective feature at the appropriate level of representation." Haegeman and Zanuttini (1990) restate this specifically for negation cases as, "Each negative phrase must be in a Spec-head relation with a negative head"[86] and note that the appropriate level of representation for the constraint is

---

[86]Note that both Rizzi's and Haegeman and Zanuttini's formulations correspond only to Clause A of the *Wh*-Criterion, thus not requiring the presence of a negative phrase with every negative head. This is also true of Zapotec, as seen in (219). My formulation in (225) includes a revised Clause B which does not require the presence of a negative phrase but does require that the negative head be in Neg⁰ at S-structure. Haegeman (1991) proposes a Clause B fully parallel to that in the *Wh*-Criterion for West Flemish, since the clitic negative head in that language is insufficient to express negation without the support of a fronted negative phrase.

8.2 Analysis of the obligatory fronting

]S-structureS-structure for West Flemish, though LF is the generally required level. Aissen (1992b) relates that fronting of *wh*-words is also required by S-structure in Tzotzil, whether they are used as *wh*-pronouns or as negative indefinite pronouns. This is the case for most Zapotecan languages as well; both *wh*-phrases and negative indefinite pronouns must front at S-structure. The Negative Criterion for QZ can therefore be formalized as:[87]

(225) The Negative Criterion for QZ

a. A negative operator must be in a specifier-head configuration with an $X^0_{[+neg]}$ at S-structure.

b. An $X^0_{[+neg]}$ must occupy Neg^0 at S-structure.

As it stands, (225) says nothing about whether multiple negative indefinite pronouns may be fronted, only that they must front. Since only a single *wh*-phrase may be fronted in QZ, it is surprising to find that a second negative indefinite pronoun is allowed to be fronted. (226) shows the ways that the QZ equivalent of "Nobody saw nothing" (meaning the same as "Nobody saw anything" in standard English) may be expressed. (226a–b) show that multiple fronting is allowed as long as the subject or human pronoun is first. (226c–d) verify that neither of the negative indefinite pronouns may remain in situ. (226e) shows that there is a different form of the indefinite pronoun meaning "nothing", *betee* (a combination of *bet* + *tee* 'nothing-one'), which is allowed to remain in place. This form may only show up in this construction where there is another negative indefinite pronoun already fronted. I therefore analyze *betee* as a strong type of Negative Polarity Item, requiring m-command by both a negative head and a negative indefinite pronoun.[88] Finally, (226f) shows the way this negative construction could be expressed without using two negative

---

[87] Clause B of the Negative Criterion proposed here for QZ (and other Zapotecan languages) is not entirely parallel to the *Wh*-Criterion which was proposed by May (1985) and updated by Rizzi (1991) to be compatible with the theory of COMP in Chomsky (1986). This change eliminates the need to posit a null negative operator in the specifier of NegP position for cases where the negation is simply marked by the head Neg^0. Such clauses are parallel to Yes/No questions which were not treated under the version of the *Wh*-Criterion for QZ since they are [+q] but [-wh].
As discussed in §7.1 for *wh*-operators, I use the term "negative operator" here to mean all XPs that are [+neg].

[88] I assume that *betee* is a fairly recent addition to the language. There is no equivalent form (*rutee*) available for the indefinite pronoun meaning 'nobody'.

indefinite pronouns. This is parallel to the only way available for expressing such a thought in question form, shown in (226g).[89]

(226) a. **rut   bet   wii-t**
nobody nothing c/see-NEG
"Nobody saw nothing, i.e., nobody saw anything."

b. ***bet   rut   wii-t**
nothing nobody c/see-NEG
(Nobody saw nothing.)

c. ***rut   wii-t   bet**
nobody c/see-NEG nothing
(Nobody saw nothing.)

d. ***bet   wii-t   rut**
nothing c/see-NEG nobody
(Nobody saw nothing.)

e. **rut   wii-t   betee**
nobody c/see-NEG nothing/one
Nobody saw anything.

f. **bet   wii-t   men te-tee   men**
nothing c/see-NEG 3   one-one 3
They each saw nothing.

g. **pa   gos   wii   men te-tee   men**
what thing c/see 3   one-one 3
What thing did they each see?

This difference in how many items may be fronted in questions versus negative constructions shows up in other languages as well. For example, Tzotzil allows the fronting of multiple negative indefinite pronouns, whereas fronted interrogative pronouns are limited to one and none may remain in situ. West Flemish also allows multiple fronting of negative phrases at S-structure. In contrast, only one *wh*-phrase may (and must) front at S-structure but others are allowed to remain in situ until LF (Haegeman 1991). MZ, however, allows only a single negative phrase to be present per clause, and it must be fronted, completely parallel to the

---
[89]The phrase *men te-tee men* is an example of the special number-marking construction analyzed in chapter 12.

8.2 Analysis of the obligatory fronting

situation in *wh*-questions. These differences may be accounted for simply by parameterization of whether or not adjunction to the specifier of NegP position is allowed; QZ, Tzotzil, and West Flemish allow such adjunction whereas MZ does not. (See the appendix for a parallel parameterized account of the adjunction possibilities in both the specifier of CP and adjoined to IP positions for *wh*-questions.)

The required relation of specifier-head agreement holding at S-structure (Clause A of the Negative Criterion), coupled with this parameterization of adjunction to the specifier of NegP, will correctly account for the obligatory fronting of the negative indefinite pronouns and the language specific allowance of whether one or more may front. The proposed accounts for both *wh*-questions and negative constructions are thus quite parallel.

The analysis of *bat* 'nowhere' and *nunk* 'never' (=no when) can be accounted for by a straightforward extension of the analysis given for the negative indefinite pronoun in subject position in (224). In this case, the pronoun is in a nonargument position at D-structure, most likely right-adjoined to VP, and moves to the specifier of NegP by S-structure. Thus, the analysis for both *bat* and *nunk* also follows from the clause structure and the Negative Criterion.

Analyses for the negative existential verb *yët* and the negative adverb *gart* remain to be given. The morphological makeup of the negative existential verb is unclear. It could conceivably be made up of three separate morphemes *y-ë-t* 'P-exist-NEG', with the Potential marking on the verb root, and the negative marker cliticizing to this. This account does not require any change in the analysis given above, since it would fit right into the configuration in (224). However, the "root" *ë* is not used to indicate existence on its own (i.e. without negation; instead the copular verbs *uu* 'be' or *ak* 'become' are used). Further, only Potential marking ever occurs. A second possibility is that *yë* is an existential verb which does not take aspect marking but must co-occur with negation. Head movement of the verb to Neg⁰ would account for the surface realization as *yët*. The final possibility is to say that *yët* is simply an inherently negative verb that does not take aspect marking. In this case, the basic clause structure would be the same, except that Neg⁰ and I⁰ would both be empty at D-structure. The negative verb would be forced to move to Neg⁰ by Clause B of the Negative Criterion, where it could then be in a specifier-head relationship with a negative phrase, if present, as in (222a).[90] See §8.2.2 for further discussion of negative existential verbs with respect to MZ.

---

[90]The Minimalist Program (Chomsky 1995) assumes this type of checking of the inflectional features which are morphologically spelled out on the verb.

For the negative adverb *gart* 'still no', I simply assume that it is base generated as Neg⁰. This accounts for the fact that it cannot co-occur with either the verbal clitic *-t* or the negative existential verb, while it may co-occur with a negative indefinite pronoun. The fact that negative indefinite pronouns precede *gart*, as in (223b), further verifies that *gart* occupies the Neg⁰ position in the clause structure shown in (224).[91]

8.2.1.2 Future Mood as an Affirmative Polarity Item. In addition to lacking free negative words simply meaning 'no', QZ also lacks negative quantifiers which could be used to negate a nominal phrase.[92] There are no words meaning 'yes' or 'no' either. Positive and negative responses to Yes/No questions are formed by repeating the complete IP, with or without the negative marker as appropriate. This is shown in (227).

(227) a. *pe s-oo   de nis*
   Q F-drink 2 water
   Will you drink water?

   b. *s-oo   noo nis*
   F-drink 1EX water
   I will drink water.

   c. *g-oo-t   noo nis*
   P-drink-NEG 1EX water
   I will not drink water.

Note that the aspect/mood marking on the negative response in (227c) is the Potential, while the question and positive response carry the Future marker. This is a requirement; in Yes/No questions about events yet to occur and in statements about possible events (such as 'perhaps...'), the Potential mood is used with negation, whereas the Future mood is used in positive contexts (see §2.2.1.6).

Potential mood can be used in other positive contexts and other aspects can be used with negation in other negative contexts, so the clear restriction seems to be that Future mood may never co-occur with negation. This

---

[91] Only V⁰-to-I⁰ movement is assumed in this case.

[92] I found two examples in the texts (Regnier 1989a) in which the negative quantifier from Spanish *ni* 'not even' is used. In each case the DP containing *ni* is fronted and co-occurs either with the verbal clitic *-t* or with *gart*. It can therefore be assumed that the $DP_{[+neg]}$ has fronted to the specifier of NegP, just like the negative indefinite pronouns must. So, like *nunk*, this Spanish loan word is being incorporated into QZ syntax.

8.2 Analysis of the obligatory fronting   159

fact could be accounted for by saying that Neg⁰ selects IPs having any aspect/mood except Future. Alternatively, Future mood could be viewed as a type of Affirmative Polarity Item, which resists being in the same clause m-command domain of negation. Either view requires that NegP be above IP in the clause structure.[93]

8.2.2 The more complete negation system of Mitla Zapotec

The analysis for the negation system of MZ follows directly from the basic analysis given for QZ. MZ also has a negative enclitic *-di* which normally attaches to the verb. In addition, MZ has the negative indefinite pronouns *rut* 'nobody' and *xhet* 'nothing'. As in QZ, these pronouns must be fronted and must co-occur with the negative marker, as shown in (228).[94]

(228) a. ***rut*** bi-ääd-***di*** lo guejdx
    nobody C-come-NEG to village
    Nobody came to the village.

   b. ***xhet*** r-lajz-***di***-ni g-un-ni
    nothing H-want-NEG-3 P-do-3
    They don't want to do anything.

Further, MZ does not allow more than one negative indefinite pronoun to be present in a clause, either fronted or in situ, as shown in (229).

(229) a. ??*rut* rut ba-hui
    nobody nobody C-see
    (Nobody saw nobody/anybody.)

   b. *rut ba-hui *rut*
    nobody C-see nobody
    (Nobody saw nobody/anybody.)

---

[93]The precise position of NegP with respect to the other Infl projections is most likely a language-specific parameter. Pollock (1989) and Laka (1990) propose that TenseP must be above NegP, while AgrP is below it; Rizzi (1991) follows Belletti (1990) in assuming that AgrP is above NegP and TenseP is below NegP; Zanuttini (1991) argues for two NegP projections in Romance, one above and one below TenseP.

[94]The description and data from MZ are taken mainly from Stubblefield and Stubblefield (1991), with a few clarifying examples provided directly by Morris and Carol Stubblefield (p.c.).

c. *rut   zhet   ba-hui
nobody nothing C-see
(Nobody saw nothing/anything.)

d. *zhet   rut   ba-hui
nothing nobody C-see
(Nobody saw nothing/anything.)

e. *rut   ba-hui zhet
nobody C-see   nothing
(Nobody saw nothing/anything.)

f. *zhet   ba-hui rut
nothing C-see   nobody
(Nobody saw nothing/anything.)

The analysis of the negative indefinite pronouns can be exactly the same for MZ as that proposed for QZ, except that MZ does not allow adjunction to the specifier of NegP.

8.2.1.1 Free Negative words and the Negative Criterion. As noted, most Zapotecan languages have at least one free negative word; MZ has three such words. *Di* 'no' is the most common. *Di* always appears first, generally with the subject immediately following it, as shown in (230a).[95] The negative enclitic *-di* is optional with the free negative words and usually does not occur in single clause constructions. (230b) shows its use with the free negative *di* in an auxiliary construction.

(230) a. *di Juan ch-ää Lua*
no Juan P-go   Oaxaca
Juan will not go to Oaxaca.

b. *di g-ac-di   g-un Juan-ni*
no P-can-NEG P-do Juan-3
Juan cannot do it.

This same pattern is seen with the second free negative word *gajd* or *gad* 'still not', as shown in (231).

---

[95] An analysis for this position of the subject is given later in this section.

8.2 Analysis of the obligatory fronting   161

(231) a. *gajd-ni   g-un   dzuunga*
        still.not-3 P-do work
        He still has not done the work.

b. *gad   g-ac-di   ch-a'a*
   still.not P-can-NEG P-go/1EX
   I still cannot go.

The third free negative word in MZ is *na'c* 'no'. It is used mostly in negative imperatives, as shown in (232). In addition, *na'c* can be used by itself as a negative response to a question, suggestion, or command.

(232) *na'c ch-ää-lu*
      no   P-go-2
      Don't go!

None of these three free negative words can co-occur with the negative pronouns, either fronted or in situ.[96] If we say that the three free negative words must also meet the requirement of the Negative Criterion at S-structure, we have an explanation for this fact. I assume that the free negative words, like the negative indefinite pronouns, are themselves maximal projections. Since all five negative words (or phrases) are licensed at S-structure only if they are in the specifier of NegP, and since there is only one specifier for that projection (and no adjunction allowed), only one of the five may occur in a given clause.[97]

The fact that the negative clitic *-di*, which corresponds to the head Neg⁰ in the analysis given for QZ, is not required with the three free negative words can be accounted for by allowing the three free negative words (but

---

[96]Ladusaw pointed out that this is reminiscent of the incompatibility between the French negative *pas*, which seems parallel to the free negative words, and the French indefinites *personne* and *rien*.

[97]There is some variation across the Zapotecan languages. For example, in IZ when the negative pronouns occur alone in a sentence or with the negative clitic only, they must be fronted. IZ also has a free negative word *ke* 'not' which may co-occur with the negative clitic. The difference is that the negative pronouns may co-occur with *ke*, and when they do, they remain in situ. Further, IZ is like MZ in disallowing multiple fronting of the negative indefinite pronouns. As long as one negative item is occupying the specifier of NegP, however, other negative indefinite pronouns may remain in situ.

In this respect, IZ is quite similar to Italian (i.e., *ke* is the analogue of *non*). If IZ only requires one negative phrase (rather than all negative phrases) to occupy the specifier of NegP at S-structure, and if *ke* is base generated in the specifier of NegP position, it follows that no movement of the negative pronouns is required when *ke* is present. This type of variation between languages is the same as that seen with question formation, which is treated more fully in the appendix.

not the negative indefinite pronouns) to license a null Neg^0, following Ladusaw (1993). These negative words could be base generated in the specifier of NegP position. Further, the three negative words and the null Neg^0 only co-occur with clauses inflected for either Potential or Unreal moods. This can be seen as selection by Neg^0 of specific types of IP (see also Zanuttini 1991), again showing that NegP must be positioned above IP for Zapotec.

The fronting of the subject which is required to co-occur with the presence of one of the free negative words and the null Neg^0 needs to to be considered also. (233) presents data showing the distribution of this subject fronting. (233a) shows the widely attested order with the fronted subject following the free negative word *di* and no negative clitic on the verb. (233b) verifies that the subject is required to front in this situation; it cannot remain in place. (233c) then shows that the object instead of the subject may not be fronted to follow *di* and (233d) demonstrates that even when the subject is fronted to come after the free negative word *di*, another constituent may not normally be focused before *di* (such a construction could only be used in a contrastive context where the emphasis is on *Oaxaca* as opposed to some other city). Finally, (233e–f) show that the subject may not surface before the verb if the negative clitic is also present.

(233) a. ***di*** *Juan ch-ää Lua*
     no Juan P-go Oaxaca
     Juan will not go to Oaxaca.

   b. *****di*** *ch-ää Juan Lua*
      no P-go Juan Oaxaca
      (Juan will not go to Oaxaca.)

   c. *****di*** *Lua   ch-ää Juan*
      no Oaxaca P-go Juan
      (Juan will not go to Oaxaca.)

   d. ??*Lua **di** Juan ch-ää*
      Oaxaca no Juan P-go
      (To Oaxaca Juan will not go.)

   e. *****di*** *Juan ch-ää-**di** Lua*
      no Juan P-go-NEG Oaxaca
      (Juan will not go to Oaxaca.)

8.2 Analysis of the obligatory fronting   163

f. *di* ch-ää-*di* Juan Lua
   no P-go-NEG Juan Oaxaca
   Juan will not go to Oaxaca.

How can we make sense of this distribution? The fact that fronting of the subject to follow the free negative word cannot occur when the negative clitic is present on the verb (233e–f) is predicted by the analysis that the free negative word is in the specifier of NegP and the negative clitic is in Neg⁰. Once the verb moves to Neg⁰ there is no place for the subject to be between the free negative word and the verb carrying the negative clitic. Neither multiple specifiers for NegP nor adjunction to the specifier of NegP is allowed in MZ.

Further, (233a–c) show that the subject, and only the subject, must occur after the free negative word and before the verb. The obvious surface position for the subject is the specifier of IP, which is otherwise unused. The specifier of IP is below the position of the free negative word (in the specifier of NegP) and above the verbal complex, which is in I⁰ if V ⁰-to-I⁰ movement has taken place. We can assume that the verbal complex only moves on to Neg⁰ if there is an overt negative clitic needing a host.

But what causes the subject to move and why is it only the subject that can move? As shown in chapter 6 any DP can be fronted in a focus construction; there is no limitation to subjects as we see in the negative constructions here. Furthermore, negative indefinite pronouns are fronted regardless of their grammatical function. Both focus movement and the fronting of negative indefinite pronouns are clearly Ā-movement, distinct from the subject fronting seen in these negative constructions. This movement is reminiscent of the analysis that subjects in SVO languages raise from the specifier of VP to the specifier of IP under the Internal Subject Hypothesis. Perhaps for Zapotec, such movement only occurs in negative clauses, but the difficult question of determining whether the subject moves to the specifier of IP in all negative clauses, or only when Neg⁰ is not overt needs to be addressed. In (233f) the subject could also be in the specifier of IP position, but the movement of the verbal complex to Neg⁰ obscures the fronting. Likewise, since the negative clitic is normally present on the verb in QZ, movement to Neg⁰ is required for negative clauses. Any fronting of the subject to the specifier of IP in these QZ negative clauses would therefore not be visible in the surface order. The one place where empirical evidence can be found is in QZ sentences using the negative adverbial *gart* 'still no' in Neg⁰. Though only a limited number of examples are available, it is clear in (234) that the subject has not moved in front of the verb to the specifier of IP.

(234) a. *por fabor gu-cheree x-kwiich   noo g-an* CARTA 7
  por favor IMP-return POS-paper 1EX P-know

  *pa   gos   r-zak   de ne   **gart**   chiid   **de***
  what thing H-happen 2 that still.no P/come 2
  Please answer my letter so I can know what happened to you
  that you still haven't come.

 b. *Jasint   nunk   **gart**   ts-a   **Jasint** Pwert.* BENIT 29
  Jacinto never still.no P-go Jacinto Salina.Cruz
  As for Jacinto, he had never gone to Salina Cruz.

We can therefore assume that movement of the subject to the specifier of IP only takes place in IPs selected by the null Neg^0 in MZ.

We might simply say that the specifier of IP is an A-position (argument-position) to which the subject moves under selection by Neg^0. I assume that the specifier of IP would have to be an A-position rather than an Ā-position to properly restrict its occupants to subjects only.[98] We could then assume descriptively that the null Neg^0 in MZ would select an IP with an "activated" A-specifier of IP (which otherwise must be empty) so that these negative clauses would have subjects in the specifier of IP at S-structure. What forces the movement of the subject from the specifier of VP to the specifier of IP is still a question. In English, such movement is required by Case theory. In Zapotec, the subject receives Case in the specifier of VP position, however, so Case theory cannot be involved.

It seems better to tie this movement to the special characteristics of the null Neg^0 itself. The null Neg^0 in MZ was already seen to specially select an IP that was headed by either Unreal or Potential mood. Further, the null Neg^0 needs to be licensed by a free negative word in the specifier of NegP. This null Neg^0 could have two licensing requirements. In addition to the requirement that it co-occur with a free negative word in the specifier of NegP, we could assume that it must also minimally govern[99] the subject of the clause. Thus, the A-specifier of IP would be "activated" and A-movement of the subject would be forced if and only if Neg^0 is not overtly filled.

The term "activated" is useful as a descriptive metaphor, but we need to formalize the notion further. Even though it would be completely invisible morphologically, we could assume that this "activation" is really forced agreement between the null Neg^0, its specifier, and the specifier of

---

[98]Diesing (1990) argues that the specifier of IP must be an A-position that subjects only can move to in certain constructions in Yiddish.

[99]No adverbials or other adjoined elements may intervene between the free negative word, the null Neg^0, and the subject.

8.2 Analysis of the obligatory fronting

IP that it minimally governs. Such an analysis is a straightforward extension of the proposal for agreement in COMP by Rizzi (1990:51–60) to account for such phenomena as the alternation between *que* and *qui* in French questions. Just as C^0 must simultaneously agree with its specifier and with the specifier of IP under Rizzi's analysis, the null Neg^0 in MZ must simultaneously agree with a free negative word in its specifier (via specifier-head agreement) and with the subject in the specifier of IP (via the minimal government relationship).

The S-structure tree for (233a) is given in (235) to clarify the proposed analysis. The free negative word *di* is base generated in the specifier of NegP position, licensing a null Neg^0 and thus meeting the Negative Criterion. This null Neg^0 both meets the specifier-head agreement relationship with its specifier *di* and "agrees" with the specifier of the selected IP, which the subject DP *Juan* has fronted to, in the required minimal government relationship. V^0-to-I^0 movement has also taken place, but I^0-to-Neg^0 movement is not motivated since it is not necessary to provide a host for a negative clitic in Neg^0.

(235)   S-structure

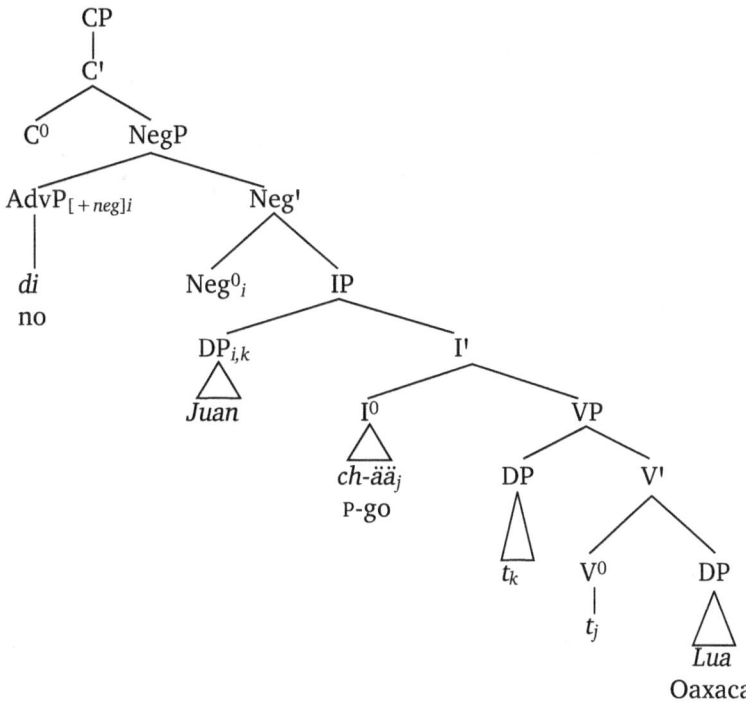

8.2.2.2 Negative quantifiers and the Negative Criterion. MZ also has two types of negative quantifiers which can be used to negate a nominal phrase or an adverbial. The first of these is *et* 'not'. The entire phrase negated by *et* appears at the front of the clause, just as the negative indefinite pronouns do. I assume that this negative phrase occupies the specifier of NegP, since it cannot co-occur with any of the other negative words or negative indefinite pronouns. In this case, the negative clitic *-di*, analyzed to be in Neg⁰, cliticizes to the end of the fronted phrase, as shown in (236a). This negative constituent may also be the head of a small clause itself with a copular reading (i.e. it may serve as the predicate of a clause where no verb is present). In this case the subject clitic attaches to the predicate, as (236b) shows.

(236) a. et   ro'c-**di**   s-ää-ni
       not there-NEG C-go-3
       It wasn't there that he went.

  b. et   xten-ä-**di**-ni
     not belongs.to-1EX-NEG-3
     It isn't mine.

These sentences can thus also be seen as following from the clause structure and Negative Criterion analysis given above, where *-di* is in Neg⁰ at D-structure and the negative phrase marked by *et* must move to the specifier of NegP by S-structure to meet the Negative Criterion. I assume that *et* is like the focus marker (analyzed in chapter 6) in that it can either fill the D⁰ position or adjoin to it.

The structures for (236b) are given in (237), where I assume the X^{max} over XP structure for small clauses argued for by Koopman and Sportiche (1991).[100]

---

[100] I show the subject as a right-specifier of D^{max} in (237) since NP and DP (or D^{max}) have their specifiers on the right (see chapter 11).
An empty IP projection could also be assumed to be present, though not shown in (237).

8.2 Analysis of the obligatory fronting

(237)

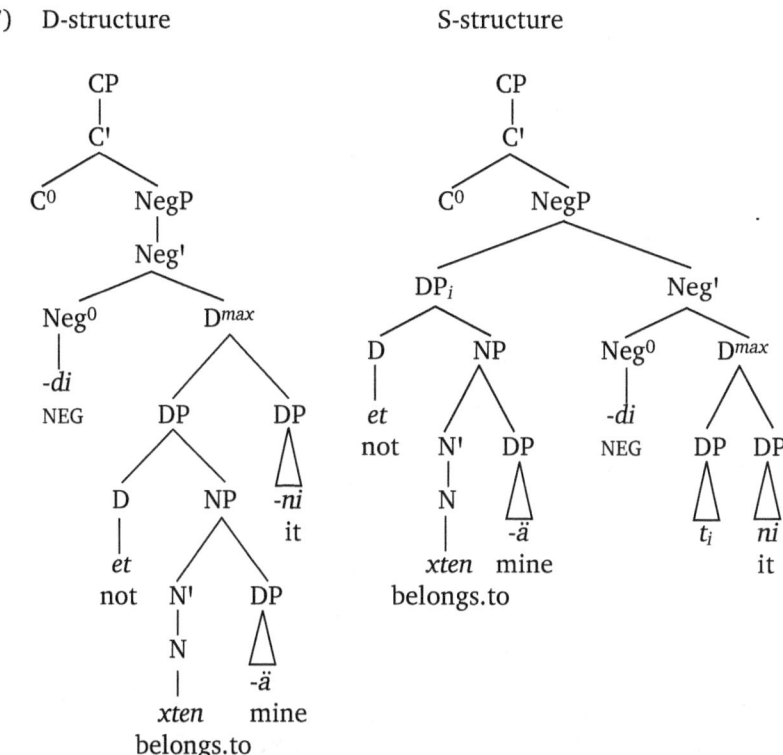

Note that due to the movement required by the Negative Criterion of the portion *et xten-ä*, which does not include the subject clitic, the more usual assumption that the subject of the small clause DP is simply the specifier of DP cannot be used. In that case, *et xten-ä* would be a D' which can neither move nor occupy a specifier position, as shown in (238).

(238)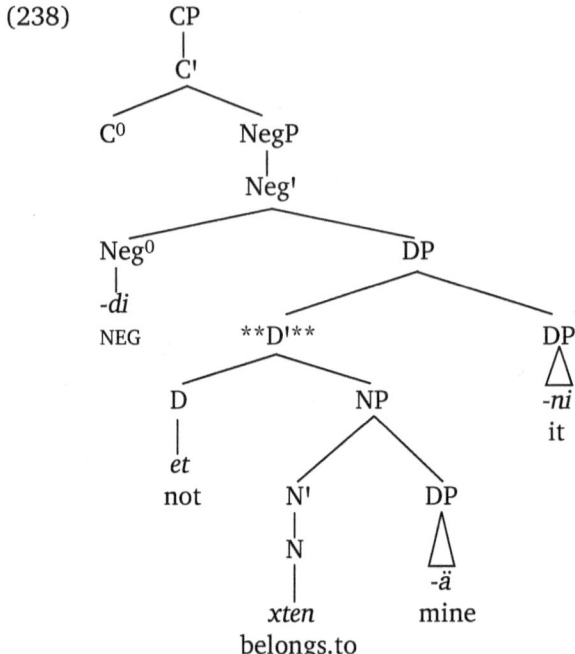

The second type of negative quantifier likewise follows the pattern shown by *et*. This involves the use of the negative indefinite pronouns *rut* and *xhet* as negative quantifiers meaning 'none' or 'not one' which agree in animacy or humanness with the nominal they are quantifying. The examples in (239) show again that the negated phrase is fronted and the negative clitic has attached to the end of the nominal phrase.

(239) a. **rut** gunaa-**di** huij
 none woman-NEG C-come
 No women came.

 b. **xhet** bisia-yas-**di** bi-dxäjl
 none bean-black-NEG C-be.found
 No black beans were found.

Also, like the case of *et* used as a copular clause without a verb, *ruti* (which may be *rut* + *di*) is used as a negative existential with human subjects and *xheti* (probably *xhet* + *di*) is used as a negative existential with inanimate subjects. Examples are given in (240), showing the negative existential fronted in its only allowed position.

8.2 Analysis of the obligatory fronting   169

(240) a. **ruti**   bej*n*   lo   nezyuj
         not.exist people face street
         There aren't any people on the street.

   b. **xheti**   guii   rolizä
      not.exist flowers house
      There aren't any flowers in the house.

Assuming that *rut* and *xhet* have the category D^0 allows a comprehensive account of their use as negative indefinite pronouns, negative quantifiers, and negative existentials. In the case of the negative pronouns, they are simply determiners which do not take a complement (see Postal 1969). As negative quantifiers they also fill the head of DP position, as do all other quantifiers in Zapotec, taking an NP complement. The requirement that the quantifier and NP must agree in humanness is accounted for by the head D^0 selecting the appropriate complement. The negative existentials *ruti* and *xheti* could also be included under this unitary analysis if we break them down into their component parts of *rut+di* and *zhet+di*. We would then assume a derivation for the examples in (240) parallel to (237), where *-di* is in Neg^0 and the head D^0 does not take a complement but does have a subject.[101] Looking at this case alone, either $D^0_{[+neg]}$ could move to Neg^0 via head movement or $DP_{[+neg]}$ could move to the specifier of NegP. The second option proves the most viable overall, since head movement is only assumed for clauses with [+V] predicates (see §10.2). The required agreement in humanness between the head D^0 and its S-structure subject is accounted for through specifier-head agreement.[102]

8.2.2.3 The interpretation of constituent negation as clausal negation.
We still need to consider how the instances of constituent negation are interpreted, especially where a negative quantifier takes an NP complement. If the arguments in Ladusaw (1992, 1993) and the analysis presented here are correct, then all the clauses in MZ and QZ which have any

---

[101]It would also be possible to assume that *rut* and *xhet* are unaccusative heads in that they select only a Theme θ-role and no Agent θ-role. As such, they would select a complement but no subject, with movement to the subject position in the specifier of D^{max} subsequently occurring. From that point, the derivation could follow similarly to that in (237).

[102]MZ also has a negative existential verb, *yu'-di*, which is very similar to the QZ form *yët*. In the MZ case it is clear that *-di* is the negative clitic because *yu'* is found alone when the negative clitic has attached to the constituent in the specifier of NegP. (See example (242c).) Further, *yu'* can be used as an existential in nonnegative contexts, as shown in (i).

(i) **yu'** xob ne*n* rojb
     exist corn in container
     There is corn in the container.

negative word at all count as clausal negation. Since there is a NegP projection, clausal negation is expressed.

What, then, is the difference in interpretation between clauses with negation only expressed on the head Neg⁰ or negation expressed by a free negative word versus the cases where there is a negative indefinite pronoun or a full negative DP in the specifier of NegP? As Ladusaw (1993) suggests, the difference is simply that in the case where a negative DP occupies the specifier of NegP position, that DP forms the restriction for the negative operator, whereas with only negative words or heads there is no restriction on the negative operator (at least none that is codified by the sentence structure). To illustrate this, the interpretation for an example of each type of sentence is shown in (241).

(241) a. **rut** bi-ääd-**di** lo guejdx
nobody C-come-NEG to village
Nobody came to the village.
Interpretation: $(\forall x{:}body'(x)) \neg [came.to.village'(x)]$

b. **di** Juan ch-ää Lua
no Juan P-go Oaxaca
Juan will not go to Oaxaca.
Interpretation: $\neg [go.to.Oaxaca'(Juan)]$

We could still question whether the fact that the negative marker -*di* attaches to the fronted constituent rather than to the verb indicates a difference in the scope of the negation. Some relevant examples are given in (242), showing that we do get a sense of negation of the fronted constituent only, since negation is not marked on the verb.[103]

(242) a. **et** ro'c-**di** s-ää-ni
not there-NEG C-go-3
It wasn't there that he went.

b. **xhet** bisia-yas-**di** bi-dxäjl
none bean-black-NEG C-be.found
No black beans were found.

---

[103]Example (253a) with *et* carries the presupposition that he went somewhere, whereas (253b) does not presuppose that something was found (Carol Stubblefield, p.c.). I do not have an account for this difference.

8.2 Analysis of the obligatory fronting

c. **xhet**-lii-**di**   yu'   roguidoo
   nothing-absolutely-NEG exist plaza
   There is absolutely nothing in the plaza.

However, the same interpretation strategy seems to give the correct readings for these sentences. (242a) would mean: restricting yourself to considering 'there', it is not the case that he went 'there'. Similarly, in (242b–c) the fact that the clitic -di is attached to the fronted constituent rather than to the verb does not change the interpretation; (242b) still means:

$$(\forall x: bean'(x) \land black'(x)) \neg [be.found'(x)]$$

The fact that the negative clitic attaches to the fronted constituent rather than to the verb might instead be a prosodic phenomenon. The negative clitic may be a combination of clitic types (Klavans 1995): it normally attaches to the raised verbal head unless the constituent in its specifier position contains "enough material" (e.g., a branching structure). In this case, it attaches to the end of the second constituent (= the end of the phrase in the specifier of NegP).

Therefore, constituent negation is equivalent to clausal negation in these languages where fronting to the specifier of NegP is required.[104] The interpretation that negation is a semantic operator with the familiar tripartite structure, where the XP in the specifier of NegP fills the restriction of the operator and the complement of Neg⁰ is the nuclear scope, accounts for the various configurations (Ladusaw 1993).

8.3 The negation constructions and Verb Movement versus Subject Adjunction

The clause structure analysis of the negative constructions presented in the previous section assumed the movement of V^0-to-I^0-to-Neg^0 in cases where the negative clitic is overt. This accounts coherently for both the fronting of the negative phrases and the fact that negation is normally marked on the verb (especially in QZ). This head movement of the verb provides important evidence for the choice between the Verb Movement and Subject Adjunction proposals for obtaining VSO word order. The next

---

[104] This fronting of negative phrases is distinct from the normal focus movement which was the topic of chapter 6. A negative phrase may not contain the focus marker. Further delineation of the interaction between negative fronting, focus movement, and wh-movement can be found in chapter 9.

subsections will clarify the Verb Movement account of the negation constructions and then contrast it with the account necessary under the Subject Adjunction hypothesis.

We saw in chapter 5 that the two proposals for obtaining VSO word order are distinct in terms of both the clause structure and the movement that is proposed. We will see here that the main difference empirically between the proposals is how they account for both the aspect marking and negation surfacing on the verb.

8.3.1 The Verb Movement account

The Verb Movement proposal for VSO clause structure assumes that the subject occupies the (left) specifier of VP, and head movement of V^0-to-I^0 occurs over the subject to produce the correct surface order. The fact that the aspect marking surfaces on the verb is accounted for via this syntactic head movement as well. (244) illustrates this account of the simple sentence in (243).

(243) *w-eey Benit mël*   BENIT 4
      C-take Benito fish
      Benito took a fish.

(244)   D-structure   S-structure

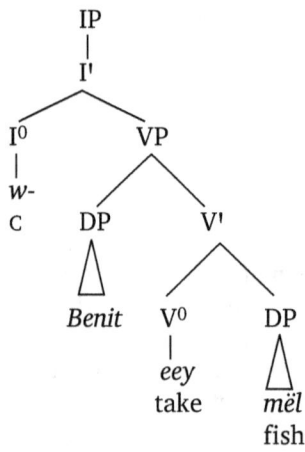 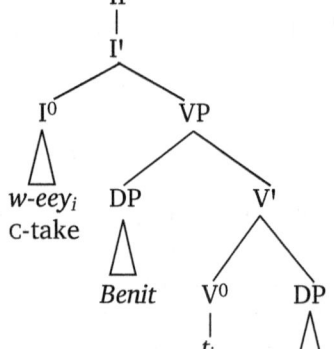

In a simple negated clause, as in (245), we only need to assume that the negative clitic heads its own projection above IP, and that head movement

8.3 Verb Movement versus Subject Adjunction 173

occurs one step higher. This movement from V^0-to-I^0-to-Neg^0 also accounts for the negative marker surfacing on the verb, as shown in (246).

(245) *w-eey-t   Benit   mël*
 c-take-NEG Benito fish
 Benito didn't take a fish.

(246)   D-structure   S-structure

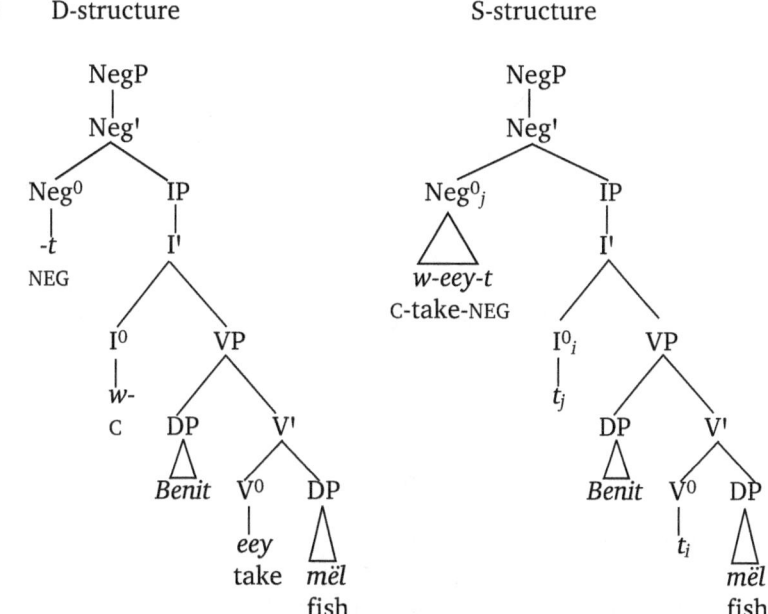

We saw that this NegP projection accounts for the licensing and co-occurrence restrictions between the various negative elements. For example, the same head movement of the verb through Infl to Neg^0 occurs when a negative indefinite pronoun fronts to the specifier of NegP to meet the requirements of the Negative Criterion, as shown in (248) for example (247).

(247) *bet   w-eey-t   Benit   __*
 nothing c-take-NEG Benito
 Benito didn't take anything.

(248)   D-structure   S-structure

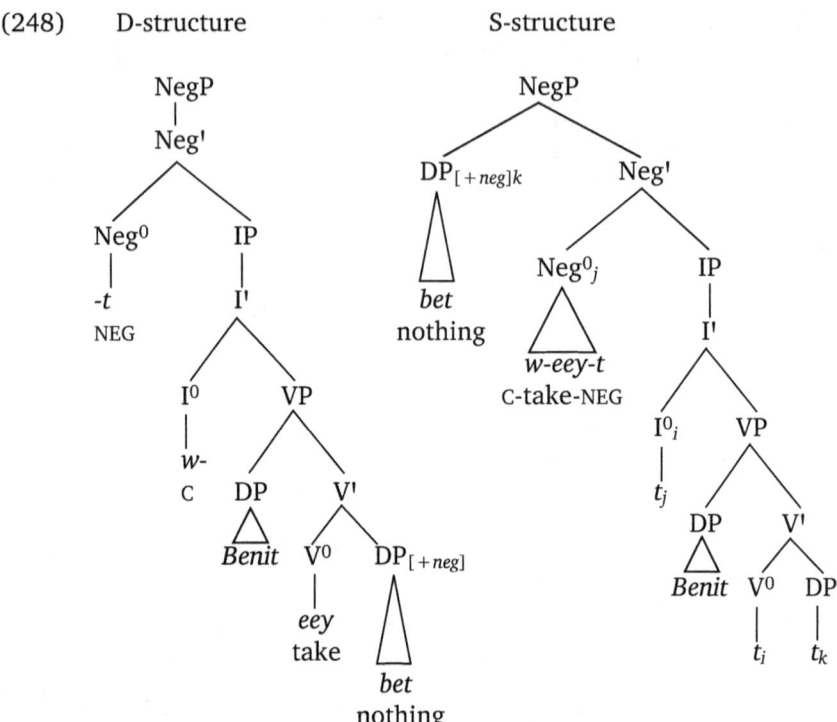

The Verb Movement proposal thus provides a coherent account for both negative and affirmative clauses. Head movement of the verb to each of the functional heads that surface attached to the verb is both motivated by the attachment and accounts for the surface form.[105] Such head movement does not take place when it is not needed to host a morphologically dependent form (Rizzi and Roberts 1989). For example, the verb moves only to I^0 and not on to Neg^0 when Neg^0 is filled by *gart* 'still.no', as in (249). (This must also be the case when there is a null Neg^0 in MZ, or the wrong surface order would be obtained.) The S-structure for (249) is given in (250), showing that only V^0-to-I^0 movement occurs; *gart* is base generated in Neg^0 and *nunk* is base generated in the specifier of NegP. The initial *Jasint* is a topic phrase.

(249) *Jasint   nunk   gart   ts-a   Jasint   Pwert*   BENIT 29
      Jacinto never   still.no P-go   Jacinto Salina.Cruz
      As for Jacinto, he had never gone to Salina Cruz.

---

[105]See §5.2.1 for more detailed discussion of the motivation for Verb Movement.

8.3 Verb Movement versus Subject Adjunction

(250)
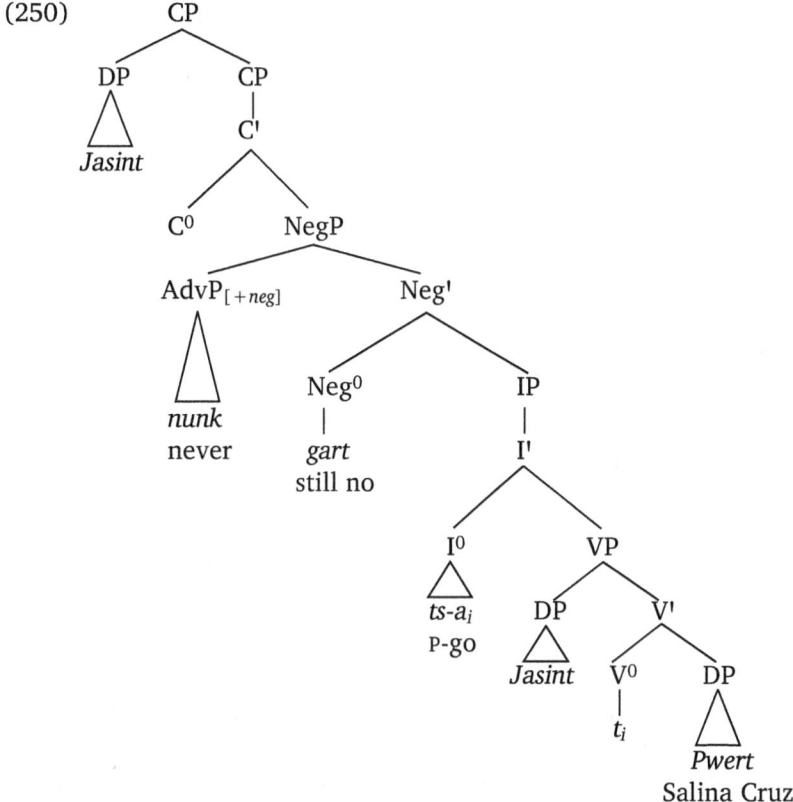

8.3.2 The Subject Adjunction account

What is necessary under the Subject Adjunction proposal to account for the same facts? The Subject Adjunction proposal for VSO clause structure assumes that the subject begins in the specifier of IP and then right-adjoins to the verb to produce the correct surface order, leaving behind a coindexed expletive *pro*. This is illustrated in (251) for the simple declarative sentence in (243).

(251) D-structure   S-structure

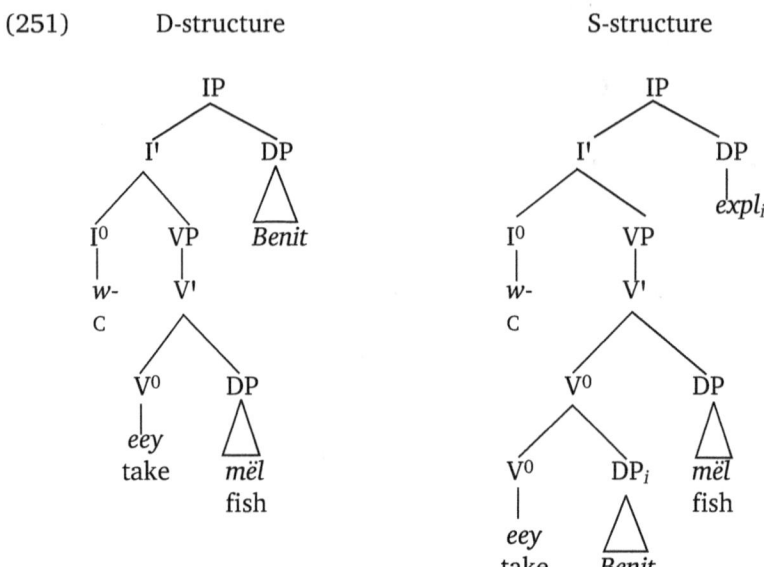

Recall that the main difference between the two proposals is in how aspect marking and negation end up being realized on the verb. In a simple clause like that diagrammed in (251), we could appeal to the clitic nature of the aspect markers to explain the fact that they surface attached to the predicate. Such an analysis is attractive (and is adopted in this work) to account for the distribution of the clitic pronouns which fill their appropriate syntactic argument position, as do the free pronouns, but simply attach to whatever is in front of them due to their dependent phonological status (see §2.3). Thus, a sentence like (252), which surfaces as a single word, would have the syntactic structure shown in (253) under the Subject Adjunction hypothesis, with the attachment being left to the phonology.

(252) g-e-m-o
   P-say-3R-3I
   One says it.

8.3 Verb Movement versus Subject Adjunction

(253)

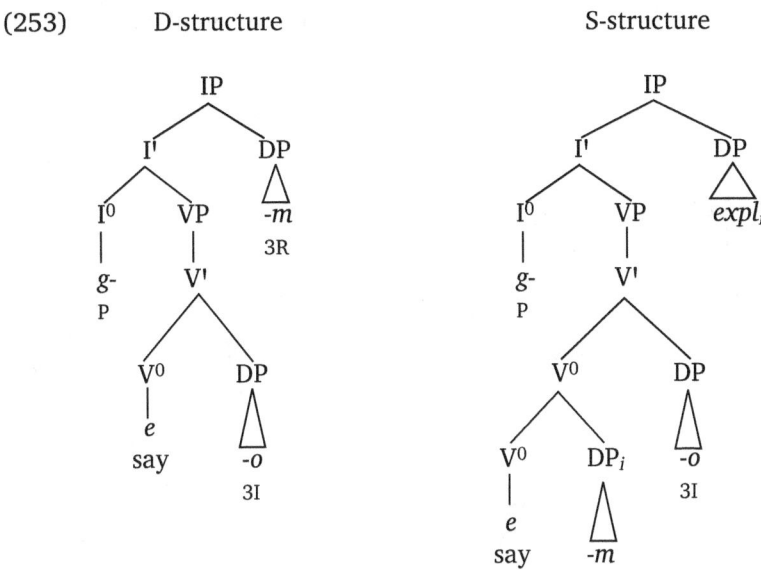

In a negative clause, however, we cannot rely on phonological attachment to account for the surface position of the negative marker. In order to maintain the basic analysis of a NegP projection above IP with the obligatory fronting accounted for by the specifier-head agreement required by the Negative Criterion, the negative marker -*t* would have to be in Neg⁰ at S-structure. Subsequent lowering of at least the negative marker (and perhaps also the aspect marker) onto V⁰, via Affix Hopping would be required, as shown in (254) for the simple negative clause in (245).

(254)   D-structure   S-structure before lowering

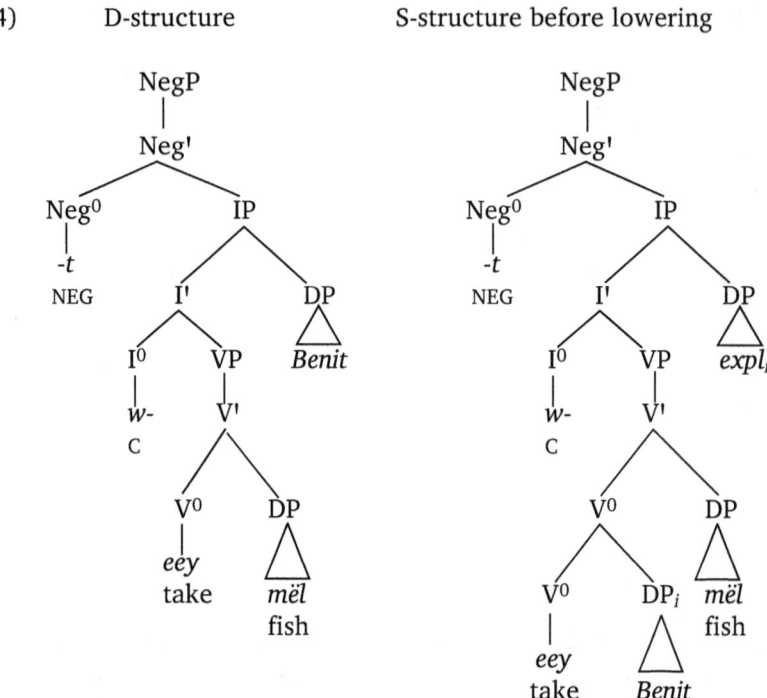

We saw that the NegP projection was especially needed to account for the obligatory fronting of negative indefinite pronouns via specifier-head agreement with the negative marker in Neg⁰. The Subject Adjunction account of example (247) is given in (255), showing that lowering of the negative marker to surface attached to the right of the verb is again necessary.

8.3 Verb Movement versus Subject Adjunction

(255)

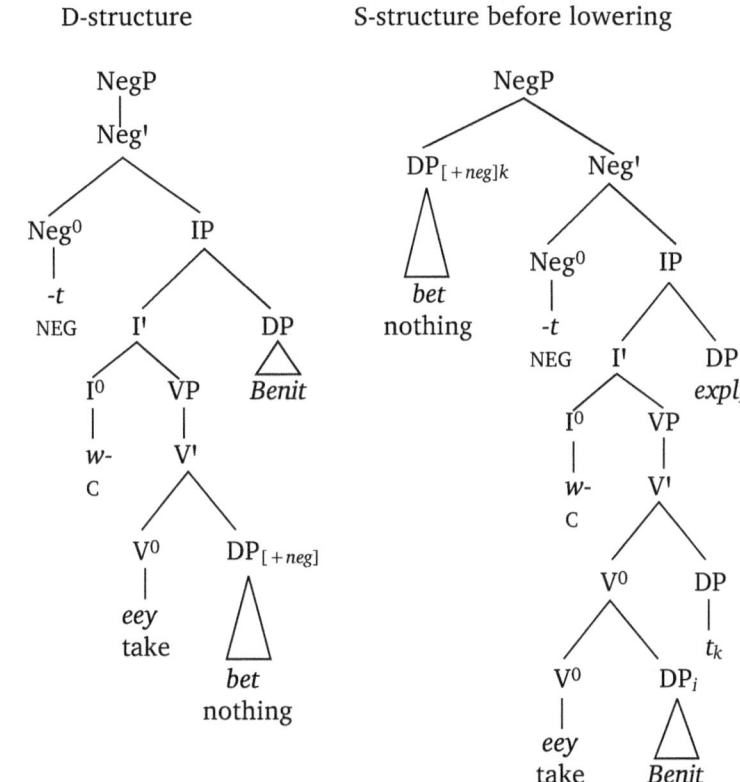

Thus, in addition to the lowering of the subject to adjoin to the verb, lowering of the negative marker to surface on the verb is also required under the Subject Adjunction proposal. This adds further unattractiveness to the use of the Subject Adjunction proposal for QZ, since lowering is in general disfavored. I do not seriously consider the possibility of applying Subject Adjunction and then using Verb Movement rather than Affix Hopping to account for the aspect marking and negation surfacing on the verb, since it offers no advantages over the simpler and theoretically superior account of Verb Movement alone.

At this point, I adopt the Verb Movement proposal for obtaining VSO word order in QZ. The overall clause structure will be further investigated and modified in the next chapter. Although chapters 9, 10, and 11 present some further challenges to the Verb Movement proposal, alternative accounts are found for the problematic constructions. The Verb Movement proposal thus proves to be workable for QZ, and most likely also for the other Zapotecan languages.

9

Interaction Between the Various Ā-Constructions

We have seen in chapters 6–8 that focus phrases, *wh*-phrases, and negative phrases are fronted in QZ. This chapter looks at the interaction between these constructions to determine the relative positions of the fronted phrases and the co-occurrence restrictions between them.

In §9.1 the fact that questions and focus constructions may not co-occur in a single clause leads to the proposal that fronted *wh*-phrases and focused phrases occupy the same position. The crucial relationship is with the C^0 which minimally governs the *wh*-phrase or focused phrase, not with any following head. In contrast, §9.2 shows that questions may co-occur with the fronting of negative phrases. The question word is always first, demonstrating that the projection containing the negative phrase must be below the adjoined position for the *wh*-phrase. The same ordering is shown to hold between focused phrases and negative phrases in §9.3.

Section 9.4 looks at the interaction between clausal coordination and negation. I conclude that it is preferable to propose the presence of a Polarity phrase in every case, rather than allowing coordination between IP and NegP. The overall clause structure proposal is then summarized in §9.5.

9.1 Questions and focus constructions may not co-occur in a clause

There are no examples in the QZ texts (Regnier 1989a) of questions which contain a separate focused phrase. (256)–(257) show the results of checking with my language consultant whether *wh*-questions and focus constructions can interact in matrix or embedded clauses. The (a) examples are the text questions without a separate focused phrase and the remaining examples demonstrate that a focused phrase may not occur either before or after the *wh*-phrase. Note that (257) shows that the presence or absence of the focus marker makes no difference.

(256) a. pa go r-laa de   GRING 34
  what thing H-do 2
  What are you doing?

 b. *pa go **de** r-laa
  what thing 2 H-do
  (What are you doing?)

 c. ***de** pa go r-laa
  2 what thing H-do
  (What are you doing?)

(257) a. n-an-t men pa nëz z-a Biki   AGOSTO 59
  S-know-NEG 3 what road PR-go Virginia
  They don't know which way Virginia is going.

 b. *n-an-t men pa nëz **la Biki** z-a
  S-know-NEG 3 what road FM Virginia PR-go
  (They don't know which way Virginia is going.)

 c. *n-an-t men pa nëz **Biki** z-a
  S-know-NEG 3 what road Virginia PR-go
  (They don't know which way Virginia is going.)

 d. *n-an-t men **la Biki** pa nëz z-a
  S-know-NEG 3 FM Virginia what road PR-go
  (They don't know which way Virginia is going.)

9.1 Questions and focus constructions may not co-occur in a clause

 e. *n-an-t men **Biki** pa nëz z-a
   S-know-NEG 3 Virginia what road PR-go
   (They don't know which way Virginia is going.)

It might be reasoned that the lack of co-occurrence between a focused phrase and a *wh*-phrase is due to the semantic fact that the *wh*-phrase is in focus in a question. This does not give a complete account, however, since fronting of a focused phrase may not occur even in a Yes/No question, where there is no fronted *wh*-phrase. This is demonstrated in (258)–(259), where again the (a) example is the text question. Different types of nominal phrases are attempted to be focused, but co-occurrence is not allowed in any case between a question and a separate focused phrase.

(258) a. r-e Javyer pe w-u maa nii de   SAMUEL 28
   H-say Javier Q C-eat 3A foot 2
   Javier asked, "Did the snake eat your foot?"

  b. *r-e Javyer pe **maa** w-u nii de
   H-say Javier Q 3A C-eat foot 2
   (Javier asked, "Did the snake eat your foot?")

  c. *r-e Javyer **maa** pe w-u nii de
   H-say Javier 3A Q C-eat foot 2
   (Javier asked, "Did the snake eat your foot?")

  d. *r-e Javyer pe **y-rup nii de** w-u maa
   H-say Javier Q P-two foot 2 C-eat 3A
   (Javier asked, "Your two feet did the snake eat?")

  e. *r-e Javyer **y-rup nii de** pe w-u maa
   H-say Javier P-two foot 2 Q C-eat 3A
   (Javier asked, "Your two feet did the snake eat?")

(259) a. g-an pe s-na Susan g-aa Susan lyu TRIPTOQ 8A
   P-know Q F-want Susan P-lie.down Susan land

   o g-aa Susan lo daa
   or P-lie.down Susan face petate
   We'll see if Susan wants to lie down on the ground or lie down on a petate.

b. *g-an   pe **la Susan** s-na   g-aa   Susan lyu
   P-know   Q   FM Susan   F-want   P-lie.down   Susan land
   (We'll see if Susan wants to lie down on the ground...)

c. *g-an   pe **Susan** s-na   g-aa   Susan lyu
   P-know   Q   Susan   F-want   P-lie.down   Susan land
   (We'll see if Susan wants to lie down on the ground...)

d. *g-an   **la Susan** pe s-na   g-aa   Susan lyu
   P-know   FM Susan   Q F-want   P-lie.down   Susan land
   (We'll see if Susan wants to lie down on the ground...)

e. *g-an   **Susan** pe s-na   g-aa   Susan lyu
   P-know   Susan   Q F-want   P-lie.down   Susan land
   (We'll see if Susan wants to lie down on the ground...)

This data reveals that a focused phrase cannot be present in any type of question. If we posit that *wh*-phrases and focused phrases occupy the same position, we have an account for their lack of co-occurrence in *wh*-questions. We saw in chapter 7 that the position for focused phrases is directly after the complementizer in embedded clauses (see (154c), §6.2.1). Since chapter 7 gave evidence that the Yes/No question marker, *pe*, acts as a complementizer in embedded clauses and that the *wh*-phrases which co-occur with *pe* in *wh*-questions must directly follow it, we can conclude that the position for both focused phrases and *wh*-phrases is directly below the complementizer C^0. Further, we have seen no evidence leading to the positing of a full projection below C^0 for either the *wh*-phrases or the focused phrases to reside. The focus marker was shown to be a type of determiner which precedes a discourse-linked phrase. It is not a complementizer nor is it the head of a Focus phrase. Similarly, the *wh*-word *zh* seems to be best analyzed as a discourse-linked *wh*-demonstrative. If a Focus phrase were posited, the head Foc^0 would always be null. The crucial relationship in these constructions is minimal government between the C^0 and the fronted phrase, not a specifier-head relationship. I therefore assume that the fronted phrase is simply adjoined to IP (or whatever phrase is immediately below CP in the clause), as shown in (260).

9.1 Questions and focus constructions may not co-occur in a clause 185

(260)

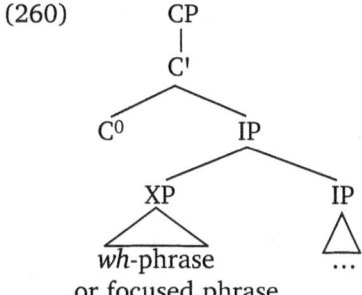

wh-phrase
or focused phrase

To restrict the occurrence of focused phrases in Yes/No questions we can appeal to the fact that the focused phrase must be in a minimal government relationship with a C^0 that agrees with it in its question feature and its focus feature (i.e. $[-q, +foc]$). Further, though chapter 3 showed that both long-distance focusing and long-distance wh-movement are possible (with an example of each type given in (261)), it is not possible to focus out of an embedded question (262a), nor to move a wh-phrase out of an embedded focus structure (262b).

(261) a. *lo   Jose r-e   Mblid y-dee   men/Mblid liber _*
         face José H-say Mary   P-give 3/Mary   book
         To José, Mary said she will give the book.

   b. *txu   n-a   Jose wii   noo _*
      who   s-say José c/see 1EX
      Who does José say that I saw?

(262) a. **la   Biki   n-an   men pa   nëz   z-a _ _*
         FM   Virginia s-know 3   what road   PR-go
         (Virginia, they know which way she is going.)

   b. **pa   nëz   zhe n-a   xe-mgyeey noo*
      what road WH   s-say POS-man   1EX

      xuz   Dolf   y-nëëz   _ _ ne   ts-a   men den
      father Rodolfo P-take   that P-go   3   ranch
      (What road did my husband say Rodolfo's father should take to go to the ranch?)

The ungrammaticality of the examples in (262) confirms that focused phrases and wh-phrases occupy the same position in the clause. These examples also provide evidence that long-distance focus movement and *wh*-movement must apply cyclically. This requirement for cyclic movement reduces to the antecedent government required by the ECP. In (262a), the *wh*-phrase counts as a closer antecedent governor for the trace of the focused phrase. Thus, by Relativized Minimality (Rizzi 1990), antecedent government of the trace of the focused phrase is blocked. Similar reasoning holds for the trace of the *wh*-phrase in (262b).

This co-occurrence restriction between focused phrases and questions does not apply to topics. A topic phrase may be present in the matrix clause of a question, as shown in (263), where the argument which is coreferent with the topic maintains its normal place in the clause. This is predicted by the analysis that topics are adjoined to a matrix CP; the C⁰ in this case may be [$+q, \pm wh$] allowing either a Yes/No question or a *wh*-question following the topic phrase.

(263) re   Jasint   **laa de naa**   BENIT 23
      H-say Jacinto   FM 2 DEM

   pe r-laan de y-laa de dxiin nee
   Q   H-want 2   P-do 2   work here
   Jacinto said, "And you, do you want to work here?"

9.2 Relative positions of *wh*-phrases and negative phrases

Unlike the co-occurrence restriction between questions and focus constructions, negative constructions, including the fronting of negative indefinite pronouns, freely occur in questions. The relative order of the two types of fronted phrases is fixed, however, showing that the NegP projection must be below the adjoined position occupied by *wh*-phrases.

This fixed ordering is demonstrated in (264)–(265) for Yes/No questions. (264a) shows a text example containing a simple Yes/No question. As expected, the negative counterpart is formed by simply adding the negative marker to the verb, as shown in (264b). Likewise, (265a) is a negative declarative containing a fronted negative indefinite pronoun. (265b–c) demonstrate that such a negative declarative can be turned into a negative Yes/No question just by adding the question complementizer *pe* to the front of the sentence. In all cases, the negative constituent is below *pe*.

9.2 Relative positions of *wh*-phrases and negative phrases

(264) a. *r-e   Javyer pe   w-u   maa nii   de*   SAMUEL 28
         H-say Javier Q   C-eat 3A   foot 2
         Javier asked, "Did the snake eat your foot?"

   b. *r-e   Javyer pe   w-u-t   maa nii   de*
       H-say Javier Q   C-eat-NEG 3A   foot 2
       Javier asked, "Didn't the snake eat your foot?"

(265) a. ***bet   wii-t   Jose***
         nothing C/see-NEG José
         José saw nothing. *or* José didn't see anything.

   b. ***pe bet   wii-t   Jose***
       Q nothing C/see-NEG José
       Didn't José see anything?

   c. **bet   pe wii-t   Jose*
       nothing Q   C/see-NEG José
       (Didn't José see anything?)

Examples (266)–(267) demonstrate the interaction between the fronting of negative indefinite pronouns and *wh*-phrases in matrix clauses. (266a) and (267a) exemplify the individual constructions before combining them. The remaining examples reiterate the facts that both types of phrases are required to front and that the *wh*-phrase must be before (or above) the negative indefinite pronoun.

(266) a. ***pa   gos   wii   men***
         what thing C/see 3
         What thing did they see?

   b. ***pa   gos   rut   wii-t***
       what thing nobody C/see-NEG
       What thing did nobody see?

   c. **pa   gos   wii-t   rut*
       what thing C/see-NEG nobody
       (What thing did nobody see?)

    d. *****rut**   *wii-t*   **pa**   **gos**
       nobody C/see-NEG what thing
       (What thing did nobody see?)

    e. *****rut**   **pa**   **gos**   *wii-t*
       nobody what thing C/see-NEG
       (What thing did nobody see?)

(267) a. **bet**   *wii-t*   men
       nothing C/see-NEG 3
       They saw nothing.

    b. **txu**   **bet**   *wii-t*
       who nothing C/see-NEG
       Who saw nothing?

    c. *****txu** *wii-t*   **bet**
       who C/see-NEG nothing
       (Who saw nothing?)

    d. *****bet** *wii-t*   **txu**
       nothing C/see-NEG who
       (Who saw nothing?)

    e. *****bet**   **txu** *wii-t*
       nothing who C/see-NEG
       (Who saw nothing?)

In sentences with embedded clauses, exemplified below in (268)–(271), we see the expected interactions between negation and *wh*-questions. (268) first reiterates that negative indefinite pronouns must front to be in the proper relationship with a Neg^0. This requires long-distance fronting (with pied-piping and inversion) in some cases. *Wh*-phrases must also front to be in the proper relationship with a $C^0_{[+wh]}$, but no higher.

(268) a. ??***rut***   *wii-t*   Jose w-gwet Susan kart lo _
       nobody C/see-NEG José C-give Susan letter face
       (José didn't see Susan give the letter to anybody.)

9.2 Relative positions of wh-phrases and negative phrases

b. *lo   rut   wii-t   Jose w-gwet   Susan kart __
   face nobody c/see-NEG José c-give Susan letter
   (José didn't see Susan give the letter to anybody.)

c. rut   lo   wii-t   Jose w-gwet   Susan kart __
   nobody face c/see-NEG José c-give Susan letter
   José didn't see Susan give the letter to anybody.

d. *wii-t   Jose rut   lo   w-gwet   Susan kart __
   c/see-NEG José nobody face c-give Susan letter
   (José didn't see Susan give the letter to anybody.)

e. wii   Jose ne   rut   lo   w-gwed-et   Susan kart __
   c/see José that nobody face c-give-NEG Susan letter
   José saw that Susan didn't give the letter to anybody.

(269a) shows that a wh-phrase can be fronted out of an embedded negative clause and (269b) demonstrates that a negative indefinite pronoun can be fronted out of an embedded question. This contrasts directly with the inability to focus out of an embedded question, and can be accounted for by the fact that the wh-phrase and the negative indefinite pronoun occupy different positions in the clause. Successive cyclic movement is possible in this case.[106] Again this reduces to the ECP requirement for antecedent government filtered by Relativized Minimality (Rizzi 1990). We can assume that adjoined antecedents can interfere with one another, and that Ā-specifiers can interfere with one another, but that an Ā-specifier cannot count as a closer antecedent governor than an adjoined XP (or vice versa). Specifically, focused phrases and wh-phrases would get in each other's way (as we saw in (262), but either would be transparent to the negated element in the specifier of NegP, as seen in (269).[107]

---

[106]I am following the segment theory of adjunction (May 1985), whereby the second instance of the maximal projection created by adjunction is not a separate projection, but merely another segment of that projection. This is crucial to enable the negative PP rut lo to move out of an embedded NegP to which a wh-phrase has adjoined.

[107]This distinction could not be made if the focused phrases and wh-phrases were analyzed as occupying the specifier of FocP, since then all the fronted phrases would be in Ā-specifiers.

(269) a. **pa nëz zhe** n-a   xe-mgyeey noo
what road WH S-say POS-man 1EX

   rut   y-nëëz-t   _ _ ne   ts-a men den
   nobody P-take-NEG   that P-go 3   ranch
   What road did my husband say that nobody should take to go to the ranch?

b. **rut**   lo   wii-t   Jose g-an   **txu** w-gwet _ kart _
   nobody face C/see-NEG José P-know who C-give   letter
   José didn't see who gave the letter to anybody.

The examples in (270)–(271) verify that both the licensing requirements for a fronted phrase and the correct ordering between fronted phrases must be met for a sentence to be grammatical. As in matrix clauses, when both a *wh*-phrase and a negative indefinite pronoun are fronted within an embedded clause (271d–e), the *wh*-phrase is first.

(270) a. **txu** wii   _ ne   **rut**   lo   w-gwet-et Susan kart _
   who C/see   that nobody face C-give-NEG Susan letter
   Who saw that Susan didn't give the letter to anybody.

b. **txu rut**   lo   wii-t   — w-gwet Susan kart _
   who nobody face C/see-NEG   C-give   Susan letter
   Who didn't see Susan give the letter to anybody.

(271) a. **rut**   wii-t   _ g-an   **pa gos** r-laa Susan _
   nobody C/see-NEG   P-know   what thing H-do   Susan
   Nobody saw what Susan did.

b. *****pa gos rut**   wii-t   — g-an   r-laa Susan _
   what thing nobody C/see-NEG   P-know H-do   Susan
   (Nobody saw what Susan did.)

c. ***rut pa   gos** wii-t   — g-an   r-laa Susan _
   nobody what thing C/see-NEG   P-know H-do   Susan
   (Nobody saw what Susan did.)

d. **rut**   wii-t   — g-an   **txu bet**   r-laa-t   _ _
   nobody C/see-NEG   P-know who nothing H-do-NEG
   Nobody saw who did nothing/anything.

9.2 Relative positions of wh-phrases and negative phrases

e. *rut   wii-t   _   g-an   bet   txu r-laa-t   _ _
   nobody C/see-NEG   P-know nothing who H-do-NEG
   (Nobody saw who did nothing/anything.)

The observed interaction between questions and negation can be accounted for by positing that the projection which houses the negative marker and the negative indefinite pronouns at S-structure (NegP here) is below both C^0 and the adjoined position for wh-phrases. The S-structure for example (266b) is given here as an illustration. (V^0-to-I^0-to-Neg^0 movement is also shown.)

(272)

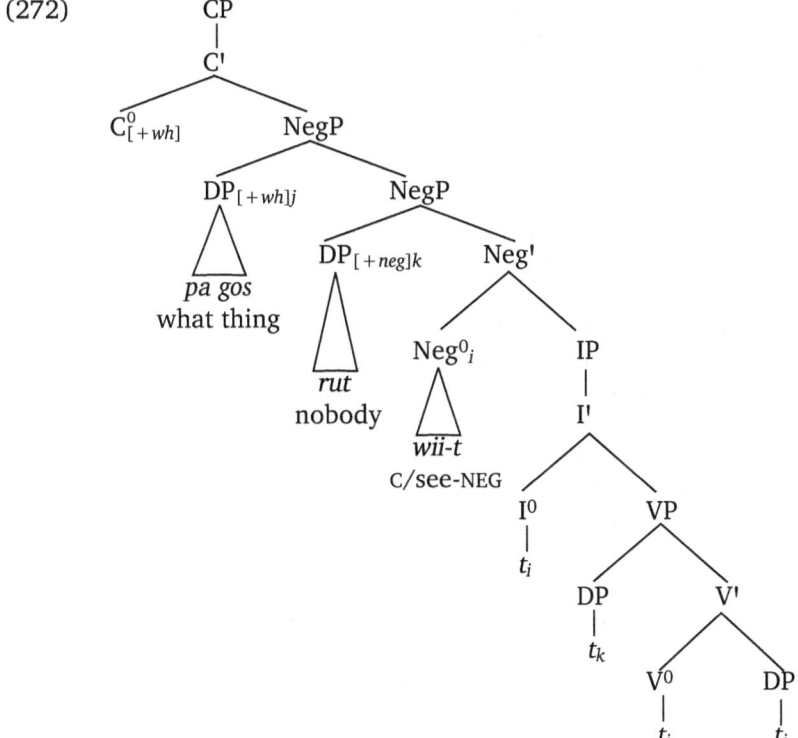

9.3 Relative positions of focused phrases and negative phrases

In §9.1 I posited that the position for wh-phrases and focused phrases is the same to account for their lack of co-occurrence. Given this, then, the interaction between focus constructions and negation constructions should yield the same results as seen for questions and negation. The available evidence shows that this is indeed the case, though semantic factors clearly limit the contexts where negation and focus may interact in a single clause. Focus constructions may co-occur with negative constructions where the negation is simply marked on the verb, as shown in (273). As expected, the focused phrase occurs before the negative-marked verb. Due to the tendency for scope relations to be read directly from S-structure in Zapotec, examples like (273) would only be used when the focus takes scope over the negation. In this case, the focus is clearly contrastive, giving a reading of 'the soldiers didn't take **José**, but they did take others' in (273a).[108] Similarly, (273b) would only be used to express the reading that '**the deer** didn't leave through the door, as the lions did' and (273c) emphasizes that 'the deer didn't leave through **the door**, but escaped through the window.' The normal case where negation has wide scope requires that all nonnegative arguments remain in situ with no phrase receiving particular focus.

(273) a. *le   Jose   w-eey-t   soldad*   SOLDADOS 32A
       FM   José   C-take-NEG soldier
       José, the soldiers didn't take.

  b. *le   mdxin   nunk   w-ruu-t   por   ru   yuu*   RYENEGU 38A
     FM   deer   never C-leave-NEG by   mouth house
     The deer never left through the door.

  c. *por   ru   yuu   nunk   w-ruu-t   mdxin*   RYENEGU 38B
     by   mouth house never C-leave-NEG deer
     Through the door the deer never left.

Checking with my language consultant whether a focused phrase and a negative indefinite pronoun may both be present yielded the judgements shown in (274). (274a) shows the normal construction without focus. (274b–c) are grammatical but they would not be used in normal situations; such constructions may only be used to signal contrastive emphasis in the proper context. (274d–e) are ungrammatical in any context because the focused phrase cannot appear between the negative indefinite pronoun and the negative-marked verb. The ungrammaticality of (274d–e) is predicted by

---

[108]The focus marker is thus more likely to occur in such examples, but it is not required. Its use in (273a) indicates that the others that were taken were previously mentioned by name. In (273c), the alternative route of escape has not been previously noted; instead, the next sentence in the story explains how the deer got out.

9.3 Relative positions of focused phrases and negative phrases

the analysis that the negative verbal complex is in Neg⁰ and the negative indefinite pronoun is in the specifier of NegP at S-structure.

(274) a. **bet**   r-laa-t   Jose
  nothing H-do-NEG José
  José does nothing.

  b. **Jose bet**   r-laa-t
  José nothing H-do-NEG
  José does nothing.

  c. **le   Jose   bet**   r-laa-t
  FM José nothing H-do-NEG
  José does nothing.

  d. *bet   Jose r-laa-t
  nothing José H-do-NEG
  (José does nothing.)

  e. *bet   le   Jose   r-laa-t
  nothing FM José H-do-NEG
  (José does nothing.)

As we saw with questions, it is possible to focus out of a negative clause (275a) and to move a negative indefinite pronoun out of a clause containing a focused phrase (275b).

(275) a. **lo   Jose** r-e   Mblid **bet**   y-dee-t   men/Mblid _ _
  face José H-say Mary nothing P-give-NEG 3/Mary
  To José, Mary said she will not give anything.

  b. **rut**   lo   wii-t   Jose ne   **Susan** w-gwet _ kart _
  nobody face C/see-NEG José that Susan C-give   letter
  José didn't see Susan give the letter to anybody.

All the available data are thus consistent with the analysis that focused phrases move to an adjoined position directly below C⁰ and above NegP, just as *wh*-phrases do.

It should also be noted here that topic phrases may occur on negative clauses quite freely, without requiring any special contrastive context.

(276) gives some text examples. This is expected by the analysis that topic phrases are simply adjoined to a matrix clause.

(276) a. ***per noo*** *w-la-leedx-t   noo-w*   SNAKHAIR 11
but 1EX C-call-liver-NEG 1EX-3I
But as for me, I hadn't believed it.

b. ***per men*** *r-on-t   men diiz*   SOLDADOS 4
but 3 H-hear-NEG 3 word
But as for the men, they didn't understand Zapotec.

9.4 Polarity phrase needed to account for clausal coordination

Up to this point, we have determined that the structure of a negative clause is as shown in (277a) whereas an assertive clause has the simpler structure shown in (277b). The types of phrases that may occupy each position at S-structure are noted.

(277) a. Negative clause   or   b. Assertive clause

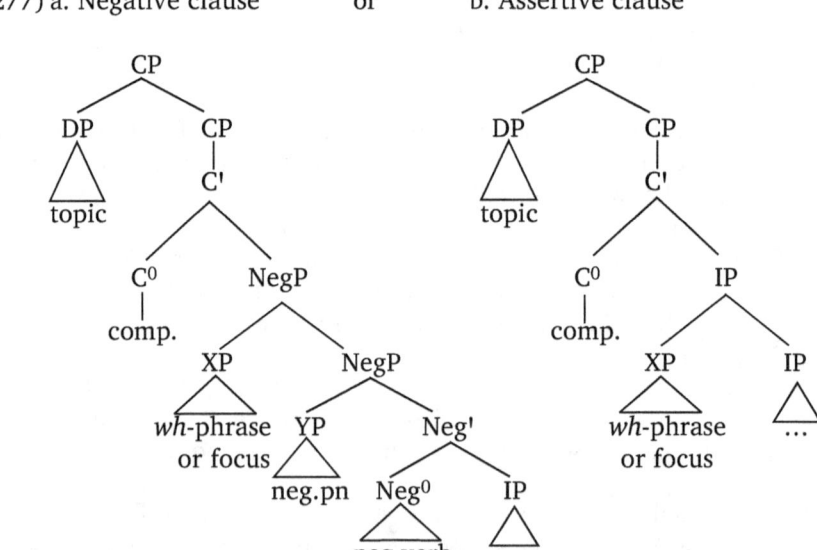

We turn now to evaluate the two different clause structures by considering how they interact under coordination.

9.4 Polarity phrase needed to account for clausal coordination

QZ has the overt conjunctions *no* 'and' and *o* 'or'. Coordination is attested at many levels. We will only deal with coordination of IP and above here. (See chapters 10 and 11 for discussion of the possibilities for Across the Board Extraction and examples of lower-level coordination.) In each example in this section the conjuncts are bracketed and the conjunction, if overt, is in bold type.

The normal higher-level coordination is between coordinate IPs, as the examples in (278) show. Note that in (278c–d) the coordination is between embedded IPs.

(278) a. che-bel   r-laan   de gaz   de [sob   de]   BATHROOM 8
when-if H-want 2 P-bathe 2   F/sit 2

   o   [*su-li*   *de*]
   or   F/stand-straight 2
When you want to bathe, sit or stand.

b. [*gu-g-eey*   *ngob*   *y-kaa* *men* *gyët*]   CWENT 21
IMP-P-take masa P-do   3   tortilla

   no [*gu-g-eey*   *ngwaan*]
   and IMP-P-take poison
Take masa, so they can make tortillas, and take poison.

c. *s-ak*   [*ts-a* *de* *lo*   *lbanyil*]   BENIT 57
F-become P-go 2   face builder

   o [*ts-a* *de* *y-chux* *de* *mëlbyuu*]
   or P-go 2   P-peel 2   shrimp
It could be that you can go to the builders or go to peel shrimp.

d. *g-an*   *pe* *s-na*   *de* [*g-aa*   *de* *lyu*]   TRIPTOQ 8
P-know Q F-want 2   P-lie.down 2   land

   o [*g-aa*   *de* *lo*   *daa*]
   or P-lie.down 2 face mat
We'll see if you will want to lie down on the ground or on a mat.

Example (279) shows that coordination may also be at the CP level, if the clause meaning 'if you bring your car' is analyzed as either being in the specifier of CP position or adjoined to CP in the second conjunct, as I assume is the normal position for adverbial phrases.[109] Coordination of two matrix questions, as shown in (280), is clearly coordination at the CP level.

(279) [ts-a de nii de] o [bel ts-a-no   de koch   TRIPTOQ 82
      P-go 2   foot 2   or if   P-go-take 2   car

      ts-a de y-deb koch de]
      P-go 2   P-one car   2
      You can walk, or if you bring your car, you can go in your car.

(280) [pe-zee w-u   maa nii   de]   no   [pa   or   w-u   maa-w]
      Q-how   C-eat 3A   foot 2   and   what hour C-eat 3A-3I
      How did the snake eat your foot and when did he do it?

The situation gets more complex when negation is added to one of the conjuncts. The only text example of this is given in (281) (though in the course of the story this particular construction is repeated three times.)

(281) laa de y-na   pe [s-u   noo   men]   MANSNAKE 43
      FM   2   P-say Q   F-eat   1EX   3

      o   [g-u-t   noo   men]
      or P-eat-NEG   1EX   3
      You say whether I should eat him or I should not eat him.

Example (281) seems to be a clear case of coordination under the embedded complementizer *pe*. The key issue is what category is being coordinated. Under the assumption—illustrated in (277)—that the NegP projection is present only in negative clauses, example (281) is a case of coordination of unlike categories: IP and NegP.

There seem to be three possible solutions to this dilemma. First, we could simply allow coordination of IP and NegP by stipulation. Or, we could question whether there is any difference between IP and NegP and attempt to collapse them back into one projection. The third possibility is to posit that there is always a projection present in all clauses, such as a polarity phrase (similar to the proposal in Laka 1990), that would encompass NegP and allow the coordination in (281) to be at the polarity phrase level. Each of these alternatives will be considered in turn.

---

[109]Alternatively, assuming that the *if* clause is left-adjoined to IP would allow this example to be analyzed as IP coordination.

9.4 Polarity phrase needed to account for clausal coordination

The first solution of simply stipulating that IP and NegP can coordinate is the least satisfactory theoretically.[110] Though there are known cases of coordination of unlike categories, the strong generalization is that only like categories coordinate. I therefore reject this option in search of a more principled proposal.

The second alternative is much more interesting for the theorist. Prior to work by Pollock (1989), negation was simply assumed to be part of Infl, and many linguists still hold the view that IP is projected from a single functional head (as opposed to a nested sequence of functional heads). Thus, example (281) would simply be a case of IP coordination, with the second conjunct carrying the feature [+neg].

This option needs to be seriously considered for QZ, especially since there is no normal use for the specifier of IP. If we assume that the S-structure position for the negative clitic (along with the rest of the verbal complex) is I⁰ rather than Neg⁰, the Negative Criterion could be restated to require specifier-head agreement within IP based on the [+neg] feature. The negative indefinite pronouns would move to the specifier of IP rather than the specifier of NegP, and the two clause structures shown in (277) could be collapsed into one, as illustrated in (282).

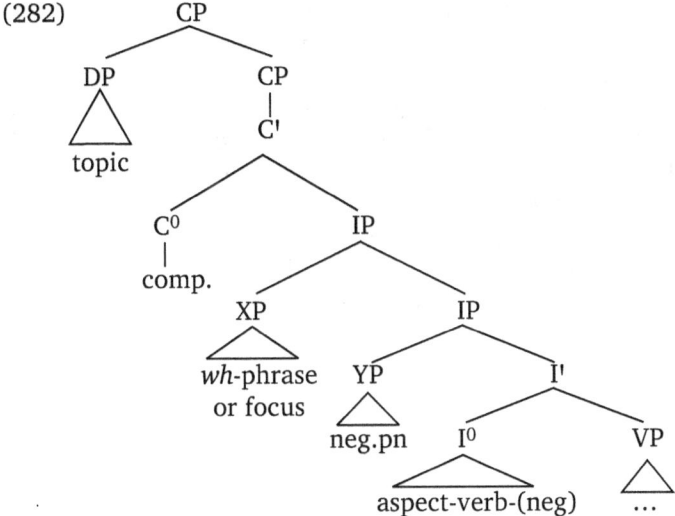

(282)

The clause structure in (282) has several clear advantages over the two clause structures in (277). The unified analysis of clause structure is very

---

[110]This might be a reasonable approach if we allowed coordination to be restricted by semantic type as opposed to syntactic category.

favorable and the problem of coordination of unlike categories disappears. Further, the specifier of IP now has a specific use and one less functional projection is needed.

In QZ, the only empirical reason to reject the proposed clause structure in (282) is found in sentences containing the negative adverbial *gart*, as in (283).

(283) *Jasint* **nunk gart** *ts-a Jasint Pwert* BENIT 29
Jacinto never still.no P-go Jacinto Salina.Cruz
As for Jacinto, he had never gone to Salina Cruz.

In order to achieve the required specifier-head relationship between the head *gart* and the negative indefinite pronoun *nunk*, *gart* would have to occupy I^0 in the configuration in (282). There would then be no position available for the Potential mood marker, and the normal V^0-to-I^0 movement could not occur.

A further problem arises if we broaden the task to analyzing Zapotec in general. Recall from chapter 8 that the same analysis given for negation in QZ was straightforwardly extendable to MZ. For MZ, we made use of the specifier of IP position as an A-position to which the subject moves in a clause which is negated by one of the free negative words. These negative words were assumed to be base generated in the specifier of NegP. (See §8.2.2.1, example (233a) and tree (235).) In order to preserve the same basic analysis, if there is no NegP projection then the free negative word must be base generated in the specifier of IP. This leaves no position available for the subject to surface in front of the verb, which has moved to I^0 to obtain the aspect marking. We could possibly say that the subject moves to adjoin directly to the free negative word in the specifier of IP, but then we have lost the account for why the subject may not precede the verb when the negative clitic is overtly present on the verb. This account is illustrated in (284) for (233a).

9.4 Polarity phrase needed to account for clausal coordination

(284)   S-structure

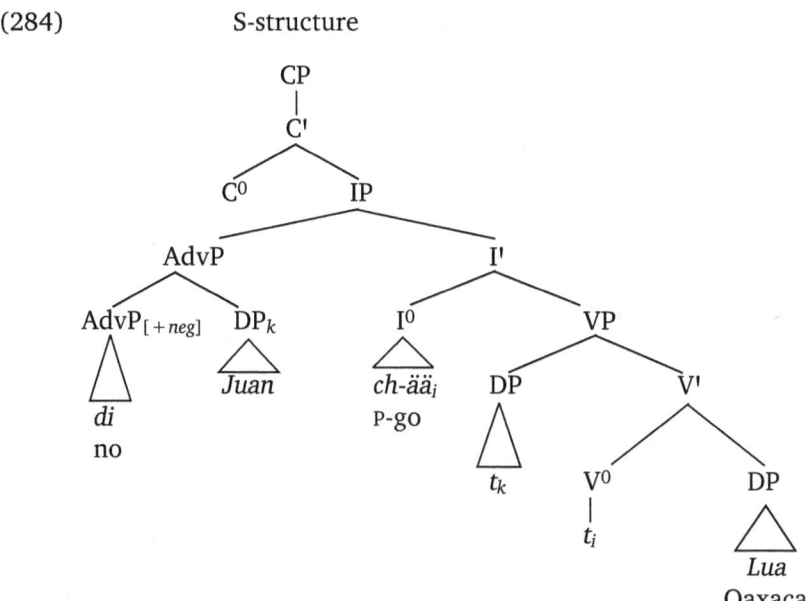

This adjunction seems somewhat strange and hard to motivate, especially since it would have to be stipulated that it occurs only when a free negative word occupies the specifier of IP and the negative clitic is not present in I^0.

The third hypothesis unifies the two clause structures in (277) by expanding the structure of the assertive clauses. I propose that there is a polarity phrase (PolP) between CP and IP in every clause. When the polarity of the clause is negative, PolP is headed by the negative clitic -*t* (or *gart* 'still no' or the negative existential verb *yët*), and the negative indefinite pronouns surface in the specifier of PolP. Positive polarity seems to be completely unmarked, so each position within PolP is null in such a case.[111]

Laka (1990:chapter 2) proposes a functional projection which she calls ΣP (following a suggestion by Pesetsky) to encompass the speech acts of affirmation and denial. Laka claims that at least some natural languages have overt morphemes or special processes to express emphatic affirmation (such as **do** and **so** in English) that can be seen as the counterpart to

---

[111]This might seem inconsistent with my rejection of a FocP projection because Foc^0 is never overtly realized. In that case, however, the focused phrases and especially the *wh*-phrases that would occupy the specifier position bear a crucial relationship with C^0 rather than Foc^0. It is also quite possible that there are morphemes associated with positive polarity or emphatic affirmation in other Zapotecan languages. I do not know of any in QZ.

negation. My proposal of a polarity phrase is distinct from Laka's ΣP. I propose that every clause, including embedded ones, has a polarity phrase while Laka does not claim that there is any such projection for regular declarative sentences and it is unclear whether or not ΣP is a property of matrix clauses only. It may well be that the items that Laka claims are part of ΣP could be incorporated into the polarity phrase I am proposing. The declarative sentences could still be the unmarked case and negative constructions would still mark negative polarity. Strong affirmation could simply be a marked case of positive polarity.

The benefits of adopting the polarity phrase for both negative and assertive clauses are that the analysis of negative fronting can be maintained for MZ as well as all negative clauses in QZ and the problem of coordination between NegP and IP is eliminated. The coordination seen in (280) is now simply coordination of embedded polarity phrases. Whether or not such a phrase is needed in other languages is dependent upon the analysis chosen for the position and category of negation, the word order, and the interaction between negation and other aspects of the grammar of a given language. For example, Chung and McCloskey (1987) and McCloskey (1991) analyze negation as always being realized in C^0 in Irish (also a VSO language). Such an analysis allows an example like (281) to simply be coordination at the CP level, making PolP unnecessary. Placing negation in C^0 is not an option in QZ since negative elements occur after an overt complementizer.

9.5 Proposed clause structure for QZ

To reiterate, the clause structure I am proposing for QZ is given in (285), showing the number of projections and the S-structure positions of the various types of phrases. This clause structure accounts for the lack of co-occurrence between *wh*-phrases and focused phrases and for the relative ordering required between complementizers, *wh*-phrases or focused phrases, and negative elements. The Polarity Phrase unifies assertive and negative clauses and allows for attested coordination at the PolP-level.[112]

---

[112] The verbal complex moves to Pol^0 from I^0 only if the negative clitic is present.

9.5 Proposed clause structure for QZ

(285)

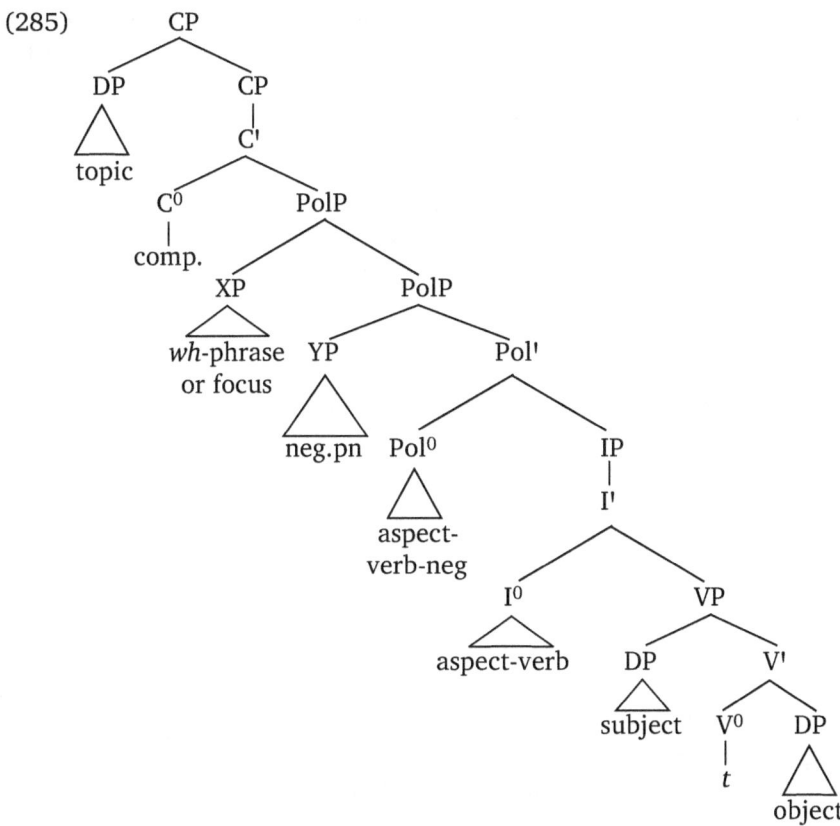

All three constructions involving Ā-movement (focus, question formation, and negation) require the relevant element to be fronted. This fronting achieves the result that scope relations are determined at S-structure, with only very limited LF-movement being allowed.

I posited (following Rizzi 1991, Haegeman and Zanuttini 1990, and Zanuttini 1991) that such fronting is motivated not only by the desire for scope relations to be readable at S-structure, but also by the adjacency requirements between an affective operator and a head bearing that particular feature. For QZ, only the negation constructions follow the usual specifier-head relationship; both *wh*-phrases and focused phrases must be governed by the appropriate head (C^0) and must be strictly adjacent to it.

Strict adjacency holds between a verb and its subject and other arguments. This required adjacency still holds even when the verb has moved to I^0 and to Pol^0 (in the case of negation) and serves to effectively limit the possible adjunction sites. For example, adverbials may not be left-adjoined to either

VP or IP, since this would violate the adjacency required between the verb and its subject. (286) shows that a free adverbial such as *yzhe* 'tomorrow' may not occur between the verb and the subject nor between the subject and the other complements; only the sentence-initial or clause-final positions are allowed.

(286) a. *yzhe*   *ts-a*   *noo*   *Mejiko*
         tomorrow   P-go   1EX   Mexico
         Tomorrow I will go to Mexico City.

     b. *ts-a yzhe   *noo Mejiko*
         P-go tomorrow 1EX   Mexico
         (I will go tomorrow to Mexico City.)

     c. *ts-a noo yzhe   *Mejiko*
         P-go 1EX   tomorrow Mexico
         (I will go tomorrow to Mexico City.)

     d. *ts-a   noo   Mejiko   yzhe*
         P-go   1EX   Mexico   tomorrow
         I will go to Mexico City tomorrow.

     e. *Mejiko   ts-a   noo   yzhe*
         Mexico   P-go   1EX   tomorrow
         To Mexico City I will go tomorrow.

(287) verifies that a similar adjacency requirement between the verb and its subject (and other complements) holds even when the verb is negated. This means that left-adjunction to both VP and IP is disallowed.

(287) a. *nak*   *w-a-t*   *noo*   *Mejiko*
         yesterday   C-go-NEG   1EX   Mexico
         Yesterday I did not go to Mexico City.

     b. *w-a-t   *nak*   *noo Mejiko*
         C-go-NEG   yesterday   1EX   Mexico
         (I did not go yesterday to Mexico City.)

     c. *w-a-t   *noo   nak*   *Mejiko*
         C-go-NEG   1EX   yesterday   Mexico
         (I did not go yesterday to Mexico City.)

9.5 Proposed clause structure for QZ

    d. *w-a-t   noo Mejiko   nak*
       C-go-NEG 1EX Mexico yesterday
       I did not go to Mexico City yesterday.

    e. *Mejiko w-a-t   noo nak*
       Mexico C-go-NEG 1EX yesterday
       To Mexico City I did not go yesterday.

McCloskey (1991) explores similar restrictions in Irish. He concludes that they are due to the strong adjacency requirement between the verb and subject imposed by Case assignment taking place under government. Just as a verb and its object normally require adjacency in SVO languages, the same holds true between a verb and its subject in VSO languages.

This restriction against left-adjunction to VP brings up a potential problem for the Verb Movement proposal for VSO clause structure that was adopted for QZ. Recall from chapter 8 that the Verb Movement proposal accounts for the fact that both aspect marking and the negation marker surface on the verb via head movement. We need to consider this account more closely with respect to a fully affixed verb, as in (288), where the negative marker appears inside of the two adverbial suffixes.

(288) *g-oo-t-re-ke   noo nis*
      P-drink-NEG-MORE-ASSOC 1EX water
      I will not drink more water either.

Under the account proposed in §8.2.1, the negative marker *-t* is in Neg^0, and V^0-to-I^0-to-Neg^0 movement causes the negation to be realized on the inflected verb. This means that the adverbial suffixes must be left-adjoined to VP, since they must precede the subject in the specifier of VP and, as is clear when there is no negation and hence only V^0-to-I^0 movement takes place, follow I^0. We must also assume that their dependent phonological status is responsible for their attachment to V^0. The S-structure for (288) under this account is given in (289), with Neg^0 changed to Pol^0 and NegP to PolP.

(289)   S-structure

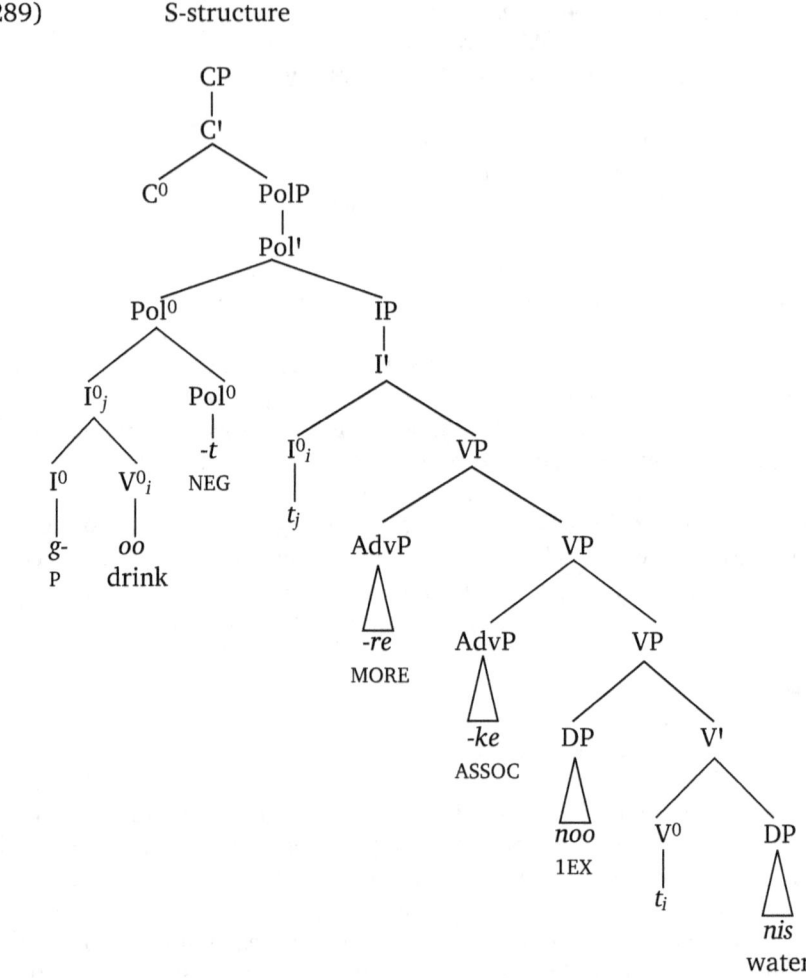

The structure in (289) is problematic for two reasons. First, if the adverbials are simply adjoined to VP, we have no account for the fact that -*re* 'MORE' and -*ke* 'ASSOC' must be realized in that order only. The second and more crucial problem is that the two adverbial "phrases" intervene between the inflected verb and its subject. We saw above that this position is not allowed for free adverbials.

These two problems with the structure in (289) lead to the alternative proposal that the adverbial suffixes -*re* 'MORE' and -*ke* 'ASSOC' are simply verbal suffixes, thus part of V⁰ syntactically. I appeal to the affixal nature of the suffixes to distinguish them from the free adverbials. This appeal to

9.5 Proposed clause structure for QZ

the morphology makes it necessary to treat the QZ negative marker -*t* as a verbal suffix and thus also part of V⁰ syntactically, since the adverbial suffixes occur outside of the negative marker.[113] This V⁰ complex would bear the feature [+*neg*] when the negative marker is present and therefore would be required to move to Neg⁰ (Pol⁰) by S-structure by Clause B of the Negative Criterion (225). This alternative derivation for (288), shown in (290), eliminates the two problems noted with the configuration in (289) while maintaining the rest of the analysis. (For instance, the obligatory fronting of a negative indefinite pronoun would be accounted for exactly as before.) This type of featural checking under syntactic head movement, based upon the morphology, is legitimized in the Minimalist Program (Chomsky 1995). The alternative analysis allows us to resolve the apparent complication and maintain the Verb Movement proposal. At the same time, treating the negative marker -*t* simply as a verbal suffix, rather than a separate syntactic head, represents a significant weakening of the hypothesis that each inflectional affix transparently reflects a syntactic head (both in hierarchical structure and in linear order).

---

[113]In MZ, the negative marker is clearly a clitic rather than simply a verbal suffix, since it appears at the end of V⁰ or at the end of a fronted constituent which is marked with a negative quantifier. For MZ, then, we can retain the analysis that the negative clitic -*di* is in Neg⁰ at D-structure.

(290)   S-structure

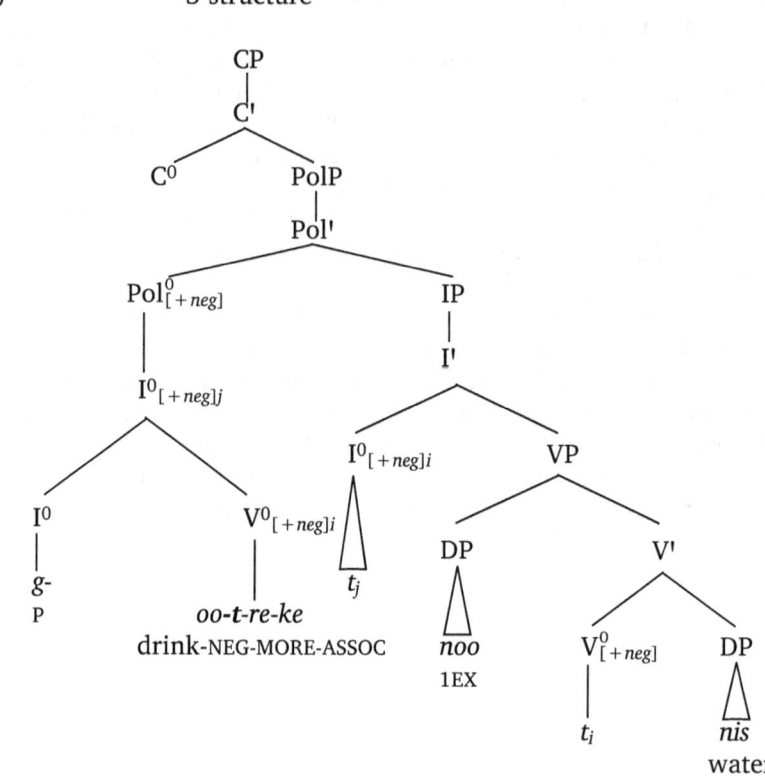

Returning to the issue of the possible positions for adverbials, we saw that the two most common positions are clause-initial and clause-final. Neither of these are problematic for any of the adjacency requirements. The only other position where adverbials can surface is after a focused phrase or *wh*-phrase but before the verb, as shown in (291). I analyze this as left-adjunction to PolP, since (291c) verifies that the adverbial occurs above the negated verb.

(291) a. laad   x-unaa   Dolf   **dxe**   zu   nga   HORTENS 37
         FM   POS-woman   Rodolfo already   PR/stand   there
         Rodolfo's wife was already standing there.

   b. txu   **dxe**   zu   nga   HORTENS 37A
       who   already   PR/stand   there
       Who was already standing there?

9.5 Proposed clause structure for QZ

c. *pe **rsil** w-u-t   maa nii de*   SAMUEL 28A
   Q morning C-eat-NEG 3A foot 2
   Didn't the snake eat your foot this morning?

Left-adjunction to PolP below the focused phrase or *wh*-phrase is allowed since it does not violate any adjacency requirement; the focused phrase or *wh*-phrase is strictly adjacent to C^0 and the adjacency requirement for negation is met inside the minimal PolP in the specifier position.

Part III

Phrase Structure and Constituent Constructions

10

Structure of Verb Phrases and Nonverbal Predicates

Since the Verb Movement proposal provides the best account of the sentences involving negation, we need to see what is necessary to extend that account to the structure of the predicate phrase. Verbal predicates are considered first in §10.1; additional support for the Verb Movement proposal for QZ is found in the ordering restrictions in the VP complements of the auxiliary constructions, presented in §10.1.1. On the other hand, the apparent examples of VP coordination shown in §10.1.2 are impossible to generate under the Verb Movement analysis, while falling out straightforwardly under the Subject Adjunction hypothesis. An alternative analysis of the few problematic examples salvages the Verb Movement proposal for QZ: they are simply cases of the null third person pronoun that may occur when the antecedent is a full DP (discussed in §4.2.2).

Section 10.2 then looks at clauses with nonverbal predicates. The structure of these clauses seems to split along the lines of the [±V] feature. In general, the [+V] projections pattern just like the clauses with verbal predicates in their predicate-specifier-complement order, while the clauses headed by [−V] predicates have their subject or specifier rightmost, coming after any complements, possessors, and adjoined elements like adjectives. (The related internal structure of argument DPs is treated in chapter 11.)

10.1 The structure of VP

The Verb Movement proposal for clause structure includes the assumption that the subject occupies the specifier of VP (or V^{max}), and that this specifier is on the left. The next section presents supporting evidence from auxiliary constructions. Section 10.1.2 then addresses the challenge posed by apparent VP coordination constructions and provides a feasible alternative analysis which is consistent with the Verb Movement proposal.

10.1.1 Auxiliary constructions with VP complements

QZ has no auxiliary verbs of the type found in English or the European languages, such as modals or *have*.[114] There are two closed classes of verbs, however, that can be considered auxiliaries. The first set is composed of five intransitive verbs of motion: *zob* 'sit', *zu* 'stand', *a* 'go to nonbase', *ya* 'go to base', and *dxiid* 'come'. These motion auxiliaries appear in three constructions:

1. They can be compounded with the participle form of another verb.

(292) *r-a-y-aan   noo x-kuch xnaa   noo*   ESCUELA 19
H-go-PRT-feed 1EX POS-pig mother 1EX
I go feed my mother's pigs.

(293) *w-on   men w-zob-tsaa te   maa*   MANSNAKE 2
C-hear 3   C-sit-shout one   3A
He heard an animal sitting shouting.

(The participle marker *y-*, shown in (292), only appears before vowel-initial verb roots.)

2. They can take a small clause VP complement, as will be discussed in this section.

3. They may select an IP complement and assign their own external argument, thus being full verbs as well as auxiliaries.

---

[114]Some Zapotecan languages, such as MZ, have a modal verb meaning 'can'. (See (230b) in §8.2.2.) This verb acts just like the verb *laan* 'want' in QZ in that it takes an IP complement, with aspect marking on the selected verb, rather than only a VP complement. The modal is therefore treated simply as a full verb.

10.1 The structure of VP

The loan marker *un* acts as an auxiliary which is used with all the borrowed Spanish verb forms. The loan marker can also be analyzed as taking a small clause VP complement. The structure of these VP complements deserves a closer look.

A few examples of the motion auxiliary *a* 'go to nonbase' are given in (294). In each case the subject immediately follows the auxiliary (unless it is focused as in (294c)) which, in turn, is followed by the base form of another verb and its complements.

(294) a. *ts-a noo wii gyoow roo*   TRIPTOQ 49
   P-go 1EX see river big
   I'll go see the big river.

  b. *lex w-a noo wii led-ne n-ak   te gyëël* MTLEMON 43
   later C-go 1EX see body-that S-become one lake
   Later we went to see where there is a lake.

  c. *laad mee-bzaan   noo w-a ye x-yuz* OLDMAN 23
   FM   boy-sibling.opp.sex 1EX C-go search POS-cattle
   My brother went to look for his cows.

The same construction is seen with the loan marker. In QZ whenever a Spanish verb is used, a loan marker *un* is also present. The loan marker, which appears first, carries the aspect marking. The subject immediately follows the loan marker, followed by the Spanish verb and any complements. The form of the Spanish verb used is closely related to the Spanish infinitive form. Examples showing this construction are given in (295). Note that the negative suffix is also carried by the loan marker.

(295) a. *r-un-t men gan ndal med*   GRANDMA3 15
   H-LM-NEG 3 able lots money
   They were not able to earn much money.

  b. *r-un-t noo gan y-tsaa noo leter*   ESCUELA 30
   H-LM-NEG 1EX able P-write 1EX letter
   I didn't know how to write a letter.

  c. *r-un men inbitar y-ra x-kompanyer men* LIFEINUS 51
   H-LM 3   invite   P-all POS-companion   3
   They invite all their companions [over].

d. *bel   r-laan   de g-un   de konoser y-ra   men ne*   TRIPTOQ 87
   if   H-want 2 P-LM 2   know   P-all   3   that

   n-uu nëz-ro   y-dxiin   yner   ts-a-b
   S-be   road-this   P-arrive   January   P-go-1I
   If you want to get to know everyone on this road, when January comes, we'll go.

e. *per bel-ne   g-un-t   de   gan   y-niiz-t   noo*   CWENT 8
   but if-that   P-LM-NEG 2   able P-give-NEG   1EX

   nzeb lo   de
   girl face 2
   But if you can't, I will not give the girl to you.

The pattern seen above with the lower verb preceding its complements is the normal case. Several examples have been found, however, where the object of the Spanish loan verb directly follows the subject, preceding the Spanish loan verb. These are shown in (296). In each case, the Spanish loan verb is *inbitar* 'invite'. The difference seems to be that the object in each case in (296) is a pronoun, whereas in (295c), where the object is a full quantified nominal phrase, the usual pattern is observed, even though the same Spanish verb is used in both cases. The object pronoun is in bold type in each example.

(296) a. *w-un   te   x-mig   x-patron   noo **noo** inbitar*   MTLEMON 2
        C-LM one   POS-friend POS-patron   1EX 1EX   invite

        w-a   noo   teb   gyëël
        C-go   1EX   one   night
        My patron's friend invited me to spend the night.

    b. *r-e   meedx lo   mdxin g-un   noo   **de** inbitar*   RYENEGU 7
        H-say lion   face   deer   P-LM   1EX   2   invite

        ts-a-b   ru   x-yuu   noo
        P-go-1I   mouth   POS-house   1EX
        The lion said to the deer, "I invite you to go to my house."

10.1 The structure of VP

c. *g-un noo **de** inbitar porke na dxe-ree*   RYENEGU 12
   P-LM 1EX 2 invite because which day-this

   n-ak xa-lni noo
   S-become POS-party 1EX
   I invite you because today is my birthday party.

We can analyze the six auxiliary-type verbs as selecting VP complements. This immediately accounts for the fact that the second verb exhibits no aspect marking ($=I^0$). If we assume that the auxiliary verbs do not assign an external argument themselves, then the upper subject position will simply be empty under the Verb Movement approach. (Recall from §3.3 that there is only very limited A-movement and no 'raising' in QZ.) Since the Verb Movement proposal makes use of the Internal Subject Hypothesis, the VP complement includes the subject or external argument assigned by the lower verb. Assuming head movement of the auxiliary to I^0 (and on to Pol^0 when it is [+neg]) allows the surface order to be obtained effortlessly, as shown in (297).

(297)   S-structure

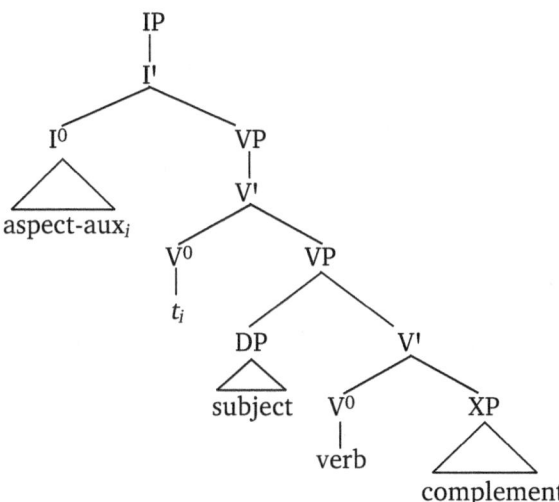

The underlying SVO order for verb phrases (McCloskey 1983) is justified by these examples, confirming the choice of the Verb Movement proposal for QZ.

Further, we can account for the examples in (296) where an object pronoun occurs between the subject and the lower verb as A-movement of the pronominal object to the specifier of VP (= sister of V'). Koopman and Sportiche (1991:239-244) give examples from Bambara, Dutch, and French participles to show that direct objects can appear in the specifier of VP. This, they argue, means that subjects are not in the specifier of VP, but of V^{max}. We already saw that such a move was needed to give a satisfying account of the possibility of moving the DP except for the subject in a negative construction (see example (236b) and trees (237)-(238) in §8.2.2.2). Making this move for VPs allows the structure in (298) for example (296c). Note that all the specifiers of V^0 are on the left.

(298)   S-structure

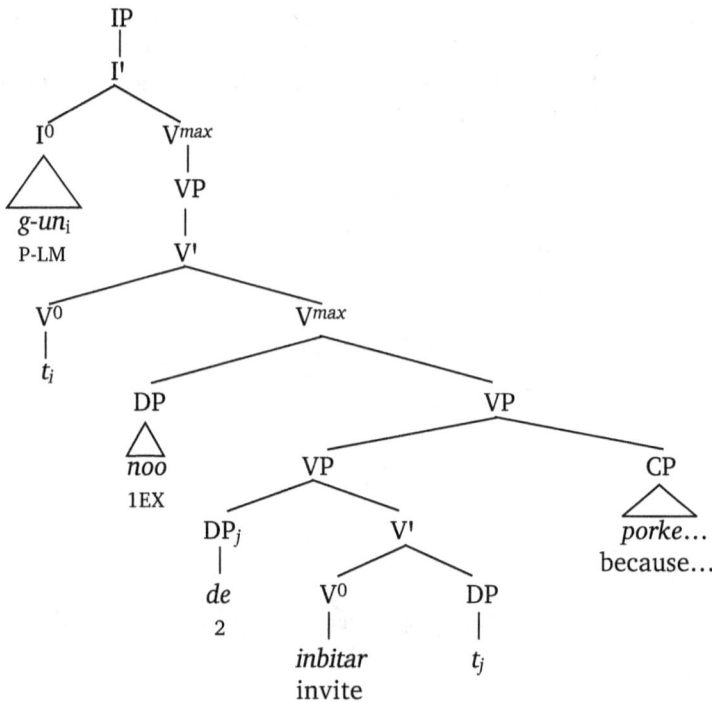

As we found with the negation constructions, these auxiliary constructions are more difficult to deal with under the Subject Adjunction proposal. Since this proposal places the subject in the specifier of IP, we must either assume that the auxiliaries select an external argument themselves

10.1 The structure of VP

(with the requirement that the verb they subcategorize for has the same external argument), or that they do not select an external argument but the one selected by the lower verb occupies the (single) specifier of IP. This subject must then right-adjoin to the auxiliary, as shown in (299), necessitating a stipulation that the subject must adjoin to the leftmost (or highest in terms of hierarchichal structure) V^0 for QZ. Movement of a pronominal object to the specifier of the lower VP is unproblematic.

(299)   S-structure

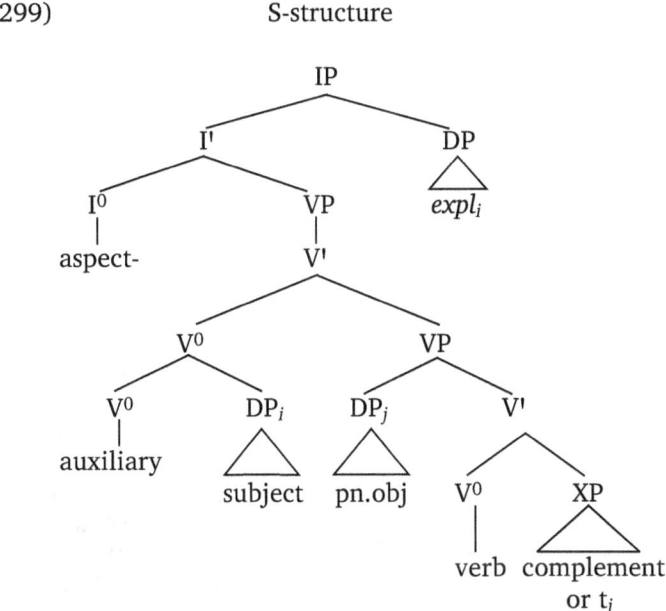

10.1.2 Analysis of the apparent VP coordination constructions

The constructions involving apparent VP or I' coordination pose the greatest challenge to the Verb Movement proposal for QZ. These constructions are easily accounted for under the Subject Adjunction hypothesis, since the subject begins in the specifier of IP which is outside the coordinated structure. In contrast, they are problematic for the Verb Movement proposal for two reasons. First, the subject is internal to the VP; and second, the proposed movement of the verb up to I^0 violates the Coordinate Structure Constraint (Ross 1967). Even if the subject is posited to be in the specifier of IP position and thus outside the coordinate structure, Verb Movement is still problematic. However, a closer look at the data reveals that true VP coordination is not attested in QZ. Instead, the problematic examples are simply cases of the appearance of the null third person pronoun. This analysis enables the Verb Movement proposal to be maintained in fully general form.

We saw in §9.4 that the normal higher-level coordination is between coordinate IPs, as exemplified in (300) for both matrix and embedded IP coordination.

(300) a. che-bel   r-laan   de gaz   de [sob de]   BATHROOM 8
when-if   H-want 2   P-bathe 2   F/sit   2

      o   [su-li   de]
      or F/stand-straight 2
When you want to bathe, sit or stand.

b. g-an   pe s-na   de [g-aa   de lyu]   TRIPTOQ 8
P-know Q   F-want 2   P-lie.down 2   land

      o   [g-aa   de lo   daa]
      or P-lie.down 2   face mat
We'll see if you will want to lie down on the ground or on a mat.

Alongside these clausal coordination examples, there are also examples like those given in (301) which appear to be examples of VP or I' coordination. The key difference between the examples in (301) and those in (300) is that the subject does not appear after the second verb in (301). The presence of a single subject for two or more VPs leads to the assumption that coordination of some category lower than IP is at work in these examples.

(301) a. dxe   w-luzh   w-az   maa [w-zob maa lo   MARTRIST 20
already C-finish C-bathe 3A   C-sit   3A   face

      ngbis] [bwich led   maa]
      sun   C/dry   body 3A
When he had finished bathing, he sat in the sun and dried his body.

10.1 The structure of VP

  b. *lux lo [g-aa noo lër]   [zoob-ke   noo niz]* LIFEINQ 16
    finish face P-wash 1EX clothes F/shell-also 1EX corn

    [g-eey nil   s-te ne y-kaa gyët   yzhe]
    P-cook corn.meal F-one that P-do   tortilla tomorrow
    After that, I will wash the clothes and also shell the corn and cook more corn meal that will make tortillas tomorrow.

  c. *la xnaa   noo [r-yaan x-kuch] [r-yaan x-kyed]*   LIFEINQ 14–15
    FM mother 1EX H-feed POS-pigs H-feed POS-chickens
    My mother feeds the pigs and the chickens.

  d. *[bweree x-yag   men] [w-nii   lo   xuz   nzaap gin* CWENT 6
    C/return nephew 3   C-speak face father girl   this

    ne y-ka men xsaap   men]
    that P-buy 3   daughter 3
    His nephew$_i$ returned and said to this girl's father$_k$ that he$_i$ would marry his$_k$ daughter.

  e. *chene [w-yab te   mër   gos]   [r-e   lo   maa]*   MARTRIST 2
    when   C-fall one pigeon female H-say face 3A
    When a female pigeon landed and said to him...

The examples in (301) deserve a closer look to determine whether there are obvious reasons which can account for the missing subject in the second conjunct. Therefore, each example will be discussed in turn.

Example (301a) is actually not a clear example of VP coordination, since there are two very plausible alternative explanations for why the subject of the second conjunct is "missing." The best explanation is that no external argument is assigned by the verb, so the subject is not really "missing" at all. *Bich* 'dry' is an unaccusative verb, so no argument involving an Agent θ-role is selected, as discussed in §3.3. The conjunct simply reads 'his body dried'. The sun, not the pigeon, did the actual drying. Alternatively, if there were an Agent argument present, it could be covert since it would be coreferent with the possessor of the object. Throughout most of the Zapotecan languages, a subject may be unexpressed if it is coreferent with the possessor of the object of the same verb. See §§4.1 and 12.2.1.1 for further discussion of this phenomenon.

Example (301b), likewise, has two plausible alternative explanations for the "missing" subject after the verb *g-eey* 'P-cook'. This verb is also unaccusative, so no Agent θ-role is selected. Strictly speaking, (301b) is noncommittal about who will do the cooking. As discussed in §3.3, the Agent θ-role associated with the verb *eey* 'cook' is only expressed when the Causative morpheme is added, as shown in (302).

(302) chene r-beree   noo lët me dxe   w-gw-eey   kafe   LIFEINQ 4
when H-return 1EX FM 3R already C-CAUS-cook coffee
When I returned, she (my mother) had made the coffee.

The other alternative in this case would be to assume that (301b) is a control construction with *PRO* as the subject of *g-eey* 'P-cook', since the Potential mood marker can signal a nonfinite construction.

In (301c) a focused phrase is the subject of two VPs which are headed by the same verb and have the same Habitual aspect marking. This can be analyzed as IP coordination with Across the Board Extraction of the subjects to the focus position, as shown in (305).

(301a–c) can therefore be analyzed instead as cases of IP coordination. These alternate analyses are not available in examples (301d–e), however. Further, QZ is not a *pro*-drop language so we cannot assume the subject of the second conjunct is *pro* (VanValin 1986, Godard 1989).

In (301d) the subject is in its normal place following the first verb, but it is interpreted as the subject of the second VP as well. In this example there are two distinct verbs but both are in the Completive aspect. Example (301e) has both distinct verbs and distinct aspect marking, again with the subject of both VPs appearing only after the first verb. These constructions thus appear to involve VP and/or I' coordination. We consider next how each of the proposals for clause structure can account for such constructions.

10.1.2.1 The Subject Adjunction account. Chung (1990) argues for the Subject Adjunction proposal for Chamorro based primarily on the attested VP coordination constructions, which are quite a bit more robust in Chamorro than in QZ. No movement out of the coordinate VP or I' structure is required under this proposal, and lowering of the subject to adjoin to the verb in the first conjunct will account for the surface word order.[115]

Chung (1990) shows that the Subject Adjunction hypothesis provides an account of all the variation in the VP coordination structures attested in Chamorro. Such a hypothesis can also account quite well for the QZ examples (301c–e) by treating them as cases of either VP or I' coordination.

---

[115]Here again as in the auxiliary constructions, QZ requires the stipulation that the subject may only adjoin to the first or leftmost verb. In contrast, Chamorro allows the subject to adjoin to any projection of V^0 in either conjunct.

10.1 The structure of VP

For example, (301d) could be analyzed as having coordinate VPs with the D-structure shown in (303). The subject then right-adjoins to the leftmost verb, producing the correct surface order.

(303)   D-structure

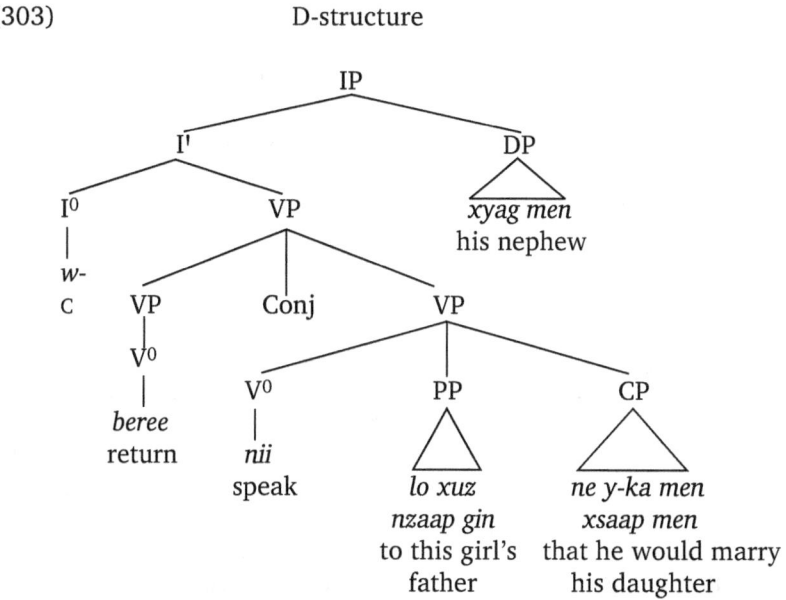

In order to claim that (301d) is correctly analyzed as having coordinate VPs, some explanation must be given to account for the aspect marking appearing on both verbs in the conjoined structure. Such an account would require the inflection feature to pass to the head(s) of its complement and be overtly realized there. I claim that an analysis of the aspect markers as morphological and syntactic words but as phonological clitics would be more correct for QZ overall, however, making the aspect markers parallel to the phonologically dependent pronouns. This means that the aspect marker would simply occupy I^0 in the syntax, with the phonological component determining which parts join together to be realized as single words.

Under this analysis of the aspect markers, (301d) would be analyzed as coordinate I's instead. Further, the coordinate I' structure will allow for cases where the aspect is different on the two verbs in the conjoined structure, as in (301e). The analysis of sentence (301d) as coordinate I's can also be easily accounted for under the Subject Adjunction proposal, since the subject also originates above I'. In this case the D-structure would be as shown in (304).

(304)   D-structure

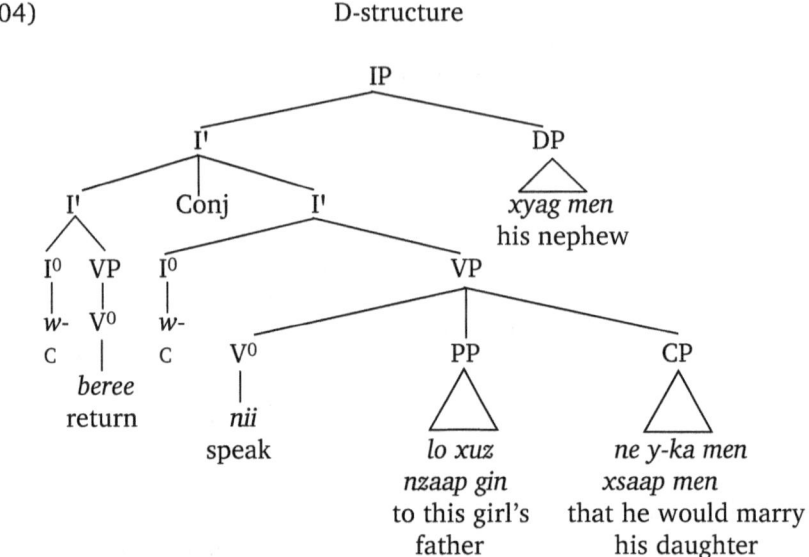

The subject still right-adjoins to the leftmost verb, and the correct surface order is obtained, showing that the Subject Adjunction proposal can account quite nicely for these coordination constructions.

10.1.2.2 The Verb Movement dilemma. On the other hand, VP or I' coordination is quite problematic for the Verb Movement proposal. (301c) can be accounted for under the Verb Movement hypothesis because it can be analyzed as coordinate IPs where the subject has been focused via Across the Board Extraction (Williams 1978). The D-structure for (301c) under this analysis is shown in (305).

10.1 The structure of VP   223

(305)   D-structure

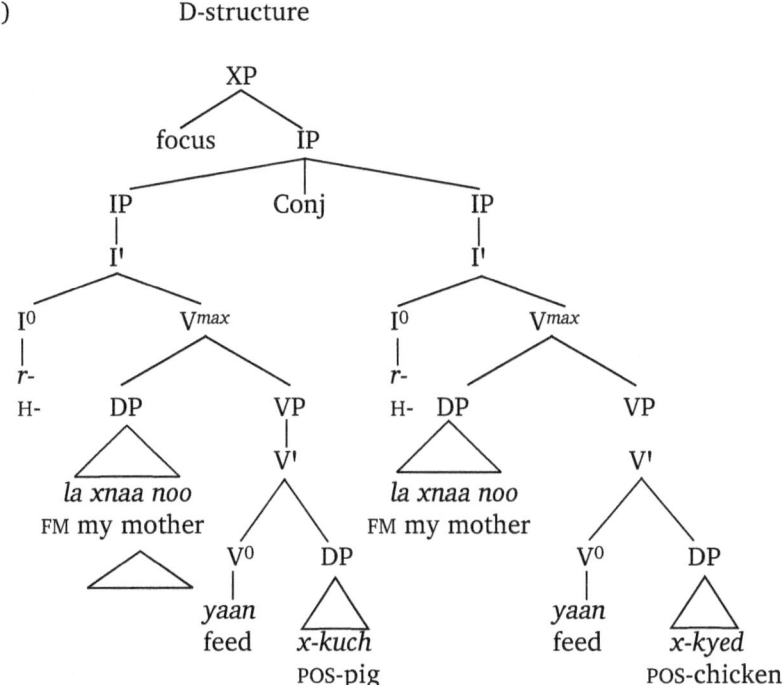

From this D-structure, V^0-to-I^0 movement within each conjunct and Across the Board Extraction of both subjects to the focus position will give the correct surface order.

McCloskey (1991) shows that the Verb Movement proposal can also account for coordination examples which have the same verb heading each conjunct, as in example (306), since the V^0-to-I^0 movement can apply as an Across the Board Extraction.[116]

---

[116]Though (306) is possible in QZ, full clausal coordination with the verb repeated in each conjunct is preferred. This example might also be assumed to be an instance of Gapping. Section 10.1.2.3 shows that the only types of constructions analyzable as Gapping that are attested in QZ are those that can be accounted for via Across the Board Extraction of the verb to Infl, as in (306).

(306) [r-yaan xnaa   noo x-kuch che-mart]   **no** [x-kyed
       H-feed mother 1EX POS-pig day-Tuesday and POS-chicken

   che-myerk]
   day-Wednesday

My mother feeds her pigs on Tuesday and her chickens on Wednesday.

The D-structure assumed for (306) is given in (307), where the coordination is at the VP level within V^{max}.

(307)   D-structure

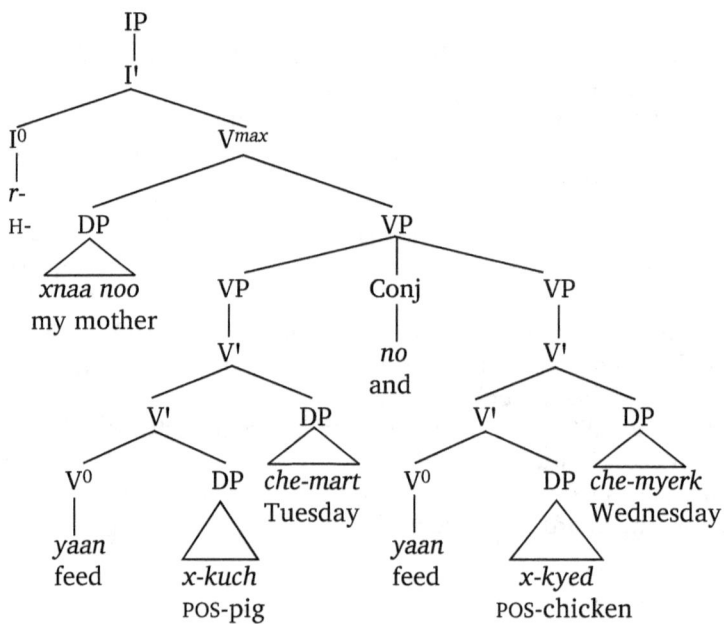

V^0-to-I^0 movement can apply from this D-structure as an Across the Board Extraction from the coordinate structure to produce the surface order given in (306). Such movement is not possible when the two verbs are distinct, though.[117] McCloskey (1991) shows that this is the correct prediction for Irish, since examples such as (301d) are ungrammatical in that language.

---

[117]Similar results hold for coordination of IP under negation; both the verbs and the aspect marking must be identical for V^0-to-I^0-to-Pol^0 movement to occur as an Across the Board Extraction. Even in this case, coordination of PolP, with repetition of the negated verb in both clauses, is preferred.

10.1 The structure of VP

Examples (301d–e) are grammatical in QZ, however, so the correct analysis must have an account for them. We can explore a few more options under the Verb Movement approach with different levels of coordination before abandoning a straight coordinate structure account for these problematic examples.

Since the Verb Movement proposal has the subject starting and remaining internal to VP, one analysis is to posit that (301d) simply has coordinate verbs at D-structure,[118] as shown in tree (308).

(308)   D-structure

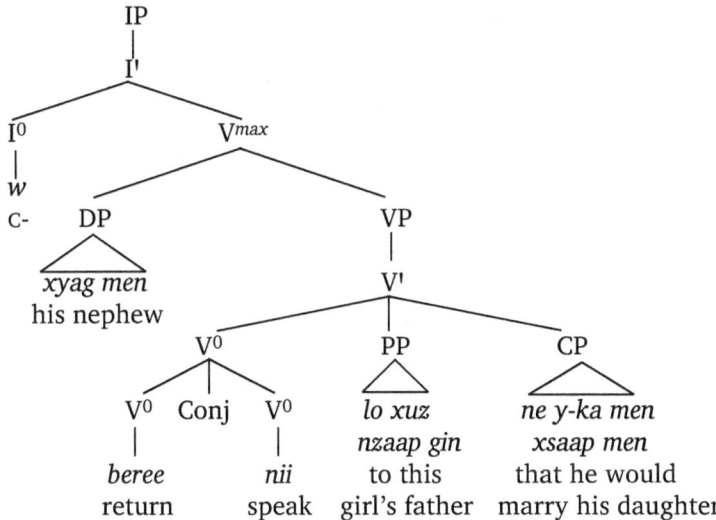

The proposed movement of the coordinate verb structure to right-adjoin to Infl will not produce the correct surface order, however. Instead, only the order given in (309) would obtain, which is ungrammatical. The subject must follow the first verb in a nonparticiple construction.

---

[118](301d) is also grammatical with the overt conjunction *no* 'and' between the conjuncts (i.e., after the subject), casting further doubt on the credibility of a coordinate verb analysis.

(309) *bwere-nii   xyag   men lo   xuz   nzaap gin
      C/return-speak nephew 3   face father girl   this

   ne   y-ka   men xsaap   men
   that P-buy 3   daughter 3
   (His nephew returned speaking to this girl's father that he would marry his daughter.)

Further, the Verb Movement proposal provides no way to account for the different aspects marked on the two verbs in (301e). To allow for the differing aspects, this coordination must be at either the I' or IP level. But this means each conjunct has its own VP complement, which again requires that there be two overt subjects. (310) shows the resulting S-structure tree after Verb Movement has applied to a coordinate I' structure, but this only generates a version of (301e) in which each predicate has its own overt subject (as in the normal case of IP coordination).

(310)   S-structure

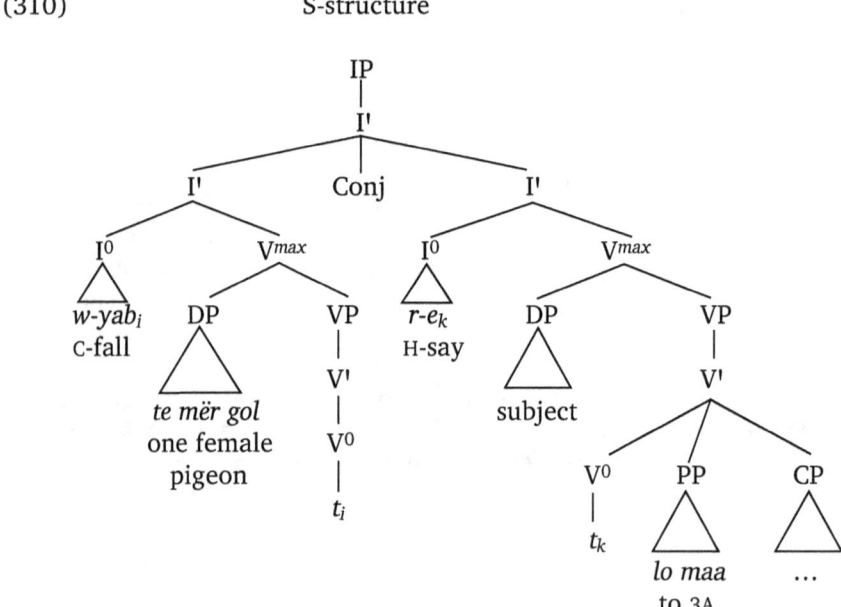

The problem with deriving examples like (301d–e) is not simply that the subject begins inside the coordinate structure. Even if the subject occupies the specifier of IP position above a coordinate I' structure, as in (311) for (301e), either by being base generated there or by being extracted Across the

10.1 The structure of VP

Board from the coordinate structure, it is still impossible to obtain the attested surface order under the Verb Movement hypothesis. The crucial problem is still the needed movement of the first verb out of the coordinate structure to precede the subject, violating the Coordinate Structure Constraint (Ross 1967), which QZ otherwise follows.

(311)   *S-structure

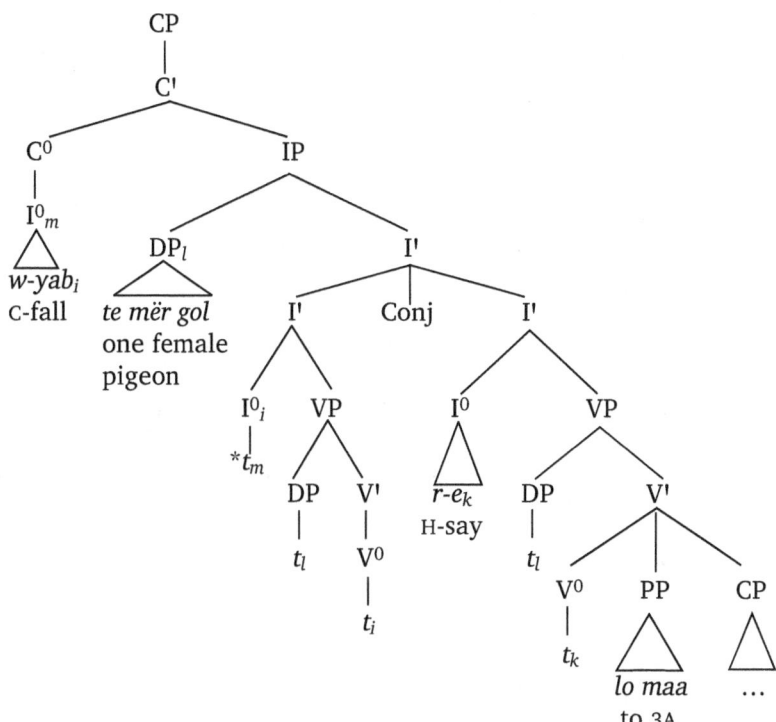

The Verb Movement proposal simply cannot account for examples like (301d–e) as coordination structures. If it is truly the correct proposal for QZ, there must be some alternative account of the problematic examples.

10.1.2.3 Possible alternative analyses. The first alternative that comes to mind is a deletion analysis, such as Gapping or Stripping. Examples like (312a) cannot be accounted for by a level of coordination below the sentence level. In this sense, (312a) is parallel to the problematic QZ examples (301d–e).

(312) a. Greg hit the ball to Jeff and Bill to Sam.

b. Greg hit the ball to Jeff and Bill hit the ball to Sam.

A deletion analysis, commonly referred to as Gapping, is proposed for these cases by Ross (1970), Jackendoff (1971), Hankamer (1970, 1979), Neijt (1979) and others. We need to take a closer look at the characteristics of Gapping constructions, to see if the QZ constructions can be analyzed as Gapping.

The basic properties of Gapping are given in (313),[119] with illustrative examples following in (314).[120]

(313) Basic Properties of Gapping:

a. The coordinate structure must involve direct coordination; neither coordinate may be embedded (314b). Only 'and' and 'or' can be the conjunctions.

b. The conjuncts must have parallel structure (314l).

c. Coreferent elements are deleted from the nonleftmost conjuncts, usually leaving behind only two constituents (314a,c,g–h,j). The verb is usually deleted; if it is, all auxiliaries and preverbal adverbs must also be deleted (314c–e, g–h).

d. Island constraints are obeyed (314k–l).

(314) a. Bob likes salmon and Bill roast beef.

b. *Bob likes salmon and Sue said Bill roast beef.

c. Bob really likes salmon and Bill roast beef.

d. *Bob really likes salmon and Bill really roast beef.

e. *Bob really likes salmon and Bill sort of roast beef.

f. *Beth ate yogurt and Norma at midnight.

---

[119]I am indebted to Jorge Hankamer for discussion of the information on Gapping and Stripping. Some of it is also found in Hankamer (1979:chapter 3).

[120](314f) is taken from Goodall (1987:79) and (314k–l) are from Neijt (1979:24).

10.1 The structure of VP

g. I lent Harvey a nickel and Sue a dime.

h. I might lend Harvey a nickel and Sue a dime.

i. *I might lend Harvey a nickel and should Sue a dime.

j. I lent Harvey a nickel last week and Sue a dime on Tuesday.

k. *That Alfonse ate the rice is fantastic and Harry the beans.

l. *Alan discussed the question of which rice we would eat and Harry which beans.

Stripping is very similar to Gapping, except that it only strands one maximal projection. Stripping constructions are most frequently found in the elliptical responses to questions, thus extending beyond the sentence level. The close adjacency required in these question-answer pairs is parallel to the direct coordination requirement for Gapping.

(315) a. Where did you go yesterday?

b. To the beach.

c. What did you do there?

d. Dug for sand crabs.

Gapping and Stripping constructions are unique in that they seem to care more about what type of constituent is left behind than about what is deleted. This is in contrast to constructions such as VP-deletion, Sluicing, and N'-deletion in possessed noun phrases, and to gaps in relative clauses and comparative clauses.[121] Identity is still required for deletion.

The Gapping rule is basically "Delete under identity in parallel coordinate structures, leaving behind only maximal projections." (See Hankamer 1979 and Neijt 1979 for alternative formulations.) If, as Neijt argues, there is no limitation to exactly two constituents left behind, then Stripping in parallel

---

[121]It is possible to assume that the gaps in VP-deletion, Sluicing, and N'-deletion in possessed noun phrases are a type of null pronominal, and that the gaps in relative clauses and comparative clauses are a type of null anaphor such as a trace (Jorge Hankamer, p.c.). The missing elements in the Gapping and Stripping constructions are more problematic, however, since they need not form a constituent and they do not pattern with any other known type of gap. I know of no analysis of Gapping or Stripping constructions within the Principles and Parameters framework.

coordinate structures can also be subsumed under this rule. The QZ examples (repeated in (316) in bracketed form) do not really have parallel structure, however, making a Subject Gapping account seem rather dubious. In each case, the structure is V S V_IO CP.

(316) a. *[bweree   [x-yag   men]] (no) [w-nii   _ [lo   xuz   nzaap*
       C/return nephew   3   (and) C-speak   face father girl

   gin] [ne   y-ka   men xsaap   men]]
   this that P-buy 3   daughter 3
   His nephew$_i$ returned and said to this girl's father$_k$ that he$_i$ would marry his$_k$ daughter.

b. *chene [w-yab [te   mër   gos]]   [r-e   _ [lo   maa] [CP...]]*
   When C-fall one   pigeon female H-say   face 3A   ...
   When a female pigeon landed and said to him,...

I therefore reject a Subject Gapping analysis due to the lack of parallel structure in the problematic examples.[122]

As a second alternative, one might wonder whether the first verb must always be an intransitive verb of motion, as in the two problematic examples. Perhaps *beree* 'return' and *yab* 'fall' should be added to the motion auxiliaries listed in the last section. We saw there that in the auxiliary construction, the single subject appears directly after the first (auxiliary) verb, as it does in (316) (repeated from (301d–e)). Note, however, that the second verb in each example carries aspect marking. Those examples therefore cannot be auxiliary constructions taking a VP complement. The fact that an overt conjunction is allowed before the second verb further rules out an auxiliary construction analysis.

The crucial fact to note is that VP/I' coordination is not generally productive in QZ. Normally the subject must be repeated in each conjunct. The examples in (316) are the only text examples found without a repeated subject. What makes these examples special is that the subject is a full nominal phrase. Recall from chapter 4 that there is a hierarchy of types of nominal phrases. Quantified nominal phrases are at the top and pronouns are at the bottom of this hierarchy, with modified or possessed nominals, proper names, and common nouns in the middle. Whereas

---

[122]Rosenbaum (1974:21–37) claims that a wide range of Gapping constructions are possible in Valley Zapotec, as responses to questions like "What do they have?", "What will they eat?", and "What did they make there?".

Only the VSO + SO + SO pattern he cites, which is obtainable by Across The Board Extraction of V^0-to-I^0, is attested in QZ.

10.1 The structure of VP

pronouns must always be repeated, those nominals higher in the hierarchy may antecede a null third person pronoun. I believe this null third person pronoun is present in the two problematic examples.

This is illustrated in the following paradigm. (317a) again contains the text example, where the subject is missing in the second conjunct. (317b), with the full subject from the first conjunct repeated, is also acceptable, though my language consultant prefers using an overt pronoun, as in (317c) over both (317a) and (317b). If the subject in the first conjunct is instead a proper name, such as *José*, then it may either be "missing" in the second conjunct (317d), or *José* may be repeated (317e), or an overt pronoun may be used (317f). In this case, my language consultant prefers repeating *José* to avoid conflict with an alternative reference for the pronoun. Finally, as predicted under this analysis, if the initial subject is a pronoun, it must be repeated (317g–h).

(317) a. *[bweree x-yag   men] [w-nii – lo   xuz   nzaap* CWENT 6
       c/return nephew 3   c-speak   face father girl

   gin ne   y-ka   men xsaap   men]
   this that P-buy   3   daughter 3
   His nephew$_i$ returned and said to this girl's father$_k$ that he$_i$ would marry his$_k$ daughter.

   b. *[bweree x-yag   men] [w-nii   x-yag   men lo   xuz*
       c/return nephew 3   c-speak nephew 3   face father

   nzaap gin ne   y-ka   men xsaap   men]
   girl this that P-buy   3   daughter 3
   His nephew$_i$ returned and his nephew$_i$ said to this girl's father$_k$ that he$_i$ would marry his$_k$ daughter.

   c. *[bweree x-yag   men] [w-nii   men lo   xuz   nzaap*
       c/return nephew 3   c-speak   3   face father girl

   gin ne   y-ka   men xsaap   men]
   this that P-buy   3   daughter 3
   His nephew$_i$ returned and he$_i$ said to this girl's father$_k$ that he$_i$ would marry his$_k$ daughter.

d. [bweree **Jose**] [w-nii – lo xuz nzaap gin
    c/return José   c-speak   face father girl this

   ne y-ka Jose xsaap men]
   that P-buy José daughter 3

José$_i$ returned and said to this girl's father$_k$ that he$_i$ would marry his$_k$ daughter.

e. [bweree **Jose**] [w-nii **Jose** lo xuz nzaap gin
    c/return José   c-speak José face father girl this

   ne y-ka Jose xsaap men]
   that P-buy José daughter 3

José$_i$ returned and José$_i$ said to this girl's father$_k$ that he$_i$ would marry his$_k$ daughter.

f. [bweree **Jose**] [w-nii **men** lo xuz nzaap gin
    c/return José   c-speak 3   face father girl this

   ne y-ka men xsaap men]
   that P-buy 3 daughter 3

José$_i$ returned and he$_i$ said to this girl's father$_k$ that he$_i$ would marry his$_k$ daughter.

g. *[bweree **noo/men**] [w-nii – lo xuz nzaap gin
    c/return 1EX/3   c-speak   face father girl this

   ne y-ka noo/men xsaap men]
   that P-buy 1EX/3 daughter 3

(I/he$_i$ returned and said to this girl's father$_k$ that I/he$_i$ would marry his$_k$ daughter.)

h. [bweree **noo/men**] [w-nii **noo/men** lo xuz nzaap
    c/return 1EX/3   c-speak 1EX/3 face father girl

   gin ne y-ka noo/men xsaap men]
   this that P-buy 1EX/3 daughter 3

I/he$_i$ returned and said to this girl's father$_k$ that I/he$_i$ would marry his$_k$ daughter.

10.1 The structure of VP

A very similar distribution is seen with the other problematic example. Again, (318a) is the text example with the missing subject in the second clause.[123] (318b) verifies that the quantified nominal phrase may not be repeated, but without the quantifier, as in (318c), the rest of the phrase is fine as the subject. (318d) shows that a pronoun may also be used in the second clause, though it is somewhat confusing to have two pronouns in the clause with two different referents. Further, if the first subject is a pronoun, the second subject cannot be "missing" (318e), but must be overtly filled (318f). This follows from the analysis that the null third person pronoun requires a nonpronominal antecedent.

(318) a. *chene [w-yab te **mër** **gos**] [r-e _ lo maa]* MARTRIST 2
   when C-fall one pigeon female H-say face 3A
   When a female pigeon landed and said to him,...

   b. **chene [w-yab te **mër** **gos**] [r-e te **mër** **gos***
   when C-fall one pigeon female H-say one pigeon female

   lo maa]
   face 3A
   (When a female pigeon landed and the female pigeon said to him,...)

   c. *chene [w-yab te **mër** **gos**] [r-e **mër** **gos***
   when C-fall one pigeon female H-say pigeon female

   lo maa]
   face 3A
   (When a female pigeon landed and the female pigeon said to him,...)

---

[123]Note that under the analysis that the "missing" subject is simply an instance of the null third person pronoun, example (318a) could instead be analyzed as consisting of an adverbial clause and a main clause, as in "When a female pigeon landed, she said to him..." We saw in chapter 4 that the null third person pronoun is not required to be c-commanded by its antecedent. This allows its presence in a coordinate structure as well as in the adverbial phrase, main clause alternative mentioned here.

d. *chene* [*w-yab* **te** **mër** **gos**] [*r-e* **maa**
   when   c-fall one pigeon female h-say 3A

   lo   *maa*]
   face 3A
   When a female pigeon landed and she said to him,...

e. *chene [*w-yab* **maa**] [*r-e* _ *lo*   **mër**]
   when   c-fall 3A   h-say face pigeon
   (When she/it landed and said to the pigeon,...)

f. *chene* [*w-yab* **maa**] [*r-e* **maa** *lo*   **mër**]
   when   c-fall 3A   h-say 3A face pigeon
   When she/it landed and she/it said to the pigeon,...

With the analysis that the examples of apparent VP or I' coordination are really cases of IP coordination with a null third person pronoun in the subject position in the second conjunct, we can maintain the Verb Movement proposal both for the overall clause structure and for the structure of VP. Further, the Verb Movement proposal correctly predicts that true, productive coordination of either VP or I' is impossible.

10.2 The structure of nonverbal predicates

When we look at the structure of other types of predicate phrases, it is clear that their ordering restrictions are dependent upon the category of the predicate. In copular clauses which do not contain one of the verbal copulas *uu* 'be' or *ak* 'become', the predicate may be an adjective which takes the Stative aspect marker, as illustrated in (319a–c), an adjective which does not take aspect marking (319d),[124] a prepositional phrase (319e), or a nominal phrase (319f).

(319) a. *n-gaa*   *den*   MEXICO 21
     s-green ranch
     The ranch is green.

   b. *n-dux* *xnaa*   *noo* *lo*   *noo*   SNAKHAIR 4
     s-angry mother 1EX face 1EX
     My mother was angry with me.

---

[124]The motivating factor behind this division among the adjectives is unclear.

10.2 The structure of nonverbal predicates

c. *kesentyent   n-yag   x-too   gyeey   gin*   LIFEINUS 68
   much   s-cold   POS-head   mountain   this
   It was very cold on the mountain top.

d. *te   park   win*   BENIT 51
   one   park   small
   One park is small.

e. *Pwert   gex-ndxoo   ruu   nis-too*   BENIT 40
   Salina.Cruz   near-very   mouth   water-head
   Salina Cruz is very near the ocean.

f. *per   x-bur   noo   maa*   BRU 27
   but   POS-burro   1EX   3A
   But it's my burro.

The word order restrictions clearly distinguish between the [+V] and the [−V] predicates. This can be illustrated by comparing (319b) with (319e). (319b) has the order adjective-subject-complement. Further, while the subject can be fronted by focusing, it cannot appear in final position, after the prepositional phrase complement. In contrast, (319e) has the subject, *Pwert*, before the prepositional predicate. The underlying order is with the subject final.[125] The subject cannot appear between the preposition and its complement. Therefore, focusing aside, the required word order in clauses with [−V] predicates is predicate-complement-subject, not predicate-subject-complement.

Across the VSO languages it seems to be a consistent pattern that the word order of clauses with nominal predicates (at least) differs from the usual predicate-subject-complement order. In these clauses, the subject is always final. I begin here by examining the proposals that have been put forth to account for this order difference by Doherty (1992) for Modern Irish within the general Verb Movement hypothesis framework and by Chung (1990) for Chamorro within the Subject Adjunction proposal. We will then be able to propose an account for QZ based upon this theoretical background and the QZ-specific empirical facts.

Doherty (1992) reports that Irish distinguishes between verbal clauses and copular clauses. He gives examples of the two copular elements in Irish to illustrate this distinction. The verbal copula *tá* 'be' is shown in

---

[125]This sentence is much better with the subject fronted as given, since ambiguity arises if the subject is final. In that position, the reading could also be 'very near the Salina Cruz Ocean' (i.e., the ocean named Salina Cruz).

(320a), while the copula used with non-verbal predicates (glossed 'COP') is shown in (320b).

(320) a. *tá seán ar meisce*
be Seán drunk
Seán is drunk.

b. *is dochtúir seán*
COP doctor Seán
Seán is a doctor.

In the verbal clauses, the predicate is a substantive verb which begins in V^0 and undergoes Verb Movement to obtain the VSO order manifested, as shown in (321a) (taken from Doherty 1992:66 where he follows Chung and McCloskey 1987 in assuming that the complement of I^0 is a small clause (SC) containing the subject). In contrast, (321b) (also from Doherty 1992:66) illustrates that the copular clauses are headed by a copular element that Doherty claims is in I^0. This copula takes an XP predicate as its complement and the subject of the clause appears in the right-specifier of IP (321b) with no movement of the predicate (or the subject).

(321)   a. Verbal Clauses   b. Copular Clauses

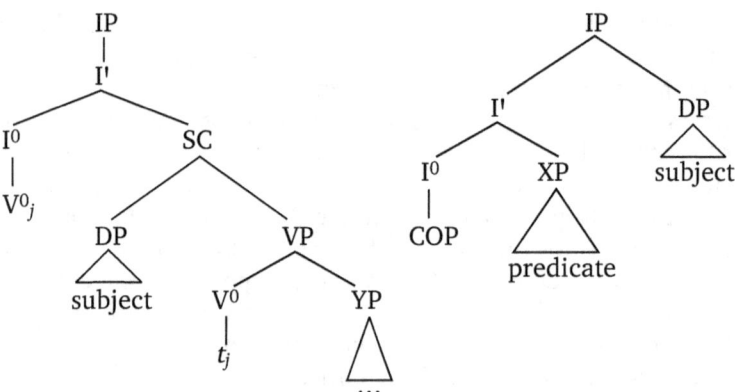

Doherty (1992) claims that the radically different clause structure proposed for copular clauses (321b) is rationalized by the fact that the copula only selects individual-level predicates. This fact then brings his analysis in line with work by Kratzer (1989), who argues that the subjects of

10.2 The structure of nonverbal predicates

individual-level predicates originate in the specifier of IP whereas the subjects of stage-level predicates originate as the specifier of the predicate itself.

The structure proposed for nonverbal predicates in Irish (321b) is almost identical to that proposed under the Subject Adjunction hypothesis by Chung (1990). Chung notes that predicates headed by both verbs and adjectives normally surface with (Infl) predicate-subject-complement order, although order variations are allowed in Chamorro. She analyzes this by allowing Subject Adjunction to adjoin the subject to any projection of the predicate X^0. In contrast, when the predicate is either a noun or a preposition, the required surface order is (Infl) predicate XP-subject, where the predicate XP includes all the complements and modifiers of the predicate. The only difference needed here is to state that Subject Adjunction may not apply in [−V] predicates; otherwise the clause structure is identical, as shown in (322).

(322)   a. [+V] Clauses   b. [−V] Clauses

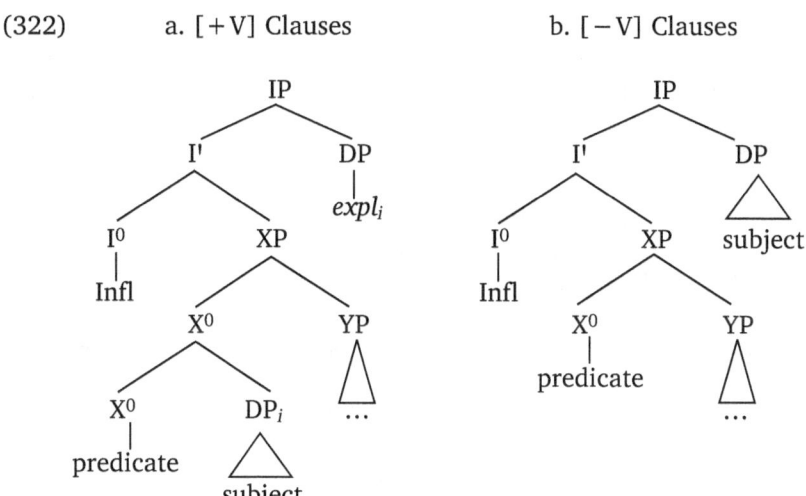

It seems that, theoretically, the Subject Adjunction proposal has a better account for the different word order attested in nonverbal predicates (both ±V) than the Verb Movement hypothesis does. However, since we have seen that the Verb Movement proposal provides the best account of the restrictions on negative constructions in Zapotec (chapter 8), and of the ordering within VP complements (§10.1.1), I extend that account to the nonverbal predicates.

First, the account for QZ must be different from the account given for Irish by Doherty (1992) since there is no distinction in clause type based on the individual-level versus stage-level predicate distinction (Kratzer 1989). As we saw in chapters 2–3, QZ has two copular verbs, *uu* 'be' and *ak* 'become'. As the glosses indicate, *uu* is used mostly with individual-level predicates while *ak* is used mostly with stage-level predicates. This distinction is not always clear, however, as shown in the examples in (323)–(324).

(323) a. n-uu gyët   GRANDMA3 24
        S-be tortilla
        There were tortillas.

     b. n-uu ndal yag bduu ru   lgyëëz Santyoo   TRIPTOQ 63
         S-be   lots   tree banana mouth town   Santiago
         There are lots of banana trees at the town of Santiago.

     c. le mdxin n-uu len   yuu   RYENEGU 31
        FM deer   S-be inside house
        The deer is in the house.

     d. barat n-uu zhob   GRANDMA3 25
        cheap S-be   elote
        Elote (corn) was cheap.

     e. kontent n-uu lextoo mër   gol   MARTRIST 40
        content S-be liver   pigeon male
        The male pigeon was content.

(324) a. ndal play   n-ak   ru   nis   BENIT 41
        lots   beach S-become mouth water
        There are many beaches at the shore of the water.

     b. zhaandxe n-ak   estados unidos   LIFEINUS 4
        pretty   S-become States   United
        The United States is pretty.

     c. g-ak   men x-unaa   de   MARTRIST 29
        P-become 3   POS-woman 2
        She will become your wife.

     d. pur   mëël   w-ak   gits   x-too   noo   SNAKHAIR 10
        pure snake C-become hair POS-head 1EX
        My hair had become pure snakes.

10.2 The structure of nonverbal predicates

Both *uu* 'be' and *ak* 'become' are clearly verbs. Clauses containing either copular verb surface with VSO order (unless focusing has fronted one constituent). This means that, under a Verb Movement account, the subject cannot originate in the specifier of IP, regardless of the individual-level or stage-level attributes of the predicate.

I incorporate the distinction between [+V] and [−V] predicates into the Verb Movement hypothesis by positing a different structure for the predicate phrase itself, rather than for the clause structure. This means that all [+V] predicates will have left specifiers and $X^0_{[+V]}$-to-I^0 movement will apply. In the case of [−V] predicates, however, all specifiers will be on the right.[126] (We shall see in chapter 11 that all specifiers are also on the right in the structure for nominal phrases.)

Head movement of the [−V] predicate would appear to be vacuous, but there is one case which indicates that such head movement cannot apply. This case, involving a negation construction in Mitla Zapotec, was seen in §8.2.2. The crucial example is repeated here.

(325) [et   xten-ä]-di-ni
      not belongs.to-1EX-NEG-3
      It isn't mine.

Recall that the account of this example involved movement of the DP$_{[+neg]}$ (bracketed in (325)) to the specifier of NegP (or PolP). Head movement of the D^0 *et* to Neg^0 (Pol^0) would not allow this attested example to be generated. Instead, the order obtained would be as shown in (326a). Applying both head movement of D^0 to Neg^0 (Pol^0) and fronting the remaining DP$_{[+neg]}$ (i.e. without the subject) to the specifier of NegP (PolP) also yields incorrect results, as shown in (326b). We must therefore insure that head movement does not apply in [−V] predicates.

(326) a. *et-di   xten-ä-ni
         not-NEG belongs.to-1EX-3
         (It isn't mine.)

     b. *xten-ä   et-di-ni
        belongs.to-1EX   not-NEG-3
        (It isn't mine.)

---

[126] I assume following Grimshaw (1990) that all functional projections in the main backbone of the clause are [+V]. The quantifiers used in the special number-marking constructions analyzed in chapter 12 will also need to be [+V], whereas when used as determiners the quantifiers are [−V].

My proposal to account for the variation in word order between [±V] predicates is illustrated in (327). All phrase-level projections are uniformly head-initial. The [+V] projections are also specifier-initial, while the [−V] projections have their specifiers on the right. Head movement of the predicate X^0 is tied to those projections which are specifier-initial, i.e., [+V].

(327)   a. [+V] Clauses   B. [−V] Clauses

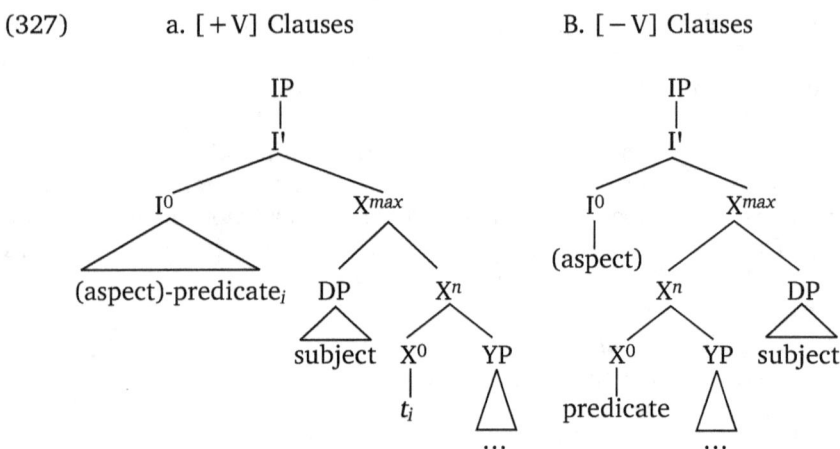

This proposal thus makes the [±V] distinction on predicate type noted under the Subject Adjunction account work within the Verb Movement framework by proposing different structures for the predicate phrases.

11
Structure of Nominal Phrases

It has been widely assumed that there is a parallelism between the structure of the clause and the structure of nominals, where the possessor of the noun is seen as parallel to the subject of the clause (Chomsky 1970).[127] Therefore, the Verb Movement and Subject Adjunction proposals each have corresponding proposals for the structure of nominals discussed in §11.1. Both of these proposals follow the DP Hypothesis (Abney 1987, Stowell 1989) in which nominal phrases are headed by a determiner, which selects a noun phrase as its complement, as sketched in (328b). This DP structure is proposed to replace the basic NP structure assumed earlier, shown in (328a).

---

[127]Not all languages demonstrate this parallelism. For example, in Chinese, even the position of the head differs: verbs precede their objects but nominals are head-final.

(328)   a. NP structure   ⇒   b. DP structure

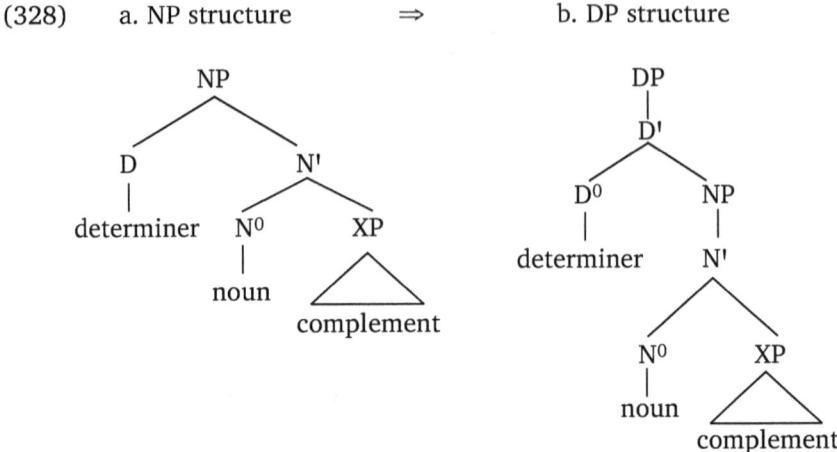

The DP Hypothesis is designed to directly reflect the assumed parallelism between the clause structure and the structure of nominals. Just as the clause is projected from a functional head (I^0) which takes a lexical phrase (VP) as its complement, nominals are projected from a functional head (D^0) and take a lexical phrase (NP) as their complement.

Section 11.2 then presents the DP structure proposed for QZ, which is distinct from both the Verb Movement and Subject Adjunction proposals. This DP structure is parallel to the structure of clauses with [−V] predicates, maintaining the [±V] division in structure noted in chapter 10. Section 11.3 then explores the coordination possibilities within nominals, which serves to reinforce the proposed structure for nominal phrases.

11.1 The DP structures parallel to the clause structure proposals

The DP structures proposed by the Verb Movement and Subject Adjunction theories of clause structure will be briefly presented and evaluated in turn.

11.1.1 The Verb Movement account

According to the version of the DP Hypothesis associated with the Verb Movement proposal, the possessor occupies the specifier of NP position, and then N^0-to-D^0 movement occurs. This head movement accounts for the fact that the possessor follows the noun, as shown in (329). (Adjoined elements such as adjectives and relative clauses are omitted here.)

11.1 The DP structures parallel to the clause structure proposals

(329) Proposed DP structure under the Verb Movement hypothesis

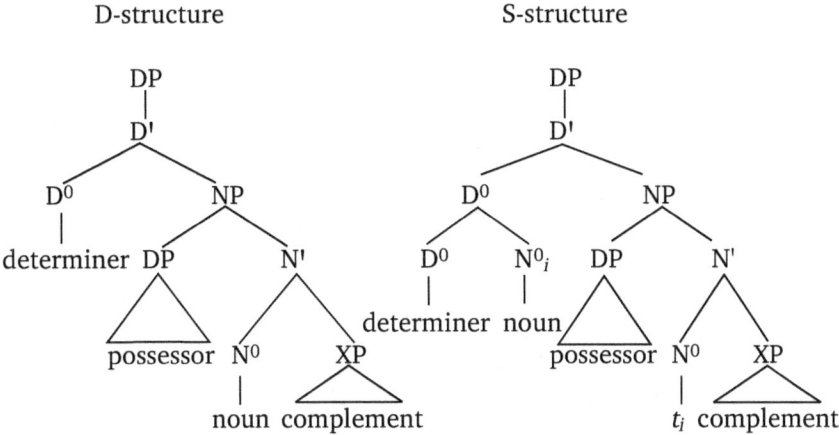

In evaluating this proposal, we can note already a difference between the proposed head movement from V^0-to-I^0 and from N^0-to-D^0: the complex unit resulting from V^0-to-I^0 movement forms a single word, and therefore such movement can be seen as resulting from morphological subcategorization (Rizzi and Roberts 1989). This is not the case with N^0-to-D^0 movement, since the determiner and the noun remain separate words. Structurally, though, the clause structure and nominal structure proposals are quite parallel, including the fact that the specifier of the functional projection is not used as an argument position.

11.1.2 The Subject Adjunction account

Under the Subject Adjunction version of the DP Hypothesis, the possessor begins in the specifier of DP and then right-adjoins to the noun, in a similar manner to the subject adjoining to the verb. This is shown in (330), again omitting adjoined constituents. Under this theory neither adjunction is assumed to form a single word, since in both cases a maximal projection adjoins to a head.

(330) Proposed DP structure under the Subject Adjunction hypothesis

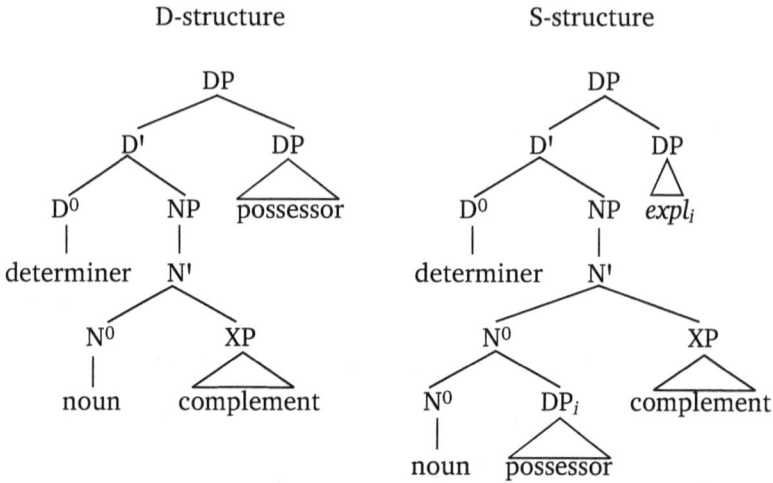

This structure is completely parallel to the corresponding proposal for clause structure and carries the same inherent strengths and weaknesses noted in §5.2.2.

Neither of these proposals, however, can account for all the possible orders and relationships within nominals in QZ. Instead, an alternative version of the DP Hypothesis is proposed which does not involve movement of any constituent.

11.2 Proposed DP structure for QZ

As seen in §2.1, nominal phrases do not carry any morphological case marking in QZ, nor is there any number marking except through the use of quantifiers. As to determiners there are no clear cases of definite nor indefinite articles; *pa,* however, seems to be a *wh*-determiner and the focus marker acts somewhat like a determiner as well. In QZ nominal phrases the quantifier or determiner comes first, followed by the noun. This in turn may be followed by one or more adjectives, a possessor, a demonstrative, and one or more relative clauses. Normally, though, only one post-modifier is used. Examples of some of the more complex nominal phrases found in the texts are given in (331), where the relative clauses in (331a–b) and the constituent being possessed in (331c) are bracketed for clarity.

11.2 Proposed DP structure for QZ

(331) a. *ndal ngyed gol [w-u mëëz]*   RANCHO 12
     lots chicken old S-eat fox
     lots of old chickens that the fox ate

  b. *te x-mig noo [ne r-laan te men*   HORTENS 4
     one POS-friend 1EX that H-want one 3

     ne r-nii disa]
     that H-speak language
    a friend of mine that wants a person that speaks the language

  c. *porke w-et [x-pëëk win] nzeb*   SYANODEN 16
     because C-die POS-dog small girl
     because her little dog had died

The fact that relative clauses come after the possessor (331b) is problematic for the Subject Adjunction account where the possessor is in the specifier of DP. The relative clause would then have to be adjoined to DP, but this violates the prohibition against adjunction to arguments (Chomsky 1986:6). The position of adjectives to the left of the possessor (331c) is also a problem, since the adjunction of the possessor cannot be directly to the noun (N^0), but instead must be to the projection directly above the adjective. Chung (1990) argues for Chamorro that Subject Adjunction may adjoin the subject to any projection of V^0. A similar claim for Possessor Adjunction within nominals would allow adjunction to any projection of N^0. The QZ case is much more fixed: the subject must immediately follow the verb (with adjunction to V' instead being disallowed), yet the possessor must follow any adjectives modifying the noun. A stipulation to this effect would be necessary to make the Subject Adjunction account of DP structure work for QZ.

Besides the proposed N^0-to-D^0 movement not meeting the usual morphological restrictions on head movement, as noted above, the position of the possessor with respect to adjectives is also problematic for the DP analogue of the Verb Movement proposal. In order to obtain the surface word order shown in (331c) for instance, the adjective would have to be left-adjoined to NP (above the possessor in the specifier of NP), as diagrammed in (332).

(332)   S-structure

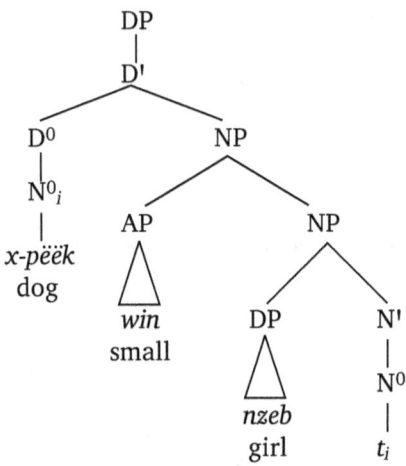

The structure in (332) is very similar to the structure ruled out for the adverbial suffixes -re 'MORE' and -ke 'ASSOC' in (289) (§9.5), due to the ordering restrictions between the suffixes and to the strict adjacency requirement between the inflected verb and the subject which is necessary for Case assignment under government.

The situation is somewhat different with respect to adjectives and nouns, though parallels with the verbal case remain. First, there are not normally ordering restrictions between adjectives. This makes the adjectives parallel to the free adverbials. We saw, however, that free adverbials could not be left-adjoined to VP due to the adjacency required by Case assignment. In order for assignment of Case to the possessor by the noun to be parallel to the assignment of Case to the subject by the verb, thus motivating the N^0-to-D^0 movement, the same strict adjacency requirement for Case assignment under government should hold (McCloskey 1991). This rules out the left-NP-adjoined position for the adjective(s) in (332), leaving the Verb Movement version of the DP Hypothesis with no account of the word order within QZ nominals.

I argue instead that Case is assigned to the possessor via specifier-head agreement with the noun, where the x- 'POS' prefix that shows up on alienably possessed nouns is the overt reflex of this agreement. We have already seen that QZ needs to be mixed with respect to the mechanism under which "case" (referring here to both regular Case and the relationship required by semantic operators) is assigned: main clauses, questions, and

11.2 Proposed DP structure for QZ 247

focus constructions use the minimal government relationship, whereas negative constructions and nominals use specifier-head agreement.[128]

The phrase structure needed for nominals would be clearer if we could check the position of the possessor with respect to complements of N, since the position of complements is fixed. This would eliminate the need to consider so many possible places that adjectives may adjoin. Unfortunately, QZ does not have true noun complement constructions in which the main noun is possessed, such as the English example *Bill's letters to Sue*; instead such sentences are expressed either with embedded possessors (333a–b) or with relative clauses (333c).

(333) a. *x-kwent   x-bur   noo*   BRU 25
         POS-account POS-burro 1EX
         on account of my burro

   b. *ru   x-yuu   x-mig   x-patron   noo*   MTLEMON 11
      mouth POS-house POS-friend POS-patron 1EX
      at the house of my patron's friend

   c. *te   x-liber   noo ne   ziid   kwent lo   lgyëz*
      one   POS-book   1EX that   PR/come   story face   village
      my book of stories about the village

Some examples of noun complement constructions which do not involve possession are given in (334).[129] These fall into two categories: those in which the main noun is a body part, used to express a location (334a and b, second line), and those in which the main noun is a classifier (334b, first line and c–e).

(334) a. *ruu   tank nga   zob   tapet*   BATHROOM 19
         mouth tub   there PR/sit rug
         On the side of the tub sits a rug.

---

[128]Use of the specifier-head relationship for Case assignment to the possessor within the Verb Movement proposal would allow the adjectives to be left-adjoined to NP, but the proposed N^0-to-D^0 movement would then be unmotivated.

[129]Actually, *x-too gyeey* 'POS-head mountain' (334b, second line) has 'mountain' as the possessor of 'head' as in 'the mountain's top' rather than being 'the top of the mountain'.

b. *chene w-dxiin mëëw disyember* LIFEINUS 62
   when C-arrive month December

   kesentyent r-ak nyag x-too gyeey
   much H-become cold POS-head mountain
   When December comes it will be very cold at the top of the mountain.

c. *n-ak-t men ze n-ak men Mejiko* LIFEINUS 28
   S-become-NEG 3 how S-become 3 Mexico
   They are not like the people of Mexico.

d. *n-uu tson klas bnii* MEXICO 5
   S-be three kind light
   There are three kinds of lights.

e. *w-ats te tla tabel lo pwent* OLDMAN 15
   C-break one piece plank face bridge
   A piece of the planking of the bridge broke.

Instead of either of the proposals for the structure of nominals mentioned above, the structure shown in (335), with no movement at all, seems to account best for the QZ nominals.

(335)
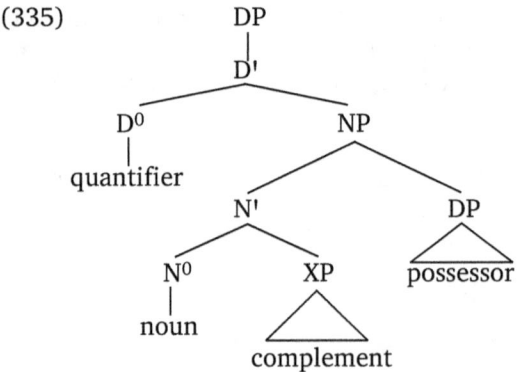

In this structure the position preceding the noun, which is normally filled by quantifiers, is the head of the DP. As Kuroda (1986) has proposed for English, I posit that the possessor fills the specifier of NP position, since this accounts for the ordering of the possessor following the noun (but after any modifying adjectives as shown below in (336)) and also allows the

11.2 Proposed DP structure for QZ

x- prefix found on alienably possessed nouns to be accounted for by the normal mechanism of specifier-head agreement.

We can extend the proposal further, again in line with the spirit of Kuroda's proposal, and posit that the specifier of D^0 position is filled by the subject of nominal small clauses. Movement evidence such as that presented in §8.2.2 and discussed in chapter 10 indicates that the predicate phrase without the subject is itself a maximal projection. I therefore posit that the subject actually occupies the specifier of D^{max} above DP; there is then no specifier directly above D', as shown in (336).

Besides the head and specifier positions in each phrase, there are several possibilities for adjoined elements. I posit that adjectives may adjoin to N', while demonstratives and relative clauses adjoin either to NP or to D'.[130] This fuller structure including the possible positions of adjoined elements is illustrated in (336).

(336)

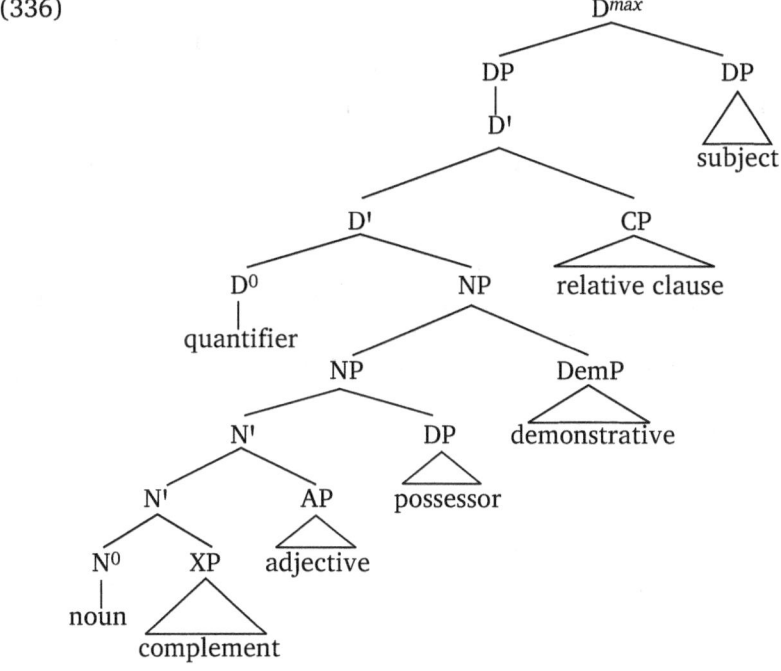

---

[130]Clearly, I do not follow the specific statement of Chomsky's (1986) theory of adjunction, since it only allows adjunction to maximal projections. The position of adjectives with respect to possessors and relative clauses could not be accounted for if the only adjunction site within the DP was adjunction to NP.

This phrase structure is consistent with the division between [±V] predicates seen in the last chapter where it was shown that the phrase structure of the predicate phrase itself is dependent upon its [±V] feature. The phrases projected from [+V] heads are uniformly head-initial and specifier-initial, whereas those projected from [−V] heads are head-initial and specifier-final. Further, head movement only occurs in clauses projected from [+V] predicates. This distinction is further verified by the fact that the phrase structure of both DP and NP is head-initial and specifier-final and that no head movement occurs.

11.3 Attested coordination within DP

The possibilities for coordination of DPs and within DP are examined here. In each example in this section, the conjuncts are bracketed and the conjunction is in bold type.

QZ has the overt conjunctions *no* 'and' and *o* 'or'. Some examples of coordinate DPs using these overt conjunctions are given in (337). Note that (337c) provides an example of a coordinate DP in focus position.

(337) a. *r-kandil   men-o   [te   xman]   o   [chip   gbiz]*   QUESO 23
H-colgar 3-3I   one   week   or   ten   day
She hangs it for a week or ten days.

b. *r-ap   noo   [ndal   yaa   ngyed]   **no**   [te   bur]*   AGOSTO 41
H-have 1EX   lots   very   chicken   and   one   burro
I have lots of chickens and one burro.

c. *[dxit]   **o**   [gyët-guu   bzaa]   n-uu*   TRIPTOQ 24
egg   or   tortilla-tamale   bean   S-be

porke   ne-guin   r-u   men-o
because   that-this   H-eat   3-3I
There are eggs or bean tamales, because from this they eat.

In addition, two DPs may coordinate without any overt conjunction, as seen in (338).

(338) *per w-see   men [y-ra x-kayet   Biki]*   GRING 32
     but C-throw 3   P-all POS-cracker Virginia

   [y-ra x-nex   Biki]
   P-all POS-fruit Virginia
   But they threw away all Virginia's$_i$ crackers and all her$_i$ fruit.

Some of these text examples can be used as starting points for determining what constituents within DP may be coordinated. (339a) is the coordinate DP from (338), where each conjunct consists of a quantifier, a noun, and its possessor. (339b–c) show that expressing the possessor in only one of the two conjuncts is ungrammatical or highly questionable.[131] The form given in (339d), where a coreferent pronoun replaces the second occurrence of the proper name possessor, could be used instead of (339a).

(339) a. *[y-ra x-kayet   Biki]   (no)   [y-ra x-nex   Biki]*
        P-all POS-cracker Virginia (and) P-all POS-fruit Virginia
        all Virginia's crackers and all her fruit

   b. *??[y-ra x-kayet]   Biki   (no)   [y-ra x-nex]*
        P-all POS-cracker Virginia (and) P-all POS-fruit
        (all Virginia's crackers and all her fruit)

   c. **[y-ra x-kayet]   (no)   [y-ra x-nex]   Biki*
        P-all POS-cracker (and) P-all POS-fruit Virginia
        (all Virginia's crackers and all her fruit)

   d. *[y-ra x-kayet   Biki]   (no)   [y-ra x-nex   men]*
        P-all POS-cracker Virginia (and) P-all POS-fruit 3
        all Virginia's crackers and all her fruit

The inability to coordinate quantified noun phrases under a single possessor is further evidence against using the Subject Adjunction proposal for QZ. If the possessor is in the specifier of DP, it should be possible to coordinate under it at the D' level and then adjoin the possessor to the first noun, as in (339b). This is correct for Chamorro, since comparable examples to both (339b–c) are grammatical there (Chung 1990, 1991), but is impossible for QZ. In contrast, if the possessor is in the specifier of NP as

---

[131] I assume the slight difference in judgement is due to the possibility of using the null third person pronoun in (339b). My language consultant's personal preference is to use overt pronouns in all cases.

proposed in (336), the attempted coordination of a quantified noun phrase under a possessor is correctly predicted to be ungrammatical.

Even without a quantifier in either conjunct, thus attempting to coordinate at the N'-level, it is not possible to have only a single possessor. (340a) shows that the possessor cannot be expressed only in the first conjunct and (340b) shows that it cannot simply remain in final position. Instead, (340c–e) show grammatical expressions where either the possessor is repeated in both conjuncts (340c), or a coreferent pronoun is used in the second conjunct (340d), or two distinct possessors are present (340e). Coordination at the N'-level is not possible in QZ.

(340) a. ??*[x-kayet]*   Biki   *(no)*   *[x-nex]*
              POS-cracker Virginia (and) POS-fruit
         (Virginia's crackers and fruit)

   b. **[x-kayet]*   *(no)* *[x-nex]*   Biki
          POS-cracker   (and) POS-fruit Virginia
       (Virginia's crackers and fruit)

   c. *[x-kayet   Biki]*   *(no)*   *[x-nex   Biki]*
          POS-cracker Virginia (and)   POS-fruit Virginia
       Virginia's crackers and her fruit

   d. *[x-kayet   Biki]*   *(no)*   *[x-nex   men]*
          POS-cracker Virginia (and)   POS-fruit 3
       Virginia's crackers and her fruit

   e. *[x-kayet   Biki]*   *(no)*   *[x-nex   Gecha]*
          POS-cracker Virginia (and)   POS-fruit Lucrecia
       Virginia's crackers and Lucrecia's fruit

It is possible to coordinate under a single quantifier, as shown in (341). Under my analysis, this is coordination at the NP-level under D^0.

(341) a. ndal *[ngyed]*   *(no)* *[bur]*
          lots chicken   (and)   burro
          lots of chickens and burros

   b. *txup-tson* *[ngyed]*   *(no)* *[bur]*
       two-three   chicken   (and)   burro
       a few chickens and burros

11.3 Attested coordination within DP   253

    c. *ndal* [*x-kyed*   *noo*] **(*no*)** [*x-bur*   *noo*]
       lots POS-chicken 1EX (and) POS-burro 1EX
       lots of my chickens and my burros

    d. *txup-tson* [*x-kyed* *xnaa* *noo*] **(*no*)** [*x-bur* *men*]
       two-three POS-chicken mother 1EX (and) POS-burro 3
       a few of my mother's chickens and her burros

Strictly speaking, the examples in (341) are ambiguous, in that one really does not know how many burros are being referred to. This is because two different levels of coordination are possible. The bracketing shown in (341) indicates coordination at the NP-level under D^0, as diagrammed in (342a) (for (341c)). The other reading is that coordination is at the DP-level, with the quantifier only a part of the first conjunct, as sketched in (342b). Without a quantifier in the second conjunct, the number of burros can be one or two or many, just as with any other nominal which is not explicitly marked for number by a quantifier.

(342)   a. NP Coordination   or   b. DP Coordination

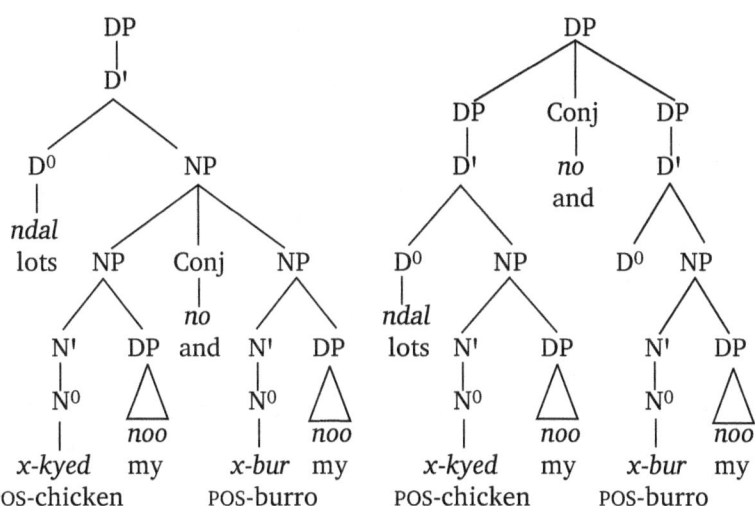

Although I have not completely researched this area, it seems that QZ does not allow zero-level or single-bar-level coordination. Only maximal phrases may coordinate. This generalization is consistent with the impossibility of coordinating different verbs under a single subject seen in §10.1.2 (though it is the movement out of the coordinate structure that is most problematic there). It is also impossible to coordinate two verbs with the same direct object. Of the attempts in (343) to express the English construction *My sister washed and ironed the clothes* in QZ, only full sentential coordination (343d) is successful. It is ungrammatical to have coordinate verbs before the subject and object (343a), or to have the subject follow the first verb and the object follow the second verb (343b), or to place both the subject and the object only in the first conjunct (343c).

(343) a. *[w-aa]   **no**   [w-gu-planch] bzaan noo lër
       C-wash and C-CAUS-iron   sister 1EX clothes
       (My sister washed and ironed the clothes.)

   b. *[w-aa]   bzaan noo **no** [w-gu-planch] lër
       C-wash sister 1EX and C-CAUS-iron   clothes
       (My sister washed and ironed the clothes.)

   c. *[w-aa]   bzaan noo lër   **no** [w-gu-planch]
       C-wash sister 1EX clothes and C-CAUS-iron
       (My sister washed the clothes and ironed.)

   d. [w-aa   bzaan noo lër]   **no** [w-gu-planch men-o]
       C-wash sister 1EX clothes and C-CAUS-iron 3-3I
       My sister washed the clothes and she ironed them.

Coordination at the D^0-level is not possible either, though this might be questioned in examples like (341b and d). Although *txup-tson* is literally 'two-three' it is a fixed form used to indicate 'a few'. True coordination would allow any two numbers to coordinate, which is not possible. Further, the other two possible determiners, *pa* 'what' and the focus marker *laa* must occur to the left of any quantifier, thus being accounted for by adjunction rather than coordination.

Given the limitation on coordinate structures in QZ to maximal projections, we can note whether there are further restrictions on which maximal projections may coordinate. We saw in chapter 10 that predicate phrases may not coordinate, except where the verbs are identical (and even this is not preferred). Likewise, IP may not coordinate under negation unless both the verbs and the aspect marking are identical (again the preferred method is to fully coordinate at the PolP level with each conjunct fully specified). This is predicted by the Verb Movement analysis: movement of the predicate to I^0 and possibly to Pol^0 violates the Coordinate Structure Constraint, unless it can be accomplished via Across the Board Extraction of identical elements.

11.3 Attested coordination within DP

We have seen examples of coordination at the CP, PolP, and DP levels. It is also possible to coordinate adjective phrases, adverbial phrases, and prepositional phrases used as modifiers. Therefore, all maximal projections may coordinate, subject to the restrictions due to Verb Movement.

12

Special Number-Marking Constructions

This chapter ties together much of the analyses of the previous chapters in giving both a semantic and a syntactic analysis for the unique constructions used to mark number, as exemplified in (345) and following.[132] Examples of regular quantified DPs are given first to highlight the contrast.

As noted in chapter 2, the only method available for marking number in QZ is through the use of quantifiers. When no quantifier is used, a noun phrase or pronoun is ambiguous between singular and plural. Use of a quantifier signals that the speaker wishes to make the number explicit.

In addition to number words, QZ has the general quantifiers *ra* 'all', *zhi* or *zhindxe* 'few',[133] *txup-tson* 'two-three' or 'some, a few', *ndal* 'lots' (used with count nouns), and *naal* 'much' (used with mass nouns). In addition, *ni*, borrowed from Spanish, is beginning to be used as a negative quantifier.[134]

---

[132]Much of the material presented in this chapter first appeared in Black (1992), though the syntactic analysis given there is in terms of a Subject Adjunction view of QZ clause structure rather than the Verb Movement proposal adopted here. Clarifying data obtained from additional field work is also included in this chapter.

[133]Phrases using either of these forms for the quantifier meaning 'few' must be fronted, as shown in §6.3.

[134]In accord with the analysis in chapter 8, a phrase marked by the negative quantifier must be fronted and must co-occur either with negation marked on the verb or with another negative head, e.g., *gart* 'still.no' in (344d).

These quantifiers can be used in regular quantificational DPs, as shown in (344).[135]

(344) a. r-ap   noo **ndal yaa** **ngyed** no te **bur**   AGOSTO 41
H-have 1EX lots very chicken and one burro
I have lots of chickens and one burro.

b. w-ak   **naal** **nis**   gyoow   OLDMAN 13
C-become much water river
There was much water in the river.

c. **zhi** maa **gin** r-dil   noo   BENIT 19C
few 3A this H-fight 1EX
Those few animals are bothering me.

d. **ni** **tla** **gyët** gart g-u noo axta-ge xsil   MENMAAC 22
not piece tortilla still.no P-eat 1EX until-that morning
I haven't eaten a piece of tortilla since this morning.

Of these quantifiers which can be used in quantificational DPs, only *ra* 'all' and the numbers 'one' through 'four' are allowed to fill the quantifier position in the constructions which are the focus of this chapter. These special number-marking constructions abound in QZ texts and speech. In these constructions, a nominal phrase is followed by a quantifier which is, in turn, followed by (usually) two nominal phrases. An example is shown in (345), where the parts of the construction are in bold.

(345) r-oo   **men** **y-rup** **men** **Biki**   nisgaal   AGOSTO 8A
H-drink 3   P-two 3   Virginia soda
She and Virginia drink soda pop.

Recall that pronouns in QZ are not specified for number, gender, or case, so the third person pronoun *men* can mean 'he/she/they' or 'him/her/them' or 'himself/herself/themselves' or 'his/her/their' depending upon its position in the sentence. Therefore the full meaning conveyed by the construction in (345) might be expressed in English as 'they, she and Virginia, just the two of them...'. The basic form of these constructions is diagrammed in (346), where the subscripts indicate required coindexing.

---

[135] I assume that *yaa* 'very' in (344a) is an intensifier that may adjoin to some quantifiers as well as to adjectives and adverbs.

(346)   DP₁   (aspect-)quantifier DP₁ DP₂
        ‾‾‾   ‾‾‾‾‾‾‾‾‾‾‾‾‾‾‾‾‾‾‾‾‾‾‾
        head   adjunct

I claim that these QZ constructions can be seen as elaborate versions of the Plural Pronoun Construction (PPC) analyzed by Schwartz (1988). A PPC is composed of a plural pronoun followed by either a nominal phrase or a prepositional phrase, depending upon the language. The plurality of the pronoun may or must be taken to express the number of the entire construction, rather than the number of only the pronoun itself. An example from Mokilese is given in (347).

(347) *kamwa Davy inla duhdu*   SCHWARTZ 4C
      2DUAL   Davy go   swim
      You (SG) and Davy went swimming.

In English we might say 'the two of you, you and Davy...' to convey the same information. Schwartz analyzes these constructions as asymmetric single-headed complex nominal phrases with the constituent structure diagrammed in (348)

(348)

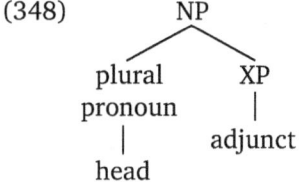

Ladusaw (1989) gives a semantic interpretation for the PPC which requires that the referent of the adjunct be properly included in the reference of the head pronoun. This is in contrast to a regular coordination relationship, where the conjuncts must be disjoint in reference. Ladusaw's interpretation entails the properties noted by Schwartz as universals for the PPC, including the plurality of the head pronoun and the Person Hierarchy Effect. The latter says that the person feature of the head must be greater or equal to the person feature of the referent of the adjunct on a hierarchy of $1 > 2 > 3$. In order for the referent of the adjunct to be properly included in the reference of the head pronoun, two things must be true. First, the number of the pronoun must be large enough to include the referent of the adjunct as well as the reference of the head, so it must be minimally dual in number. Second, the person feature of the head pronoun must also be high enough to include the referent of the adjunct. For example, a second or third person pronoun head cannot include a first person adjunct in its reference. The inclusion requirement thus entails these two properties of the PPC.

Since the Person Hierarchy Effect is also a strong constraint in the QZ constructions, the semantic interpretation for the PPC provides a starting point for understanding them. Section 12.1 looks at the semantics of these special QZ number-marking constructions further.

The syntactic issues raised are addressed in §12.2, where I present an analysis for the version of the construction where all the parts are contiguous.

The analysis is complicated by the fact that there is also a completely synonymous, separated version of (345) (repeated here as (349a)), which is shown in (349b). Whereas the construction appears to be a single constituent in (349a), only the head is in subject position in (349b), while the adjunct is at the end of the clause.

(349) a. *r-oo* **men y-rup men Biki** *nisgaal* AGOSTO 8A
H-drink 3 P-two 3 Virginia soda
She and Virginia drink soda pop.

b. *r-oo* **men** *nisgaal* **y-rup men Biki** AGOSTO 8B
H-drink 3 soda P-two 3 Virginia
She and Virginia drink soda pop.

Section 12.3 discusses whether a syntactic movement analysis or a semantic construal analysis is preferable for the separated version of the QZ number-marking construction.

12.1 Semantic interpretation

For the PPC, the requirement that the referent of the adjunct be included in the reference of the plural pronoun head entails the Person Hierarchy Effect (Ladusaw 1989). In that construction, both the person feature and the number feature are determined by the head plural pronoun.

QZ does not have plural pronouns, so the relevant person feature and number feature are found separately. Section 12.1.1 verifies that the quantifier provides the number feature for the entire construction. The meaning of the Potential marking on the quantifier is also explained. Section 12.1.2 discusses how inclusion can be seen as partially extending to

12.1 Semantic interpretation

nonpronominal or nonplural pronoun heads for Mesoamerican languages. Section 12.1.3 then shows that an extension of Ladusaw's interpretation for the PPC based on group reference correctly entails the Person Hierarchy Effect for the QZ constructions.

12.1.1 The quantifier contribution

Since the only method available for marking number in QZ is through the use of quantifiers,[136] the number-marking role of the quantifier in the special constructions under consideration is crucial to the correct interpretation of the construction. There is substantial evidence that the quantifier marks the number of the entire constituent. For example, while (350a) can have either of the first three readings given (with the first one being correct from the context), the last reading is impossible. In contrast, only that reading is possible if the quantifier is changed to *y-rup* 'P-two' as in (350b). What is crucial to understanding this is that *y-ra* 'P-all' cannot be used in contexts where there are only two participants, since *y-rup* 'P-two' provides an alternative way of expressing that. Instead, the plurality expressed by *y-ra* entails that there are at least three participants.

(350) a. *sabt   w-a-xee   noo*   MTLEMON 6
       Saturday C-go-rise   1EX

   w-xa-ndxen   noo   y-ra   x-patron   noo
   C-eat-breakfast   1EX   P-all POS-patron   1EX
   Saturday I got up and ate breakfast with all my patrons.
   Saturday we got up and ate breakfast with our patron.
   Saturday we got up and ate breakfast with all our patrons.
   *(Saturday I got up and ate breakfast with my patron.)

---

[136]Marlett and Pickett (1985) report that outside of the southern group, all of the Zapotecan languages have either a plural proclitic which is used with nominals and pronouns, or a verbal prefix to pluralize the subject, or both. Within the southern group, quantifiers must be used to mark plurality for a nominal. There are variations as to whether there is a singular versus plural distinction in pronouns, though all southern dialects except QZ have at least singular and plural first person exclusive. QZ makes no singular or plural distinction at all, with the sole exception of the first person inclusive pronoun, which must include the speaker and the hearer and so is plural in that limited sense.

Though the other Zapotec languages all have quantificational DPs, the use of quantifiers in the constructions being analyzed here is only widely attested within the southern group. This complementarity certainly suggests that the proliferation of these special constructions in QZ stems from the lack of alternative methods of pluralization.

b. *sabt*   *w-a-xee*   *noo w-xa-ndxen*   **noo y-rup x-patron noo**
Saturday C-go-rise 1EX C-eat-breakfast 1EX P-two POS-patron 1EX
Saturday I got up and ate breakfast with my patron.

Though normally the distinction is made only between dual and plural, using the quantifiers meaning 'two' and 'all' respectively, these structures may also be found where the number marking is singular, as well as where a group of three or four is indicated. Singular marking is used to indicate that the action was done alone, as shown in (351).

(351) a. *teb   tir   te   mër   zob   lo   yag*   MARTRIST 1
one time one pigeon PR/sit face tree

r-oolbaan **maa** *te-tee* **maa**   OLDMAN 5
H-sing 3A one-one 3A
One time a pigeon was sitting in a tree singing all by himself.

b. *luzh   lo   g-uu* **men** *bni   dxiid* **men** *te-tee* **men**
finish face P-sow 3 seed F/come 3 one-one 3
After he plants the seed, he will come alone.

Example (352) shows that while the quantifiers meaning 'two' and 'all' may be thought of as selecting two DP arguments (and 'one' only one), the quantifiers meaning 'three' and 'four' have three and four DP argument positions, respectively (see §12.2.3 for the analysis).[137] As (352c) verifies, it is ungrammatical to have more DPs following the quantifier than the quantifier selects: *gy-on* 'P-three' only selects three DP arguments, so four DPs cannot be present.[138] Further, as (352d) shows, having less arguments filled than are selected by the quantifier is highly unnatural. Though my language consultant verifies that (352d) can be understood to mean 'there were four people including Susan and myself who came', it is not a normal, natural usage and no examples like it were found in the texts.[139]

---

[137]Thus, *gyon* and *ytap* are very close to being three- and four-place conjunction morphemes which Gazdar, Klein, Pullum and Sag (1985:170) conjectured that no language could have.

[138]The only exception to this is that the names of babies or young children are sometimes allowed to be added in additionally with a conjunction, as in the bracketed portion in (i).

(i) *w-a* **noo gy-on** *noo Dolf*   *Susan [no   Min   lee]*   MTLEMON2 2
C-go 1EX P-three 1EX Rodolfo Susan and Yazmin also
Rodolfo, Susan, and I (and Yazmin also) went.

[139]The two "missing" arguments in (352d) can be accounted for by the Redundancy Condition, discussed in the next paragraph, allowing the construction to be understood.

(352) a. xiid   **noo gy-on noo Susan Dolf**   lee   TEXAS 29
F/come   1EX   P-three   1EX   Susan   Rodolfo   also
Susan, Rodolfo, and I will come (the three of us).

b. xiid   **noo y-tap noo Susan Dolf Biki**   lee
F/come   1EX   P-four   1ex   Susan   Rodolfo   Virginia   also
Susan, Rodolfo, Virginia, and I will come (the four of us).

c. *xiid   **noo gy-on noo Susan Dolf Biki**   lee
F/come   1EX   P-three   1EX   Susan   Rodolfo   Virginia   also
(Susan, Rodolfo, Virginia, and I will come (the three of us).)

d. ??xiid   **noo y-tap noo Susan**   (lee)
F/come   1EX   P-four   1EX   Susan   also
(Susan and I will come (the four of us).)

There is also a simpler construction which is fully grammatical that acts like a plural (or dual, triple, etc.) pronoun would in other languages. I analyze this as a special case of the full construction which is subject to a Redundancy Condition. The Redundancy Condition says that if DP_2[140] is the same pronoun as DP_1 then DP_2 is not realized phonetically, since it adds no new information. Constructions illustrating this Redundancy Condition are given in (353a)–(355a); the (b) examples show that repetition of the pronoun is ungrammatical.

(353) a. s-ya   **men y-rup men**   SAMUEL 13
PR-go   3   P-two   3
They both were going.

b. *s-ya   **men y-rup men men**
PR-go   3   P-two   3   3
(They both were going.)

(354) a. g-u-sëë   **noo y-ra noo**   LIFEINQ 20
P-eat-dinner   1EX   P-all   1EX
We all will eat dinner.

b. *g-u-sëë   **noo y-ra noo noo**
P-eat-dinner   1EX   P-all   1EX   1EX
(We all will eat dinner.)

---
[140]The same reasoning extends to DP_3 and DP_4 when the quantifiers meaning 'three' and 'four' are used.

(355) a. w-nëëz **noo** byon **g-yon** **noo**   TEXAS 4
       C-catch 1EX airplane P-three 1EX
       We three caught an airplane.

   b. *w-nëëz **noo** byon **g-yon** **noo** **noo** **noo**
       C-catch 1EX airplane P-three 1EX 1EX 1EX
       (We three caught an airplane.)

This simplified version has the same distribution as the fuller versions of the construction, including the synonymous separated version shown in (355). Versions of the special number-marking construction which follow the Redundancy Condition are quite common. They can be found not only in subject position, but also as objects, possessors, objects of prepositions, and in focus position, just as the fuller version of the construction can. This distribution will be displayed further in §12.2.2.

This simpler construction can also be used appositively, as in (356), where the number feature of the quantifier must match the number of persons referred to in the appositive construction (bracketed),[141] thus further confirming that the quantifier specifies the number of the entire structure.

(356) a. xiid **noo gy-on noo** [txup bech Dolf noo lee]
       F/come 1EX P-three 1EX two brother Rodolfo 1EX also
       The three of us will come, Rodolfo's two brothers and I.

   b. *xiid **noo gy-on noo** [Susan no txup bech
       F/come 1EX P-three 1EX Susan and two brother

       Dolf noo lee]
       Rodolfo 1EX also
       (The three of us will come, Susan, Rodolfo's two brothers and I.)

   c. w-a **men y-tap men** [tson bech Dolf no Susan lee]
       C-go 3 P-four 3 three brother Rodolfo and Susan also
       They four went, Rodolfo's three brothers and Susan.

   d. *w-a **men y-tap men** [tson bech Dolf]
       C-go 3 P-four 3 three brother Rodolfo
       (They four went, Rodolfo's three brothers.)

---

[141] The appositive construction is not used with the quantifier y-ra 'P-all'.

12.1 Semantic interpretation

Note that this appositive construction is the only way to express the meaning conveyed by examples such as (356a and c). In the regular construction, DP_2, DP_3, or DP_4 may not be filled by a nominal phrase that refers to more than one person,[142] as (357) verifies, giving further evidence for the selection of a specific number of arguments by the quantifier.

(357) a. *xiid   noo   gy-on   noo   txup   bech   Dolf
       F/come   1EX   P-three   1EX   two   brother   Rodolfo
       (Two of Rodolfo's brothers and I will come (the three of us).)

   b. *xiid   noo   y-tap   noo   Susan   txup   bech   Dolf
      F/come   1EX   P-four   1EX   Susan   two   brother   Rodolfo
      (Susan, two of Rodolfo's brothers, and I will come (the four of us).)

   c. *w-a   men   y-tap   men   tson   bech   Dolf
      C-go   3   P-four   3   three   brother   Rodolfo
      (He and three of Rodolfo's brothers went (the four of them).)

We move now to the question of the purpose and meaning of the aspect/mood marking on the quantifier. The forms of the aspect prefixes which can appear on quantifiers are identical to those found on verbs, but their semantic significance is altered somewhat. In regular quantificational DPs, three aspect markers are attested on the quantifiers which can be used in these special constructions, i.e., the numbers 'one' through 'four' and the quantifier meaning 'all'. The other quantifiers never carry aspect marking nor any other affixes. Each marker will be described in turn. Only the Potential marker, given last here, is attested in the special number-marking constructions.

The Completive aspect marker *w-* can be used to indicate a finished period of time, as in (358a-b), or to form an ordinal number as in (358c).

---

[142] This restriction does not seem to hold with the quantifier *y-ra* 'P-all', since (i) is grammatical. (The DP_1 following the quantifier can be omitted due to either the Subject = Possessor of Object Condition or the Nonpronominal Head Condition, to be discussed in §§12.2.1.1 and 12.2.1.2.)

   (i) w-tap   Jesus   y-ra   chip-txup   x-tisipulo   Jesus   LUCAS 9:1
       C-reunite Jesus   P-all   ten-two   POS-disciple   Jesus
       Jesus and all his twelve disciples came back together.

However, this example may alternatively be analyzed as a coordinate structure without an overt conjunction.

(358) a. ***w-ra*** *gyëël w-a-xee   noo* MTLEMON 37
         C-all night C-go-rise 1EX
         The next day we got up.

   b. ***w-deb*** *iz   w-ya   x-mig   noo   lgyëz* MARTIN 1
      C-one year C-go   POS-friend 1EX   town
      Last year my friend came to the village.

   c. *per chene w-ya Jose **w-rup** tir* AGOSTO 20
      but when C-go José C-two time

      w-za-no   Jose   Jwan
      C-walk-take   José   Juan
      But when José went the second time, he took Juan.

Likewise, the Future marker *s-* may be used to indicate 'another' (359a–b) or 'again' (359c–d) as many times as the cardinality of the quantifier indicates. The marking on the quantifier is independent of the aspect marking on the main verb.

(359) a. *por **s-teb**   koo   zob   **s-te**   giblew* BATHROOM 31A
         on   F-one   side   PR/sit F-one   faucet

         ne   r-naa   men
         that   H-wash.hands   3
         On the other side sits another faucet at which they wash their hands.

   b. *nes   **s-yon**   iz* HORTENS 48A
      inside F-three year

      y-tsoow men   te   Biblya   na   disa
      P-make   3   one   Bible   which   language
      Within another three years, they will make a Bible in Zapotec.

   c. *xiid   noo   **s-te**   x-yuu   de* MARTIN 47
      F/come   1EX   F-one   POS-house   2
      I will come again to your house.

12.1 Semantic interpretation 267

    d. *r-lux   lo   nga   r-kaa   giib   s-te*   ESCUELA 20
       H-finish face there H-touch bell F-one
       After this the bell rang again.

The third aspect/mood marker that can appear on these quantifiers is the Potential *y-* or *gy-*. Its use indicates that the number expressed by the quantifier is that of the whole group, whereas a number without the aspect/mood marking gives a partitive reading. For example, the use of the Potential marking in the quantificational DP in (360a) indicates that the three rifles were all the rifles that the thieves had. Without the aspect/mood marking, as in (360b), the reading is that the man carried three out of a larger group of rifles that the thieves had.

(360) a. *w-eey   men   **gy-on**   x-kwiib   ngbaan*   CWENT 41
      C-take 3   P-three POS-rifle thief
      He carried the thieves' three rifles.

    b. *w-eey   men   **tson**   x-kwiib   ngbaan*
      C-take 3   three   POS-rifle thief
      He carried three of the thieves' rifles.

In the special number-marking constructions, only the Potential marker may occur. It is almost always present and carries the same holistic meaning as in regular quantificational DPs (361a). If the Potential marker is not present, a partitive reading is conveyed, as seen in example (361b).

(361) a. *s-ya   **men**   **y-rup**   **men***   SAMUEL 13
      PR-go 3   P-two 3
      They both were going.

    b. *s-ya   **men**   **txup**   **men***
      PR-go 3   two   3
      Two of them (out of the group) were going.

Consistent with this holistic versus partitive meaning of the Potential marking, *ra* 'all' always carries the Potential marking in these special constructions, since the meaning of the quantifier is inconsistent with a partitive reading.

Note that the use of the construction without the Potential marker does not change any of the requirements regarding the number of arguments which can/must appear after the quantifier. Specifically, removing the

Potential marker from (352d) does not make it grammatical; it remains highly unnatural. Dropping the Potential marker does not license identifying only part of that particular group. Instead, it indicates that the group referred to is only part of a larger group. In contrast, use of the Potential marker indicates that the identified group is the total group relevant to the context.

12.1.2 Head type and inclusion

In the QZ constructions, the head DP$_1$ can be filled by any referential nominal phrase, including proper names, common noun phrases, or quantified noun phrases, as well as by pronouns. Some examples of each type are given in (362). Pronoun heads are the most common in the full construction, which has all the DPs overt, due to the optionality conditions to be discussed in §§12.2.1.1–12.2.1.2.

(362) a. *tempran r-a-xee* **noo y-rup noo xnaa** **noo** LIFEINQ 1
early H-go-rise 1EX P-two 1EX mother 1EX
Early my mother and I would get up.

b. *nga ts-uu de y-rup de Susan* TRIPTOQ 6
there P-be 2 P-two 2 Susan
There you'll be with Susan.

c. *w-zhoon men y-ra men x-pëëd noo* MARTRIST 6
C-run 3 P-all 3 POS-baby 1EX
She and my children ran away.

d. *w-ya maa y-rup maa x-mig mër gos* MARTRIST 35
C-dance 3A P-two 3A POS-friend pigeon female
He danced with the female pigeon's friend.

e. *w-guu Jose y-rup Jose xuz noo* AGOSTO 44A
C-sow José P-two José father 1EX

   leen x-yuu xuz noo
   inside POS-house father 1EX
José and my father put it inside my father's house.

12.1 Semantic interpretation 269

f. *w-nëëz mëëk* **ngyed** *y-rup* **ngyed** *konej*   AGOSTO 49
 C-catch dog   chicken P-two chicken rabbit
 The dog caught a chicken and a rabbit.

g. *te* **men** *y-rup* **x-pëëk men** *z-a*   *x-ten*   *men* MENMAAC 1A
 one 3   P-two POS-dog 3   PR-go POS-ranch 3
 A man and his dog were going to his ranch.

The pronominal examples (362a–d) show how these QZ constructions are similar to the PPC. If the number marked by the quantifier is superimposed on the head pronoun, it has the effect of a plural pronoun Then, the referents of the pronoun and second DP in the adjunct can be seen as included in the reference of the "plural pronoun" head, as shown in the readings given in (363a–d) for (362a–d), respectively.

(363) a. Early we two, I and my mother, would get up.

b. There will be you two, you and Susan.

c. They all, she and my children, ran away.

d. The two animals, he and the female pigeon's friend, danced.

The notion of inclusion within the reference of a pronoun can be formalized as Set-theoretic inclusion, which forms the lattice shown in (364).[143] The lattice shows that combining a first person exclusive pronoun and a second person pronoun yields a first person inclusive pronoun. A first person exclusive pronoun may add a third person referent and still remain first person exclusive. Likewise, a second person pronoun may add a third person referent and remain second person. Finally, the combination of a first person exclusive pronoun, a second person pronoun, and a third person pronoun requires the use of first person inclusive. First person inclusive is thus the top or upper-bound of the lattice, while the empty set is the bottom or lower-bound.

---

[143] I am grateful to Bill Ladusaw for pointing out the lattice properties of pronominal systems. For details regarding the mathematical properties of lattices, see Partee, ter Meulen, and Wall (1990:chapter 10).

(364)

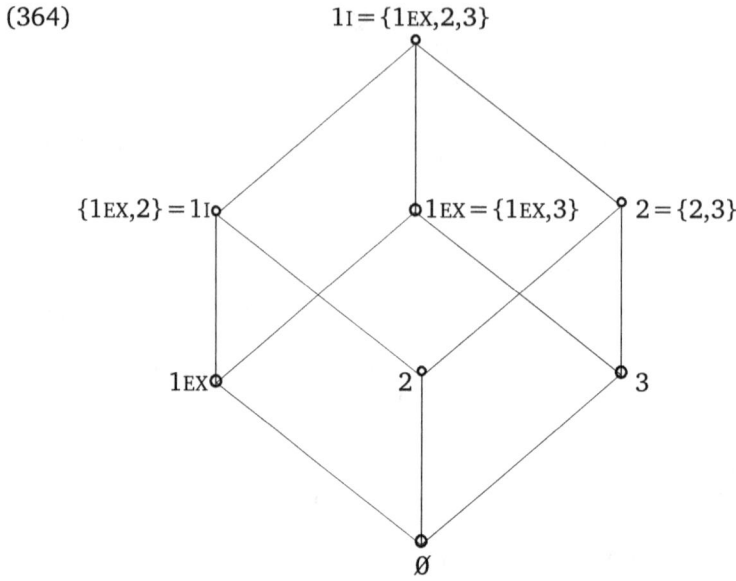

Looked at from the point of view of the semantic interpretation for the PPC given by Ladusaw (1989), the requirement that the referent(s) of the adjunct be included in the reference of the pronoun head entails the Person Hierarchy Effect, due to the meaning of the person features of the pronouns. For example, since a second person pronoun refers to a group which includes the hearer but excludes the speaker, a construction with a second person pronoun as head could not have a first person adjunct. Likewise, a third person pronoun refers to a group which excludes both the speaker and the hearer, so neither a first person nor a second person adjunct is allowed. The inclusion interpretation thus accounts for the Person Hierarchy Effect without a separate stipulation that the person feature of the head must be greater or equal to the person feature of the adjunct on a scale of 1 > 2 > 3.

The distinction in usage of the first person exclusive and inclusive pronouns in QZ provides additional evidence that the inclusion relationship entails the Person Hierarchy Effect for constructions with pronominal heads. In the QZ constructions which include both first and second person, it is ungrammatical to use the first person exclusive pronoun *noo* as the head, as shown in (365a) and (366a). The grammatical counterpart of each of these is shown in (365b) and (366b), where the first person

12.1 Semantic interpretation

inclusive pronoun is the head. This data accords with the lattice showing the inclusion relation in (364).[144]

(365) a. *g-ux-sëë   **noo y-ra noo de**   LIFEINQ 20A
P-eat-dinner 1EX P-all 1EX 2
(We(inc) all will eat dinner.)

b. *g-ux-sëë-b   y-ra-b*
P-eat-dinner-1I P-all-1I
We(inc) all will eat dinner.

(366) a. *g-ux-sëë   **noo y-rup noo de**   LIFEINQ 20B
P-eat-dinner 1EX P-two 1EX 2
(You and I will eat dinner (together).)

b. *g-ux-sëë-b   y-rup-e*
P-eat-dinner-1I P-two-1I
You and I will eat dinner (together).

Once we move away from pronoun heads, however, the inclusion interpretation seems more problematic. Giving a reading similar to those in (363) for (362e–g) yields the bizarre results shown in (367a–c), respectively. In each of these examples, the reference of the head and of the adjunct seem to be disjoint.

(367) a. ??The two José's, José and my father, put it inside my father's house.

b. ??The dog caught two chickens, a chicken and a rabbit.

---

[144]Recall that the first person inclusive pronoun *-be* is a phonological clitic which attaches to the preceding word whenever possible. In (365b) it has attached to the quantifier *y-ra* and the final vowel has dropped to form a closed syllable. In (366b) it has again attached to the quantifier, this time *y-rup*. Since degemination applies to the *p-b* combination, the word surfaces as *y-rup-e*. The final vowel cannot drop in this case or there would be no evidence for the pronoun.

Note also that it is not possible to use the first person inclusive pronoun as the head but have the first person exclusive pronoun and the second person pronoun in the adjunct, as in (i).

(i)   *g-ux-sëë-b   y-ra noo de*
P-eat-dinner-1I P-all 1EX 2
(We(inc) all will eat dinner.)

This is due to the required coindexing between the head and the first DP following the quantifier. See §12.3.3.

c. ??Two 'one man's, including a man and his dog, were going to his ranch.

One approach we could try is to analyze the QZ structures with nonpronominal heads as versions of the Comitative Coordination construction proposed by McNally (1993) for Russian. An example is given in (368).

(368) **Anna**   s   **Petej**   napisali   pis'mo   MCNALLY 1
Anna.NOM with Peter.INSTR wrote-PL letter
Anna and Peter wrote a letter.

McNally proposes that the NP *Anna* and PP *s Petej* in (368) form a single-headed asymmetric constituent which has a semantics practically identical to that of a symmetric coordinate structure. She analyzes the structure of these Comitative Coordination structures as shown in (369), which is almost identical syntactically to Schwartz' analysis for the PPC.

(369)
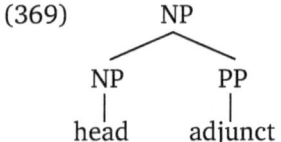

McNally further notes that the fact that the verb in (368) has plural agreement marking argues for the constituency of the construction. The number marking is not found on the head of the construction, but rather is semantically determined. She claims that the Comitative Coordination construction denotes a group, with an implicature requiring that the action was done together, where the referent of the adjunct must be disjoint from the referent of the head.

A major problem with adopting a Comitative Coordination analysis for the QZ structures would be that it does not explain the fact that the Person Hierarchy Effect is a strict requirement, even in the constructions with nonpronominal heads. There is no reason under the Comitative Coordination analysis that one could not say *John with me*, but the QZ counterpart of this is ungrammatical. Thus, the idea of disjoint reference seems incorrect for the QZ constructions.

Surprisingly, in Mesoamerican languages the inclusion relationship may still be workable. Judith Aissen (p.c.) found that PPC-type constructions in

12.1 Semantic interpretation

Tzotzil which have proper names rather than plural pronouns as the head are also grammatical and receive basically the same interpretation as regular PPCs. This is possible since, in Tzotzil as in QZ, a proper name may denote not only that individual, but also his family or close associates.

Following up on this reasoning, we could assume that the correct extension of Ladusaw's semantic analysis of the PPC would be that the referent(s) in the adjunct must be included in the reference of the head, with the number feature of the group being given by the quantifier. Under this analysis, proper names and common noun phrases become simply special types of third person pronouns. Therefore, just as a third person animate (but nonhuman) pronoun *maa* could not include reference to a person (similarly, *it* cannot refer to John), *John* could not include reference to someone, say, in his enemy's family. This analysis might be made to work for (362e), since 'José' and 'my father' could be close associates, and for (362g), since a man's dog certainly belongs to him. It does not seem workable for (362f), however, since the reference of 'chicken' does not seem in any way to include the reference of 'rabbit'. Therefore, more needs to be said to entail the Person Hierarchy Effect for nonpronominal heads; inclusion alone is not sufficient.

12.1.3 The Person Hierarchy Effect and group reference

In addition to the case of (362f), where the inclusion relation does not hold between the reference of the head and the reference of the adjunct, there are problematic cases where inclusion does hold. Examples (370)–(371) show that the inclusion analysis does not entail the Person Hierarchy Effect for nonpronominal heads. If the person referred to by the second person pronoun is a member of Susan's family, the inclusion interpretation would predict that (370b) is grammatical, but it is not, since it violates the Person Hierarchy Effect. The correct order is given in (370a).

(370) a. *ts-a de y-rup de Susan* TRIPTOQ 80
P-go 2 P-two 2 Susan
You can go with Susan.

b. **ts-a Susan y-rup Susan de*
P-go Susan P-two Susan 2
(Susan can go with you.)

Similarly, *xnaa noo* 'my mother' should be able to head a construction which includes 'me', but as (371b) shows, the Person Hierarchy Effect again rules this out.

(371) a. *tempran r-a-xee* **noo y-rup noo xnaa noo**   LIFEINQ 1
early   H-go-rise 1EX P-two 1EX mother 1EX
Early my mother and I would get up.

b. **tempran r-a-xee* **xnaa noo y-rup xnaa noo noo**
early   H-go-rise mother 1EX P-two mother 1EX 1EX
(Early my mother and I would get up.)

Clearly, it is the person feature of the head that is crucial. In order to ensure that the Person Hierarchy Effect is met we need the person feature of the head to be the person feature for the entire structure. Also, we saw in §12.1.1 that the quantifier marks the number for the construction. I capture both of these properties in the semantic interpretation given in (372), where the phrase "the mother DP" signifies the whole construction.[145]

(372) Proposed Semantic Interpretation

> The mother DP defines a group which has the person feature of the head DP_1 and the number feature of the quantifier. The referents of all the arguments of (i.e., DPs following) the quantifier must be included in the defined group.

This means that, as before, a first person exclusive head would require that the hearer (second person) could not be part of the group, whereas a first person inclusive head would require that both the speaker and the hearer be included. A second person head would mean that the speaker (first person) could not be included, and a third person head would exclude both the speaker and the hearer. For example, the makeup of the group X referred to by *Susan y-rup Maria* 'Susan P-two Mary' would be calculated as follows:

Susan $\in X$, person $= 3 \Rightarrow 1 \notin X, 2 \notin X$
Mary $\in X$
$|X| = 2$

---

[145]We could appeal to the Correspondence Principle (Zwicky 1977) to correlate the syntactic and semantic features on the mother DP, though no overt morphosyntactic marking is present in QZ.

12.1 Semantic interpretation

There seems to be one hole remaining: pronominal heads are preferred over nonpronominal heads. Thus, even when a third person pronoun is used, it cannot be in DP_2 while a nonpronominal is the head. Chung (1981) reports that there is a similar hierarchical ranking of pronouns over nonpronominal DPs in Chamorro. In this case the subject of a transitive irrealis clause is required to be equal or superior to the object on this hierarchy. In these Chamorro clauses, if a nonpronominal subject (like our DP_1 head) is present, the object (comparable to DP_2) cannot be a pronoun.

If nonpronominals are treated as lower than third person pronouns (i.e., as if they have 'fourth' person feature rather than third person on an appropriately expanded lattice), then the given interpretation will also assure that a pronominal head is chosen over a nonpronominal head.

The proposed interpretation thus entails both the Person Hierarchy Effect and the number resolution for the structure. It covers both pronominal and nonpronominal heads, thus clarifying and extending Ladusaw's analysis beyond the limited domain of the PPC.

An account of the construal between the head and the adjunct will be postponed until §12.3.3.

12.2 Syntactic analysis of the contiguous structure

Before a syntactic analysis can be given, more of the properties of the construction must be covered. Section 12.2.1 presents the two conditions on the optionality of the repeated DP_1; the first provides evidence for the clausal nature of the quantifier and following DPs.

In §12.2.2, more data is given showing the distribution of the construction. Here two possible analyses are contrasted: one where the whole construction is a single DP which fills an argument role, versus an account of the quantifier as a predicate which is embedded under the verb in the preceding clause. I argue that the former analysis is superior.

Section 12.2.3 then deals with the questions of where the quantifier clause attaches within the DP and what its internal structure is.

12.2.1 The clausal nature of the quantifier phrase

In addition to the basic properties of the special number-marking constructions described in §12.1, there are two other conditions under which the DP_1 following the quantifier can be optionally omitted. (The head DP_1

preceding the quantifier is always overt.)[146] These two conditions, which are shown to be part of the grammar of QZ rather than being specific to the special number-marking constructions, will be covered in the next two subsections. A discussion of the ordering restrictions among the DPs follows. These conditions point toward a clausal analysis of the quantifier and the DPs following it.

12.2.1.1 The Subject = Possessor of Object Condition. In addition to the examples of the full construction we have seen where all the DPs are overt, there are many examples where there is no repeated DP_1 after the quantifier. One condition allowing this repeated DP_1 to be phonetically silent is the Subject = Possessor of Object Condition, which says that DP_1 may be absent after the quantifier if it is also the possessor of DP_2. Example (373) shows this optionality when both DP_1 and the possessor of DP_2 are proper names and in (374) both are pronominal.[147] Example (375) verifies that this optionality is not possible when the possessor of DP_2 is different from DP_1.

(373) a. *Biki z-a g-un kompanyar*   GRING 6
   Virginia PR-go P-LM accompany

    Gecha y-rup x-pëëd Gecha
    Lucrecia P-two POS-baby Lucrecia
   Virginia went to accompany Lucrecia$_i$ and her$_i$ baby.

  b. *Biki z-a g-un kompanyar*
   Virginia PR-go P-LM accompany

    Gecha y-rup Gecha x-pëëd Gecha
    Lucrecia P-two Lucrecia POS-baby Lucrecia
   Virginia went to accompany Lucrecia$_i$ and her$_i$ baby.

(374) a. *tempran r-a-xee noo y-rup noo xnaa noo* LIFEINQ 1
   early H-go-rise 1EX P-two 1EX mother 1EX
   Early my mother and I would get up.

---

[146]Except that the quantifier and following DPs may stand alone as the answer to an appropriate question.
[147]Recall from chapter 4 that Principle C of the Binding theory must be parameterized for QZ; proper names may be repeated throughout the sentence rather than changing all references after the first to pronouns. Further, there is no marking on the pronouns to indicate reflexivity.

12.2 Syntactic analysis of the contiguous structure

    b. *tempran r-a-xee* **noo** *y-rup xnaa* **noo**
       early   H-go-rise 1EX P-two mother 1EX
       Early my mother and I would get up.

(375) a. *w-zhoon* **men** *y-ra* **men** *x-pëëd* **noo**   MARTRIST 6
       C-run   3   P-all 3 POS-baby 1EX
       She and my children ran away.

    b. *w-zhoon **men** *y-ra x-pëëd* **noo**
       C-run   3   P-all POS-baby 1EX
       (She and my children ran away.)

This optionality is the same phenomenon seen in regular transitive sentences when the subject and the possessor of the object are coreferent (presented in chapter 4 as the reflexive of possession construction, following Butler 1976a). See §4.1.2 for YZ examples and §4.1.3 for examples from QZ.

There is clearly a special relationship between the subject and the possessor of the object in QZ and other Zapotecan languages. Unfortunately, framing a theoretical analysis for these constructions where the subject may be null when it is coreferent with the possessor of the object is extremely challenging. I will only be able to detail some of the challenges and tentatively suggest a possible account here.

Binding theory recognizes c-command as the key relationship necessary in anaphoric constructions (Reinhart 1981, Chomsky 1981, etc.). The anaphor, or referentially dependent element, must be c-commanded by its antecedent in order to obtain its reference from the antecedent. Likewise, a full DP cannot be c-commanded by its antecedent (though we have seen in chapter 4 that QZ allows violations of this Principle C requirement). The referentially independent element normally precedes and c-commands the referentially dependent element, making the term "antecedent" meaningful. In these Zapotecan constructions, however, it is the preceding and c-commanding element, the subject, that is referentially dependent on the possessor of the object.

As verified in the S-structure trees in (376), there is no way under either the Verb Movement or Subject Adjunction Hypotheses to have a normal c-command relationship between the possessor of the object and the subject. In the Verb Movement account, the subject is in the specifier of V^{max}, well above the possessor of the object. In the Subject Adjunction account, the subject starts even higher, as the specifier of IP. The S-structure position after Subject Adjunction has taken place is much lower in the tree, but the possessor, being the specifier of NP within the object DP, is still unable to c-command even the lowered subject.

(376) Verb Movement   or   Subject Adjunction

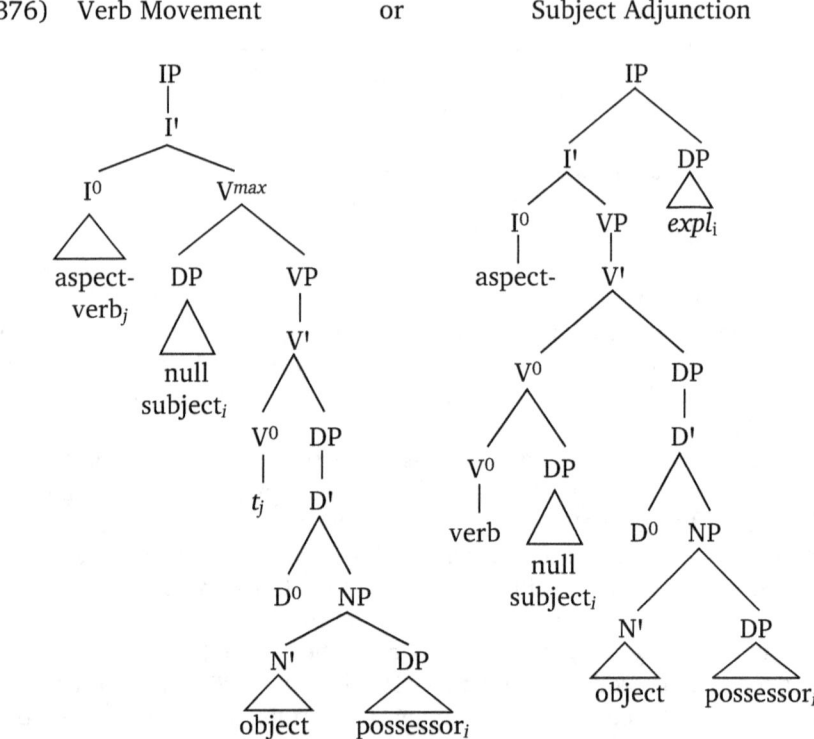

We need to verify that these problematic constructions really consist of a verb followed by a null subject and then an object with its possessor and are not instead simply examples of VOS order. All of the available evidence points to the conclusion that the final element is indeed the possessor and not the (displaced) subject.

First, the object and its possessor can be focused together, as in the YZ example (377), indicating that they form a single constituent. A coindexed pronoun must overtly mark the subject on the verb when this focusing occurs, however, showing that the null subject is only licensed very locally.

(377) liš   Bed-ən?   ba-ǰ-gʷia-bo?
      paper Peter-the already-H-look.at-3F
      Peter$_i$'s paper, he$_i$ is already looking at.

12.2 Syntactic analysis of the contiguous structure

Further, strict VSO order is required for the correct interpretation of grammatical functions within the clause since there is no overt case marking. VOS order, which could be obtained by either rightward movement of the subject or by the optionality of Subject Adjunction movement, is unattested in Zapotec.

Woolford (1991) notes that Jacaltec avoids the problem of the reflexive c-commanding its antecedent by incorporating the reflexive into the verb instead of placing it in object position, as shown in (378) (taken from Craig 1977:148). *Sba* is argued to have incorporated into the verb, since VOS order is never allowed in Jacaltec either.

(378) [xil sba] naj Pel
 saw self CL Peter
 Peter saw himself.

One might wonder, therefore, if an incorporation analysis would work for the Zapotec constructions, which have the same superficial word order. Unfortunately, though initially attractive, such an analysis does not account for all the facts.

First, the "incorporated" object is a noun requiring a possessor. The DP following this object serves as the possessor, not as the subject (though coreferent with the subject). This is confirmed in JZ, where some of the subject and possessor pronouns differ. Nellis and Nellis (1983:379–380) note that in these constructions for both reflexive and reciprocal uses, it is always the possessive pronoun form that appears, rather than the subject form of the pronoun. (379) illustrates this: the possessive pronoun is used in the simple grammatical example (379a), but replacing the possessive pronoun with a subject pronoun yields ungrammaticality (379b).

(379) a. *quiê-ní?í*
 wash-hand/3POS
 He$_i$ washed his$_i$ hands.

 b. **quiê-ná?-a*
 wash-hand-3SUBJ
 (He$_i$ washed his$_i$ hands.)

There is also a syntactic argument against an incorporation analysis for these constructions. This comes from the position of negation with respect to the object. In a regular incorporation construction the object appears inside the negative marker, as shown in (380). This accords with the Verb

Movement proposal for clause structure adopted here, where the whole verbal complex, including the incorporated object, moves to I^0, across the subject (which is required in negative commands), and then to Neg^0 (or Pol^0).

(380) g-ix-**nii**-t   de   lo   pis   BATHROOM 18
      P-put-foot-NEG   2   face   floor
      Don't step on the floor.

In contrast to the order in (380), negation is marked **before** the object in a Subject = Possessor of Object construction, as shown in (381). The incorporation analysis is thus unlikely, since the object is not part of the verbal complex which undergoes head movement.

(381) a. r-dxiin-t   _   x-ten   men   RANCHO 9
       H-arrive-NEG   POS-ranch   3
       They$_i$ didn't arrive at their$_i$ ranch.

      b. w-tsalo-t   _   x-mgyeey   men   RANCHO 43
       C-meet-NEG   POS-man   3

         s-teb   koo   z-a   x-mgyeey   men
         F-one   side   PR-go   POS-man   3
         She$_i$ didn't meet her$_i$ husband, because he went the other way.

Given that the final element is the possessor and the subject is null, we are left with a need to redefine the binding relationship for these particular constructions. This binding relationship allowing the null subject is very local; it only holds within a single clause and cannot even survive focusing or other Ā-movement. Further, although the possessor of the object does not c-command the null subject, the reverse is true. Since these two elements are also coindexed, an A-chain is formed and the null subject A-binds the possessor of the object. Clearly, a local A-chain is still required in these Zapotec constructions, but it is the tail rather than the head of the chain that is identified. Judith Aissen (1992 class lectures) reported a similar identification requirement in Tzotzil, where the tail of an A-chain which is first or second person must be identified with respect to number, while the head is so marked.

As in Black (1996), I propose that the Principles of Binding theory be reworded in terms of A-chains instead of A-binding to allow parameterization of whether the head or tail of the A-chain is the referentially dependent

12.2 Syntactic analysis of the contiguous structure 281

element. The dependent element is identified by the referentially independent element through the A-chain. The revised principles would read as in (382), where {head/tail} indicates a parameter to be set.

(382) Principles of Binding theory

A. Anaphors must be the {head/tail} of a local A-chain.

B. Pronouns must not be the {head/tail} of a local A-chain.

C. Nominal phrases must not be the {head/tail} of an A-chain.

Setting the parameter to 'tail' in each case would yield the equivalent to Chomsky's principles. The null subject in these Zapotec constructions requires that the parameter in Principle A be set to 'head'.

A more abstract alternative (but which does not require parameterized Principles of Binding theory) is that the null subject is an expletive-type element in the A-chain, parallel to the analysis of the scope-markers in *wh*-chains in the partial *wh*-movement analyzed by McDaniel (1989) (see also the appendix), allowing it to locally c-command the overt possessor. If this analysis proves viable, it will provide an interesting point of connection between A-chains and Ā-chains.

Returning to the analysis of the special number-marking constructions, it is sufficient to note that the optionality of the repeated DP_1 due to the Subject = Possessor of Object Condition is part of a general constraint in Zapotec grammar. Most importantly, it gives evidence for a clausal analysis of the quantifier and following DPs, since the relationship between the DP_1 and the possessor of DP_2 is exactly the same as that between the subject and the possessor of the object in a clause.[148]

12.2.1.2 The Nonpronominal Head Condition. The second condition which allows the repeated DP_1 following the quantifier to be omitted distinguishes between pronouns and nonpronominals. If DP_1 is a pronoun not meeting the Subject = Possessor of Object Condition then it must be overt after the quantifier. In the case of a nonpronominal head DP_1, the repeated DP_1 may be optionally omitted. With proper name or common

---

[148]To my knowledge, there is no similar relationship between the possessor of the head noun and the possessor of its complement in an ordinary nominal phrase, as in (i), which licenses a null possessor.
  (i) $John_i$'s love for his_i mother
This is expected given the lack of parallelism in structure between clauses headed by [+V] predicates and nominal phrases (chapter 11).

noun heads, the overt realization of the repeated DP$_1$ appears to be truly optional, whereas the preference is clearly not to repeat the DP$_1$ in constructions with more complex heads, as in (387c–f). Since it is also possible to replace the second instance of DP$_1$ with a coreferent pronoun, I claim that the Nonpronominal Head Condition is simply an instantiation of the null third person pronoun and the hierarchy of DP-types seen in chapter 4. As such, it does not need to be stated separately in the grammar.

Examples (383)–(385) illustrate this Nonpronominal Head Condition. When the head DP$_1$ is a pronoun, DP$_1$ must be repeated after the quantifier, as verified by the (b) examples. In (385) the two different pronouns used indicate two groups being combined, giving a reading of 'we all, I with them,...'.

(383) a. *ts-a* **de y-rup** *de Susan* TRIPTOQ 80
P-go 2 P-two 2 Susan
You can go with Susan.

b. **ts-a* **de y-rup** *Susan*
P-go 2 P-two Susan
(You can go with Susan.)

(384) a. *r-oo* **men y-rup men** *Biki nisgaal* AGOSTO 8
H-drink 3 P-two 3 Virginia soda
She and Virginia drank soda pop.

b. **r-oo* **men y-rup** *Biki nisgaal*
H-drink 3 P-two Virginia soda
(She and Virginia drank soda pop.)

(385) a. *nga w-u-gwe* **noo y-ra noo men** MTLEMON2 45
there C-eat-lunch 1EX P-all 1EX 3
There we all ate lunch.

b. **nga w-u-gwe* **noo y-ra men**
there C-eat-lunch 1EX P-all 3
(There we all ate lunch.)

The repeated DP$_1$ may be omitted, however, when both DP positions are filled by nonpronominals. (386) illustrates this optionality when DP$_1$ is filled by a proper name and (387a–b) verifies that it also holds for

12.2 Syntactic analysis of the contiguous structure

common nouns. With more complex nominal phrases, the preference is not to repeat the full DP_1 (387c), but instead to use the common noun only (387d), a coreferent pronoun (387e), or the null third person pronoun (387f) (i.e., omitting the second DP_1).

(386) a. xna-ydoo   x-pee   Manwel n-ak   AGOSTO 12
mother-church POS-son Manuel S-become

Katalina y-rup Tomas
Catherine P-two Thomas
The godparents of Manuel's son are Catherine and Thomas.

b. xna-ydoo   x-pee   Manwel n-ak
mother-church POS-son Manuel S-become

Katalina y-rup Katalina Tomas
Catherine P-two Catherine Thomas
The godparents of Manuel's son are Catherine and Thomas.

(387) a. w-nëëz mëëk **ngyed y-rup ngyed konej**   AGOSTO 49
C-catch dog chicken P-two chicken rabbit
The dog caught a chicken and a rabbit.

b. w-nëëz mëëk **ngyed y-rup konej**
C-catch dog chicken P-two rabbit
The dog caught a chicken and a rabbit.

c. ??w-nëëz mëëk **te ngyed win y-rup te ngyed win konej**
C-catch dog one chicken small P-two one chicken small rabbit
The dog caught a small chicken and a small rabbit.

d. w-nëëz mëëk **te ngyed win y-rup ngyed konej**
C-catch dog one chicken small P-two chicken rabbit
The dog caught a small chicken and a rabbit.

e. w-nëëz mëëk **te ngyed$_i$ win y-rup maa$_i$ konej**
C-catch dog one chicken small P-two 3A rabbit
The dog caught a small chicken and a rabbit.

f. *w-nëëz mëëk te ngyed win y-rup konej*
   C-catch dog one chicken small P-two rabbit
   The dog caught a small chicken and a rabbit.

The versions of the construction where the second DP₁ is not phonetically realized, such as *Katalina yrup Tomas* in (386a), look something like regular coordination constructions. A coordination analysis is not tenable as a general solution for all the special number-marking constructions, however, and it does not even account well for the examples of the form DP₁ quantifier DP₂. I show this by demonstrating the problems encountered by two possible versions of a regular coordination construction.

First, since an overt conjunction is not required between the conjuncts in DP coordination (as seen in §11.3), one might assume that the quantifier is really only a part of the second conjunct, as shown in (388a). Alternatively, in the special number-marking constructions the quantifier itself could be assumed to act as the conjunction, as in (388b).

(388) a. *Quantifier in 2nd conjunct   or   b. *Quantifier as conjunction

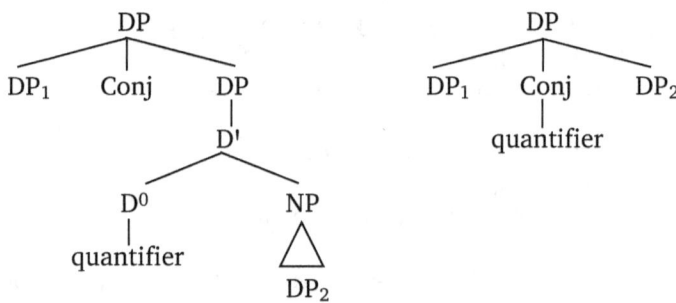

The best chance of success for the analysis that the quantifier is part of the second conjunct in a regular DP coordination structure (388a) would be in examples like those given in (389)–(390). In each case, the attested reading as a special number-marking construction is given in (a). The reanalysis as a coordinate structure is shown in (b) (with the two coordinates bracketed), but this reading is noted as unattested (*), since it is not the reading given by the QZ speaker, nor is it correct from the context.

(389) a. *te men y-rup x-pëëk men z-a x-ten men* MENMAAC 1A
       one 3   P-two POS-dog 3   PR-go POS-ranch 3
       A man and his dog were going to his ranch.

b. *[te   men]   [y-rup x-pëëk   men] z-a   x-ten   men
   one 3   P-two POS-dog 3   PR-go   POS-ranch 3
   (A man and two of his dogs were going to his ranch.)

(390) a. z-a   x-unaa   men y-rup x-pëëd   x-unaa   men RANCHO 34
         PR-go POS-woman 3   P-two POS-baby POS-woman 3
         She$_i$ (his woman) and her$_i$ baby were going.

   b. *z-a   [x-unaa   men] [y-rup x-pëëd   x-unaa   men]
      PR-go POS-woman   3   P-two POS-baby POS-woman   3
      (She$_i$ (his woman) and her$_i$ two babies were going.)

The cases which can be syntactically analyzed both ways are very limited: the repeated DP$_1$ must be omitted subject to one of the conditions given above, the second DP must be a noun which can be quantified, and the construction must not be separated. Also, the quantifiers *te* 'one', *tson* 'three' and *tap* 'four' cannot be used, since they select the "wrong" number of arguments. For the vast majority of cases, the construction we are considering cannot be analyzed alternatively as a regular coordinate structure without an overt conjunction. Therefore, in addition to providing an unattested reading in the few cases where such an alternate analysis is available, a coordination analysis of this type does not account for the full distribution of the construction.

The analysis that the quantifier is a conjunction (388b) runs into similar distribution problems. It could possibly be used to account for the examples which have the form DP$_1$ quantifier DP$_2$, as in (386a), (387b), (389a) and (390a), but it provides no account for the many examples where the DP$_1$ following the quantifier is overt, as in (386b) and (387a), nor for the examples which use the quantifiers meaning 'three' or 'four'.

In the next section, we look at two more analyses involving coordination that attempt to solve the problem encountered here of accounting for more than one DP being possible after the quantifier. These analyses are also ruled out by their inability to account for the required ordering and number of the DPs.

12.2.1.3 Ordering restrictions between the DPs. Coindexation of the head DP and the first DP after the quantifier (the two DP$_1$s) is required. This coindexation is almost always shown by identity between the two DP$_1$s if the second instance is overt. However, in addition to allowing the repeated DP$_1$ to be null due to one of the optionality conditions given, the second instance of DP$_1$ may be a coreferent pronoun (at least in the contiguous structure), as shown in (392c). Further, DP$_1$ and DP$_2$ may not be in reverse order after the quantifier, as shown in (391)–(392), nor may the DP$_1$ after the quantifier add new information, as (393c) verifies.

(391) a. *nga   ts-uu **de y-rup de Susan**   TRIPTOQ 6
       there P-be 2   P-two 2 Susan
       There you'll be with Susan.

   b. **nga ts-uu **de y-rup Susan de**
       there P-be 2   P-two Susan 2
       (There you'll be with Susan.)

(392) a. xna-ydoo   x-pee   Manwel n-ak   AGOSTO 12
       mother-church POS-son Manuel S-become

       Katalina y-rup Katalina Tomas
       Catherine P-two Catherine Thomas
       The godparents of Manuel's son are Catherine and Thomas.

   b. *xna-ydoo   x-pee   Manwel n-ak
       mother-church POS-son Manuel S-become

       Katalina y-rup Tomas Katalina
       Catherine P-two Thomas Catherine
       (The godparents of Manuel's son are Catherine and Thomas.)

   c. xna-ydoo   x-pee   Manwel n-ak
       mother-church POS-son Manuel S-become

       Katalina$_i$ y-rup men$_i$ Tomas
       Catherine P-two 3 Thomas
       The godparents of Manuel's son are Catherine and Thomas.

(393) a. *lex   bweree-ke   **men y-ra men**   MTLEMON2 57B
       later C/return-ASSOC 3   P-all 3
       Then they all returned also.

   b. *lex   bweree-ke   **men y-ra men Susan**
       later C/return-ASSOC 3   P-all 3 Susan
       Then they all, including Susan, returned also.

12.2 Syntactic analysis of the contiguous structure

c. *lex   b-weree-ke   men   y-ra   Dolf   Susan
   later C/return-also 3 P-all Rodolfo Susan
   (Then they all, including Rodolfo and Susan, returned also.)

The unattested examples above where the first DP following the quantifier is not coindexed with the head DP_1 are simply uninterpretable in QZ. The reason for this restriction ties in with the need for assuring correct semantic construal of the adjunct, especially in the separated structure. This construal will be discussed in §12.3.3.

The ordering restriction between the DPs following the quantifier is a key factor in ruling out two possible syntactic configurations where there is always only one DP following the quantifier. This DP would have to be a coordinate structure to account for the cases where more than one DP is present following the quantifier (thus improving on the two analyses rejected in the last section). Under one version of such an analysis, the quantifier would act as a conjunction between the head DP_1 and the coordinate DP, as shown in (394a). Alternatively, the full configuration would be an asymmetric DP structure where the adjunct QP takes a single DP complement, which is itself a coordinate DP, illustrated in (394b).[149]

(394) a. *Double coordination   or   b. *Adjunct coordination

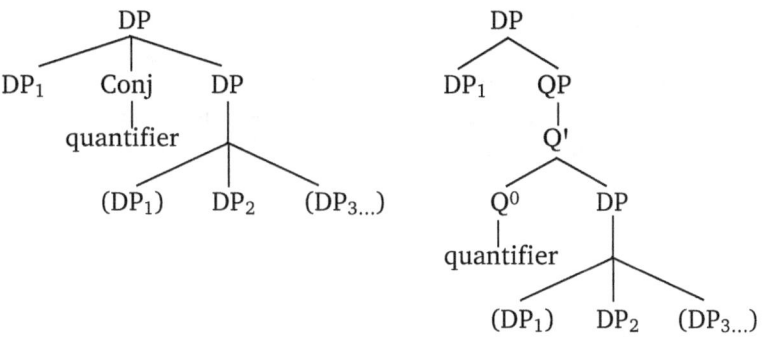

These analyses where the quantifier is always followed by only a single DP might seem advantageous over the account where it may take one to four complements. However, the coordinate DP analyses in (394) would not have any mechanism for assuring that the proper number of DPs will be coordinated in the single DP. The examples given in (395) are predicted incorrectly to be grammatical. The fact that *y-rup* 'P-two' and *y-ra*

---

[149]Here I abstract away from the issue of whether the adjunct attaches to the head DP or somewhere within it. That issue will be dealt with in §12.2.3.

'P-all' may only have two DPs following them while *gy-on* 'P-three' must have three DPs is unaccounted for under either coordinate DP analysis in (394), but it falls out nicely under a clausal analysis of the QP adjunct where the quantifier is normally a multiargument predicate.

(395) a. *w-nëëz mëëk **ngyed y-rup ngyed konej mëël**
   c-catch dog chicken P-two chicken rabbit snake
   (The dog caught a chicken, a rabbit, and a snake.)

   b. *w-nëëz mëëk **ngyed y-ra ngyed konej mëël**
   c-catch dog chicken P-all chicken rabbit snake
   (The dog caught a chicken, a rabbit, and a snake.)

   c. *w-nëëz mëëk **ngyed gy-on ngyed konej**
   c-catch dog chicken P-three chicken rabbit
   (The dog caught a chicken and a rabbit.)

Further, if the DP following the quantifier were a regular coordinate DP, we should be able to insert *no* 'and' between DP_1 and DP_2. This, however, is not allowed (396a). Also, as seen above within a regular coordinate DP, the order of the conjoined DPs is reversible, but reversing the order within the special number-marking constructions makes the sentence ungrammatical (396b).

(396) a. *w-nëëz mëëk **ngyed y-rup ngyed no konej**
   c-catch dog chicken P-two chicken and rabbit
   (The dog caught a chicken and a rabbit.)

   b. *w-nëëz mëëk **ngyed y-rup konej ngyed**
   c-catch dog chicken P-two rabbit chicken
   (The dog caught a chicken and a rabbit.)

It should be noted that the structure in (394b) has several advantages over the other coordination structures considered thus far. It is clearly an asymmetric structure with a head and an adjunct, and as such it parallels the structure of the PPC. This allows both the semantics and the syntax to be similar between the two constructions. Further, the quantifier is treated as the head of the adjunct. Both of these advantages will also be included in the analysis I adopt. Instead of the single (coordinate) DP complement for the quantifier shown in (394b), however, I assume that the quantifier heads a clausal adjunct and subcategorizes for one to four

12.2 Syntactic analysis of the contiguous structure

complements. This accounts for the various properties and restrictions on these special constructions in a way that is consistent with the rest of QZ syntax. The proposed internal structure of this clausal adjunct will be given in §12.2.3.

12.2.2 The constituency of the construction

This section presents more data to show that the construction as a whole fills all the normal DP positions. This distribution, coupled with the fact that the whole construction can be focused as a unit, argues for its constituency as a DP. I will use this to specifically argue against the alternative proposal that the QP is an embedded predicate.

These structures are found in subject position in the vast majority of cases. A few representative examples are given in (397).

(397) a. *s-ya* **men** *y-rup* **men**   SAMUEL 13
PR-go 3   P-two 3
They were both going.

b. *nga*   *w-u-gwe*   **noo** *y-ra* **noo men**   MTLEMON2 45
there C-eat-lunch 1EX P-all 1EX 3
There we all ate lunch.

c. *tempran r-a-xee*   **noo** *y-rup* **noo xnaa**   **noo**   LIFEINQ 1
early   H-go-rise 1EX P-two 1EX mother 1EX
Early my mother and I would get up.

d. *nga*   *ts-uu de y-rup de Susan*   TRIPTOQ 6
there P-be 2 P-two 2 Susan
There you'll be with Susan.

e. *z-a*   **x-unaa**   **men** *y-rup* **x-pëëd**   RANCHO 34
PR-go POS-woman 3   P-two POS-baby

    x-unaa   **men**
    POS-woman 3
She$_i$ (his woman) and her$_i$ baby were going.

The examples in (398) show that the structure can also be focused, giving evidence that it forms a constituent.

(398) a. laa **xnaa**   **noo yrup xuz**   **noo** r-laa-w   AGOSTO 21
FM mother 1EX P-two father 1EX H-do-3I
My mother and my father did it.

b. *noze* **noo** *y-ra* **noo** *s-ya den*   SYANODEN 8
only 1EX P-all 1EX PR-go ranch
Just the rest of us go to the ranch.

An example of the construction used in a stative sentence is given in (399).

(399) *xna-ydoo*   *x-pee*   Manwel *n-ak*   AGOSTO 12
mother-church POS-son Manuel S-become

Katalina   y-rup Tomas
Catherine P-two Thomas
The godparents of Manuel's son are Catherine and Thomas.

These structures can also be the object of a regular declarative sentence. (400a–b) show single clause examples, whereas in (400c–d) the construction is the object of an embedded clause. Again, constructions subject to the various conditions are exemplified.

(400) a. *w-nëëz mëëk* **ngyed**   **y-rup ngyed** *konej*   AGOSTO 49
C-catch dog chicken P-two chicken rabbit
The dog caught a chicken and a rabbit.

b. *w-nache*   *meedx* **men** *y-ra* **men**   ANIMAL 49
C-frighten lion 3 P-all 3
The lion frightened everyone.

c. *y-niiz* **noo** *txup chamar* o *tson chamar*   TRIPTOQ 9
P-give 1EX two blanket or three blanket

y-ral   **de y-rup de Susan**
P-cover 2 P-two 2 Susan
I'll give you two or three blankets to cover you and Susan.

12.2 Syntactic analysis of the contiguous structure

d. *Biki   z-a   g-un kompanyar*   GRING 6
   Virginia PR-go P-LM accompany

   Gecha   y-rup x-pëëd   Gecha
   Lucretia P-two POS-baby Lucretia

   ne   ts-a-loo   Gecha   x-kiich   Gecha
   that P-go-extract Lucretia POS-paper Lucretia
   Virginia went to accompany Lucretia$_i$ and her$_i$ baby so that
   Lucretia$_i$ could get her$_i$ visa.

Though no text examples were found, (401) gives various examples from my language consultant where the special number-marking construction is acting as the object of a preposition.

(401) a. *r-e   Jasint   lo   **Rafayel y-rup Lawer***
         H-say Jacinto face Ralph   P-two Larry
         Jacinto said to Ralph and Larry...

   b. *r-e   Jasint   lo   **men y-rup men** Biki*
      H-say Jacinto face 3   P-two 3   Virginia
      Jacinto said to her and Virginia...

   c. *w-gwed Benit   mëlbyuu lo   **men y-ra men***
      C-give Benito fish   face 3   P-all 3
      Benito gave fish to all of them.

   d. *w-eey Danyel gyët   por **noo y-ra noo** men*
      C-take Daniel tortillas for 1EX P-all 1EX 3
      Daniel took tortillas for all of us.

Finally, the contiguous structure can be a possessor, as shown in (402). This exemplifies the optionality allowed by the Nonpronominal Head Condition.

(402) w-dxiin men led-ne   ts-oo   men   GRING 8
     C-arrive 3   body-that P-extract 3

   x-kiich   Gecha   y-rup Karmita
   POS-paper Lucretia P-two Carmita
   They arrived at the place where they get Lucretia's and Carmita's
   visas.

The distribution of the construction leads to the conclusion that the head, at least, is a DP, since it may fill all the normal DP positions. The fact that the whole construction can be focused (398) argues for its constituency as a DP. The alternative account which assumes that the quantifier clause is actually embedded under the main verb, rather than being a DP adjunct, cannot account for this focusing.

Such an alternative embedded predicate account deserves a closer look, however, since it holds promise in explaining the required coindexing between the head DP_1 and its counterpart after the quantifier. We would assume that the main verb selects a quantifier clause that has an external argument (i.e. the DP_1 following the quantifier) which is coindexed with the verb's external argument (which is what I have been calling the head DP_1). Though such a construction in English requires a nonfinite embedded clause with a null subject, as in the free translation of (403), the QZ equivalent usually has both subjects overtly expressed.

(403) r-laan   Jose s-ya   Jose den
      H-want   José PR-go José ranch
      José wants to go to the ranch.

If we consider the quantifier as filling the same position and role as the embedded transitive verb in (403), then an example such as (404) would have the D-structure shown in (405).

(404) w-a   Jose y-rup Jose zux   noo
      C-go José P-two José father 1EX
      José went together with my father.

12.2 Syntactic analysis of the contiguous structure

(405)   D-structure

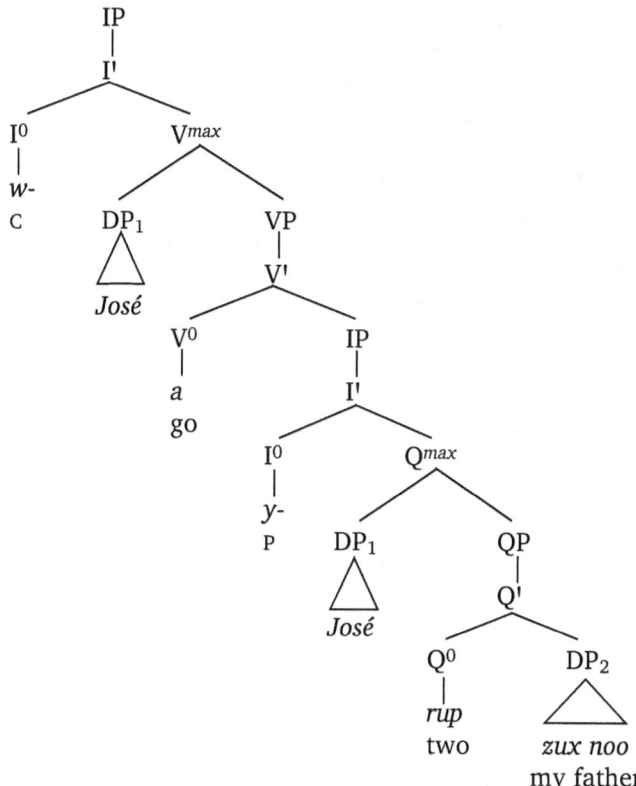

As mentioned, such an account would provide a nice explanation for the required coindexing between the two instances of DP_1. This is true as long as the head DP_1 occupies the subject position in the clause. Coindexation between the external arguments of the verb and the quantifier is not required nor correct when the head DP_1 is the object, possessor, or object of a preposition in a clause, since the head DP_1 is not the external argument of the verb in these cases. Further, there is nothing about the main verb a 'go' that is selecting the quantifier clause; such phrases can go with any verb as long as the coindexation requirement between the two DP_1s is met. The quantifier clause must therefore be an adjunct.

The amended alternative that the quantifier clause is a VP adjunct can also be ruled out by the full distribution of the special number-marking construction. Such an analysis would be equivalent to assuming that all the contiguous versions of these special number-marking constructions have the same

D-structure as the separated structures, if a base generated analysis were used for the separated constructions (see §12.3). For example, in the separated structure in (406a) the quantifier and following DPs clearly form an adjunct clause. The adjunct is not necessary, since without it the sentence conveys the information 'One time I/we went to bathe at the river'. The adjunct adds the specific details that the group who went to bathe included 'me' and 'my mother' (and other female relatives, as indicated by the use of *y-ra* 'P-all' rather than *y-rup* 'P-two'). Further, the S-structure position of the adjunct in (406a) would be right-adjoined to VP (or possibly to V^{max}), as shown in (407). The question is whether the structure in (407) is also the D-structure of both (406a and b), as would be the case under the VP-adjunct analysis, rather than allowing the whole construction to be a constituent at least in the contiguous construction (406b).

(406) a. teb   tir   w-a   **noo**   gos   ru   gyoow   SNAKHAIR 1
        one time C-go 1EX bathe   mouth   river

     y-ra noo   xnaa   noo
     P-all 1EX   mother 1EX
     One time I went to bathe at the river together with my mother (and others).

  b. teb   tir   w-a   **noo y-ra noo xnaa   noo**
    one time C-go 1EX P-all 1EX mother 1EX

     gos   ru   gyoow
     bathe   mouth   river
     One time my mother and I (and others) went to bathe at the river.

12.2 Syntactic analysis of the contiguous structure

(407)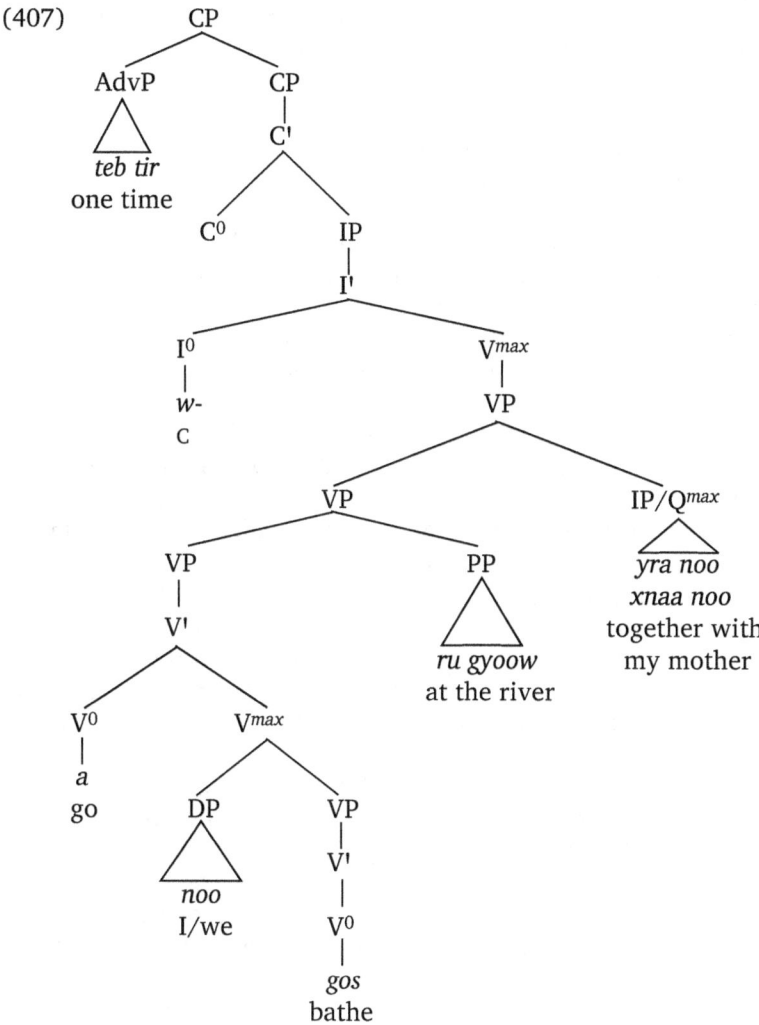

The structure in (407) seems clearly wrong as a D-structure for (406b) at least. In order to obtain the surface order of (406b), movement to adjoin the quantifier clause to the subject DP would be necessary. Such adjunction to an argument would violate the prohibition in Chomsky (1986:6). Also, since the head and the adjunct do not ever form a constituent under the VP-adjunct analysis, there remains no account for the fact that they can be focused together.

The analysis I propose where the head and the adjunct form a single DP constituent is therefore superior to both the controlled embedded predicate account and the VP-adjunct analysis, at least for the contiguous structure.

12.2.3 The internal structure of the mother DP and of the clausal adjunct

We have established so far that the quantifier and following DPs form an adjunct clause and that the head DP_1 and this adjunct clause together comprise a single constituent. The remaining questions to be dealt with in giving a syntactic analysis of the contiguous structure are where the quantifier clause attaches within the DP and what the internal structure of the quantifier clause is.

Instead of positing that the adjunct attaches to the head DP itself (as assumed by Schwartz (1988) for the PPC, McNally (1993) for the Comitative Coordination constructions, and Black (1992) in my earlier analysis of these QZ constructions), I propose here that the adjunct clause attaches within the DP, most likely adjoined to D', just as relative clauses do (see (336) in §11.2). This base generated adjunction within DP has the advantage of not violating Chomsky's (1986) prohibition against adjunction to arguments even when it is applied to base generated structures.[150] The parallel to relative clauses is in accord with the fact that relative clauses may also be separated from their heads, just like these quantifier clauses may.

As for the internal structure of the adjunct, I assume that it is an IP which is headed by the Potential marker on the quantifier, just as normal clauses are headed by the aspect marking in I^0. The I^0 in this case selects a quantifier phrase (Q^{max}) which has a [+V] predicate. As such, this quantifier predicate head has its specifiers on the left and undergoes movement to I^0 (recall the discussion in chapter 10 of the distinction between [±V] predicates).

Independent evidence for the characterization of these special quantifiers as [+V] comes from the surprising fact that they can carry the normal verbal suffixes when the construction is focused and the emphasis is on whether the action specified was done together or not, as shown in (408) and (411). These suffixes must occur on the main verb when the

---

[150]Though it does violate his specific statement of the prohibition that limits adjunction to maximal projections only. I assume here and throughout this study (see especially the structure required for nominals in §11.2) that adjunction to nonmaximal projections is allowed.

12.2 Syntactic analysis of the contiguous structure 297

construction is in its normal position in the clause, as (409)–(410) and (412)–(413) verify.[151]

(408) led **Rafayel y-rup-t** Lawer w-tsoow mezh
FM Ralph P-two-NEG Larry C-make table
It wasn't together that Ralph and Larry made a table.
(i.e., Ralph made it alone.)

(409) *r-oo **men y-rup-t men Biki** nisgaal
H-drink 3 P-two-NEG 3 Virginia soda
(She and Virginia drink soda pop, not together.)

(410) r-oo-t **men y-rup men Biki** nisgaal
H-drink-NEG 3 P-two 3 Virginia soda
She and Virginia don't drink soda pop together.

(411) **Martin y-rup-ke Biki** r-oo nisgaal
Martin P-two-ASSOC Virginia H-drink soda
Martin and Virginia also drink soda pop.

(412) *r-oo **Martin y-rup-ke Biki** nisgaal
H-drink Martin P-two-ASSOC Virginia soda
(Martin and Virginia also drink soda pop.)

(413) r-oo-ke **Martin y-rup Biki** nisgaal
H-drink-ASSOC Martin P-two Virginia soda
Martin and Virginia drink soda pop also.

In addition, as a [+V] predicate, the quantifier subcategorizes for a certain number and type of arguments, just as verbs do. Therefore, the quantifiers meaning 'two' and 'all' are like transitive verbs, whereas the quantifier meaning 'one' is like an intransitive verb in its subcategorization requirements, and the quantifiers meaning 'three' and 'four' take that number of arguments, respectively. I further assume that the first argument after the quantifier is the external argument (or subject) in each case, which accords

---

[151] The fact that the negative marker can occur on the quantifier when the special number-marking construction is focused (408) indicates that the adjunct clause headed by the quantifier may be a Polarity Phrase (PolP) rather than simply an IP. Since examples of the quantifier carrying the negative marker are so rare (no such examples were found in the texts (Regnier 1989a), probably due to the special context required) and they are restricted to focus position, I leave it as an IP in the discussion and trees.

with the ordering restrictions among the DPs and the Subject = Possessor of Object Condition.

The structure I propose for a simple sentence like (414) is given in (415).

(414) w-a   Jose y-rup   Jose   zux   noo
      C-go   José P-two   José   father   1EX
      José went together with my father.

(415)   D-structure

```
                        IP
                        |
                        I'
                      /    \
                    I⁰      Vmax
                    |      /    \
                    w-    DP     VP
                    C     |      |
                          D'     V'
                         / \     |
                        D₁' IP   V⁰
                       / \  |    |
                      D⁰ NP I'   a
                         △ / \   go
                       José I⁰ Qmax
                            |  / \
                            y- DP₁  QP
                            P  △    |
                              José  Q'
                                   / \
                                  Q⁰  DP₂
                                  |   △
                                 rup  zux noo
                                 two  my father
```

Note that this structure is very similar to the embedded predicate analysis (405) except that the "embedded" IP is adjoined to D' within the subject DP here, instead of being a complement of the verb. The structure in (415) has the distinct advantage that the whole construction is a constituent, while maintaining the clausal nature of the adjunct. An account for the

12.3 Analysis of the separated construction

Having given the semantic interpretation for these special number-marking constructions and a syntactic analysis for its contiguous structure, we are now ready to address the analysis of the separated version of the construction.

Consider again the pair of sentences in (416), repeated from earlier.

(416) a. *r-oo*   **men** *y-rup* **men** *Biki*   *nisgaal*   AGOSTO 8A
H-drink 3   P-two 3   Virginia soda
She and Virginia drink soda pop.

b. *r-oo*   **men** *nisgaal* **y-rup** *men* *Biki*   AGOSTO 8B
H-drink 3   soda   P-two 3   Virginia
She and Virginia drink soda pop.

Example (416b) looks exactly like (416a), except that the object intervenes between the head and the adjunct in (416b). Otherwise, the separated construction is identical to the contiguous construction, both in its interpretation, the restrictions on the optionality of the DPs, and the fact that the Person Hierarchy Effect is a strict requirement.

Data illustrating these separated constructions are given in (417)–(421). There are numerous examples where the head is in the subject position, immediately following the verb, but the quantifier phrase comes after the direct object or locative phrase, as shown in (417).

(417) a. *w-tsoow* **Rafayel** *te*   *mezh*   *y-rup*   **Rafayel Lawer** AGOSTO 43
C-make Ralph one table P-two Ralph Larry
Ralph and Larry made a table.

b. *r-ya* **xuz** *noo* *den*   *y-ra* **xnaa** *noo*   QUESO 3
H-go papa 1EX rancho P-all mother 1EX

    r-boo   *me gyezh*
    H-extract 3F cheese
My father and mother go to the ranch and she makes cheese.

c. *chene w-uu **noo** lgyëz **y-ra xnaa noo*** SANJOSE 1
   when C-be 1EX town P-all mother 1EX

   r-a xnaa noo San Jose
   H-go mother 1EX San Jose
   When I lived in town with my mother (and family), my mother went to San Jose.

d. *w-a **noo** wii lo gyëël **y-ra noo men*** MTLEMON 50
   C-go 1EX see face lake P-all 1EX 3
   We all went to see the lake.

e. *bweree **noo** nëz **y-rup noo men*** LIFEINUS 67
   C/return 1EX road P-two 1EX 3
   We two returned by the road.

Example (418) shows that this separated construction may also have its head in the subject position of a deeply embedded clause, with the adjunct following the object.

(418) *dxe-bel r-laan de ts-a de g-e **noo** lo men xiid* HORTENS 5
      already-if H-want 2 P-go 2 P-say 1EX face 3 F/come

   *men g-u de diiz **y-rup** de men*
   3 P-chat 2 word P-two 2 3
   If you want to go, I will tell him to come, so that you can talk with him.

There are also many cases where only the head is in focus position and the adjunct is clause final, as shown in (419).

(419) a. *te **men** z-a x-ten **y-rup** x-pëëk men* MENMAAC 1
       one 3 PR-go POS-ranch P-two POS-dog 3
       A man was going to his ranch with his dog.

   b. *le **Jose** w-zhoon **y-rup** x-unaa Jose* AGOSTO 69
      FM José C-run P-two POS-woman José
      José$_i$ ran away with his$_i$ wife.

12.3 Analysis of the separated construction

    c. *le* **xuz** *noo w-guu bni* **y-ra**   SYANODEN 19
       FM papa 1EX C-sow seed P-all

      mee bzaan   *noo*
      boy sibling.opp.sex 1EX
      My father planted seed with all my brothers.

Example (420) is the only unambiguous one in the texts[152] of a separated construction where the head is in object position. In this case a locative phrase intervenes between the head and the adjunct.

(420) *lex w-a-ron men* **noo** *x-yuu x-mig men*   MTLEMON 8
     later C-go-leave 3 1EX POS-house POS-friend 3

    y-rup x-pëëd *noo*
    P-two POS-baby 1EX
    Then they took me and my baby to their friend's house.

Example (421) is ambiguous, though (421a) is the preferred reading due to semantic considerations. The ambiguity comes about because the repeated DP_1 is missing after the quantifier, and two different conditions can account for this. In (421a), the Nonpronominal Head Condition has applied where 'my mother' is the head in subject position and the adjunct includes 'my father' in the sending process. In (421b), we can assume that the first person exclusive pronoun *noo* is the head in object position. The Subject = Possessor of Object Condition allows the pronoun to be missing in the quantifier phrase in this case, giving a reading that 'my father and I' were sent to school.

(421) a. *dxe win noo r-xaal* **xnaa** **noo** *noo skwel*   ESCUELA 1
      already small 1EX H-send mother 1EX 1EX school

     y-rup xuz noo
     P-two papa 1EX
     When I was young, my mother and my father sent me to school.

---

[152]My QZ language consultant assures me that separated counterparts of the contiguous structure in object position are generally grammatical as long as the intervening material is within the same clause.

b. *dxe   win   noo r-xaal   xnaa   noo **noo** skwel*   ESCUELA 1
already small 1EX H-send mother 1EX 1EX school

y-rup xuz noo
P-two papa 1EX
When I was young, my mother sent me and my father to school.

All of these variations in the position of the head and the adjunct in the separated QZ construction can be accounted for straightforwardly with a derivational syntax. The D-structure for the separated construction can be the same as proposed for the contiguous structure. The only movements necessary are Extraposition from DP of the adjunct quantifier clause (relative clauses may also undergo this movement) and the independently needed fronting for focus. This analysis is demonstrated in §12.3.2.

First, though, we look at the reasons that base generated analyses have been preferred over movement analyses in similar constructions in other languages.

12.3.1 Arguments for a base generation analysis in other languages

McNally's analysis of the Russian Comitative Coordination constructions was given in §12.1.2, where it was noted that plural number agreement marking is found on the verb. McNally (1993) shows that the verbal agreement marking is singular, rather than plural, when the parts of the construction are separated in what she calls a Comitative VP Adjunct construction. Examples of this are shown in (422) where (a) is the Comitative Coordination construction like that shown earlier, (b) is the Comitative VP Adjunct construction, and (c) verifies the ungrammaticality of plural verbal agreement marking in the separated version of the construction.[153]

(422) a. ***Anna**   s   **Petej**   pridut*   MCNALLY
Anna.NOM with Peter.INSTR come-3PL
Anna and Peter are coming.

b. ***Anna**   pridët   s   **Petej***   MCNALLY 6A
Anna.NOM come-3SG with Peter.INSTR
Anna is coming with Peter.

---

[153]Example (422a) is taken from an earlier version of the paper.

12.3 Analysis of the separated construction

c. *Anna   pridut   s   Petej   MCNALLY 6B
Anna.NOM come-3PL with Peter.INSTR
(Anna are coming with Peter.)

McNally gives further arguments regarding the constituency of the Comitative Coordination construction versus the nonconstituency of the Comitative VP Adjunct construction. These include the facts that sentences like (422a) are ungrammatical when the NP and PP are separated by adverb interpolation or extraposition whereas adverbs may normally intervene in the separated version (422b), and that the PP in constructions like (422a) may not be extracted via *wh*-movement while the PP in (422b) may be easily extracted. She thus gives compelling evidence that the Comitative Coordination construction does form a constituent, but the Comitative VP Adjunct construction is base generated separately.

These arguments do not apply to the QZ constructions, however, since there is no number marking on the verb at all in QZ, much less different number markings to distinguish the different constructions. The number marking for the group remains on the quantifier in all cases. Further, there is no discernible difference in extraction possibilities.

Turning now to Plural Pronoun Constructions in Tzotzil, Aissen (1989) shows that an ambiguity is created by adding a comitative PP to a sentence. The plural pronoun head may be interpreted either as referring to a single individual, thus including the referent of the comitative PP in its plurality, or as being plural itself, with the referent of the comitative PP simply added on. Examples (423) and (424) illustrate this, where the (a) examples show the verb form and its meaning[154] and the (b) examples show the ambiguity between the PP-included and PP-excluded readings created by adding the comitative PP.

(423) a. *libatotikotik*   AISSEN 1
we(exc).went
We went.

b. *libatotikotik   xchi7uk   li   Petule*
we(exc).went with   def Petul
(i) I went with Petul. (PP-included reading)
(ii) We(exc) went with Petul. (PP-excluded reading)

---

[154]Tzotzil is a *pro*-drop language and the predicate agrees with both the subject and the direct object. The unmarked word order is VOS.

(424) a. *chajtojik* AISSEN 2
   I.pay.you(pl)
   I'll pay you(pl).

b. *chajtojik   xchi7uk li   Xune*
   I.pay.you(pl) with   def Xun
   (i) I'll pay you(sg) and Xun. (PP-included reading)
   (ii) I'll pay you(pl) and Xun. (PP-excluded reading)

The PP-included reading is simply that of the Plural Pronoun Construction. Under the PPC analysis, the PP-included reading for (423) would have the structure shown in (425).[155]

(425)

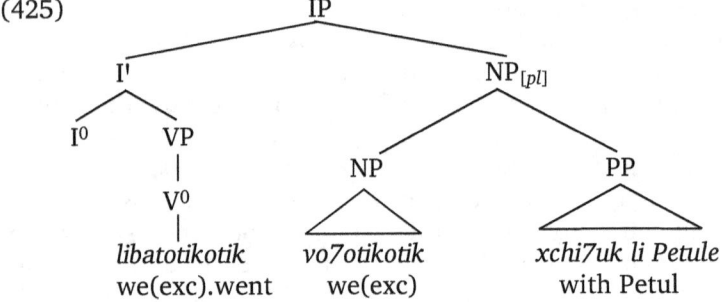

In (425) the subject is first person plural exclusive because its head is; thus the verb is inflected for a first person plural exclusive subject. However, based upon the semantic interpretation given by Ladusaw (1989), the subject really means 'we, including Petul' or 'Petul and me'. All that is necessary to yield (423b) is to assume that the pronominal head of the construction can drop, like other personal pronouns in Tzotzil.

In contrast, the PP-excluded reading can be represented as in (426), where there is no Plural Pronoun Construction, and the PP is instead base-generated as a VP dependent. In computing who went in (426), *Petule* is added to the subject which is already plural, so more than two people must have gone. Again, *pro*-drop will yield (423b).

---

[155] The subject is shown here in the specifier of IP, though it could instead be a right-specifier of VP (or V^{max}).

12.3 Analysis of the separated construction

(426)

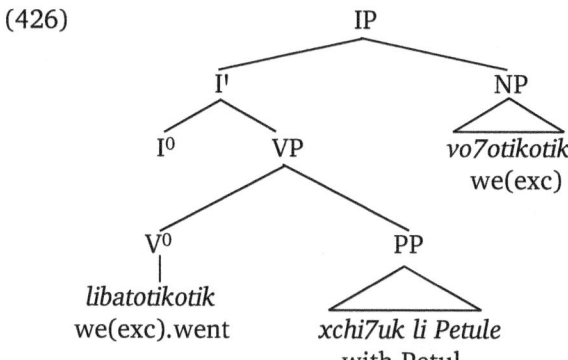

The ambiguity in the readings for these Tzotzil sentences is thus explained as a phrase-structural ambiguity if we assume that the PP-excluded readings are base-generated as shown in (426). Again, we do not see this type of ambiguity in the QZ constructions; so there is no reason to assume that the separated constructions cannot be generated by movement.

12.3.2 Predictions made by a movement analysis

Since nothing in the QZ grammar necessitates that the separated structure be base generated, I propose a derivational analysis which provides a natural account for the fact that the Person Hierarchy Effect and other properties of the construction hold for the separated structure as well as for the contiguous structure.

In this section, the observed distribution of the data for the separated structure is shown to fall out automatically from mechanisms independently needed in the QZ syntax, namely Extraposition from DP and focusing. The analysis will be presented first, followed by discussion of the few problematic examples noted in the literature for assuming that Extraposition from DP is accomplished via movement.

We begin by comparing the account for the contiguous structure in (427a) with the separated structure (427b).

(427) a. *r-oo* **men y-rup men Biki** *nisgaal* AGOSTO 8A
   H-drink 3   P-two 3   Virginia soda
   She and Virginia drink soda pop.

   b. *r-oo* **men** *nisgaal* **y-rup men Biki** AGOSTO 8B
   H-drink 3   soda   P-two 3   Virginia
   She and Virginia drink soda pop.

Under a derivational analysis, the D-structure for both examples in (427) is the same, as shown in (428), thus accounting naturally for their synonymy.

(428)   D-structure for (427a–b)

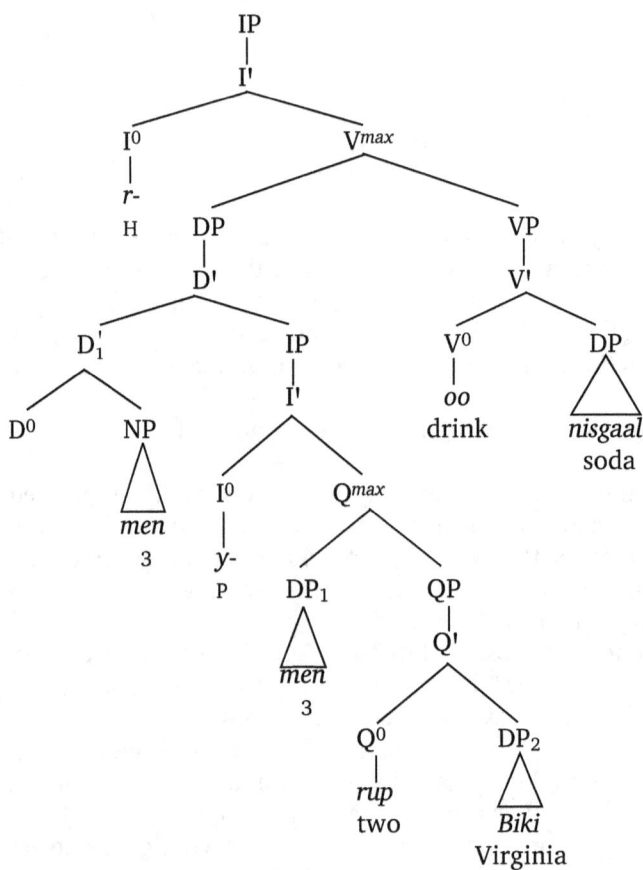

All that is necessary to obtain the S-structure for (427a) is for V^0 to move to I^0 in the main clause and for Q^0 to move to I^0 in the adjunct, as shown in (429).

12.3 Analysis of the separated construction 307

(429)   D-structure for (427a)

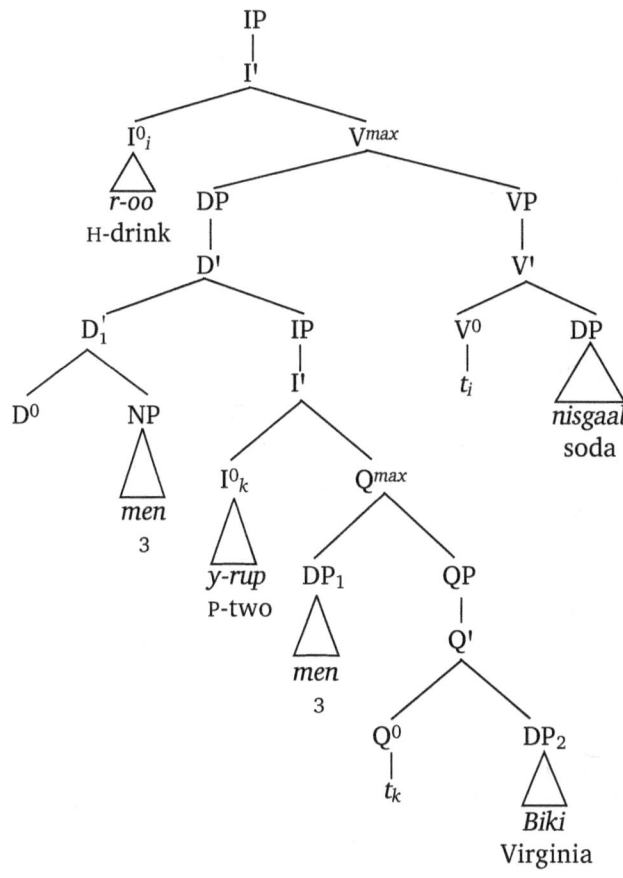

Both of these head movements also take place in (427b). In addition, the IP adjunct undergoes Extraposition from DP movement to obtain the S-structure for (427b) shown in (430).

(430)   S-structure for (427b)

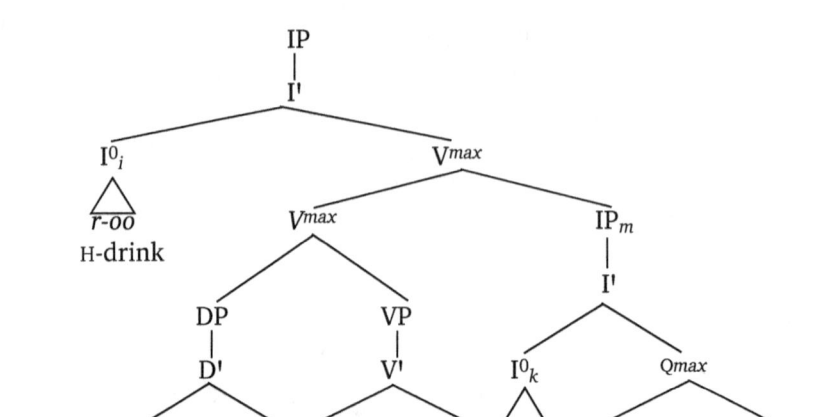

Similar Extraposition from DP will also account for the cases where the head is in object position and the adjunct is clause final, as in (420).

We still need an account for the separated structures where the head is in focus position, such as (431b). Again, the separated structure can be compared with the contiguous structure, which has been focused as a constituent (431a).

(431) a. *le xuz noo y-ra mee bzaan   noo*   SYANODEN 19A
         FM papa 1EX P-all boy   sibling.opp.sex 1EX

   w-guu bni
   C-sow   seed
   My father and all my brothers planted seed.

12.3 Analysis of the separated construction

b. **le xuz noo** w-guu bni **y-ra mee**   SYANODEN 19
   FM papa 1EX C-sow seed P-all boy

   bzaan   **noo**
   sibling.opp.sex   1EX
   My father planted seed with all my brothers.

I assume again that the D-structure for both variations of (431) is as given in (432).

(432)   D-structure for (431a–b)

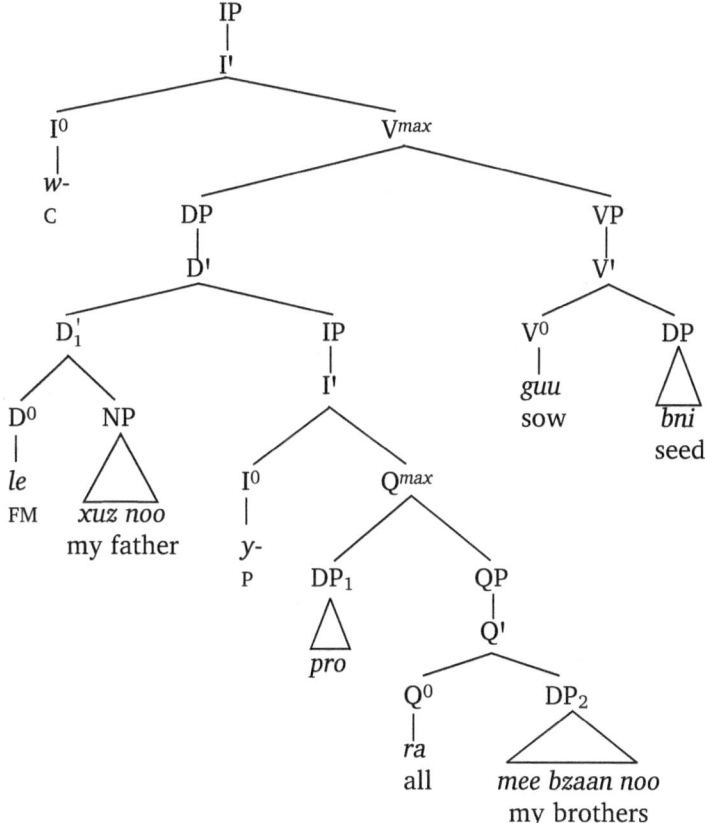

In (431a), the focusing operation moves the entire subject DP to adjoin to PolP below C⁰, as shown in (433). (Head movement to I⁰ also occurs as before.)

(433)   S-structure for (431a)

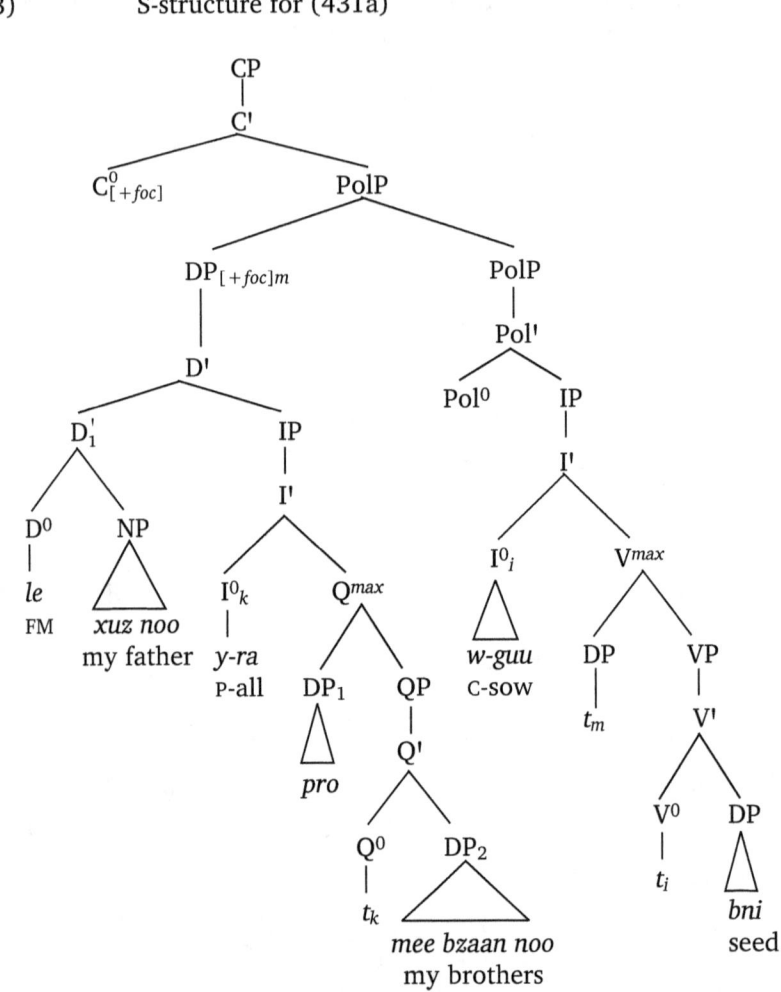

To obtain the S-structure for (431b) instead, we must first apply Extraposition from DP to the adjunct clause, and then focus the head, which is all that remains overtly in the subject DP. This is illustrated in (434).

12.3 Analysis of the separated construction

(434) S-structure for (431b)

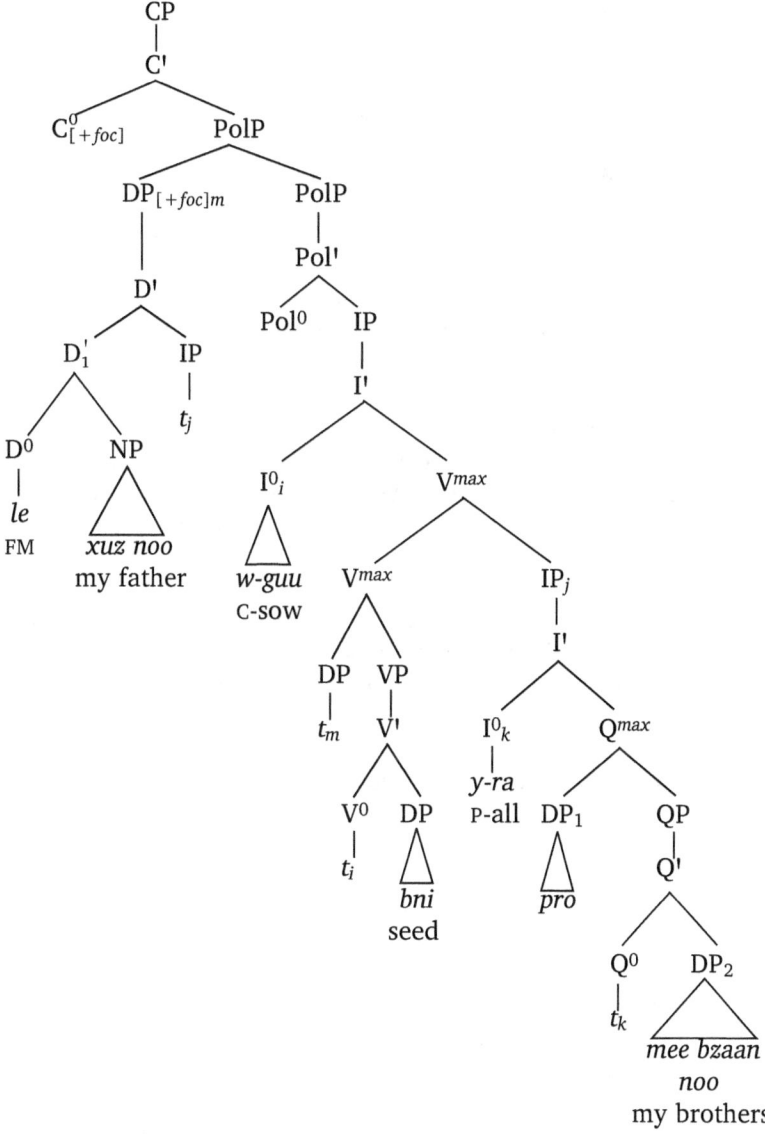

This separation involving Extraposition from DP and then focusing is also found with relative clauses, as shown in the following examples (see also §7.3).

(435) a. *[s-te   giblew]* zob   gya   *[ne   regader]*   BATHROOM 7
F-one faucet PR/sit high that showerhead
Another faucet that is the showerhead sits higher.

b. *[chup maa]* n-ak   *[ne   r-e   g-u*   MANSNAKE 74
two   3A   S-become that H-say P-eat

maa noo]
3A 1EX
There were two animals that said the snake should eat me.

c. *[koyot]* n-ak   *[ne   w-sa-laa   x-bit   noo]* MANSNAKE 77
coyote S-become that C-fall-escape POS-life 1EX
The coyote was the one that saved my life.

The attested separation of relative clauses is more restricted than the separation in the special number-marking structures is, however. In every case where Extraposition from DP may apply in relative clauses, the matrix verb is either an unaccusative, stative, or copular verb. This restriction is verified in (436).

(436) a. r-a   me r-ka   me *[gyus na   g-eey   x-nisyaa me]*   SANJOSE 2
H-go 3R H-buy 3R pot which P-cook POS-food 3R
She went to buy a pot which her food would cook in.

b. **r-a me [gyus]* r-ka   me *[na   g-eey   x-nisyaa me]*
H-go 3R pot   H-buy 3R which P-cook POS-food 3R
(She went to buy a pot which her food would cook in.)

c. **[gyus]* r-a   me r-ka   me *[na   g-eey   x-nisyaa me]*
pot   H-go 3R H-buy 3R which P-cook POS-food 3R
(She went to buy a pot which her food would cook in.)

In contrast, the separated version of the special number-marking construction is attested in sentences with all types of matrix verbs. I have no concrete account to offer for this difference, but simply suggest that the separation in the number-marking constructions is freer due to the required coindexation between the head and the DP$_1$ following the quantifier, which assures correct construal of the separated clause.

The distribution of the separated structure also gives credence to a movement analysis. We saw that the head of the separated structure is

12.3 Analysis of the separated construction

found in all the same positions that the contiguous structure is found in, with two notable exceptions. While the contiguous structure can be a possessor, as in (437a), the separated version (437b) is ungrammatical. Likewise, the contiguous structure can serve as the object of a preposition, as in (438a), but it is impossible to have only the head in that position, with the quantifier clause appearing clause-final (438b).

(437) a. w-oo men x-kiich **Gecha** **y-rup Karmita** *ofisin*
   C-extract 3 POS-paper Lucretia P-two Carmita office
   They got Lucretia's and Carmita's visas at the office.

 b. *w-oo men x-kiich **Gecha** *ofisin* **y-rup Karmita**
   C-extract 3 POS-paper Lucretia office P-two Carmita
   (They got Lucretia's and Carmita's visas at the office.)

(438) a. w-eey Danyel gyët por **noo y-ra noo** Danyel x-too
   C-take Daniel tortillas for 1EX P-all 1EX Daniel POS-head

   gyeey
   mountain
   Daniel took tortillas for all of us (including himself) to the mountain top.

 b. *w-eey Danyel gyët por **noo** x-too gyeey **y-ra**
   C-take Daniel tortillas for 1EX POS-head mountain P-all

   noo Danyel
   1EX Daniel
   (Daniel took tortillas for all of us (including himself) to the mountain top.)

This lack of a synonymous separated structure in the possessor and object of preposition positions only can be explained by the failure of these positions to be properly governed in QZ. Neither the possessor nor the object of a preposition can be extracted by either *wh*-movement or focusing (except with pied-piping of the entire phrase). I assume this is due to P^0, D^0 and N^0 not being proper governors, eliminating the possibility of proper government of the trace from within DP or PP. Further, the position of the possessor as specifier of NP (see §11.2) makes it too low to be properly governed from outside of the DP, and the same is true of the object of a preposition. Both the positions which the head and adjunct can move to and the positions which this separation can occur from are thus explained by a derivational analysis.

There are two main reasons that some (such as Culicover and Rochemont 1990) prefer not to allow Extraposition from DP as a movement option, but instead to assume that such constructions are base generated. First is the fact that Extraposition from DP involves rightward movement, which is somewhat dispreferred within the Principles and Parameters framework. However, the separated structures in QZ display the same clause-boundedness noted in other languages for constructions involving rightward movement. The trace left by adjunction to VP (or V^{max}) will therefore be antecedent governed.

Further, a few examples have been noted (e.g., by Perlmutter and Ross 1970 and Gazdar 1981) which are problematic for assuming that separated relative clause constructions are generated by movement. One such example is given in (439a). While (439b) could be assumed to be generated by movement from a D-structure with the order shown in (439c), (439a) could not be so generated.

(439) a. A man came in and a woman went out who look quite similar.
b. A man and a woman came in who look quite similar.
c. A man and a woman who look quite similar came in.

Examples such as (439a) have been used to argue for an account in which the relative clause is base generated as an adjunct to the coordinate structure, with the construal and coindexing requirements being determined by the semantics.

Due to the nature of the coindexing requirement between the DP_1s in the QZ constructions, examples with split heads as in the problematic (439a) are not possible, nor are examples with conjoined heads as in (439b–c). QZ does not seem to allow separated relative clauses with the problematic structure either. The only available way to express the same basic meaning as in (439a–c) is given in (440a–c), respectively. Note that in (440a) a coordinate DP structure is used, where each conjunct contains a relative clause. In (440b–c), however, the special number-marking construction is used to express the meaning of the English coordinate structure, and it in turn serves as the head of a relative clause. The main verb in each case expresses the notion 'to look alike', while the movement into and out of the store is now expressed within a relative clause. A more direct translation of the English examples in (439) is not possible in QZ. I have attempted to make the unproblematic structure of these examples clear via labeled bracketing.

12.3 Analysis of the separated construction

(440) a. *tese r-zak-lo*   [_{DP}[_{DP} *mgyeey* [_{CP} *ne w-dee leen tyent]]*
same H-appear-face   man   that C-enter inside store

[_{DP} *wnaa* [_{CP} *ne w-ruu leen tyent]]]*
woman   that C-leave inside store

The man that entered the store and the woman that left the store look alike.

b. [_{DP} **te mgyeey y-rup te wnaa** [_{CP} *ne w-dee leen tyent]]*
one man   P-two one woman   that C-enter inside store

tese r-zak-lo   **men y-rup men**
same H-appear-face 3   P-two 3

A man and a woman that came inside the store look like each other.

c. *tese r-zak-lo*   [_{DP} **te mgyeey$_i$ y-rup men$_i$ te wnaa**
same H-appear-face   one man   P-two 3   one woman

[_{CP} *ne w-dee leen tyent]]*
that C-enter inside store

A man and a woman that came in the store look alike.

Though a base generated account of the separated structure is certainly possible, the account would need to be more complex. For instance, the semantics would have to include not only the construal and coindexation requirements, but also stipulations as to what positions the head could occupy, amounting to a re-creation of the ECP. Such stipulations are unnecessary in a derivational account, since the possible positions are determined by otherwise needed principles of the syntax. In addition to this complication of the semantics, the syntax would have to allow the quantifier clause to adjoin at D-structure to VP for the separated structure but to D' for the contiguous structure. The semantics would then have to also provide an account for the synonymy between the two variations of the construction. I therefore prefer the derivational analysis as the simpler and more natural account of the separated structures for QZ.

12.3.3 The required coindexation and semantic construal

The purpose of the repeated DP_1 after the quantifier is to assure proper construal between the head and adjunct parts of the construction. When the repeated DP₁ is overt, this linking is assured. The specific conditions on its optionality make the identity of the missing DP₁ recoverable, thus eliminating ambiguity in most cases.

As we have seen, coindexation of the head and the first DP after the quantifier (the two DP₁s in the configurational diagram) is required. DP₁ and DP₂ may not be in reverse order after the quantifier (441a–b), nor may the DP₁ after the quantifier add any new information (441c). These sentences are uninterpretable in QZ.

(441) a. *nga ts-uu **de y-rup Susan de**   TRIPTOQ 6A
there P-be 2 P-two Susan 2
(There you'll be with Susan.)

    b. *xna-ydoo   x-pee   Manwel n-ak   AGOSTO 12A
mother-church POS-son Manuel S-become

       Katalina y-rup Tomas Katalina
Catherine P-two Thomas Catherine
(The godparents of Manuel's son are Catherine and Thomas.)

    c. *lex bweree-ke   **men y-ra Dolf   Susan**   MTLEMON 2, 57A
later C/return-ASSOC 3   P-all Rodolfo Susan
(Then they all, including Rodolfo and Susan, returned also.)

When there is more than one DP in a sentence, the coindexing restriction determines which DP the QP is construed with, in either a contiguous construction or a separated construction.

The QP may not simply be construed with the closest nominal, as shown in (442). Though the possessor immediately precedes the adjunct, the order of the DPs following the quantifier prohibits construal with the possessor *xuz noo* 'my father' in (442a), since the first DP following the quantifier may not be coindexed with the possessor. In contrast, this construal is required in (442b), where the order of the DPs following the quantifier has been reversed.

12.3 Analysis of the separated construction

(442) a. *w-guu **Jose** leen   x-yuu   xuz   noo*   AGOSTO 44
       C-sow José inside POS-house father 1EX

       y-rup Jose xuz   noo
       P-two José father 1EX
       José and my father put it inside my father's house.
       *(José put it inside my father's and José's house.)

   b. *w-guu Jose leen   x-yuu   **xuz**   **noo***
       C-sow José inside POS-house father 1EX

       y-rup xuz   noo Jose
       P-two father 1EX José
       José put it inside my father's and José's house.
       *(José and my father put it inside my father's house.)

Construal is not determined by marking certain verbs for construal with subjects and others for construal with objects either.[156] In (443a), the only possible natural reading construes the adjunct with the object.[157] The third person pronoun subject cannot be coindexed with the missing DP_1 in the quantifier adjunct, since the Nonpronominal Head Condition would require the repeated DP_1 to be overt in that case. The first person pronoun object may be coindexed with the missing DP_1, however, because it is the same as the possessor of DP_2, thus satisfying the Subject = Possessor of Object Condition on optionality. By changing the positions of the subject and object pronouns in (443b), we now have the adjunct construed with the subject as the only possible reading.

(443) a. *lex   w-a-ron   men **noo** x-yuu   x-mig   men*   MTLEMON 8
       later C-go-leave 3   1EX POS-house POS-friend 3

       y-rup x-pëëd   noo
       P-two POS-baby 1EX
       Then they took me and my baby to their friend's house.

---

[156]This constitutes another argument against the hypothesis that the quantifier serves as an embedded predicate whose external argument is controlled by the matrix verb.

[157]Technically, it is possible to construe the quantifier adjunct with the possessor of the locative in a contiguous structure based on the optionality of the repeated DP_1 allowed by the Nonpronominal Head Condition (i.e., the head DP_1 *x-mig men* 'their friend' could antecede the null third person pronoun). This would give the reading 'Then they took me to [their friend and my baby]'s house', which is not an expected rendering of the sentence.

b. *lex   w-a-ron   **noo** men x-yuu   x-mig   men*
later C-go-leave 1EX 3   POS-house POS-friend 3

y-rup x-pëëd   noo
P-two POS-baby 1EX
Then I with my baby took them to their friend's house.

Thus, verbs meaning 'take' or 'send' do not have required construal in these special number-marking constructions. Instead, we would need a QZ particular construal rule for these Quantifier clause adjuncts under a base generated view of the syntax of the separated structures.

Under a derivational syntax, the construal is really accomplished via D-structure adjunction, with the correct interpretation of a separated structure being determined by the trace of movement. Pollard and Sag (1994) claim that the adjunct "subcategorizes" for the category of the head it can attach to (e.g., Adjectives "subcategorize" for an N' and relative clauses "subcategorize" for an NP). Further restrictions may also need to be added to this "subcategorization," such as coindexing requirements between the head and the relative pronoun in a relative clause. Pending further development of formalism in the theory of adjunction, I suggest that both the coindexing requirement and correct construal can be captured for the special number-marking construction by the Adjunct Admissibility Filter given in (444). Informally, this filter requires that a Quantifier clause may only adjoin at D-structure to a D' which is coindexed with the external argument of the quantifier.

(444) Quantifier Adjunct Admissibility Filter
Let Q(x)   = x is a Quantifier clause
Let D'(x)   = x is labelled D'
Let Ext(x)   = the external argument of x
Let Adjoin (x,y) = x is adjoined to y at D-structure
Let Coindexed(x,y) = x is coindexed with y

(Q(x) $\wedge$ Adjoin(x,y)) $\Rightarrow$ (D'(y) $\wedge$ Coindexed(y, Ext(x)))

In combination, the syntactic and semantic analyses given for the special number-marking constructions thus account for all the properties and requirements of both the contiguous and separated structures.

Appendix

A Parametric Account of Question Formation

In this appendix, the treatment of *wh*-questions given in chapter 7 is expanded. The analysis given here serves to bring together the various accounts of facets of *wh*-question formation given by May (1985), Rizzi (1991), Rudin (1988), and McDaniel (1989). At the same time, it verifies that QZ fits squarely within the boundaries of the cross-linguistic variation attested. I use the *Wh*-Criterion as a starting point for this exploration. We see that parameterization of the level of representation at which each clause of the *Wh*-Criterion applies is not sufficient to account for the full distribution of question formation cross-linguistically. Instead, a parameterization of the positions available for *wh*-movement at each level of representation, coupled with a well-formedness principle for *wh*-constructions is proposed. This account is then extended to encompass the partial *wh*-movement constructions in German and Romani (McDaniel 1989) by rewording the principle in terms of *wh*-chains.

The *Wh*-Criterion alone is not sufficient

As seen in chapter 7, the Wh-Criterion is a general well-formedness condition on *wh*-constructions. The *Wh*-Criterion was originally proposed by May (1985) and updated to conform with the theory of COMP in Chomsky (1986) by Rizzi (1991), as given in (445).

(445) The *Wh*-Criterion

    A. A *wh*-operator must be in a Spec-head configuration with an $X^0_{[+wh]}$.
    B. An $X^0_{[+wh]}$ must be in a Spec-head configuration with a *wh*-operator.

May (1985) allowed for parameterization of the level at which each clause of the *Wh*-Criterion must hold to account for a large portion of the cross-linguistic variation. For example, May assumed that Clause B of the *Wh*-Criterion is required at S-structure in English to assure the fronting of one *wh*-phrase, but that Clause A holds only at LF, thus allowing one or more *wh*-phrases to remain in situ in multiple *wh*-questions. We can extrapolate from this example to the general case and see that the following implications hold:

(446) a. No visible fronting ⇒ Clause B holds at LF
      b. One or more fronted ⇒ Clause B holds at SS
      c. None may be in situ ⇒ Clause A holds at SS
      d. One or more in situ ⇒ Clause A holds at LF

Of course, the world's languages display much more variation in their patterns of question formation than just the difference between the English and the QZ patterns. We can differentiate five distinct patterns or types of languages, each of which will be exemplified here.

First, we look at languages which allow fronting of multiple *wh*-phrases. These languages further divide into two types. There are languages like Bulgarian and Romanian, which require all *wh*-phrases to be fronted; none may remain in situ. (447) demonstrates this with both single clause and multiple clause constructions in Bulgarian (taken from Rudin 1988:449–450).

(447) a. **koj kogo** vižda
      who whom sees
      Who sees whom?

     b. ***koj** vižda **kogo**
      who sees whom
      (Who sees whom?)

c. **koj kŭde** misliš [če e otišŭl _ _]
   who where think-2S that has gone
   Who do you think (that) went where?

d. ***koj** misliš [če e otišŭl _ **kŭde**]
   who think-2S that has gone where
   (Who do you think (that) went where?)

e. ***koj** misliš [**kŭde** (če) e otišŭl] _ _
   who think-2S where that has gone
   (Who do you think (that) went where?)

Directly contrasting with Bulgarian and Romanian are languages like Serbo-Croatian, Polish, and Czech, in which multiple fronting is allowed in single clause questions but (for most speakers) a second *wh*-phrase cannot be fronted out of an embedded clause. (448) gives examples from Serbo-Croatian (taken from Rudin 1988:449, 453–454). Example (448a) shows multiple fronting in a matrix question. Multiple fronting, however, cannot occur from an embedded clause. In Serbo-Croatian, the "in-situ" *wh*-word is normally placed to the left of the verb, which is the focus position, as exemplified in (448b–c). It is not possible to front two *wh*-phrases to the matrix clause, as shown in (448d–e). It is also ungrammatical to front one *wh*-phrase to the matrix clause and place the second *wh*-phrase in the specifier of the lower CP$_{[-wh]}$, as examples (448f–g) verify.

(448) a. **ko koga** vidi
       who whom sees
       Who sees whom?

   b. **ko** želite [da vam **šta** kupi _]
      who want-2P to you what buy-3S
      Who do you want to buy you what?

   c. **šta** želite [da vam **ko** kupi _]
      what want-2P to you who buy-3S
      "What do you want who to buy you?"

   d. ***ko šta** želite [da vam kupi _ _]
      who what want-2P to you buy-3S
      (Who do you want to buy you what?)

e. *šta ko želite [da vam kupi _ _]
   what who want-2P to you buy-3S
   (What do you want who to buy you?)

f. *ko želite [šta da vam kupi _ _]
   who want-2P what to you buy-3S
   (Who do you want to buy you what?)

g. *šta želite [ko da vam kupi _ _]
   what want-2P who to you buy-3S
   (What do you want who to buy you?)

The second major group of languages to consider are those which require the fronting of a single *wh*-phrase. Again, this group divides into two types: those which allow other *wh*-phrases to remain in situ and those which do not. The latter do not allow multiple *wh*-questions at all. We saw that QZ is an example of the type that requires fronting of a single *wh*-phrase (and only one), but does not allow any others to remain in situ. Other languages of this type are Italian, Irish, and Tzotzil. Some representative QZ examples are given in (449).

(449) a. **pa go** r-laa de   GRING 34
       what thing H-do 2
       What are you doing?

   b. *r-laa de **pa go**
      H-do 2 what thing
      (You are doing what?)

   c. *pe r-laa de **pa go**
      Q H-do 2 what thing
      (You are doing what?)

   d. *pa go r-laa de lo txu
      what thing H-do 2 face who
      (What are you doing to who?)

   e. *pa go txu lo r-laa de
      what thing who face H-do 2
      (What are you doing to who?)

f. *r-laa de **pa** **go** lo **txu**
H-do 2 what thing face who
(What are you doing to who?)

The QZ pattern directly contrasts with that of English, which allows multiple *wh*-questions as long as one and only one *wh*-phrase is fronted. English also allows questions with the *wh*-phrase in situ, but only if accompanied by the question intonation pattern and contrastive stress is placed on the *wh*-phrase.

(450) a. What are you doing?
  b. You are doing **what**?
  c. *You are doing what?
  d. What are you doing to whom?
  e. *What who are you doing to?
  f. *You are doing what to whom?

West Flemish is another language which patterns like English with respect to question formation.

French has the option of fronting one *wh*-phrase or leaving them all in situ, as shown in (451) (taken from Rudin 1988:445).

(451) a. **qu'** as-tu donné à **qui**
  what have-you given to whom
  What have you given to whom?

  b. tu as donne **quoi** à **qui**
  you have given what to whom
  What have you given to whom?

Thus, French can pattern like English, or it may pattern like Chinese, Japanese, and the other languages which do not front *wh*-phrases at all. This is the third major group of languages: multiple *wh*-questions are allowed but all the *wh*-phrases must remain in situ. Chinese examples (taken from Huang 1982) are given in (452).

(452) a. ni xiang-zhidao Lisi **weisheme** mai-le **sheme**
  you wonder Lisi why bought what
  What do you wonder why Lisi bought (it)?

b. *sheme ni   xiang-zhidao Lisi **weisheme** mai-le __
   what you wonder   Lisi why   bought
   (What do you wonder why Lisi bought (it)?)

c. ***sheme weisheme** ni   xiang-zhidao Lisi __ mai-le __
   what   why   you wonder   Lisi   bought
   (What do you wonder why Lisi bought (it)?)

The chart in (453) summarizes these facts and shows the range of attested types of languages that we need to account for. Based upon the implications given in (446), the level at which the two clauses of the Wh-Criterion must apply is shown in the final column for each language type.

(453)

Type	Fronting	In Situ	Languages	Wh-Criterion
I	multiple	none	Bulgarian Romanian	B at SS A at SS
II	multiple	OK	Serbo-Croatian Polish Czech	B at SS A at LF
III	single	none	QZ Italian Irish Tzotzil	B at SS A at SS
IV	single	OK	English West Flemish French (opt.)	B at SS A at LF
V	none	none	**Unattested**	B at LF A at SS
VI	none	OK	Chinese Japanese French (opt.)	B at LF A at LF

The fact that type V is unattested should not be surprising; a language which did not allow fronting of a wh-phrase and did not allow any to remain in situ could not form wh-questions at all. I assume it is a universal that all languages have the ability to ask content questions. Given this, all four logical combinations allowing for the two clauses of the Wh-Criterion to apply at either S-structure or LF are accounted for, since the other three possibilities are attested.

As should be clear from the chart in (453), however, these distinctions in the level of application for each part of the criterion are not sufficient to distinguish between languages of types I and III, nor between types II and IV. Languages which allow multiple fronting and languages which require only one *wh*-phrase to be fronted cannot be distinguished via distinctions in the level at which the *Wh*-Criterion applies; the only distinction made is whether or not it is possible to have *wh*-phrases remain in situ. Clearly, something more is needed to correctly separate all four of these types of languages.

A second problem exists for languages like Chinese which do not allow fronting of any *wh*-phrases at S-structure. The requirement that Clause B holds at S-structure forces the fronting of at least one *wh*-phrase for languages of types I–IV. Since the mappings in (446) are one-way implications rather than *iff* statements, however, simply stating that Clause B is not required to hold until LF does not prohibit fronting earlier than LF in a language like Chinese. These two problems point out the need for further parameterization.

Parameterization of the *wh*-scope positions

Rudin (1988) provides a partial answer to the first problem by differentiating between languages that allow more than one *wh*-phrase to be in the specifier of CP position at S-structure from those that allow multiply-filled specifiers of CP only at LF. Rudin follows Adams (1984) in using a filter called the Condition on Comp (or SpecCP) Adjunction which is parameterized according to the level of representation at which it applies. Under this view, type I languages would be distinguished from type III languages by the fact that type I allows the specifier of CP to be multiply filled at both S-structure and LF, whereas type III languages never allow it. Likewise, type II languages allow a multiply-filled specifier of CP at both S-structure and LF, but type IV languages only allow it at LF.

Rudin shows that the picture is actually more complex than this. She carefully establishes that the multiple fronting languages (types I and II) differ in several ways which can be straightforwardly explained if only Bulgarian and Romanian truly allow more than one *wh*-phrase to be in the specifier of CP at S-structure. In contrast, Polish, Czech, and Serbo-Croatian have only a single *wh*-phrase in the specifier of CP position, while all other fronted *wh*-phrases are adjoined to IP.

This possible adjunction to IP opens the door to an account of the canonical position of fronted *wh*-phrases in QZ. Recall that some *wh*-phrases in QZ must co-occur with the question marker, *pe*, used in Yes/No questions, as shown in (454). Since the position of the fronted *wh*-phrase in these constructions is always after the question marker, which occupies C⁰, the *wh*-scope position for QZ is analyzed as adjunction to the immediately following phrase, usually IP.[158]

(454) a. ***pe-zee*** *n-a*   *no*   BENIT 32
     Q-how s-become there
     How is it there?

   b. *****zee*** *n-ak*   *no*
      how s-become there
      (How is it there?)

   c. *****zee pe*** *n-ak*   *no*
      how Q   s-become there
      (How is it there?)

Thus, adjunction to IP seems to be needed to account for the empirical facts in some languages, providing evidence for overruling the assumption in Chomsky (1986) that *wh*-phrases may not adjoin to IP.

In addition, we are close to a solution for the second problem noted above: what prevents visible (i.e. S-structure) fronting of *wh*-phrases in a language like Chinese? To fully account for the cross-linguistic variation seen, we need to parameterize not only the level of representation at which *wh*-movement applies, but also the positions available for such movement. Also, rather than distinguishing only between singly-filled and multiply-filled positions, we must be able to mark a particular position as completely unavailable for *wh*-movement. For instance, we would say that English has a single specifier of CP position available at S-structure, but allows adjunction to the specifier of CP at LF. Adjunction to IP is disallowed for *wh*-phrases at both levels in English. In contrast, QZ has a single IP-adjoined position available at S-structure, with no further adjunction and no specifier of CP position available at either S-structure or LF. Early *wh*-movement (i.e. at S-structure) in Chinese is ruled out by

---

[158] I assumed the presence of a Polarity Phrase (PolP) in chapter 9 to account for the coordination between clauses of different polarity. Under that analysis the *wh*-scope position is adjoined to PolP which is above IP. Here I abstract away from that distinction so that the two positions of specifier of CP and adjoined to IP can be discussed in more general terms cross-linguistically.

Parameterization of the *wh*-scope positions

the lack of an available position for such movement: neither the specifier of CP position nor an IP-adjoined position is available at S-structure in Chinese.

Thus, languages would be able to specify the parameters shown in (455).[159]

(455)

	Wh-scope position	Number of positions	Level
Possible values	Specifier of CP Adjoined to IP	none one multiple	SS, SS* (LF)

The specific parameters needed to account for each of the language types from (453) are detailed in (456).

(456)

Type	Fronting	In Situ	Languages	*Wh*-Crit.	*wh*-scope positions
I	multiple	none	Bulgarian Romanian	B at SS A at SS	mult-spec CP-SS* none-adj. IP-SS*
II	multiple	OK	Serbo-Croatian Polish Czech	B at SS A at LF	one-spec CP-SS* mult-adj. IP-SS*
IIIa	single	none	QZ	B at SS A at SS	one-adj. IP-SS* none-spec CP-SS*
IIIb	single	none	Italian Irish Tzotzil	B at SS A at SS	one-spec CP-SS* none-adj. IP-SS*
IV	single	OK	English West Flemish French (opt.)	B at SS A at LF	one-spec CP-SS mult-spec CP-LF none-adj. IP-SS*
V	none	none	**Unattested**	B at LF A at SS	**Unattested**
VI	none	OK	Chinese Japanese French (opt.)	B at LF A at LF	none-spec CP-SS none-adj. IP-SS* mult-spec CP-LF

This parameterization of the scope positions available at the different levels of representation, coupled with the *Wh*-Criterion (which is also parameterized by level for each clause), correctly differentiates between

[159]SS* is used to notationally indicate that a particular configuration holds at SS and LF.

types I through IV and prevents early *wh*-movement in type VI languages. However, questions of redundancy arise. Is it really necessary to have two different parameters relating to the level of representation?

We just determined that it was necessary to parameterize what scope positions are available at each level of representation to restrict the number and positions of the moved *wh*-phrases at that level. In essence, parameterizing the scope positions available sets the upper limit, preventing too early *wh*-movement from occurring. This is exactly why the parameterization was proposed: the parameterization of levels of representation at which the two clauses of the *Wh*-Criterion apply could not prevent this early movement. On the other hand, simply having scope positions available does not mean movement must take place. Motivating such movement was the purpose of the *Wh*-Criterion.

The basic generalization is that a *wh*-operator moves at the earliest level allowed by the availability of a *wh*-scope position, in order to achieve the desired configuration (or relationship) with an $X^0_{[+wh]}$. If the *wh*-scope position is the specifier of CP, then the *wh*-operator will be in the normal specifier-head relationship with a $C^0_{[+wh]}$. In the case where the *wh*-scope position is adjoined to IP, the desired configuration will be a minimal government relationship where a $C^0_{[+wh]}$ directly governs the *wh*-operator. These are referred to as licensed *wh*-configurations. The *Wh*-Criterion could therefore be replaced by the general *Wh* Well-formedness Principle given in (457).

(457) *Wh* Well-formedness Principle

> A *wh*-operator must be in a licensed *wh*-configuration with an $X^0_{[+wh]}$ at the earliest level of representation at which a *wh*-scope position is available.

The principle in (457) provides a lower limit for *wh*-movement by "forcing" the movement to apply as soon as possible, while the language-specific parameters detailing the available *wh*-scope positions serve as the upper limit.

Wh-chains account for partial *wh*-movement

McDaniel (1989) describes a construction in German and Romani which he calls partial *wh*-movement. In this construction, a *wh*-phrase moves to the specifier of a CP lower than the CP over which the *wh*-phrase takes scope. The lower CP is [-*wh*]. The normal scope position, the specifier of the

$CP_{[+wh]}$, is filled either by a "scope-marker" or by another *wh*-phrase. Examples of partial *wh*-movement where the specifier of $CP_{[+wh]}$ is filled with a scope-marker (=*was* 'WHAT' in German and *so* 'WHAT' in Romani) are given in example (458b) for German and in example (459b) for Romani, taken from McDaniel (1989:569). The (a) examples give the synonymous full *wh*-movement constructions for each language.

(458) a. *[mit wem]$_i$ glaubt [$_{IP}$ Hans [$_{CP}$ t$_i$ dass [$_{IP}$ Jakob jetzt t$_i$ spricht]]]*
   With whom does Hans think that Jakob is now talking?

   b. *was$_i$ glaubt [$_{IP}$ Hans [$_{CP}$ [mit wem]$_i$ [$_{IP}$ Jakob jetzt t$_i$ spricht]]]*
   WHAT does Hans believe with whom Jakob is now talking?

(459) a. *kas$_i$ [$_{IP}$ o Demiri mislinol [$_{CP}$ t$_i$ so [$_{IP}$ i Arìfa dikhĺa t$_i$]]]*
   Whom does Demir think that Arifa saw?

   b. *so$_i$ [$_{IP}$ o Demìri mislinol [$_{CP}$ kas$_i$ [$_{IP}$ i Arìfa dikhĺa t$_i$]]]*
   WHAT does Demir think whom Arifa saw?

Following McDaniel, the scope-markers are coindexed with the *wh*-phrase whose scope they indicate. He assumes that the scope-markers are base-generated in the specifier of $CP_{[+wh]}$ and that they are linked with a moved *wh*-phrase. The scope-markers can be thought of as *wh*-expletives, indicating that the moved *wh*-phrase is out of place. McDaniel further notes that if there are more than two clauses, the *wh*-phrase may move to an intermediate specifier of CP, as well as to the lowest or the highest one. (See McDaniel 1989 for the full range of data.)

McDaniel shows that partial *wh*-movement obeys the same subjacency restrictions with respect to island violations as does regular *wh*-movement. Partial *wh*-movement can therefore be subsumed under the same constraints and filters as full *wh*-movement, if they are restated in terms of chains. McDaniel suggests that the difference between languages which allow partial *wh*-movement and those that do not is due to the presence of an Ā-expletive in the lexicon.

We need to consider how to extend the parameterized account given above for full *wh*-movement to allow for these partial *wh*-movement constructions. If the head of the *wh*-chain must be overt, then only languages with overt scope-markers can have partial *wh*-movement.[160] In all other

---

[160] As McDaniel (1989) notes, this restriction to overt scope-markers may not hold universally. Positing of non-overt scope-markers may be necessary to account for the partial *wh*-movement allowed in Ancash Quechua (Cole 1983), Belauan (Georgopoulos 1984) and possibly also in Iraqi Arabic.

cases, the head of the chain will be the true *wh*-phrase, since traces must be c-commanded by their antecedents. Without changing the parameters regarding the scope positions available at each level of representation, a simple rewording of the well-formedness principle from (457) will correctly allow partial *wh*-movement, as shown in (460).[161]

(460) *Wh* Well-formedness Principle (Chain Version)

> The head of a *wh*-chain must be in a licensed *wh*-configuration with an $X^0_{[+wh]}$ at the earliest level of representation at which a *wh*-scope position is available. Further, a *wh*-phrase in an A-position must be part of a *wh*-chain whose head is in a *wh*-scope position.

Thus a *wh*-phrase must still move as soon as possible, subject to the availability of a *wh*-scope position. This movement is directly to the licensed *wh*-configuration in the case of full *wh*-movement. Partial *wh*-movement is allowed only if there is a scope-marker in the licensed *wh*-configuration to head the *wh*-chain.

This principle allows both full and partial *wh*-movement. (461) shows the S-structure for the full *wh*-movement construction example in (459a), where the *wh*-phrase, *kas*, has moved to the specifier of the matrix $CP_{[+wh]}$, heading a chain with its trace in the lower specifier of CP and its trace in the original argument position. Both traces are legitimate since the head of the chain is in a licensed *wh*-configuration with an $X^0_{[+wh]}$, even though one of the traces is in the specifier of a $CP_{[-wh]}$.

---

[161] As given, the *Wh* Well-formedness Principle is only the equivalent of, or replacement for, Clause A of the *Wh*-Criterion. That is, we are only requiring movement of the *wh*-phrases to the proper position to be in a licensed *wh*-relationship with an $X^0_{[+wh]}$, not requiring any movement of the $X^0_{[+wh]}$. This is because I am basically assuming that the $X^0_{[+wh]}$ is really $C^0_{[+wh]}$ and that it is base generated there. (The *Wh*-Criterion also used Clause B to motivate movement of the *wh*-phrase, but this has been replaced in the current proposal by the statement requiring *wh*-movement to take place at the earliest level at which a *wh*-scope position is available.) It is interesting to note, however, that an extension of Clause B of the *Wh*-Criterion using chains can be used to account for the distribution of Subject-Aux Inversion in English. See Rizzi (1991) for this proposal.

(461)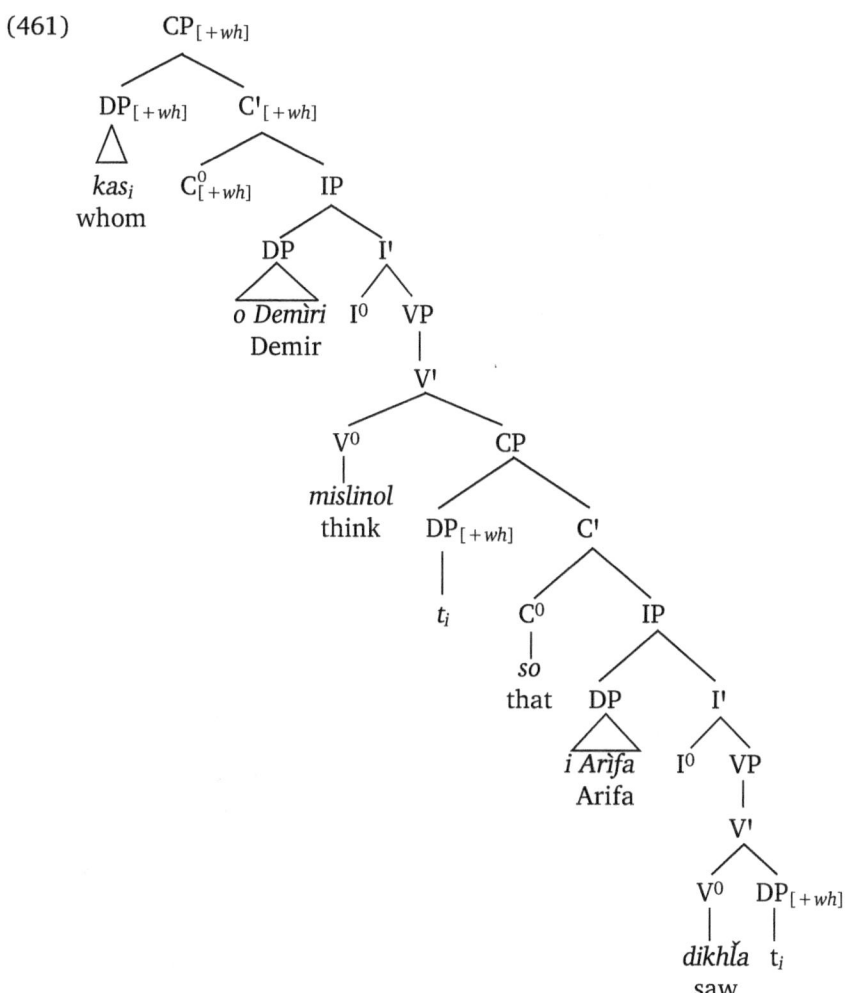

The S-structure tree, given in (462), for the partial *wh*-movement example (459b) is very similar. Instead of the true *wh*-phrase, *kas*, moving all the way to the specifier of the matrix $CP_{[+wh]}$, it has stopped in the lower CP. This is legitimized by the presence of the scope-marker, *so*, in the specifier of the top CP. Since *so* serves as the head of the *wh*-chain and it is in a licensed *wh*-configuration with an $X^0_{[+wh]}$, *kas* may surface in the specifier of a $CP_{[-wh]}$.

(462)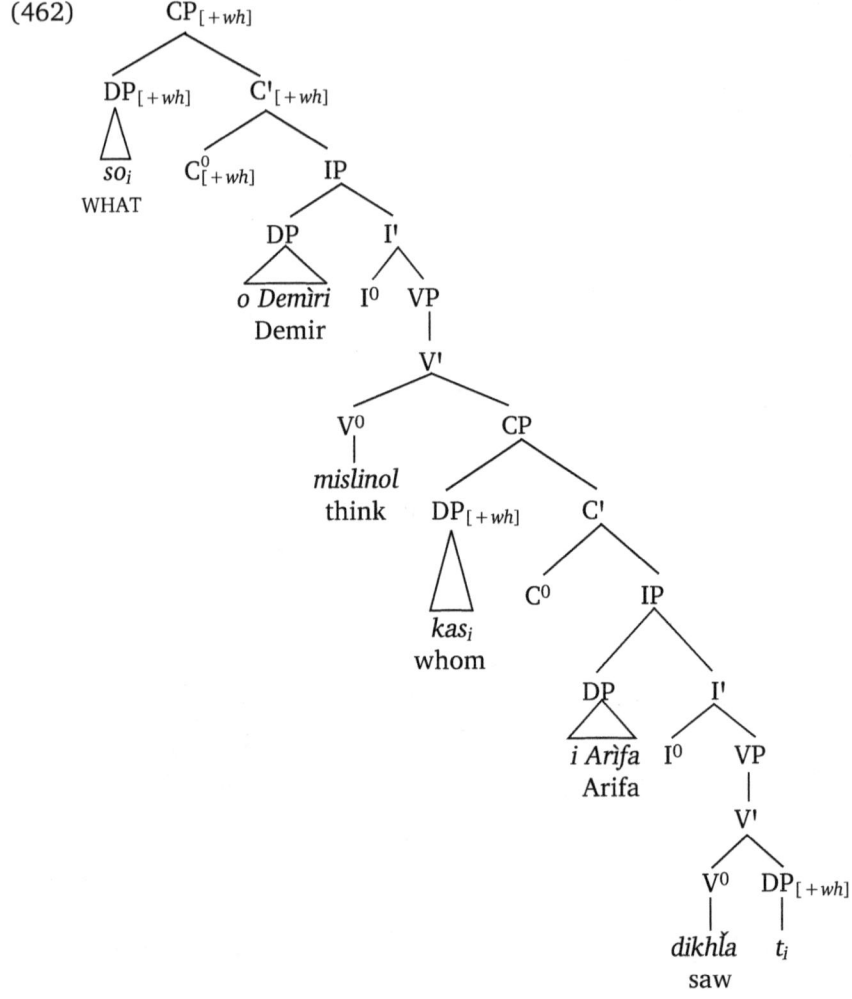

A similar distribution in the number of negative phrases allowed to be fronted at S-structure was seen in chapter 8. The parameterized analysis given here for question formation can be straightforwardly extended to that case (and possibly to other semantic operators, such as focus, if the need arises).

References

Abney, Stephen. 1987. The English noun phrase and its sentential aspect. Ph.D. dissertation. Cambridge, Mass.: MIT.

Adams, Marianne. 1984. Multiple interrogation in Italian. The Linguistic Review 4:1–27.

Aissen, Judith. 1987. Tzotzil clause structure. Dordrecht: Reidel Publishers.

Aissen, Judith. 1989. Comitative agreement in Tzotzil. SRC Working Papers, 89–102. Santa Cruz: University of California.

Aissen, Judith. 1992a. Topic and focus in Mayan. Language 68:43–80.

Aissen, Judith. 1992b. Varieties of *wh*-movement in Tzotzil. Paper presented at the Specifiers Conference. Santa Cruz: University of California.

Aissen, Judith. 1996. Pied-piping, abstract agreement, and functional projections in Tzotzil. Natural Language and Linguistic Theory 14:447–491.

Anderson, Stephen R. 1992. A-morphous morphology. Cambridge Studies in Linguistics 62. New York: Cambridge University Press.

Anonymous. 1823. Gramática de la lengua zapoteca. Edición preparada por Antonio Peñafiel. 1981. Mexico, D.F.: Editorial Innovación, S.A.

Aoun, J., N. Hornstein, and Dominique Sportiche. 1981. Aspects of wide scope quantification. Journal of Linguistic Research 1:67–95.

Baker, Mark C. 1988. Incorporation: A theory of grammatical function changing. Chicago: University of Chicago Press.

Barker, Chris and Geoffrey K. Pullum. 1990. A theory of command relations. Linguistics and Philosophy 13:1–34.
Belletti, Adriana. 1990. Generalized verb movement. Turin: Rosenberg and Sellier.
Benton, Joseph P. 1981. The completive and potential form of Chichicapan Zapotec verbs. Workpapers of the Summer Institute of Linguistics University of North Dakota Session 25:11–30.
Benton, Joseph P. 1987. Clause and sentence-level word order and discourse strategy in Chichicapan Zapotec oral narrative discourse. S.I.L. Mexico Workpapers 9:72–84. Summer Institute of Linguistics, Mexico Branch.
Berman, Stephen. 1989. An analysis of quantificational variability in indirect *wh*-questions. West Coast Conference on Formal Linguistics 8:29–43.
Black, Cheryl A. 1992. Comitative coordination using quantifiers in Quiegolani Zapotec. In Black and McCloskey (eds.), 1–33.
Black, Cheryl A. 1993. Negative Concord with obligatory fronting in Zapotec. In Pullum and Potsdam (eds.), 1–20. Santa Cruz: University of California.
Black, Cheryl A. 1994. Quiegolani Zapotec syntax. Ph.D. dissertation. Santa Cruz: University of California.
Black, Cheryl A. 1995. Laryngeal licensing and syllable well-formedness in Quiegolani Zapotec. Workpapers of the Summer Institute of Linguistics. University of North Dakota Session 39:11–32.
Black, Cheryl A. 1996. A backwards binding construction in Zapotec. Workpapers of the Summer Institute of Linguistics, University of North Dakota Session 40:75–87.
Black, H. Andrew. 1992. South American verb second phenomena: Evidence from Shipibo. In Black and McCloskey (eds.), 35–63.
Black, H. Andrew. 1993. Constraint-ranked derivation: A serial approach to optimization. Ph.D. dissertation. Santa Cruz: University of California.
Black, H. Andrew and James McCloskey, eds. 1992. Syntax at Santa Cruz, Vol. 1. Santa Cruz: University of California.
Bowers, John. 1993. The syntax of predication. Linguistic Inquiry 24(4):591–656.
Briggs, Eleanor. 1961. Mitla Zapotec grammar. Mexico: Instituto Lingüístico de Verano and Centro de Investigaciones Antropólogicas de México.
Broadwell, George Aaron. 1999. Focus alignment and optimal order in Zapotec. Paper presented at the Chicago Linguistic Society.

Burton, Strang and Jane Grimshaw. 1992. Coordination and VP-internal subjects. Linguistic Inquiry 23(2):305–313.
Burzio, Luigi. 1986. Italian syntax: A Government-Binding approach. Studies in Natural Language and Linguistic Theory. Dordrecht: Kluwer.
Butler, Inez M. 1976a. Reflexive constructions of Yatzachi Zapotec. International Journal of American Linguistics 42:331–337.
Butler, Inez M. 1976b. Verb classification in Yatzachi Zapotec. S.I.L. Mexico Work Papers 2:74–84. Summer Institute of Linguistics, Mexico Branch.
Butler, Inez M. 1988. Gramática zapoteca: Zapoteco de Yatzachi El Bajo. Serie Gramática de Linguas Indígenas de México. Mexico D.F.: Instituto Lingüístico de Verano.
Choe, Hyon-Sook. 1986. An SVO analysis of VSO languages and parameterization: A study of Berber. In S. Berman, J. Choe, and J. McDonough (eds.), NELS 16, GLSA. Amherst: University of Massachusetts.
Chomsky, Noam. 1970. Remarks on nominalization. In Roderick Jacobs and Peter Rosenbaum (eds.), Readings in English transformational grammar, 184–221. Waltham, Mass: Ginn.
Chomsky, Noam. 1977. On *Wh*-movement. In P. Culicover, T. Wasow and A. Akmajian (eds.), Formal syntax, 71–131. New York: Academic Press.
Chomsky, Noam. 1981. Lectures on Government and Binding. Dordrecht: Foris.
Chomsky, Noam. 1982. Some concepts and consequences of the theory of Government and Binding. Cambridge: MIT Press.
Chomsky, Noam. 1986. Barriers. Cambridge: MIT Press.
Chomsky, Noam. 1991. Some notes on economy of derivation and representation. In R. Freidin (ed.), Principles and Parameters in comparative grammar, 417–454. Cambridge: MIT Press.
Chomsky, Noam. 1995. The Minimalist Program. Cambridge: MIT Press.
Chung, Sandra. 1981. Transitivity and surface filters in Chamorro. In J. Hollyman and A. Pawley (eds.), Studies in Pacific languages and cultures in honor of Bruce Biggs. Auckland: Linguistic Society of New Zealand.
Chung, Sandra. 1990. VP's and verb movement in Chamorro. Natural Language and Linguistic Theory 8(4):559–620.
Chung, Sandra. 1991. Functional heads and proper government in Chamorro. In McCloskey (ed.), 85–134.

Chung, Sandra, William Ladusaw, and James McCloskey. 1994. Sluicing and logical form. LRC Working Papers, 94–101. Santa Cruz: University of California.

Chung, Sandra and James McCloskey. 1987. Government, barriers, and small clauses in Modern Irish. Linguistic Inquiry 18:173–237.

Chung, Sandra and Alan Timberlake. 1985. Tense, aspect, and mood. In Shopen (ed.), 202–258.

Cinque, Guglielmo. 1990. Types of Ā-Dependencies. Linguistic Inquiry Monograph 17. Cambridge: MIT Press.

Cole, Peter. 1983. Subjacency and successive cyclicity: Evidence from Ancash Quechua. Journal of Linguistic Research 2(4):35–58.

Comorovski, Ileana. 1986. Multiple *wh*-questions in Polish. Linguistic Inquiry 17:171–177.

Comrie, Bernard. 1985. Causative verb formation and other verb-deriving morphology. In Shopen (ed.), 309–348.

Craig, Colette. 1977. The structure of Jacaltec. Austin: University of Texas Press.

Craig, Colette. 1986. Jacaltec noun classifiers: A study in grammaticalization. Lingua 70:241–284.

Craig, Colette. 1991. A morpho-syntactic typology of classifiers. Colloquium talk presented at the University of California, Santa Cruz.

Culicover, Peter W. and Michael S. Rochemont. 1990. Extraposition and the complement principle. Linguistic Inquiry 21:23–47.

De Angulo, Jaime. 1926. The development of affixes in a group of monosyllabic languages in Oaxaca. Language 2:46–61, 119–133.

De Angulo, Jaime. 1926b. Tone patterns and verb form in a dialect of Zapotec. Language 2:238–250.

De Cordova, Juan. 1578. Arte del Idioma Zapoteco. Edición facsimilar 1886. México, D.F.: Imprenta del Gobierno en la Escuela de Artes.

Derbyshire, Desmond C. and Geoffrey K. Pullum. 1978. Object-initial languages. Presented at the Summer Meeting of the Linguistic Society of America.

Diesing, Molly. 1990. Verb movement and the subject position in Yiddish. Natural Language and Linguistic Theory 8:41–79.

Doherty, Cathal. 1992. Clausal structure and the modern Irish copula. In Black and McCloskey (eds.), 65–91

Earl, Robert. 1968. Rincon Zapotec clauses. International Journal of American Linguistics 34:269–274.

Emonds, Joseph. 1979. Word order in generative grammar. In G. Bedell, F. Muraki, and K. Kobayashi (eds.), Explorations in Linguistics. Toyko: Kenkyusha Press.

Emonds, Joseph. 1985. A unified theory of syntactic categories. Dordrecht: Foris.
Fontana, Josep M. 1993. A residual A-bar position in Spanish. West Coast Conference on Formal Linguistics XII. Santa Cruz: University of California.
Fukui, Naoki and Margaret Speas. 1986. Specifiers and projection. MIT Working Papers in Linguistics 8. Cambridge: MIT.
Gazdar, Gerald. 1981. Unbounded dependencies and coordinate structure. Linguistic Inquiry 12:155–184.
Gazdar, Gerald, Ewan Klein, Geoffrey Pullum, and Ivan Sag. 1985. Generalized phrase structure grammar. Cambridge, Mass.: Harvard University Press.
Georgopoulos, Carol. 1984. Resumptive pronouns, syntactic binding, and levels of representation in Belauan. Proceedings of NELS 14:81–97.
Godard, Danièle. 1989. Empty categories as subjects of tensed Ss in English or French? Linguistic Inquiry 20:497–505.
Goodall, Grant. 1987. Parallel structures in syntax: Coordination, causatives, and restructuring. Cambridge Studies in Linguistics 46. Cambridge: Cambridge University Press.
Greenberg, Joseph H. 1963. Some universals of grammar with particular attention to the order of meaningful elements. In Joseph H. Greenberg (ed.), Universals of Language, 73–113. Cambridge: MIT Press.
Grimes, Barbara F., ed.; Richard S. Pittman and Joseph E. Grimes, consulting eds. 1996. Ethnologue: Languages of the World, Thirteenth Edition. Dallas: Summer Institute of Linguistics.
Grimshaw, Jane. 1979. Complement selection and the lexicon. Linguistic Inquiry 10:279–326.
Grimshaw, Jane. 1986. A morphosyntactic explanation for the mirror principle. Linguistic Inquiry 17:745–749.
Grimshaw, Jane. 1990. Argument structure. Cambridge: MIT Press.
Haegeman, Liliane. 1991. Negative concord, negative heads. In LINS 250: Issues in Italian syntax, 51–71. 1991 Linguistic Institute. Santa Cruz: University of California.
Haegeman, Liliane and Raffaella Zanuttini. 1990. Negative concord in West Flemish. Ms. University of Geneva.
Haider, Hubert and Martin Prinzhorn, eds. 1986. Verb second phenomena in Germanic languages. Dordrecht: Foris.
Hale, Kenneth and Elisabeth Selkirk. 1987. Government and tonal phrasing in Papago. Phonology Yearbook 4:151–183.

Hankamer, Jorge. 1973. Unacceptable ambiguity. Linguistic Inquiry 4:17–68.
Hankamer, Jorge. 1979. Deletion in coordinate structures. Outstanding Dissertations in Linguistics 16. New York and London: Garland Publishing, Inc.
Hayes, Bruce. 1989. The prosodic hierarchy in meter. Phonetics and phonology, Volume 1: Rhythm and meter. New York: Academic Press.
Hendrick, Randall. 1991. The morphosyntax of aspect. In McCloskey (ed.), 171–210.
Huang, C.-T. James. 1982. Move *wh* in a language without *wh*-movement. The Linguistic Review 1:369–416.
Huang, C.-T. James. 1984. On the distribution and reference of empty pronouns. Linguistic Inquiry 15:531–574.
Huang, C.-T. James. 1990. Reconstruction and the structure of vp: Some theoretical consequences. Ms. Cornell University.
Hyman, Larry M. 1990. Boundary tonology and the prosodic hierarchy. In Inkelas and Zec (eds.), 109–125.
Inkelas, Sharon and Draga Zec, eds. 1990. The phonology-syntax connection. Chicago: University of Chicago Press.
Jackendoff, Ray S. 1971. Gapping and related rules. Linguistic Inquiry 2:21–35.
Jaeggli, Osvaldo and Kenneth J. Safir. 1989. The null subject parameter and parametric theory. In Jaeggli and Safir (eds.), The null subject parameter. Dordrecht: Kluwer Academic Publishers.
Kaisse, Ellen M. 1982. Sentential clitics and Wackernagel's law. West Coast Conference on Formal Linguistics 1:1–14.
Kitagawa, Yoshihisa. 1986. Subjects in Japanese and English. Ph.D. dissertation. Amherst: University of Massachusetts.
Klavans, Judith L. 1982. Some problems in a theory of clitics. Ph.D. dissertation. University College London. Reproduced by Indiana University Linguistics Club.
Klavans, Judith L. 1985. The independence of syntax and phonology in cliticization. Language 61:95–120.
Koopman, Hilda and Dominique Sportiche. 1991. On the position of subjects. In McCloskey (ed.), 211–258.
Kratzer, Angelika. 1989. Stage-level and individual-level predicates. Ms. Amherst: University of Massachusetts.
Kreikebaum, Wolfram. 1987. Fronting and related features in Santo Domingo Albarradas Zapotec. S.I.L. Mexico Workpapers 9:33–71. Summer Institute of Linguistics, Mexico Branch.
Kuroda, S. Y. 1986. Whether you agree or not. Appendix of Ms.

Ladusaw, William A. 1989. Group reference and the plural pronoun construction. SRC Working Papers, 89–102. Santa Cruz: University of California.

Ladusaw, William A. 1992. Expressing negation. SRC Working Papers, 92–103. Santa Cruz: University of California.

Ladusaw, William A. 1993. Configurational expression of negation. Talk given at the University of California, San Diego and to the Negation Seminar at the University of California, Santa Cruz. March, 1993.

Laka Mugarza, Miren Itziar. 1990. Negation in syntax: On the nature of functional categories and projections. Ph.D. dissertation. MIT.

Lasnik, Howard. 1981. On two recent treatments of disjoint reference. Reprinted in Essays on anaphora, 1989. Dordrecht: Kluwer Publishing Company.

Lasnik, Howard. 1986. On the necessity of binding conditions. Reprinted in Essays on Anaphora, 1989. Dordrecht.: Kluwer Publishing Company.

Lasnik, Howard and Mamoru Saito. 1984. On the nature of proper government. Linguistic Inquiry 15:235–289.

Lasnik, Howard and Mamoru Saito. 1992. Move alpha. Cambridge: MIT Press.

Leal, Mary and Otis Leal. 1954. Noun possession in Villa Alta Zapotec. International Journal of American Linguistics 20:215–216.

López L., Filemón and Ronaldo Newberg Y. 1990. La conjugación del verbo zapoteco: zapoteco de Yalálag. México, D.F.: Instituto Lingüístico de Verano, A.C.

Lyman, Larry. 1964. The verb syntagmemes of Choapan Zapotec. Linguistics 7:16–41.

Marantz, Alec. 1989. Clitics and phrase structure. In Mark Baltin and Anthony Kroch (eds.), Alternative conceptions of phrase structure, 99–116. Chicago: University of Chicago Press.

Marks, Donna L. 1976. Zapotec verb morphology: Categories and tonomechanics with special attention to Sierra Juarez Zapotec. M.A. thesis. University of Texas at Arlington.

Marlett, Stephen A. 1993. Zapotec pronoun classification. International Journal of American Linguistics 59:82–101.

Marlett, Stephen A. and Velma B. Pickett. 1985. Pluralization in Zapotec languages. In Mary C. Marino and Luis A. Pérez (eds.), The Twelfth LACUS Forum 1985, 246–255.

Marlett, Stephen A. and Velma B. Pickett. 1987. The syllable structure and aspect morphology of Isthmus Zapotec. International Journal of American Linguistics 53:398–422.

May, Robert. 1985. Logical form: Its structure and derivation. Cambridge: MIT Press.
McCarthy, John J. and Alan S. Prince. 1992. Edge alignment constraints. Talk presented at the University of California, Santa Cruz. December 11, 1992.
McCarthy, John J. and Alan S. Prince. 1993. Prosodic morphology I: constraint interaction and satisfaction. Ms. University of Massachusetts, Amherst and Rutgers University.
McCloskey, James. 1983. A VP in a VSO language? In Gerald Gazdar, Ewan Klein and Geoffrey K. Pullum (eds.), Order, concord, and constituency. Dordrecht: Foris.
McCloskey, James. 1991. Clause structure, ellipsis and proper government in Irish. In McCloskey (ed.), 259–302.
McCloskey, James. 1992a. Adjunction, selection, and embedded verb-second. Paper presented at the Specifiers Conference. Santa Cruz: University of California.
McCloskey, James. 1992b. On the scope of verb movement in Irish. LRC Working Papers 92–10, Santa Cruz: University of California.
McCloskey, James, ed. 1991. The syntax of verb-initial languages. Lingua Special Edition. Amsterdam.
McDaniel, Dana. 1989. Partial and multiple *wh*-movement. Natural Language and Linguistic Theory 7:565–604.
McNally, Louise. 1992. VP coordination and the VP-internal subject hypothesis. Linguistic Inquiry 23:336–341.
McNally, Louise. 1993. Comitative coordination: A case study in group formation. Natural Language and Linguistic Theory 11: 347–379.
Neijt, Anneke. 1979. Gapping: A contribution to sentence grammar. Studies in generative grammar 7. Dordrecht: Foris.
Nellis, Neil and Jane Goodner de Nellis. 1983. Diccionario zapoteco: Zapoteco de Juarez. Serie de Vocabularios y Diccionarios Indígenas, 27. México D.F.: Instituto Lingüístico de Verano. Also includes a grammar by Doris A. Bartholomew.
Nespor, Marina and Irene Vogel. 1986. Prosodic Phonology. Dordrecht: Foris.
Newberg, Ronald. 1987. Participant accessibility in Yalálag Zapotec. S.I.L. Mexico Workpapers 9:12–25. Summer Institute of Linguistics, Mexico Branch.
Partee, Barbara H., Alice ter Meulen, and Robert E. Wall. 1990. Mathematical methods in linguistics. Dordrecht: Kluwer.
Perlmutter, David and John Robert Ross. 1970. Relative clauses with split antecedents. Linguistic Inquiry 1:350.

Pesetsky, David. 1987. *Wh*-in situ: movement and unselective binding. In Eric J. Reuland and Alice G. B. ter Meulen (eds.), The representation of (in) definiteness. Current Studies in Linguistics Series. Cambridge: MIT Press.
Pickett, Velma. 1953a. Isthmus Zapotec verb analysis I. International Journal of American Linguistics 19:292–296.
Pickett, Velma. 1953b. Las construcciones de los verbos del zapoteco del Istmo de Juchitán, Oaxaca. MCCM 12: Ciencias Sociales, 191–198. México: UNAM.
Pickett, Velma. 1955. Isthmus Zapotec verb analysis II. International Journal of American Linguistics 21:217–232.
Pickett, Velma. 1959. The grammatical hierarchy of Isthmus Zapotec. Ph.D. dissertation. Ann Arbor: University of Michigan.
Pickett, Velma. 1960. The grammatical hierarchy of Isthmus Zapotec. Language Dissertation 56: Language 36.1 (part 2).
Pickett, Velma. 1967. Isthmus Zapotec. In N.A. McQuown (ed.), Handbook of Middle American Indians, 291–310. Austin: University of Texas Press.
Pickett, Velma. 1976. Further comments on Zapotec motion verbs. International Journal of American Linguistics 42:162–164.
Pickett, Velma y colaboradores. 1959. Castellano-zapoteco, zapoteco-castellano (Vocabulario zapoteco del Istmo). Serie de Vocabularios Indígenas 3. Mexico D.F.: Instituto Lingüístico de Verano.
Pickett, Velma, Cheryl Black, and Vicente Marcial C. 1998. Gramática popular del zapoteco del Istmo. Oaxaca and Tucson: Centro de Investigación y Desarrollo Binniza A.C. and Instituto Lingüístico de Verano.
Piper, Michael J. 1993. La correferencia en el zapoteco del sur: hacia una reformulacíon de la teoría de ligamiento. Paper presented at the X Congreso Internacional de la Asociación Lingüística y Filológica de la América Latina. April 11–16, 1993. Veracruz, Mexico.
Piper, Michael J. 1997. Aspectos de la sintaxis del zapoteco de Amatlán: la interacción entre la estructura de la cláusula, las categorias vacías y el ligamiento. In Mariana Pool Westgaard (ed.), Estudios de lingüística formal, 171–198. México D.F.: El Colegio de México.
Platzack, Christer and Anders Holmberg. 1989. The role of AGR and finiteness. In Working Papers in Scandinavian Syntax 43:51–76.
Pollard, Carl and Ivan A. Sag. 1992. Anaphors in English and the scope of binding theory. Linguistic Inquiry 23:261–303.
Pollard, Carl and Ivan A. Sag. 1994. Head driven phrase structure grammar. CSLI. Chicago.

Pollock, Jean-Yves. 1989. Verb movement, UG, and the structure of IP. Linguistic Inquiry 20:365–424.
Postal, Paul M. 1966. On so-called 'pronouns' in English. In D. Reibel and S. Schane (eds.), Modern studies in English: Readings in transformational grammar, 201–224. New Jersey: Prentice-Hall, Inc.
Prince, Alan and Paul Smolensky. 1991. Connectionism and harmony theory in linguistics. Lecture notes and handouts from the LSA Summer Institute at UCSC. Tech. Report CU-CS-533-91. Boulder: University of Colorado.
Prince, Alan and Paul Smolensky. 1992. Optimality: constraint interaction in generative grammar. West Coast Conference on Formal Linguistics 11.
Prince, Alan and Paul Smolensky. 1993. Optimality theory. Rutgers University Center for Cognitive Science Technical Report 2. New Jersey: Piscataway.
Pullum, Geoffrey K. 1979. Review of Universals of language (4 volumes), edited by Joseph Greenberg. Linguistics 17:925–930.
Pullum, Geoffrey K. and Paul M. Postal. 1979. On an inadequate defense of 'trace theory'. Linguistic Inquiry 10:689–706.
Pullum, Geoffrey K. and Eric Potsdam, eds. 1993. Syntax at Santa Cruz, Vol. 2. University of California at Santa Cruz.
Radin, Paul. 1930. A preliminary sketch of the Zapotec language. Language 6:64–85.
Regnier, Randy. 1989a. Collection of unpublished Quiegolani Zapotec glossed texts. Summer Institute of Linguistics, Mexico Branch.
Regnier, Randy. 1989b. Quiegolani Zapotec grammar. Ms. Summer Institute of Linguistics, Mexico Branch.
Regnier, Susan. 1993. Quiegolani Zapotec phonology. SIL-UND Workpapers Vol. XXXVII:37–63. University of North Dakota.
Reinhart, Tanya. 1976. The syntactic domain of anaphora. Ph.D. dissertation. Cambridge: MIT Press.
Reinhart, Tanya. 1981. Definite NP anaphora and c-command domains. Linguistic Inquiry 12:605–635.
Reinhart, Tanya and Eric Reuland. 1993. Reflexivity. Linguistic Inquiry 24:657–720.
Riggs, David Brent. 1987. Paragraph analysis for Amatlán Zapotec. S.I.L. Mexico Workpapers 9, 1–11. Summer Institute of Linguistics, Mexico Branch.
Rizzi, Luigi. 1982. Issues in Italian syntax. Studies in Generative Grammar 11. Dordrecht: Foris.
Rizzi, Luigi. 1990. Relativized minimality. Linguistic Inquiry Monograph 16. Cambridge: MIT Press.

Rizzi, Luigi. 1991. Residual verb second and the *Wh*-Criterion in LINS 250: Issues in Italian Syntax. Course material for the 1991 Linguistic Institute. Santa Cruz: University of California.
Rizzi, Luigi and Ian Roberts. 1989. Complex inversion in French. Probus 1:1–30.
Rosenbaum, Harvey. 1974. Language universals and Zapotec syntax. Ph.D. dissertation. University of Texas at Austin.
Ross, John Robert. 1967. Constraints on variables in syntax. Ph.D. dissertation. MIT.
Ross, John Robert. 1970. Gapping and the order of constituents. In M. Bierwisch and K. E. Heidolph (eds.), Progress in Linguistics, 249–259. The Hague: Mouton.
Rudin, Catherine. 1988. On multiple questions and multiple *wh* fronting. Natural Language and Linguistic Theory 6:445–501.
Rudin, Catherine. 1993. On focus position and focus marking in Bulgarian questions. Paper presented at FLSM IV.
Saxon, Leslie. 1989. Control and control verbs: two sources of 'control effects'. WCCFL 8:347–357.
Schwartz, Linda. 1988. Asymmetric feature distribution in pronominal 'coordinations'. In M. Barlow and J. Greenberg (eds.), Agreement in natural language: Approaches, theories, descriptions, 237–249. Stanford: CSLI.
Selkirk, Elisabeth O. 1978. On prosodic structure and its relation to syntactic structure. In T. Fretheim (ed.), Nordic Prosody II. Trondeim: TAPIR.
Selkirk, Elisabeth O. 1984. Phonology and syntax: the relation between sound and structure. Cambridge: MIT Press.
Selkirk, Elisabeth O. 1986. On derived domains in sentence phonology. Phonology Yearbook 3:371–405.
Sells, Peter. 1985. Lectures on contemporary syntactic theories. Center for the Study of Language and Information. Stanford.
Shopen, Timothy, (ed.). 1985. Language typology and syntactic description III. Cambridge: Cambridge University Press.
Smith Stark, Thomas C. 1988. 'Pied-piping' con inversión en preguntas parciales. Ms. Centro de Estudios Lingüísticos y Literarios, El Colegio de México y Seminario de Lenguas Indígenas.
Speas, Margaret. 1991. Phrase Structure in natural language. Dordrecht: Kluwer Academic Publishers.
Speck Charles H. and Velma B. Pickett. 1976. Some properties of the Texmelucan Zapotec verbs go, come, and arrive. International Journal of American Linguistics 42:58–64.

Sproat, Richard. 1985. Welsh syntax and VSO structure. Natural Language and Linguistic Theory 3:173–216.
Stenning, Keith. 1987. Anaphora as an approach to pragmatics. In Morris Halle, Joan Bresnan, and George A. Miller (eds.), Linguistic Theory and Psychological Reality. Cambridge: MIT Press.
Stowell, Tim. 1989. Subjects, specifiers, and X-Bar theory. In Mark Baltin and Anthony Kroch (eds.), Alternative conceptions of phrase structure, 232–262. The University of Chicago Press.
Stubblefield, Morris and Carol Miller de Stubblefield. 1991. Diccionario zapoteca de Mitla, Oaxaca. Serie de Vocabularios y Diccionarios Indígenas 31. México D.F.: Instituto Lingüístico de Verano. Also includes a grammar by Morris Stubblefield and Elena E. de Hollenbach.
Suñer, Margarita. 1993. About indirect questions and semi-questions. Linguistics and Philosophy 16:45–77.
Travis, Lisa. 1984. Parameters and effects of word order variation. Ph.D. dissertation. Cambridge: MIT.
Van Valin, Robert Jr. 1986. An empty category as the subject of a tensed S in English. Linguistic Inquiry 17:581–586.
Vikner, Sten. 1991. Verb Movement and the licensing of NP-positions in the Germanic languages. Ph.D dissertation. Germany: Universität Stuttgart.
Ward, Michael. 1987. A focus particle in Quioquitani Zapotec. S.I.L. Mexico Workpapers 9, 26–32. Summer Institute of Linguistics, Mexico Branch.
Williams, Edwin. 1978. Across-the-board rule application. Linguistic Inquiry 9:31–43.
Woolford, Ellen. 1991. VP-internal subjects in VSO and nonconfigurational languages. Linguistic Inquiry 22:503–540.
Zanuttini, Raffaella. 1991. Syntactic properties of sentential negation. A comparative study of Romance languages. Ph.D. dissertation. University of Pennsylvania.
Zwicky, Arnold M. 1977. Hierarchies of person. CLS 13:714–733.

Index

A

A-binding 15
A-bound 77
A-chain 280
Across the Board Extraction 222, 223, 224, 254
adjacency 13, 47, 113, 134, 136, 138, 141, 201, 202, 203, 206, 207, 229, 246
adjective 22, 36, 51, 52, 234, 244, 248, 249
adjunct 288, 293, 298, 300, 308, 310, 315
adjunction 10, 15, 96, 102, 113, 126, 127, 136, 146, 157, 160, 163, 199, 201, 243, 245, 249, 254, 295, 296, 318, 326
adverb 22, 133, 153, 157, 303
Agent 32, 53, 54, 55, 57, 59, 61, 62, 219
agreement 33, 59, 95, 137, 164, 177, 249
Amatlán Zapotec 103
A-movement 13, 14, 16, 37, 58, 59, 95, 164, 216
anaphoric 73
anaphors 73
antecedent government 186, 189, 314
appositive 264, 265
aspect 24, 153, 172, 176, 203, 213, 215, 220, 221, 230, 265, 296

ASSOC 32
auxiliary 212, 215, 216, 230

Ā

Ā-binding 15
Ā-movement 13, 14, 16, 37, 49, 90, 101, 112, 144, 163, 201

B

Bambara 216
Berber 95
binding 15, 280
Binding theory 15, 69, 75, 277
body part 46, 247
Bulgarian 320, 325
Burzio's Generalization 12, 58

C

case 12, 58, 60, 61, 95, 138, 164, 203, 246, 258, 279
Case filter 12
Case theory 11, 12, 13, 57, 94, 96, 164
causative 32, 58, 61, 220
c-command 8, 15, 277, 281
chain 12, 16

C

Chamorro 85, 95, 97, 220, 235, 237, 245, 275
Chinese 241, 323, 325, 326
Choapan Zapotec 53
Comitative Coordination 272, 296, 302, 303
commands 31
comparatives 146
complement 7
complementizer 105, 112, 122, 123, 124, 125, 127, 138, 143, 184, 186, 196, 200
Completive 26, 27, 220, 266
conjunction 195, 230, 284, 285
consonant 4, 34
construal 287, 312, 314, 315, 317, 318
control 39, 40, 42, 62
coordinate 221
Coordinate Structure Constraint 217, 227, 254
coordination 194, 195, 196, 200, 217, 218, 220, 222, 223, 224, 226, 227, 229, 230, 234, 250, 252, 253, 259, 284, 285, 287, 288
copula 235, 236
copular 238, 312
copular verb 25, 48, 49, 51
CP-recursion 127, 133
Czech 321, 325

D

demonstrative 22, 23, 36, 244, 249
determiner 108, 110, 184, 244
direct quotation 47
discourse 77, 79, 103, 110, 111
ditransitive 46, 58
DP Hypothesis 10, 23, 241, 242, 243, 244
DPs 108
D-structure 6, 12, 13, 58, 61, 95, 96, 127, 146, 157, 166, 294, 302, 306, 309, 315, 318
Dutch 216

E

ECP 14, 96, 114, 137, 186, 189, 315
embedded clause 64, 182, 184, 188, 190, 290, 300
emphatic 70
empty categories 11, 14, 16, 37
Empty Category Principle *See* ECP

English 36, 39, 43, 76, 90, 95, 114, 128, 146, 150, 164, 247, 248, 314, 315, 323
exclamations 140
existential 48, 50, 152, 153, 157, 168, 199
expletive pro 42
expletives 329
external argument 40, 55, 60, 61, 215, 293, 297, 299, 318
extraction 303
extraposition 47, 147, 303
extraposition from DP 146, 302, 307, 308, 310, 311, 312, 314

F

Faroese 42
FocP *See* focused phrases
focus 53, 62, 64, 99, 100, 102, 103, 105, 115, 135, 137, 163, 182, 183, 185, 189, 191, 192, 193, 223, 289, 295, 300, 302, 308, 309, 310, 311, 321
focus marker 99, 105, 108, 109, 110, 111, 112, 166, 182, 184
focused phrases 114, 183, 184, 185, 189, 192, 193
focusing 239, 313
French 90, 95, 216, 323
fronting 103, 107, 112, 136, 137, 147, 150, 162, 163, 171, 178, 183, 186, 188, 200, 205, 302
functional head 9, 113, 174, 242
Future 29, 158, 266

G

Gapping 228, 229
gender 258
German 42, 328, 329
Germanic 128
governed 201
governing category 16
government 9, 12, 14, 91, 95, 112, 113, 126, 136, 138, 203, 246
governor 137

H

Habitual 26, 27, 28, 81, 220
head 7, 201, 205, 249, 288, 299, 308, 315

head movement 15, 95, 97, 128, 157,
    169, 171, 172, 173, 174, 203, 239,
    242, 245, 250, 307
Head Movement Constraint 15
hierarchy of 230
hierarchy of DP-types 282
hierarchy of nominal phrases 101

I

Icelandic 42
imperative 31, 161
inclusion 269, 270, 272, 273
incorporation 56, 94, 95, 279, 280
infinitive 37, 58
Infl 150, 173
Internal Subject Hypothesis 92, 95, 163, 215
interrogative 64, 128, 129, 133
intonation 125, 126
intonational phrase 126
intransitive 46, 56, 59, 62
Irish 95, 200, 224, 235, 237, 322
Irrealis 24
Isthmus Zapotec *See* IZ
Italian 150, 161, 322
IZ 53, 69, 73, 125, 161

J

Jacaltec 37, 64, 279
Japanese 85, 323
JZ 36, 279

K

Kanjobalan 37

L

laryngealized vowels 34, 70
    vowels 5
lexical head 9, 14, 113
LF 114, 118, 120, 139, 141, 155, 201,
    320, 325, 326
loan marker 213
Logical Form 6, see LF

M

marking 261

m-command 8, 13, 150, 155, 159
meteorological constructions 43
minimal government 113, 114, 121, 134,
    138, 141, 164, 165, 184, 247, 328
Mokilese 259
mood 24
more 32
morphological case 12, 21, 36, 58, 150, 244
motion 212, 230
motion auxiliary 213
movement 96
Move-α 6, 13, 16, 114
MZ 108, 156, 159, 161, 163, 164, 166,
    169, 198, 200, 205

N

negation 97, 108, 135, 149, 151, 153,
    170, 171, 188, 191, 192, 196, 203,
    216, 239, 279
negative 30, 31, 32, 49, 66, 136, 137,
    156, 158, 160, 161, 163, 166, 170,
    171, 173, 177, 178, 186, 187, 188,
    190, 192, 198, 199, 200, 205
Negative Concord 149
Negative Criterion 91, 137, 153, 157,
    161, 165, 166, 167, 173, 177, 197
negative marker 279
NegP 89, 153, 157, 159, 160, 162, 163,
    165, 166, 169, 170, 171, 173, 177,
    178, 186, 189, 191, 193, 196, 198
nominal phrases 22, 23, 42, 75, 77, 79,
    230, 234, 239, 244
Nonpronominal Head Condition 282, 291,
    301, 317
null 37, 39, 40, 42, 73, 79, 80, 81, 83,
    85, 142, 144, 162, 164, 165, 174,
    184, 231, 233, 277, 278, 280, 282,
    292
number 21, 22, 36, 244, 257, 258, 260,
    274, 275, 303

O

object 290, 300, 301, 308
operator 13, 114, 119, 139, 141, 142,
    143, 154, 170, 171, 201, 328
OSV 91
OVS 63, 91, 100

P

Papago 126
participle 212
passive 37, 53, 55, 59
person 260, 274
Person Hierarchy Effect 259, 260, 270, 272, 273, 274, 275, 299, 305
phonetic symbol 4
Phonological Form 6
pied-piping 107, 134, 136, 137, 188, 313
Plural Pronoun Construction 259, 304
polarity phrase 90, 196, 199, 200
Polish 321, 325
possessive prefix 21
possessor 22, 23, 36, 70, 71, 73, 106, 134, 135, 137, 219, 242, 243, 244, 245, 247, 248, 252, 276, 277, 279, 280, 281, 291, 313
Potential 28, 29, 31, 38, 41, 61, 62, 157, 158, 198, 220, 265, 267, 268, 296
PPC 260, 269, 270, 272, 275, 288, 296
preposition 46, 54, 56, 137, 291, 313
prepositional phrase 134, 135, 234
Principles of Binding Theory 16
pro 16, 37
PRO 17, 37, 41, 42
Progressive 27
Projection Principle 11, 14, 95
pronoun 33, 34, 35, 36, 42, 58, 73, 77, 79, 101, 144, 152, 155, 157, 160, 166, 169, 176, 186, 187, 188, 190, 192, 258, 260, 275
proper government 14, 107, 313
proper governor 14, 107, 137, 313
proper name 273
prosodic structure 126

Q

quantifier 22, 23, 36, 48, 108, 114, 147, 166, 168, 169, 233, 244, 248, 252, 253, 257, 258, 261, 262, 264, 265, 266, 267, 274, 276, 282, 284, 285, 287, 288, 292, 296, 297, 299, 301, 303, 312, 315, 317
question 64, 140, 152, 156, 182, 183, 186, 191, 319
question marker 122, 123, 127

R

raising 60
Realis 24
reciprocal 70, 71, 279
Redundancy Condition 263, 264
reflexive 70, 279
reflexive of possession 72, 74, 277
relative clauses 22, 23, 140, 141, 143, 145, 146, 244, 245, 249, 296, 311, 312, 314
Relativized Minimality 113, 186, 189
Romani 328, 329
Romanian 320, 325
Russian 272, 302

S

San Dionicio Ocotopec Zapotec 137
Santa Catarina Xanaguía Zapotec 35
scope 114, 115, 120, 133, 138, 170, 171, 192, 201, 326, 328, 329, 330
semantics 103, 104, 129, 134, 183, 192, 259, 260, 265, 270, 272, 274, 287, 288, 301, 304, 314, 315
Serbo-Croatian 321, 325
SOV 91
Spanish 128, 129
specifier 7, 90, 119, 120, 136, 139, 143, 153, 157, 160, 163, 165, 166, 167, 169, 171, 173, 189, 193, 216, 240, 243, 249, 325, 328
specifier-head 8, 12, 91, 95, 112, 128, 134, 136, 138, 141, 149, 153, 157, 165, 169, 177, 178, 184, 197, 198, 201, 246, 247, 249, 328
S-structure 6, 12, 58, 59, 91, 95, 112, 114, 118, 119, 126, 138, 139, 141, 153, 155, 156, 161, 165, 166, 169, 174, 191, 192, 193, 201, 277, 294, 306, 310, 320, 325, 326
Stative 25, 26, 40, 48, 51, 52, 234, 312
Stripping 229
strong DPs 80, 81
subject 163, 164, 167, 169, 198, 202, 215, 218, 220, 226, 277, 279, 280, 297, 299, 300, 304
Subject Adjunction 95, 97, 127, 171, 175, 176, 178, 179, 216, 217, 220, 221, 222, 235, 237, 240, 243, 245, 251, 277

Subject = Possessor of Object Condition
276, 281, 298, 301, 317
subordinate clauses 28
SVO 62, 91, 99, 138, 163, 203, 215
SZ 108

T

Texmelucan Zapotec 53, 70
Thai 76
Theme 53, 54, 55, 57, 58, 59
Theta theory 10
Theta-Criterion 11
topic 62, 64, 101, 102, 104, 105, 106, 108, 186, 193
trace 14, 16, 37, 96, 137, 313, 318
transitive 45, 53, 56, 59, 62
Tzotzil 64, 126, 152, 157, 273, 303, 304, 322

U

unaccusative 32, 37, 43, 46, 57, 58, 59, 61, 62, 219, 312
Uniformity of Theta Assignment Hypothesis 11, 57
Universal Grammar 5, 12
Unreal 27

V

Valley Zapotec 230
Verb Movement 92, 94, 95, 97, 127, 128, 153, 171, 172, 174, 179, 203, 205, 215, 217, 222, 223, 225, 226, 227, 234, 235, 237, 239, 240, 242, 245, 254, 277, 279
Vietnamese 76

V^{max} 216, 224
VOS 46, 91, 278, 279
vowel 34
VSO 45, 46, 62, 91, 92, 93, 95, 97, 99, 103, 118, 138, 150, 171, 172, 175, 179, 203, 235, 239, 279

W

weak DPs 80, 81
weather 43
Welsh 95
West Flemish 154, 156, 157, 323
Wh Well-formedness Principle 328, 330
wh-chain 330
Wh-Criterion 13, 91, 112, 118, 119, 120, 127, 128, 137, 138, 140, 141, 154, 319, 320, 324, 325, 327
wh-movement 118, 127, 185, 313
wh-operator 120
wh-phrase 120, 122, 125, 134, 136, 138, 139, 140, 154, 156, 182, 183, 184, 185, 186, 187, 188, 189, 190, 191, 193, 321, 322, 323, 328, 329
wh-question 186

X

X-bar theory 7, 89, 93, 96, 121

Y

Yalálag Zapotec 103
Yatzachi See YZ
Yes/No questions 30, 64, 138, 140, 158, 183, 184, 186
Yiddish 64
YZ 33, 36, 37, 53, 58, 69, 71, 73, 278

www.ingramcontent.com/pod-product-compliance
Lightning Source LLC
Chambersburg PA
CBHW072119290426
44111CB00012B/1715